GCC: The Complete Reference

About the Author

Arthur Griffith has been involved with the development of compilers, interpreters, linkers, and assemblers since his first programming job in 1977, where he worked as a team member developing an assembler and linker for special-purpose computers. He then joined the maintenance group for a compiler of the PL/EXUS language, which had an underlying structure very similar to GCC. The next project was to write an interactive interpreter and compiler for a language named SATS.

The projects that followed these included the development of a Forth interpreter, extensions to a COBOL compiler, and the development of some special-purpose interpretive languages for machine control. One of these was an interactive command language providing multistation ground-based control of industrial satellite communications systems.

For the past few years, Arthur Griffith has turned to writing computer books, teaching programming online, and developing some software in Java. The programming books he has written range from *Java, XML, and Jaxp* to *COBOL for Dummies*. He has used GCC for many software-development projects, and with the inclusion of Java as one of the GCC languages, writing this book became his project of choice.

GCC:
The Complete Reference

Arthur Griffith

McGraw-Hill/Osborne

New York Chicago San Francisco
Lisbon London Madrid Mexico City
Milan New Delhi San Juan
Seoul Singapore Sydney Toronto

McGraw-Hill/Osborne
2600 Tenth Street
Berkeley, California 94710
U.S.A.

To arrange bulk purchase discounts for sales promotions, premiums, or fund-raisers, please contact **McGraw-Hill/Osborne** at the above address. For information on translations or book distributors outside the U.S.A., please see the International Contact Information page immediately following the index of this book.

GCC: The Complete Reference

1234567890 CUS CUS 0198765432

ISBN 0-07-222405-3

Publisher Brandon A. Nordin	**Copy Editor** Bart Reed
Vice President & Associate Publisher Scott Rogers	**Proofreader** John Gildersleeve
Editorial Director Wendy Rinaldi	**Indexer** Irv Hershman
Project Editor Katie Conley	**Computer Designers** Tabitha M. Cagan, Kathleen Fay Edwards
Acquisitions Coordinator Tim Madrid	**Illustrators** Michael Mueller, Lyssa Wald
Technical Editor Paul Garland	**Series Design** Peter F. Hancik

This book was composed with Corel VENTURA™ Publisher.

For Mary

Contents at a Glance

Contents

Part I

The Free Software Compiler

Part II

Using the Compiler Collection

Part III

Peripherals and Internals

Part IV

Appendixes

Acknowledgments

I must thank Wendy Rinaldi at McGraw-Hill/Osborne for giving me the opportunity to write this book, and for her patience in the early days when it looked like it was going to take forever.

I want to thank Katie Conley for keeping me on track and heading in the right direction. She has a unique ability for keeping track of the status of the various parts of the book as it moves through the editing process. Bart Reed and I have a completely different take on the English language—his is both readable and correct. I want to thank Paul Garland for checking the technical accuracy of the book and pointing out the places where my imagination overtook the facts.

I must thank Margot Maley at Waterside for keeping my feet on the ground and my hands on the keyboard.

My understanding of how compilers work was a necessity for writing this book. I want to thank Dave Rogers for introducing me to the C language many years ago, and for drafting me to write a compiler for it. I also need to thank Ron Souder and Travis Mitchell for throwing me into some very strange projects that caused me to become immersed in some of the more obscure nooks and crannies of language processing and object code generation.

Perhaps most of all, I owe a great deal of thanks to the late Fred Lewis for introducing me to the fascinating world of compilers, assemblers, and linkers.

Introduction

It can be argued that the current free-software movement is the most important thing happening in computing today. We are in the midst of a major shift from all software being proprietary and closely held by individual companies to a large body of software that can be freely acquired and used by anyone for any purpose. Free software now includes not only programming language compilers and linkers, but numerous utilities, graphical user interface environments, and even entire operating systems.

Add all this to the fact that virtually all free software is compiled by GCC, and it can be argued that GCC is the most important piece of software in the world. Of course, programs are written in many languages, and there are compilers for these languages, but for the most part these compilers are written and compiled using GCC. At some point, all free software harks back to GCC. Some computer companies have begun to drop support for their own compilers and simply install GCC instead. It's free for the taking and is constantly being extended and maintained.

With the addition of the two latest languages to the GCC family—Java and Ada—the GCC compiler is spreading its wings even further. This brings the total number of active languages in GCC to six: C, C++, Objective-C, Fortran, Java, and Ada. Development is in progress on other languages, such as COBOL, and they will be added to GCC if there is enough support behind them.

Milestones

The GNU Project was launched in 1984 for the purpose of developing a free operating system. Richard Stallman is the founder of the GNU Project and the original author of GCC.

The initial release of the first beta of GCC, release number 0.9, was on March 22, 1987. The first actual release, version 1.0, was on May 23, 1987. In all there have been 108 releases from the very beginning to the release on which this book is based—version 3.1, released on May 5, 2002. That's an average of one release every 1.7 months for the last 15 years.

What's Inside?

The purpose of this book is to provide information to those wishing to use GCC for software development. A good bit of information can be found about GCC internals that can be used to get you started in the direction of working inside the compiler, but the main idea behind this book is to guide you through the steps of installing and using the compiler to develop software. Any way that you care to measure software, GCC is huge. And like most huge software systems, it contains useful features that you can use only if you discover that they exist, determine exactly what it is they do, and figure out how to use them. That's the primary purpose of this book.

The book is divided into three parts. Part I, "The Free Software Compiler," serves as an introduction to the fundamentals of the compiler and includes instructions you can follow to download and install it. Part II, "Using the Compiler Collection," contains detailed instructions for using the compiler. A chapter is dedicated to each of the six programming languages, with several examples of each. Special chapters are included to describe the preprocessor and techniques for linking objects produced from different languages. Part III, "Peripherals and Internals," includes chapters on linking, debugging, cross-compiling, makefiles, and the GNU assembler. Part III also contains information on the inner workings of both the front end and back end of the compiler.

GCC is the world's champion in the number of command-line options available. These options are listed alphabetically in Appendix D and cross-referenced in Appendix C. Chapter 21 contains even more command-line options—the ones that have to do with the specific computer hardware for which the compiler is generating code.

To give you a better idea of the topics covered in this book, here's a short description of each chapter:

- Chapter 1 is a general introduction to the fundamental concepts of GCC, including a list of its parts and the languages it compiles.

- Chapter 2 contains procedures you can use to install GCC.

- Chapter 3 describes the workings of the preprocessor and how you can employ it to process the source code of a language.

- Chapter 4 contains examples of compiling and linking C.
- Chapter 5 contains examples of compiling and linking C++.
- Chapter 6 contains examples of compiling and linking Objective-C.
- Chapter 7 contains examples of compiling and linking Fortran.
- Chapter 8 contains examples of compiling and linking Java.
- Chapter 9 contains examples of compiling and linking Ada.
- Chapter 10 contains examples of mixing two languages to create a single executable.
- Chapter 11 explains how the internationalization facilities can be employed in your compiled program to allow its displayed strings to be modified to fit a locale.
- Chapter 12 contains examples of producing and using static and shared libraries.
- Chapter 13 explains the fundamentals of using the GNU debugger.
- Chapter 14 describes the use of make and its associated utilities.
- Chapter 15 discusses the GNU assembler and describes how you can use it in conjunction with GCC.
- Chapter 16 describes the process required to configure GCC to compile and link programs to be executed on another computer.
- Chapter 17 describes how GCC can be used to produce code for an embedded system.
- Chapter 18 contains examples of generating useful output from the compiler other than object code.
- Chapter 19 describes the rudiments of using lex and yacc to create a language front end for GCC.
- Chapter 20 describes the content of the intermediate language produced by the compiler front end and read by the compiler back end.
- Chapter 21 contains a list of the command-line options that apply versions of GCC running on specific hardware.
- Appendix A contains a copy of the GNU Public License.
- Appendix B lists the environment variables that effect GCC.
- Appendix C is a cross-reference of the command-line options by category.
- Appendix D is an alphabetical listing of the command-line options.
- Appendix E is a glossary.

The
Complete
Reference

GCC

Part I

The Free Software Compiler

Chapter 1

Introduction to GCC

The GNU Compiler Collection (GCC) is the most important piece of open source software in the world. Virtually all other open software is based on it at some level or another. Even other languages, such as Perl and Python, are written in C, which is compiled by the GNU compiler.

The GCC compiler has had a very interesting history. Its history is more than just a list of dates and events. This piece of software is more fundamental to the entire free software movement than any other. In fact, without it or something like it, there would be no free software movement. Linux is possible because of GCC.

This introduction provides an overview of what is in the compiler collection and what the tools are that surround it. Along with compiling are the tools that track the source code and the programs to edit files, control the compilation process, and provide information for debugging.

This introduction concludes with a parts list and a process description. The list contains descriptions of the files and programs that make up the compiler collection. The list is followed by a step-by-step description of the process of moving source files into a linked and executable program.

GNU

GCC is a product of the GNU Project. This project began in 1984 with the goal in mind of developing a complete UNIX-like operating system as free software. Like any project of this size, the GNU Project has taken some twists and turns, but the goal has been achieved. Today there is indeed a fully functional UNIX-like operating system, named Linux, abroad in the world and is being used with great success by countless companies, governments, and individuals. And this system, with all its utilities and applications, is based on the GNU Compiler Collection.

The range of free software available for Linux, and for other systems, is enormous and is growing every day. Software developed as part of the overall GNU Project to create a free UNIX is listed in the Free Software Directory at http://www.gnu.org/directory.

Thousands of programmers have contributed to the various GNU projects, as well as to other free software projects, and virtually all of them at some level are based on GCC.

Measuring a Compiler

Compilers can be compared in terms of speed of compilation, speed of the generated code, and the size of the generated code. It's hard to measure much else. Some numbers can be produced, but it's difficult to attach much meaning to them. For example, a count of the number of source files (makefiles, configuration files, header files, executable code, and so on) shows that there are well over 15,000 files of various types. Compiling the source files into object files, libraries, and executable programs increases the count by several thousand more. Counting the lines of code—the number of lines of text in the 15,000+ files—produces a number greater than 3,700,000. By any criteria you want to use, that's a large program.

The quality of the code varies widely because so many programmers have been involved in development. Also, the largest portion of the internal documentation consists of comments embedded in the code, so the quantity and quality of documentation also varies. Fortunately, the large number of programmers working on the code has, over time, improved both the code and the comments. Fortunately, it is not necessary for you to read the embedded comments to be able to use the compiler. However, if you decide to work on the compiler itself, you will find yourself spending time reading comments embedded in the code.

The only way to measure the quality of a compiler is to ask the people that use it. The number of users around the world will never be known (free software has that characteristic), but the number of users has to be enormous. It is used on some versions of UNIX where a native compiler is present and supported by the vendor of the UNIX system. In fact, I know of one large UNIX vendor that uses GCC for many of its own in-house projects, even though this vendor has its own very fine compiler.

The compiler is never still. As described in Chapter 2, you can install a released version of GCC by downloading the source code for a specific release, or you can download the latest (and experimental) version. The experimental version is never still for more than a few minutes—it is constantly being changed. Some of the corrections are bug fixes, some add new languages and features, and some remove things that no longer apply. If you have worked with GCC in the past and find yourself returning to it after being away for a while, you will definitely notice some changes.

Command-Line Options

Each command-line option begins with either a hyphen or a pair of hyphens. For example, the following command line will compile the ANSI standard C program named muxit.c and produce an unlinked object file named muxit.o:

```
gcc -ansi -c muxit.c -o muxit.o
```

The single-letter options that have a name following them can optionally include a space between the letter and the name. For example, the option -omuxit.o is the same as -o muxit.o.

The following command uses -v for verbosity and --help to print the available options, and it will print a verbose list of all the command-line options, including those that are specific to each language:

```
gcc -v --help
```

It is possible to construct command lines in such a way that nothing happens. For example, the following command feeds an object file to the compiler and then specifies -c to prevent the linker from being invoked:

```
gcc -c brookm.o
```

All the command-line options fall roughly into three categories:

- **Language specific** The GCC compiler is capable of compiling several languages, and some options apply to only one or two of them. For example, the -C89 option only applies to C to specify that the 1989 standard be used.

- **Platform specific** The GCC compiler can generate object code for several platforms, and some options only apply when code is being created for a specific platform. For example, if the output platform is Intel 386, the -fp-ret-in-387 option can be used to specify that floating-point values returned from function calls be stored in the hardware floating-point registers.

- **General** Many of the options have meaning for all languages and all platforms. For example, the -O option instructs the compiler to optimize the output code.

Specifying an option unknown to the compiler will always result in an error message. Specifying an option that does not apply to the target platform will also result in an error message.

The gcc program itself processes all options that are known to it and blindly passes the remaining options on to the process that is to compile a specific language. If the option passed to a language-specific process is unknown, an error will be reported.

Options are available to direct gcc to perform only certain actions (such as linking or preprocessing) and nothing else, which means that other flags that would normally be valid simply serve no purpose. Unless the -W option is used to generate extra warnings, flags that are recognized but do not apply are silently ignored.

Platforms

The GCC set of compilers runs on many platforms. A *platform* is a combination of a specific computer chip and the operating system running on it.

Although GCC has been ported to thousands of these hardware/software combinations, only a few fundamental platforms are used for testing to determine the correctness of a release. These fundamental targets, listed in Table 1-1, have been selected because they are the most popular and because they are representative of other platforms supported by GCC.

Care is taken to make certain GCC runs correctly for the primary platforms shown in Table 1-1, and a good deal of attention is paid to the secondary platforms, listed in Table 1-2.

Hardware	Operating System
Alpha	Red Hat Linux 7.1
HPPA	HPUX 11.0
Intel x86	Debian Linux 2.2, Red Hat Linux 6.2, and FreeBSD 4.5
MIPS	IRIX 6.5
PowerPC	AIX 4.3.3
Sparc	Solaris 2.7

Table 1-1. *Primary GCC Evaluation Platforms*

The reason for primary and secondary testing on such a limited number of platforms is a matter of manpower. If your platform is not represented here, you may still find that the compiler runs perfectly on your system. Also, a complete test suite comes with the source code of the compiler, so you will easily be able to verify that the compiler works properly. Another approach would be to volunteer to run tests on your platform so the compiler can be verified for it before each release.

What the Compiler Does

A compiler is a translator. It reads a set of instructions written in one form (usually the text of a programming language) and translates it into a set of instructions (usually a collection of binary hardware instructions) that can be executed by a computer.

Roughly, the compiler is divided into two parts: the front end and the back end. The front end reads the source of the program and transforms what it finds into

Hardware	Operating System
PowerPC	Linux
Sparc	Linux
ARM	Linux
Intel x86	Cygwin

Table 1-2. *Secondary GCC Evaluation Platforms*

a memory-resident table in the form of a tree. Once the tree has been constructed, the back end of the compiler reads the information stored in the tree and converts it into assembly language for the target machine.

The following is a bird's-eye view of the steps taken to perform the translation of your source into an executable program:

- Lexical analysis is at the very beginning of the compiler's front end. It reads the characters from the input and decides which ones belong together to make symbols, numbers, and punctuation.

- The parsing process reads the stream of symbols coming from the lexical scanner and, following a set of rules, determines the relationships among them. The output of the parser is the tree structure that is passed to the back end of the compiler.

- The parse tree structure is translated into a psuedo-assembly language named Register Transfer Language (RTL).

- The back end of the compiler begins by analyzing the RTL code and performing some optimizations. Redundant and unused sections of code are removed. Some portions of the tree may be moved to other locations in the tree to prevent statements from being executed more often than necessary. All in all, there are more than a dozen optimizations, and some of them have more than one pass through the code.

- The RTL is translated into assembly language for the target machine.

- The assembler is invoked to translate the assembly language into an object file. This file is not in an executable format—it contains executable object code, but not in a form that it can actually be run. Besides, it more than likely contains unresolved references to routines and data in other modules.

- The linker combines object files from the assembler (some of which may be stored in libraries filled with object files) into an executable program.

Note the complete separation of the front end from the back end. Any language with a parser that can be used to produce the tree structure can be compiled with GCC. Similarly, any machine for which a program has been written to translate the tree structure into assembly language is capable of compiling programs from any of the languages handled by the front end.

It is actually not as simple as this description makes it sound, but it works.

The Languages

GCC compiles several languages, but there is a fundamental relationship among them all. The parsers are all entirely different because the syntax of each language is unique, but with each step of the compilation process, more and more of the code becomes common among all the languages. As described in the previous sections, the GNU Compiler Collection can accept input in the form of any one of a number of programming languages and produce output that will run on one of a number of different platforms.

C Is the Fundamental Language

The fundamental language of GCC is C. The entire compiler system began as a C compiler and, over time, the other languages were added to it. This was fortunate because C is a system-level language capable of dealing directly with the elementary elements of computer programs, which, in turn, makes it a relatively easy task to build other language compilers on top of its internals.

If you are programming in a language other than C, as you become more familiar with GCC you will find that many of the things you work with are in terms of the C language. You can think of C as sort of the underlying assembly language of the GCC compiler. Most of the compiler itself is written in C.

C++ Was the First Addition

The C++ language is a direct extension (with minor modifications) of the C language, so it was a perfect candidate for the first language to be added to GCC. Everything that can be done in C++ can also be done in C, so there was no need to modify the back end of the compiler—it was only necessary to load the front end with a new parser and semantics analyzer. Once the intermediate language is generated, the rest of the compiler is exactly the same as the C compiler.

Objective-C

Objective-C is not as popular or as well known as C or C++, but it is another language that was derived from (and is based on) the C language. It is referred to as "C with objects" and, as you learn it, you realize that's exactly what it is. For the most part, you can write a C program and compile it as Objective-C and have it run. A special syntax that is distinctively different from the fundamental C syntax is used to define objects, so there is no confusion or conflict with any of the parts that are pure C code.

Fortran

Fortran does one thing that C does not do: math. The standard Fortran function library (known as the Fortran *intrinsics* because they act as if they are a part of the language) is extensive and has been perfected and extended over many years. Fortran is used extensively today in scientific computing because of its fundamental ability to perform complex calculations rapidly and correctly. Fortran even has complex numbers as one of its primitive data types, and the primitive numeric data types can be declared with extended accuracy.

The structure of the language is a bit more cumbersome than some of the more modern languages, but it contains the facilities for subroutines and functions that are needed for structured programming. The latest Fortran standard has expanded these capabilities to the point that the new Fortran is really quite a modern language.

Java

Java is the youngest of the languages included in GCC. The Java language, like C++, is based on C, but it takes a somewhat different approach to the syntax of writing classes. Where C++ is more flexible, Java removes the ambiguities of C++ by restricting object construction, destruction, and inheritance to some strictly unambiguous forms.

Java is very different from other languages included in GCC because of the form of its object code. Java compiles into a special format of object code, known as *bytecodes*, that can be executed by an interpreter (known as a Java Virtual Machine). All Java programs were executed this way until the GCC compiler added the option of generating native executable code by hooking a Java front end onto the existing GCC back end for code generation. In addition, another front end was added that is capable of reading Java bytecodes as the source code used to produce a binary native executable.

Ada

The newest addition to the GCC family is Ada. It was added as a fully functional compiler originally developed separately by Ada Core Technologies as the GNAT Ada 95 compiler, and donated to GCC in October of 2001.

The front end of the Ada compiler is different from the others, in that it is written in Ada. This is fine once you have some sort of Ada compiler installed, but it will require a special bootstrapping procedure on some systems. All the other languages are written in C and C++, so they are almost universally portable.

Ada is a language specifically designed for use by multiple programmers writing large programs. When an Ada program is compiled, it cross-references with the source code of the other portions of the program to verify correctness. The syntax of the language requires each function and procedure to be declared as being a member of a package, and the package configuration is compared against this declaration. C and C++ use prototypes to declare externally referenced functions, and Java uses a file naming convention to locate package members, but neither of these techniques is as stringent as Ada.

The Chill Is Gone

With version 3.0, the Chill language became an unsupported part of GCC. Then, just prior to the release of version 3.1, the source code of the Chill language was removed from GCC. However, GCC is very complicated, and the Chill language has been an integral part of it for quite some time, so you will see Chill language references throughout the GCC online documentation and in various locations in the source code. This book was written during the transition period, so you will find references to Chill compiler options and file types.

Parts List

GCC is made up of many components. Table 1-3 lists the parts of GCC, but not all of them are always present. Some of them are language specific, so if a particular language has not been installed, certain files will be missing from that system.

Part	Description
c++	A version of gcc that sets the default language to C++ and automatically includes the standard C++ libraries when linking. This is the same as g++.
cc1	The actual C compiler.
cc1plus	The actual C++ compiler.
collect2	On systems that do not use the GNU linker, it is necessary to run collect2 to generate certain global initialization code (such as constructors and destructors in C++).
configure	A script in the root directory of the GCC source tree. It is used to set configuration values and create the makefiles necessary to compile GCC.
crt0.o	The initialization and shutdown code is customized for each system and compiled into this file, which is then linked to each executable to perform the necessary program startup and shutdown activities.
cygwin1.dll	A shared library for Windows that provides an API that emulates UNIX system calls.
f77	The driver program used to compile Fortran.
f771	The actual Fortran compiler.
g++	A version of gcc that sets the default language to C++ and automatically includes the standard C++ libraries when linking. This is the same as c++.
gcc	The driver program that coordinates execution of compilers and linkers to produce the desired output.
gcj	The driver program used to compile Java.
gnat1	The actual Ada compiler.

Table 1-3.   *Various Installed Parts of GCC*

Part	Description
gnatbind	A utility used to perform Ada language binding.
gnatlink	A utility used to perform Ada language linking.
jc1	The actual Java compiler.
libgcc	This library contains routines that could be considered part of the compiler because they are linked with virtually every executable. They are special routines that are linked with an executable program to perform fundamental tasks such as floating point arithmetic. The routines in this library are often platform dependent.
libgcj	The runtime library containing all the core Java classes.
libobjc	The runtime library necessary for all Objective-C programs.
libstdc++	The runtime library contains all the C++ classes and functions defined as part of the standard language.

Table 1-3. *Various Installed Parts of GCC* (continued)

Table 1-4 lists software that works in conjunction with GCC to aid in the compilation process. Some are absolutely essential (such as as and ld), where others can be useful but are not strictly required. Although many of these tools are available as native utilities on various UNIX systems, you can get most of them as a GNU package known as binutils. The procedure for installing binutils is described in Chapter 2.

Tool	Description
addr2line	Given an address inside an executable file, addr2line uses the debug information in the file to translate the address into a source code file name and line number. This program is part of the binutils package.

Table 1-4. *Software Tools Used with GCC*

Tool	Description
`ar`	A program to maintain library archive files by adding, removing, and extracting files from the archive. The most common use for this utility is to create and manage object library archives used by the linker. This program is part of the `binutils` package.
`as`	The GNU assembler. It is really a family of assemblers because it can be compiled to work with one of several different platforms. This program is part of the `binutils` package.
`autoconf`	Produces shell scripts that automatically configure a source code package to compile on a specific version of UNIX.
`c++filt`	The program accepts names that have been mangled by the C++ compiler (which it does for overloading) and translates the mangled names to their original form. This program is part of the `binutils` package.
`f2c`	A Fortran-to-C translation program. It is not a part of GCC.
`gcov`	A profiling tool used with `gprof` to determine where the greatest amount of time is being spent during the execution of your program.
`gdb`	The GNU debugger, which can be used to examine the values and actions inside a program while it is running.
`GNATS`	The GNU Bug Tracking System. An online system for tracking bugs for GCC and other GNU software.
`gprof`	This program will monitor the execution of a program that has been compiled with profiling code built into it and reports the amount of time spent in each function, providing a profile from which routines can be optimized. This program is part of the `binutils` package.
`ld`	The GNU linker. This program combines a collection of object files into an executable program. This program is part of the `binutils` package.
`libtool`	A generic library support script used in makefiles to simplify the use of shared libraries.

Table 1-4.   *Software Tools Used with GCC* (continued)

Tool	Description
make	A utility that reads a makefile script to determine which parts of a program need compiling and linking and then issues the commands necessary to do so. It reads a script (named makefile or Makefile) that defines file relationships and dependencies.
nlmconv	Converts a relocatable object file into a NetWare Loadable Module (NLM). This program is part of the binutils package.
nm	Lists the symbols defined in an object file. This program is part of the binutils package.
objcopy	Copies and translates an object file from one binary format to another. This program is part of the binutils package.
objdump	Displays several different kinds of information stored inside one or more object file. This program is part of the binutils package.
ranlib	Creates and adds an index to an ar archive file. The index is the one used by ld to locate modules in the library. This program is part of the binutils package.
ratfor	The Ratfor preprocessor can be invoked by GCC but is not a part of the standard GCC distribution.
readelf	Displays information from an ELF formatted object file. This program is part of the binutils package.
size	Lists the names and sizes of each of the sections in an object file. This program is part of the binutils package.
strings	Reads through a file of any type and extracts the character strings for display. This program is part of the binutils package.
strip	Removes the symbol table, along with any other information required for debugging, from an object file or an archive library. This program is part of the binutils package.
vcg	The Ratfor viewer reads information from a text file and displays it as a graph. The vcg utility is not distributed as part of GCC, but the -dv option can be used to generate optimization data in the format understood by vcg.
windres	A compiler for Window resource files. This program is part of the binutils package.

Table 1-4. *Software Tools Used with GCC* (continued)

Contact

The home website for GNU is http://www.gnu.org, and the home website of the GCC project is http://gcc.gnu.org.

The GCC compiler scales very well—from simple batch utility programs to multimillion-line systems. Generally, as a software project gets larger or becomes specialized in some way, situations arise where odd problems are uncovered. Some of these are bugs and some are peculiarities, but there inevitably comes a time when you need clarification—or at least a nudge in the right direction. Fortunately, help is available, along with everything you would like to know about GCC.

The primary source of information is through mailing lists. An open mailing list (one in which all the members are able to both send and receive) has the advantages of being immediate and making it easy for a dialogue to take place. If it is help you are after, I would suggest subscribing to the gcc-help mailing list. A dialogue on an open list can continue until the situation is clarified and the problem is solved. Table 1-5 contains brief descriptions of all the GCC open mailing lists. The read-only mailing lists are listed in Table 1-6.

List Name	Description
gcc	A general discussion area for the development of GCC. If you only subscribe to one list, this should be the one. It should keep you abreast of the latest news and developments. This is a high volume list.
gcc-bugs	Discussions of bugs and bug reports. This is a high volume list.
gcc-help	This list is for use by people searching for answers to questions. This is a high volume list
gcc-patches	Source code patches and discussions of patches are submitted to this list. This is a high volume list.
gcc-testresults	Test results and discussions of testing and test results are posted to this list.
java	The discussion list for the development and maintenance of the Java front end of GCC, as well as the Java runtime library.
java-patches	Source code patches for the Java front end and the Java runtime library are posted to this list as well as the gcc-patches list.
libstdc++	The discussion list for the development and maintenance of the standard C++ library.

Table 1-5.   *The Open GCC Mailing Lists*

List Name	Description
gccadmin	This mailing list receives the messages issued from the cron jobs run by the gccadmin account at gcc.gnu.org.
gcc-announce	A low volume mailing list for announcements of new releases and other events of importance to GCC.
gcc-cvs	A message is sent to this list for each check-in to the CVS repository.
gcc-cvs-wwwdocs	A message is sent to this list each time there is a check-in to the CVS repository of the HTML documentation.
gcc-prs	A message is sent to this list each time a problem report is entered into the GNATS database.
gcc-regression	Messages are posted to this list containing the results of running regression testing of GCC.
java-announce	A low volume mailing list for announcements relating to the Java front end or the Java runtime routines.
java-cvs	A message is sent to this list (and the gcc-cvs list) for each check-in to the Java compiler and runtime sections of the CVS repository.
java-prs	A message is sent to this list (and the gcc-prs list) each time a Java related problem report is entered into the GNATS database.
libstdc++-cvs	A message is sent to this list each time there is a check-in to the libstc++ part of the CVS repository.

Table 1-6. *The Read-Only GCC Mailing Lists*

All the mailing lists can be accessed at the website http://www.gnu.org/software/gcc/lists.html. Entries can be made on this page to subscribe and unsubscribe to the lists. Also, each list has its own website that can be used to search and read through the archived messages of the list. The name of the list preceded by gcc.gnu.org/ml/ is the name of the website. For example, to locate the gcc-announce archive website, go to http://gcc.gnu.org/ml/gcc-announce.

Chapter 2

Acquiring and Installing
the Compiler

W hile ready-to-run binary versions of GCC are available, the most common installation procedure is to download the source code and compile it. The process of compiling GCC has become quite stable and mature because it has been refined over several years. The same basic installation process is used for installing all GNU software. In simple terms, the steps are as follows:

1. Download the source code and store it in a directory of its own.

2. Create a separate working directory to be used for compiling the source.

3. From the working directory, execute the configure script, which creates a directory tree with a collection of platform-dependent files to control the compilation process.

4. Enter the command make to compile the source into an object.

5. Enter the command make install to install the newly compiled programs and libraries on your system.

There are two ways to get the source code: You can get compressed tar files by using FTP, or you can get the individual compressed files using CVS. Using FTP you can get released and stable versions of the compiler. Using CVS gives you access to the released versions as well as the current experimental version. The FTP form is more tuned for a user of the compiler, where the CVS form is designed for use by the maintainers of GCC, but the installation procedure is almost the same for them both.

If you are on a computer that does not have other GNU software installed, you will probably find it necessary to install binutils first. Included in the binutils package are several utility programs used by GCC, including an assembler and linker that have been designed to work directly with GCC. It is possible to use native assemblers and linkers, but the GNU assembler and linker have been designed to work with the GNU compilers. The installation procedure is basically the same as for GCC, but the binutils installation process can be performed easily on a machine without binutils already installed, whereas a GCC installation may require the presence of binutils.

Like almost all GNU software, the compiler is written in C, so a C compiler must already be present on the computer before you can compile a new one. If you want to install GCC for a computer that does not already have a C compiler, it is necessary to cross-compile the compiler from the compiler installed on another machine that was specifically configured and compiled for this purpose. Chapter 16 explains the procedure of compiling for another machine.

Binary Download

If you do not already have a C compiler, you can do one of two things: You can download the source onto another computer that has a C compiler and cross compile a version for your target machine, or you can download a precompiled version. GNU does not provide precompiled versions of the compiler, but a few are available from other locations. There are too many different kinds of computers and operating systems for there to be a binary version available for every computer, but Table 2-1 lists a few that are available.

Each of these sites has download and installation instructions. The GCC compiler is portable, but the portability is designed to work across UNIX operating systems. The DOS version of the compiler is a simple port and needs only to be loaded onto a DOS machine to be run, but it is limited to only the C and C++ compilers. The Windows compiler of the Cygwin Project is a complete port that includes not only the compiler but also a set of utilities that provide a complete UNIX work environment.

Platform	Name and Location
AIX	Bull's Large Freeware and Shareware Archive for AIX at http://freeware.bull.net The University of Southern California's Public Domain Software Library for AIX at http://aixpdslib.seas.ucla.edu
DOS	DJGPP at http://www.delorie.com/djgpp
HP-UX	The Computer-Aided Engineering Center of the University of Wisconsin at http://hpux.cae.wisc.edu The HP-UX Porting and Archive Center in Utah at http://hpux.cs.utah.edu The HP-UX Porting and Archive Center in the United Kingdom at http://hpux.connect.org/uk SunSITE Central Europe at ftp://sunsite.informatik.rwth-aachen.de/pub/packages/gcc_hpux
Solaris 2	Solaris Freeware Project (both Intel and Sparc) at http://www.sunfreeware.com
SGI	SGI Freeware at http://freeware.sgi.com
UnixWare	Skunkware at ftp://ftp2.caldera.com/pub/skunkware/w7/Packages
Windows	The Cygwin Project at http://sources.redhat.com/cygwin

Table 2-1.   *Precompiled Versions of the GCC Compiler*

FTP Source Download

A number of sites provide anonymous FTP access to the GCC source files. It is possible to download the full compiler collection or select only the language (or languages) you wish to install. The files are listed in Table 2-2, but it is not necessary to download all of them. You have two choices:

- You can choose to download only the core and then select any of the languages you would like to include with it.
- You can download the entire compiler, which is the same as downloading the core, all the languages, and the test suite.

The test suite is optional. It is a collection of source code programs that you can use to verify whether the compiler you have downloaded and compiled is working properly.

The following steps can be used to download the source code and install it, making it ready to be compiled:

1. Select an FTP site. The GNU FTP site is ftp.gnu.org/gnu, but you should probably choose from among the hundreds of mirror sites located around the world. You can find a current list of mirror sites at http://www.gnu.org/order/ftp.html. To make your download as smooth as possible, you should choose a mirror site close to you.

File Name	Contains
gcc-3.1.tar.gz	The entire compiler, including the core and all the components.
gcc-ada-3.1.tar.gz	The Ada compiler.
gcc-core-3.1.tar.gz	The core contains the C compiler and the modules that are common to all compilers.
gcc-g++-3.1.tar.gz	The C++ compiler.
gcc-g77-3.1.tar.gz	The Fortran compiler.
gcc-java-3.1.tar.gz	The Java compiler.
gcc-obj-3.1.tar.gz	The Objective C compiler.
gcc-testsuite-3.1.tar.gz	The test suite.

Table 2-2. *The FTP Files Containing the Source of GCC*

2. Download the files into a work directory. This may be the same directory that you will use to compile GCC, but it is usually a temporary directory because these files can be deleted after the source has been extracted from them. It is important that you download the files with the FTP option set to binary, not text. These are compressed files, and the FTP text mode will destroy them by misinterpreting the content and converting certain values into ASCII characters.

3. Select or create a directory to be used to contain the source tree directory. When you unpack GCC, it will create its own directory in the current directory, so you can select a directory in which other source directories have been installed. For example, if you elect to install the source in a directory named /usr/local/src, unpacking all the files from that location will cause the GCC source tree to be installed as /usr/local/src/gcc-3.1.

4. Unpack the files. If your tar utility supports the gzip format (the z option), you can unpack a file as follows:

```
cd /usr/local/src
tar -xvzf /tmp/download/gcc-core-3.1.0.tar.gz
```

5. If your version of tar does not support gzip, you will need to add an extra step to the procedure, as follows:

```
cd /usr/local/src
gunzip /tmp/download/gcc-core-3.1.0.tar.gz
tar -xvf /tmp/download/gcc-core-3.1.0.tar
```

This will create a directory named /usr/local/src/gcc-3.1 that contains the source. If you have chosen to download more than one file, you will need to use the same command for each of them. In the unlikely event that you don't have a copy of gunzip, you can get a ready-to-run copy of it for your system at http://www.gzip.org.

CVS Source Download

In some respects a Concurrent Versions System (CVS) download is easier than an FTP download. It is certainly more flexible because it allows you to download different versions of GCC. The CVS system is used by the developers of GNU software to retrieve the latest experimental versions and keep track of any updates. And because CVS is a source code archive, you can use its facilities to retrieve any version of the compiler, including the current release.

There are Some slight differences in the form of the download of the tar source files and the CVS source files. To compile from CVS source, you will need to have the Bison parser and version 4 or later of Texinfo installed to produce some intermediate files. These generated files are included with the tar files but are not included among the CVS files. Another difference is that the defaults for some of the configuration options are set to provide more diagnostics in the CVS download.

The CVS repository tracks every change made to the source code. When the time comes to make a release, a *tag* is created to mark the release. The tag is associated with the current (or selected) version of every source module in the repository. When you wish to download a version of the compiler, you specify the tag name to your local cvs utility, and it will retrieve all the source files for you. The source files are downloaded to you in a compressed form (if you specify the proper command-line option) and are uncompressed and stored in the correct directory as they arrive. The result is that you get the same set of directories and files that you get from an FTP download.

The following steps describe a procedure you can follow to download a specific version of GCC:

1. Verify that you have the cvs utility installed on your system by entering the following command:

   ```
   cvs -v
   ```

   This should display the version number along with some other information. If you do not have a copy of cvs or if the version you have is 1.10.4 or older, you will need to get a copy of the latest version, which you can do at http://www.cvshome.org.

2. Specify the name of the remote CVS repository. The simplest way to do this is to define the name as an environment variable with the following command:

   ```
   CVSROOT=:pserver:anoncvs@subversions.gnu.org:/cvsroot/gcc
   export CVSROOT
   ```

   This is the location of the CVS repository. The cvs utility will look for the environment variable if the -d option is not specified on the command line. If you prefer, you can use the -d option to specify the address with every cvs command, but it must be the first option on the command line, as follows:

   ```
   cvs -d :pserver:anoncvs@subversions.gnu.org:/cvsroot/gcc
   ```

3. Log into CVS. With the CVSROOT environment variable set, you can log directly into the repository with the following command:

   ```
   cvs login
   ```

   You will be prompted for a password, so to log in anonymously with read-only access, just press RETURN. If the login completes successfully, the command-line prompt will reappear for you to enter your next cvs command.

4. Download the source files. Change to the parent directory of the one that you would like to contain the GCC source tree. Entering the following command will download all the source of the named release and store it in a new directory named gcc:

   ```
   cvs -z 9 checkout -r gcc_3_1_0_release gcc
   ```

The -z 9 option is important because it instructs cvs to compress the files, which shortens the time required to get all the files. Whether you compress the files or not, the end result is the same because cvs expands them as it stores them on the local disk.

5. Using the same tag as before, you can also retrieve the documentation that matches that particular version of the compiler. It is in the form of a set of HTML files stored in a directory named wwwdocs. The command to download the documentation is very much like the one you used to download the source files:

```
cvs -z 9 checkout -r gcc_3_1_0_release wwwdocs
```

Previous Releases

Normally you will want to get the latest release of the compiler from your CVS download, but there are tag names for a number of releases if you need a different one. The tag names listed in the following table can be used to retrieve earlier releases.

gcc_3_0_3_release	gcc_2_95_2-release	egcs_1_1_release
gcc_3_0_2_release	gcc_2_95_1-release	egcs_1_0_3_release
gcc_3_0_1_release	gcc_2_95-release	egcs_1_0_2_release
gcc_3_0_release	egcs_1_1_2_release	egcs_1_0_1_release
gcc_2_95_3	egcs_1_1_1_release	egcs_1_0_release

The Experimental Version

If you don't specify a tag name, you will get a snapshot of the latest experimental version of GCC. The following command will download the experimental version :

```
cvs -z 9 checkout gcc
```

The source code you get this way is the newest experimental version of the compiler, so it may not work correctly. In fact, there is no guarantee you will even be able to compile it.

Once you have a copy of the latest version of all the files, you can keep them current by using cvs to update them whenever you wish. The cvs command will compare the version of the files in the repository with the version you have on the local disk and download only the ones needed to make everything current. The update command looks like this:

```
cvs -z 9 update
```

As this command updates your local directories, it lists each file name preceded by a single character indicating the action taken. The letter *P* indicates that you already have the latest version. The letter *U* indicates that a new version of the file has replaced an old one. A question mark appears when there is a file in the local directory that does not match anything in the repository.

As the GCC software is being developed, the documentation is being updated to match it. You can download the latest version of it in a similar fashion:

```
cvs -z 9 checkout wwwdocs
```

If you elect to download the documentation, it will also be updated when you use cvs to update the source files.

Compiling and Installing GCC

The installation procedure of GCC has been performed thousands of times over a period of several years and on many different platforms, so it has become very mature and stable. If you intend to both compile and install GCC on the same machine, the process can be very simple. However, if you need to do something special, you have plenty of options available.

Installation Procedure

The following list is made up of the major steps required to install GCC.

1. Make certain that your current C compiler is available. Either cc or gcc should be on your path, or the CC environment variable must be set to the name of the compiler. You can verify the presence of the compiler by entering cc or gcc from the command line.

2. Verify that you have GNU make installed. It is possible for other versions of make to work properly, but it is quite likely that you will run into problems. If you elect to use another version of make and find that you get some strange error messages, you should install GNU make and try again. To verify that you have GNU make, you can enter the following command, which causes GNU make to identify itself:

   ```
   make -v
   ```

3. Create a configuration directory. This directory is to be the root of a tree of directories that will contain all the makefiles and object files they generate. It is highly recommended that you do not compile GCC anywhere in the directory tree containing the source files.

4. Select the options you wish to use on the `configure` script. There are many options to choose from, and they are all described in the next section. Each option has a default value, so you will only need to specify options for special situations.

   The most commonly used option is `--prefix`, to specify the name of the root directory of the GCC binary installation. After the installation is complete, the named *prefix* directory contains all the GCC executables and other files in subdirectories named `bin`, `include`, `info`, `lib`, `man`, and `share`. The default prefix is `/usr/local`.

   One of the most interesting things about the `configure` script is its almost infallible ability to guess the exact operating system and hardware it is running on. It does this by calling on a script named `config.guess`. If you wish, you can execute this script from the command line and see that it properly identifies your system.

5. Execute the `configure` script from inside the working directory. Because you are executing the script from another directory, it is necessary to specify its full path name. For example, if you have downloaded the source tree into `/opt/gnu/gcc`, your object directory is named `/opt/build`, and if you want to store the final executables and libraries in `/opt/usr/local`, you can execute the `configure` script as follows:

```
cd /opt/build
/opt/gnu/gcc/configure --prefix=/opt/usr/local
```

6. Compile GCC. If the `configure` script ran successfully, several files and directories are in the object directory, including one file named `Makefile`. To compile everything, enter the following command:

```
make
```

   As the compilation proceeds, you will see some error messages displayed, but this is normal as long as make ignores them and the compiler moves on to the next file. Some errors and warnings are expected—only the ones that halt the process are of any concern.

7. Test the compiler. Running the test suite is an optional step and may even require you to download some extra software to do it. If you decide to run the test suite, you can find the procedure for doing so at the end of this chapter, in the section titled "Running the Test Suite."

8. Install the compiler. With everything compiled, you can install GCC with the following command:

```
make install
```

9. Set the path. To be able to use the compilers directly, it is necessary to include the directory containing the executables in the `PATH` environment variable. Unless you made some changes to the location by specifying some of the directory name options with the `configure` script, your `PATH` variable is probably already set correctly.

10. If you want to create a cross compiler (that is, a compiler that runs on one system to compile programs that run on another), you should first build the native compiler and then follow the procedure in Chapter 16 for creating a cross compiler.

11. If you want to build the Ada compiler—which is not completely built by the steps described here—you will need to follow the procedure in Chapter 9.

Configuration Options

The installation options are the ones specified on the command line of the `configure` script. This script generates the files that control compiling and installing. Every option has a default that is correct for creating a compiler (or set of compilers) for your local machine, but there are circumstances where adjustments must be made. The following is a description of these options:

- **Enable and disable** Options that have names beginning with `--enable` all have corresponding option names beginning with `--disable`. Which one of these is the default will vary from one platform to the next. In the following alphabetical listing of the options, these are all listed under the names that begin with `--enable`.

- **With and without** Options that have names beginning with `--with` all have corresponding option names beginning with `--without`. Which of the two is the default will vary from one platform to the next. The following alphabetical listing of the options shows all the names beginning with `--with`.

- **Languages** By default, the `configure` script will prepare to compile all the languages you have installed, but you can specify which languages are actually compiled with the `--enable-languages` option.

- **Prefix directory name** The parts of the compiler are installed into a set of directories with fairly standard names, but you can specify the names to be anything you like. Even when you do elect to change the directory names, you will seldom need to use any option other than `--prefix`, because the prefix directory is the root name of all the installation directories. You should be aware that using the same directory tree as both the source and object files is not recommended because it can lead to some conflicts that cause problems.

- **File names** It is possible to specify modifications to be made to the names of the files that make up the compiler. This is particularly useful if you are developing your own experimental compiler or want to install more than one version of GCC.

- **Libraries** Part of GCC is the libraries that contain the runtime functions employed by the various languages. Both shared and static libraries are created as part of the GCC installation. Some of the libraries are required and some are optional.

■ **Assembler and Linker**   A collection of options can be used to specify the names and locations of the assembler and linker to be employed. If you do not use the options to specify their location, two steps are taken by the configuration procedure to try to locate them:

1. The `configuration` script looks in the directory named *exec-prefix*/ `lib/gcc-lib/`*target/version*, where *exec-prefix* defaults to `/usr/local`, unless it has been change by either the `--prefix` or `--exec-prefix` option for setting directory names. The *target* is the name of the target system, and the *version* number refers to GCC.

2. The `configure` script looks in the directories that are specific to the operating systems (such as `/usr/ccs/bin` for Solaris and `/usr/bin` for Linux).

■ **Code generation**   There are two categories of code generation options: One specifies the type of object code to be included as part of the compiler itself, and the other specifies the kind of code to be produced from the compiler.

■ **Platform**   The platform is also called the *target* or the *host*. Some options apply to specific hardware running specific operating systems. Although the `config.guess` script can almost always guess which platform you are using, there are certain hardware options it cannot detect. Some systems appear to be identical when, actually, slight variations exist.

--bindir=*directory*
The default is *exec-prefix*/`bin`. This is the name of the directory to contain the executables. The `PATH` environment variable normally contains this directory name, so the compiler names can be entered directly from the command line.

--build=*host*
Generates the configuration to be run on the specified host. The default is to be the same platform as the one set by the `--host` option, which defaults to the output of the script `config.guess`.

--cache-file=*filename*
The `configure` script performs numerous tests to determine the configuration and capabilities of the local machine. The named file will contain the results of the test.

--datadir=*directory*
The default is *prefix*/share. This is the name of the directory to contain data files, such as locale information.

--enable-altivec
Specifies that the target platform is a PowerPC that supports AltiVec vector enhancements. This option causes the generation of AltiVec code when appropriate.

--enable-checking=*check[,check,...]*
This option will enable the generation of code that performs some internal checks of the compiler. The checks will generate diagnostic output and increase compilation time, but they have no other effect on output from the compiler. This option is set by default when compiling from a CVS download, but it is not set when compiling a released version.

You can specify the list of checks you want by choosing among `misc`, `tree`, `gc`, `rt1`, and `gcac`. If you omit the list and just specify `--enable-checking`, the list will default to only `misc`, `tree`, and `gc`. The checks `rt1` and `gcac` are very expensive.

--enable-cpp
Specifies that the user accessible version of cpp (the C preprocessor) be installed. This is normally the default. Also see `--with-cpp-install-dir`.

--enable-languages=*language[,language,...]*
Specifies that only the named languages are to have compilers built for them. The available language names are `ada`, `c`, `c++`, `f77`, `java`, `objc`, and `CHILL`. Without this option specified, all languages are compiled. Some extra steps are required to compile Ada, as described in Chapter 9. The CHILL language is no longer supported and will not compile properly except in older versions of GCC.

--enable-libgcj
Specifies that the runtime library for Java be built. This is the default. Specifying `--disable-libgcj` makes it possible to create a Java compiler but use a runtime library from another source.

--enable-maintainer-mode
Specifies that the file named `gcc.pot` be regenerated from the source code. This file is the master message catalog containing all the error and warning diagnostic messages generated by the compiler. This file is used for internationalization, as described in Chapter 11.

 For this to work correctly, you will need the complete source tree and a recent version of gettext.

--enable-multilib
This is the default on most systems. This option specifies that multiple libraries for the target machine be built. These libraries are normally built to support the different target variants, floating point emulation, function calling conventions, and so on. Instead of suppressing the generation of all the libraries, for the platforms listed in Table 2-3 you can suppress certain libraries by name. For example, for the platform arc-*-elf*, you can use the option `--disable-biendian` to suppress the creation of that one library.

--enable-nls
Specifies that Native Language Support (NLS) be included as part of the compiler to allow for the display of warning and error messages in languages other than American English. Also see `--with-included-gettext` and `--with-catgets`.

Platform	Library Name
arc-*-elf*	Biendian
arm-*-*	fpu, 26bit, underscore, interwork, biendian, nofmult
m68*-*-*	softfloat, m68881, m68000, m68020
mips*-*-*	single-float, biendian, softfloat
powerpc*-*-*	aix64, pthread, softfloat, powercpu, powerpccpu, powerpcos, biendian, sysv, aix
rs6000*-*-*	aix64, pthread, softfloat, powercpu, powerpccpu, powerpcos, biendian, sysv, aix

Table 2-3.   *Variant Library Suppression by Platform*

--enable-shared
This is the default. Specifying `--disable-shared` will build only static libraries.

**--enable-shared[=*package[,package ...]]*
For GCC versions 2.95 and earlier, this option is necessary to have shared libraries built. In later versions, shared libraries are built by default for all platforms that support them.

Specifying a list of package names will instruct that shared libraries be built only for the named packages. The recognized package names are `libgcc`, `libstdc++`, `libffi`, `zlib`, `boehm-gc`, and `libjava`.

--enable-target-optspace
Specifies that the libraries should be optimized for size instead of speed.

--enable-threads
For some platforms, this is the default. It specifies that the target supports threads. This affects the libraries for Objective C and exception handling for C++ and Java. If there are no threads for the target system or if the compiler is not able to generate threaded code for the target system, the option `--disable-threads` is equivalent to `--enable-threads=single`.

--enable-threads=*library*
Specifies that the named library is the thread support library. Table 2-4 lists the possible library names.

--enable-version-specific-runtime-libs
Specifies that the header files for certain runtime libraries are installed in a directory named for the target and version instead of the usual places. The libraries are installed

Library	Description
aix	AIX thread support.
dce	DCE thread support.
mach	The generic MACH thread support. This option requires that you provide a copy of the gthr-mach.h header file.
no	Same as single.
posix	Standard POSIX thread support.
rtems	RTEMS thread support.
single	Disables thread support.
solaris	Sun Solaris 2 thread support.
vxworks	VxWorks thread support.
win32	Microsoft Win32 thread support.

Table 2-4.   *Names Used to Select Thread Support*

in *libdir*/gcc-lib/*target/version*. The include files for libstdc++ are installed in *libdir*/gcc-lib/*target/version*/include/g++, unless you specify the location with the --with-gxx-include-dir option.

--enable-win32-registry
Specifies that a Win32 version of GCC is not to use the Registry to locate installation paths of the compiler and its libraries by using the following Registry key:

    HKEY_LOCAL_MACHINE\SOFTWARE\Free Software Foundation*key*

The value of *key* defaults to the GCC version number. The value of the key can be set with the option --enable-win32-registry.

--enable-win32-registry=*key*
Specifies that a Win32 version of GCC locate the installation paths in the Windows Registry using the following Registry key:

    HKEY_LOCAL_MACHINE\SOFTWARE\Free Software Foundation*key*

If you do not specify this option, the default is to use the GCC version number as the key. Using the Registry this way makes it possible to install and use different versions of GCC in different locations.

--exec-prefix=*directory*
The default is *prefix*. This is the name of the top level directory to hold any architecture-dependent files.

--help
This option will print a list of the command-line options and will cause the `configure` script to terminate without doing anything else. The option list is organized by category.

--host=*host*
The name of the host computer. The default is the output of the script `config.guess`. GCC runs on a wide variety of hosts.

--includedir=*directory*
The default is `prefix/include`. This is the name of the directory to contain the C header files.

--infodir=*directory*
The default is `prefix/info`. This is the name of the directory in which to store documentation in the `info` format.

--libdir=*directory*
The default is `exec-prefix/lib`. This is the name of the directory to contain the static libraries and other internal parts of GCC.

--libexecdir=*directory*
The default is `exec-prefix/libexec`. This is the name of the directory to contain certain program executables associated with libraries.

--localstatedir=*directory*
The default is `prefix/etc`. This is the name of the directory to contain modifiable data specific to a single machine. Also see `sysconfdir`.

--mandir=*directory*
The default is `prefix/man`. This is the name of the directory to contain the man pages.

--nfp
Specifies that the machine does not have a floating point unit. This option only applies to `m68k-sun-sunos*` and `m68k-isi-bsd`.

--no-create
The configuration script will run but will not create the output files necessary to compile the code.

--norecursion
The source tree contains a separate `configure` script for each directory. Executing one `configure` script will also cause the execution of the `configure` scripts in all the subdirectories, unless this option is specified.

--prefix=*directory*
The default is `/usr/local`. This is the top level directory used for the entire installation of GCC. The default is to place all the other directories inside the *prefix* directory with the names `bin`, `include`, `info`, `lib`, `man`, and `share`. Specifying the *prefix* name specifies the path name to each of the other directories, unless one of the other naming options is used to specifically change it.

--program-prefix=*prefix*
The default is not to use a prefix. The prefix name is placed on the front of all the file names placed in the bin directory. For example, to change the installed name of the Java compiler from `gcj` to `stim-gcj`, you would use the following option:

```
--program-prefix=stim-
```

--program-suffix=*suffix*
The default is not to use a suffix. The suffix name is added to the end of all the file names placed in the bin directory. For example, to change the installed name of the Java compiler from `gcj` to `gcj-v4`, you would use the following option:

```
--program-suffix=-v4
```

--program-transform-name=*pattern*
The pattern is a `sed` script to be applied to the names of the files placed in the `bin` directory. Using `sed` scripts this way makes it possible to modify the name of each of the executable files individually. For example, to change the name of the Java compiler `gcj` to `gjava`, and to change the name of `g++` to `gcplus`, and leave all the other names as they are, you would use the following option:

```
--program-transform-name='s/^gcj$/gjava/; s/^g++$/gcplus/'
```

This option can be used in combination with the prefix and suffix options because `--program-prefix` and `--program-suffix` are always applied to the name before the pattern scripts of this option are applied. This option cannot be used when creating a cross compiler.

--sbindir=*directory*
The default is *exec-prefix*/sbin. This is the name of the directory to contain the system executables.

--silent
This option suppresses output from `configure` script, which normally lists all the tests it makes. This option is the same as `--quiet`.

--srcdir=*directory*
The named directory is expected to contain the file `configure.in`, which provides `configure` with specific information about the names and locations of the source files.

--sysconfdir=*directory*
The default is `prefix/etc`. This is the name of the directory to contain read-only data specific to a single machine. Also see `localstatedir`.

--target=*host*
The target machine (the one on which the compiler is to run) defaults to the output from the script `config.guess`.

--tmpdir=*directory*
Specifies the name of the directory to be used by the `configure` script to store its temporary work files.

--version
Prints the version number of the `autoconf` utility used to create the `configure` scripts; it takes no further action.

--with-as=*pathname*
Specifies the full path name of the assembler. This option is needed if the assembler cannot be found by following the default search procedure of the `configure` script, or if there is more than one assembler on the system and you need to specify which one to use.

--with-catgets
If NLS is enabled by `--enable-nls` but the host does not have `settext` installed, the compiler will use the host's `catgets`.

--with-cpp-install-dir=*directory*
Specifies that a copy of cpp (the C preprocessor) be installed as `prefix/directory/` cpp in addition to being installed as cpp in the directory specified by the `--bindir` option (which defaults to `exec-prefix/bin`). Also see `--disable-cpp`.

--with-cpu=*cpu*
Specifies a CPU for the target platform. If a specific CPU for a platform is selected, GCC has the opportunity to produce better code than it does when producing code for a family of processors. Table 2-5 lists the CPU names recognized for this version of GCC. New CPU names are being constantly added; therefore, if you don't find the one you need in the table, look in the configuration file `config.gcc`.

Platform	CPU Names
arm*-*-*	xarm2, xarm3, xarm6, xarm7, xarm8, xarm9, xarm250, xarm600, xarm610, xarm700, xarm710, xarm7m, xarm7dm, xarm7dmi, xarm7tdmi, xarm9tdmi, xarm7100, xarm7500, xarm7500fe, xarm810, xxscale, xstrongarm, xstrongarm110, xstrongarm1100
powerpc*-*-*	xcommon, xpower, xpower2, xpower3, xpowerpc, xpowerpc64, xrios, xrios1, xrios2, xrsc, xrsc1, xrs64a, x401, x403, x405, x505, x601, x602, x603, x603e, x604, x604e, x620, x630, x740, x750, xx801, x821, x823, x8607400, x7450, xec603e
sparc*-*-*	supersparc, hypersparc, ultrasparc, v7, v8, v9

Table 2-5.   *CPUs That Can Be Specified by Name*

--with-dwarf2
Specifies that the debugging information produced by the compiler be, by default, in the DWARF 2 format.

--with-gnu-as
Specifies that whatever assembler is found, it is assumed to be the GNU assembler. On a system sensitive to this situation, there could be problems if this option is specified and the actual assembler found is not the GNU assembler. Problems could also arise if this option is specified and the assembler found is the GNU compiler. The following is a list of platforms on which this matters:

hppa1.0-*-*   m68k-sony-bsd

hppa1.1-*-*   m68k-altos-sysv

i386-*-sysv   m68000-hp-hpux

i386-*-isc   m68000-att-sysv

i860-*-bsd   *-lynx-lynxos

m68k-bull-sysv   mips-*

m68k-hp-hpux

If you have more than one assembler on your system, you should specify which one to use with the `--with-as` option. On the following systems, if you use the GNU assembler, you must also use the GNU linker (and specify it with the `--with-ld` option):

i386-*-sysv	m68k-altos-sysv
i860-*-bsd	m68000-hp-hpux
m68k-bull-sysv	m68000-att-sysv
m68k-hp-hpux	*-lynx-lynxos
m68k-sony-bsd	mips-* (except mips-sgi-irix5-*)

--with-gnu-ld
The same as the option `--with-gnu-as`, except it is for the linker.

--with-gxx-include-dir=*directory*
The default is `prefix/`include/g++-v3. This is the name of the directory for the
g++ header files. Also see `--enable-version-specific-runtime-libs`.

--with-headers=*directory*
Specifies the directory that contains the header files of the target when building a cross
compiler. This is a required option if the directory `prefix/target/`sys-include
does not exist. The header files will be copied into the GCC installation directory and
modified so they will be compatible. Also see `--with-newlib` and `--with-libs`.

--with-included-gettext
If NLS is enabled by `--enable-nls`, this option specifies that the build process try
using its own copy of `gettext` before using the version installed on the system.

--with-ld=*pathname*
The same as the option `--with-as`, except it is for the linker.

--with-libs=*"directory [directory ...]"*
This option is for building a cross compiler. The libraries in the named directories
will be copied into the GCC install directory. Also see `--with-headers` and
`--with-newlib`.

--with-local-prefix=*directory*
The default is `/usr/local`. This is the prefix of the include directory that will be
searched by the compiler for locally installed include files. This option should be
specified only if your system already has an established convention of using some
directory other than `/usr/local/include` for locally installed header files. This
option must not be set to `/usr` because the installed header files will be intermixed
with the system header files, and the conflicts will cause some programs not to compile.

Specifying the `--prefix` option has no effect on the prefix for this option. The
`--prefix` option specifies where to install GCC, while this option tells the compiler
where to look for header files when it is running.

--with-newlib
This option is for building a cross compiler. The library newlib is used as the C library of the target machine. The function __eprintf is not included in libgcc.a on the assumption that it will be provided in newlib. Also see --with-headers and --with-libs.

--with-slibdir=*directory*
The default is *libdir*. This is the name of the directory to contain the shared libraries.

--with-stabs
Specifies that the debugging information produced by the compiler be, by default, in the stabs format instead of the standard format of the host system. Normally GCC defaults to producing debugging information in the ECOFF format, but using this flag will change the default to BSD-style stabs. This option sets the default built into the compiler, which can be overridden by using the option -gcoff or -gstabs on the compiler's command line.

The ECOFF format does not contain enough information to debug languages other than C. The stabs format of debugging information carries more information but will usually require the use of the gdb debugger.

--with-system-zlib
Specifies that the compiler should use the installed zlib instead of creating a new one. This option only applies to Java.

--with-x
Specifies that the X Window System is to be used.

--x-includes=*directory*
The name of the directory containing the X include files.

--x-libraries=*directory*
The name of the directory containing the X libraries.

The binutils

Although it is possible to use GCC with native compilers and linkers, the compiler works best, and is most compatible, with the GNU assembler, linker, and other utilities. All the binutils are briefly described, along with the rest of GCC tools, in the tools list in Table 1-4. The following is a list of the names of the utilities in the binutils package:

addr2line	grpof	objcopy	size
ar	ld	objdump	strings
as	nlmconv	ranlib	strip
c++filt	nm	readelf	windres

Several of these utilities read and write information inside object files. This is done through the facilities provided by the Binary File Descriptor (BFD) Library, which is also provided as part of the `binutils` source code. This library provides a collection of functions that are aware of several different formats of object code and can be called on to manipulate them. This makes it possible for each of the utilities to be compiled to run the same on several different platforms.

The following steps can be used to download the source code and install it so that it's ready to be compiled:

1. Select an FTP site. The GNU FTP site is `ftp.gnu.org/gnu`, but you should probably choose from among the hundreds of mirror sites located around the world. You can find a current list of mirror sites at http://www.gnu.org/order/ftp.html. To make your download as smooth as possible, you should choose a mirror site close to you.

2. Download the file named `binutils-2.9.tar.gz` into a work directory. The version number will probably be different because this package is being constantly improved and updated. It is important that you download the file with the FTP option set to binary, not text. This is a collection of compressed files, and the FTP text mode will destroy them by misinterpreting the content and converting certain values into ASCII characters.

3. Select the options you wish to use on the `configure` script. The options available are basically the same as the ones for the GCC script. Just as with the GCC script, the binutils `configure` script can be run without any options, but it is easiest to use the `--prefix` option to specify the name of the directory that will contain the binary installation of the utilities. The directory named as *prefix* will contain the subdirectories `bin`, `include`, `info`, `man`, and `share`. If no directory is named, the default prefix is `/usr/local`.

4. Execute the `configure` script from inside the working directory. Because you are executing the script from another directory, it is necessary to specify its full path name. For example, if you have downloaded the source tree into `/opt/gnu/binutils`, your object directory is named `/opt/bubuild`, and you want to store the final executables and libraries in `/opt/usr/local`, you can execute the configure script as follows:

```
cd /opt/bubuild
/opt/gnu/binutils/configure --prefix=/opt/usr/local
```

5. If it has not already been done, include the new `bin` directory in the PATH environment variable so that the utilities can be located.

As an alternative to FTP, you can get a copy of the current working version of binutils by using CVS. This is normally used only by programmers intending to make modifications to the source, but it is also the only way to keep up with current developments. The CVS access procedure is the same as described earlier for GCC. First, set CVSROOT as follows:

```
CVSROOT=:pserver:anoncvs@sources.redhat.com:/cvs/src
export CVSROOT
```

Then log in with the following command and respond with anoncvs as the password:

```
cvs login
```

The following command will download the entire source tree:

```
cvs -z 9 checkout binutils
```

Once you have everything checked out, you can retrieve updates at any time by logging in and entering the following command:

```
cvs -z 9 update
```

Win32 Binary Installation

If you wish to run GCC on a Windows operating system, you can get a version that is compiled and ready to run. You can find out more about the Cygwin compiler at the following Web site:

```
http://cygwin.com
```

Cygwin

The GNU software development tools can be run on Windows because of a shared library named cygwin1.dll, which contains an API that emulates a UNIX environment. It works on all versions of Windows from 95 on (except for Windows CE). Using these tools makes it possible to write both console and Win32 GUI applications. Writing a GUI application requires the use of the Win32 API, but command-line applications can be written based solely on the Cygwin library.

Although it is free software, the licensing of Cygwin is a mixed bag. Parts of it are covered by the GNU license, parts by the standard X11 license, and parts are public domain. None of it is shareware, so you never have to pay anyone for noncommercial

use, but you need to be aware of some licensing requirements if you are going
to use it for a commercial product (that is, if you are going to sell software that depends
on the library). You can find out how to get a commercial license by sending a query to
sales@cygwin.com.

Two kinds of programs run on Windows: the console type (those that are run from
the command line and do not display windows) and the GUI type (which can be started
from the console but are designed to be windowing programs). There is a slightly
different process for compiling each of these.

The following command will compile and link a console program:

```
gcc helloworld.c -o helloworld.exe
```

It is also possible to use the GCC compiler, along with the Windows API and
appropriate Cygwin utilities, to create Windows programs and DLLs. The process is
described in Chapter 16.

Installation

A special installation program named setup.exe can be used not only for the initial
download and installation but also to download and install updates as new versions
become available. One of the main reasons for the download utility is the fact that the
package has become very large and not everyone needs every piece of it. The setup.exe
program manages the download and lets you choose which parts to download and
specify how you would like to have the software installed.

The following list of steps are a general description of the installation process. The
procedure is mostly automated and, once you get things started, you will be prompted
for input:

1. Create an installation directory. There is much more that just GCC available
   from Cygwin, so you should probably name the directory something like
   c:\cygwin, which is the default. The installation creates a number of directories
   (such as bin and etc), so you are actually creating the root of a directory tree.

2. Download setup.exe into the new directory. Go to the Web site http://
   cygwin.com/download.html, where you will find the latest information or use
   the link to http://cygwin.com/setup.exe, which will cause your browser to
   prompt for a location for the download. On this same page, you will see a link
   to other sites that can be used for the download, which could be convenient
   depending on your location.

3. Execute the setup.exe program. You will be given the option of installing
   the software from the Internet or downloading the software and storing it in
   a directory. You will also find an option for installing the software from a
   directory if you have already downloaded a copy of the software. You can elect
   to install the software directly from the Internet or download it first and install
   it later.

4. Select a mirror site. You will be shown a list of mirror sites, and you will need to select one near you. Your selection may be rejected because a download site is too busy. If this is the case, you should select another one.

5. Select your downloads. You will be provided a list of categories of utilities. All these programs are included in the Cygwin package, and all are compiled and ready to run. You can select as many utilities from as many categories as you like, but selecting the Devel category will provide you with a list of software development utilities, including GCC. The default is for most of the packages to be labeled *Skip*, which means they will not be downloaded. Selecting Skip with the mouse will toggle among the various options—if you want to download the binary version of a program, simply toggle to the version number you would like. If you select a version number, a box will appear that you can check if you also want to download the source code.

6. If you have elected to install the software directly from the Internet, you are done. If you only downloaded the files from the Internet, you will need to run setup again and request them to be installed using the files in your download directory.

Running the Test Suite

Before you finally install a newly compiled version of GCC, you can run a suite of tests on it to verify that it works properly. This is an optional step because, generally speaking, if you are able to compile GCC so it runs at all, it will run correctly. These tests are mainly for developers to use to make certain that fixing a bug or adding a feature did not introduce another bug or remove another feature.

There are a few simple steps you can follow to run the tests on your system:

1. If you have not already done so, download and install the test suite in the same directory as the rest of the GCC source code. You can verify that it has been downloaded by the presence of the directory `gcc/testsuite`.

2. Install the latest version of DejaGnu. Be sure you have the latest version because an older version (1.3 or older) will not work.

3. Set the environment variables. If the installation of DejaGnu places `runtest` and `expect` in directories that are included in the PATH setting, you will probably not need to set these variables. If not, and assuming that DejaGnu has been installed in `/usr/local`, the following two environment variables will need to be set:

```
TCL_LIBRARY=/usr/local/tcl8.0
DEJAGNULIBS=/usr/local/dejagnu
```

4. Run the test. Change to the same directory you use to compile GCC and run whichever tests you like. If you want to run the entire test suite (which can take a very long time), enter the following command:

```
make -k check
```

The `-k` option instructs the `make` command to ignore failure conditions and continue with the next test. To run only the tests for the C front end of the compiler, enter the following command:

```
make -k check-gcc
```

To run only the tests for C++, enter the following command:

```
make -k check-g++
```

5. Check the results of the test. After you have run the tests, you will find that some new files have been created in the test suite subdirectories. The files with the `.log` suffix contain detailed listings of the actions taken by the tests. The files with the `.sum` suffix contain summaries of the test results, with each result being designated by one of the result codes listed in Table 2-6.

Result	Description
PASS	The test was expected to pass, and it passed.
XPASS	The test was not expected to pass, but it passed.
FAIL	The test was expected to pass, but it failed.
XFAIL	The test was expected to fail, and it failed.
UNSUPPORTED	The test is not supported on this platform.
ERROR	A problem was detected while running the test.
WARNING	A possible problem was detected while running the test.

Table 2-6. *Test Result Summary Codes*

The
Complete
Reference

Part II

Using the Compiler Collection

Chapter 3

The Preprocessor

The concept of the preprocessor was originally devised as part of the C programming language. The preprocessor reads the source code and responds to directives embedded in it to produce a modified version of the source, which is fed to the compiler. The preprocessor is still an important part of C, C++, and Objective-C, but it also can be used (with limitations) to preprocess the source code of other languages. For example, it can be used to implement conditional compilation for Fortran and Java.

In GNU terminology, the preprocessor is referred to as CPP. The GNU executable program is named cpp.

Directives

The instructions to the preprocessor appear in the source as *directives* and can be easily spotted in the source code because they all begin with a hash (#) character, appearing as the first nonblank character on a line. The hash character usually appears on column 1 and is immediately followed by the directive keyword. All the directives are listed in Table 3-1 and described in the paragraphs that follow the table. It is possible for the preprocessor to modify source lines other than the ones with directives, but only if there is a directive instructing it to do so.

#define

The #define directive creates the definition of a macro. The macro has a name that, when found elsewhere in the text, is replaced with the string of characters defined as the value of the macro. It is possible to specify parameters that are to be used as part of the macro expansion.

Most macro definitions are, in effect, named constants. These names are traditionally in all uppercase letters. For example, the following definition creates a macro named ARRAY_SIZE that will cause the insertion of the value 512 wherever it is used in the source code:

```
#define ARRAY_SIZE 512
```

This macro can subsequently be used to declare an array of the specified size, as follows:

```
int valarray[ARRAY_SIZE];
```

The following is a well-known macro that uses parameters to create an expression that returns the minimum of two values:

```
#define min(a,b) ((a) < (b) ? (a) : (b))
```

Directive	Description
#define	Defines a name as a macro that the preprocessor will expand in the code every place the name is used.
#elif	Provides an alternative expression to be evaluated by an #if directive.
#else	Provides an alternative set of code to be compiled if an #if, #ifdef, or #ifndef is false.
#error	Produces an error message and halts the preprocessor.
#if	Compiles the code between this directive and its matching #endif only if evaluating an arithmetic expression results in a nonzero value.
#ifdef	Compiles the code between this directive and its matching #endif only if the named macro has been defined.
#ifndef	Compiles the code between this directive and its matching #endif only if the named macro has not been defined.
#include	Searches through a list of directories until it finds the named file; then it inserts the contents of the file just as if it had been inserted by a text editor.
#include_next	The same as #include, but this directive begins the search for the file in the directory following the one in which the current file was found.
#line	Specifies the line number, and possibly the file name, that is reported to the compiler to be used to create debugging information in the object file.
#pragma	A standard method of providing additional information that may be specific to one compiler or one platform.
#undef	Removes a definition previously created by a #define directive.
#warning	Produces a warning message from the preprocessor.
##	The concatenation operator, which can be used inside a macro to combine two strings into one.

Table 3-1. *The Directives Understood by the GNU Preprocessor*

This macro can then be expanded in the source code by using its name and values to be substituted for a and b:

```
result = min(44,uplim);
```

The code expanded from this macro will look like this:

```
result = ((44) < (uplim) ? (44) : (uplim));
```

The following is a list of characteristics and rules that apply to macro definitions:

- A macro definition is contained on one line. If you need to write it on multiple lines for clarity or because of its length, you can do so by using the backslash as a line continuation character, as in the following example, which is an expression returning a random int value in the specified range:

```
#define ran(low,high) \
        ((int)random() % (high-low+1)) \
         + low
```

- The preprocessor processes the text in order and will only make macro substitutions after the macro has been defined. For example, in the following four lines of code, the macro B is used once before it has been defined and once after:

```
#define A 100
sum = A + B;
#define B 200
sum = A + B;
```

The result of preprocessing these four lines is as follows:

```
sum = 100 + B;
sum = 100 + 200;
```

- Substitutions are recursive, so they can be nested one inside the other. That is, once a substitution has been made, the preprocessor will process the same text again to make further substitutions. The following example shows how one macro can be substituted for another:

```
#define TANKARD TSIZE
#define TSIZE 100
tank1 = TANKARD;
#define TSIZE 200
tank2 = TANKARD
```

Preprocessing these five lines results in the following:

```
tank1 = 100;
tank2 = 200;
```

■ To change the definition of a macro, it is necessary to delete it and define it again, as in the following example:

```
#define MLKEYVAL 889
#undef MLKEYVAL
#define MLKEYVAL 890
```

■ For a macro to be defined as having parameters, there must be no spaces between the name of the macro and the parentheses. The following example shows one macro defined with parameters and one with a simple string substitution:

```
#define showint(a) printf("%d\n",a)
#define incrint (a) a++
showint(300);
incrint(bbls);
```

The following is the result of preprocessing the previous lines:

```
printf("%d\n",300);
(a) a++(bbls)
```

■ Macro names are not substituted inside strings, as in the following example:

```
#define BLOCK 8192
printf("The BLOCK number.\n");
```

The output looks like the following:

```
The BLOCK number.
```

■ An argument passed to a macro can be "stringized" by preceding its name with a hash (#) character. In the following example, the macro named MONCK contains a stringized version of its argument, which is combined with other strings (by being placed adjacent to them):

```
#define MONCK(ARGTERM) \
    printf("The term " #ARGTERM " is a string\n")
MONCK(A to B);
```

The output looks like the following:

```
The term A to B is a string
```

- A macro can be defined without a value. Although the macro has no value associated with it, it is still defined and can be used as a flag for testing by #ifdef and #ifndef.

- A *variadic* macro is one with a variable number of arguments. The arguments, represented by an ellipsis (three dots), are all stored as a single comma-separated string in a variable named __VA_ARGS__ that will be expanded inside the macro. For example, the following macro accepts any number of arguments:

```
#define err(...) fprintf(stderr,__VA_ARGS__)
err("%s %d\n","The error code: ",48);
```

The following is the output of the preprocessor after processing these two lines:

```
fprintf(stderr,"%s %d\n","The error code ",48);
```

A variadic macro can include named parameters as long as the variable-length list of parameters comes last. The following is an example of a macro that has two fixed arguments followed by a variable list:

```
#define errout(a,b,...) \
    fprintf(stderr,"File %s    Line %d\n",a,b); \
    fprintf(stderr,__VA_ARGS__)
```

The following is an example of using this macro:

```
errout(__FILE__,__LINE__,"Unexpected termination\n");
```

In all the previous forms of variadic macros, at least one parameter is required to be present to satisfy the requirements of the variable list of parameters, because __VA_ARGS__ is preceded by a comma where it is used in the fprintf() function call inside the macro. As a special case of the concatenation operator, you can request that the preceding comma be removed when __VA_ARGS__ is empty by inserting it in the argument list, like this:

```
fprintf(stderr, ##__VA_ARGS__)
```

#error and #warning

The #error directive will cause the preprocessor to report a fatal error and halt. This can be used to trap conditions where there is an attempt to compile a program in some way that is known not to work. For example, the following will only compile successfully if the macro __unix__ has been defined:

```
#ifndef __unix__
#error "This section will only work on UNIX systems"
#endif
```

The #warning directive works the same as the #error directive, except the condition is not fatal and the preprocessor continues after issuing the message.

#if, #elif, #else, and #endif

The #if directive evaluates an arithmetic expression and examines the result. If the result of the evaluation is not zero, it is considered to be true and the conditional code is compiled. Otherwise, the expression is considered to be false and the code is not compiled. For example, the following string is declared only if the value of the COUNT macro has not been defined as zero:

```
#if COUNT
char *desc = "The count is non-zero";
#endif
```

The following is a list of characteristics and rules that apply to the expression and to the conditional directives:

- The expression can include integer constants and macro names if the macro name has been declared with a value.

- Parentheses can be used to specify the order of evaluation of the expression.

- The expression can include arithmetic in the form of the +, -, *, /, <<, and >> operators, which work much the same as the corresponding integer arithmetic operators in C. All arithmetic is performed as the largest integer size available on the platform, which is normally 64 bits.

- The expression can include the comparison operators >, <, >=, <=, and ==, which work the same as the corresponding operators in C.

- The expression can include the logical operators && and ||.

- The not (!) logical operator can be used to reverse the result of an expression. For example, the following is true only if LIMXP is not greater than 12:

    ```
    #if !(LIMXP > 12)
    ```

- The defined operator can be used to determine whether a macro has been defined. For example, the following is true only if a macro named MINXP has been defined:

    ```
    #if defined(MINXP)
    ```

    The not (!) operator is often used in conjunction with the defined operator to test for a macro having not been defined, as in the following example:

    ```
    #if !defined(MINXP)
    ```

- An identifier that has not been defined as a macro always results in zero. The -Wundef option can be used to produce a warning in this circumstance.

- Macro names defined as having arguments always evaluate to zero. The -Wundef option can be used produce a warning in this circumstance.

- An #else directive can be used to provide alternate code that will be compiled, as in the following example:

```
#if MINTXT <= 5
#define MINTLOG 11
#else
#define MINTLOG 14
#endif
```

- An #elif directive can be used to provide one or more alternative expressions, as in the following example:

```
#if MINTXT <= 5
#define MINTLOG 11
#elif MINTXT == 6
#define MINTLOG 12
#elif MINTXT == 7
#define MINTLOG 13
#else
#define MINTLOG 14
#endif
```

#ifdef, #else, and #endif

The lines of code following the #ifdef directive are compiled only if the named macro has been defined. The #ifdef directive is terminated by an #endif. For example, the following array is declared only if the macro MINTARRAY has been defined:

```
#ifdef MINTARRAY
int xarray[20];
#endif  /* MINTARRAY */
```

The comment on the line with the #endif is not required, but it has been shown to be helpful in reading the code.

The inverse of the #ifdef directive is the #ifndef directive, which will compile the conditional code only if the macro has *not* been defined.

An #else directive can be used following an #ifdef to provide an alternative. In the following example, if MINTARRAY has been defined, the array will be of type int; otherwise, it will be of type char:

```
#ifdef MINTARRAY
int xarray[20];
#else
char xarray[20];
#endif /* MINTARRAY */
```

Other directives can be included as part of the code that is conditionally compiled. This includes `#ifdef`, `#ifndef`, and `#if`, but each one must be properly paired with its own `#endif`.

#include

The `include` directive searches for the named file and inserts its contents into the text just as if it had been inserted there by a text editor. A file that is included this way is generally referred to as a *header* file and carries a .h suffix, but it can be any text file with any name.

The `include` directive has two forms. The one most used for system header files surrounds the name with a pair of angle brackets, with the form for user header files being surrounded by quotes, as follows:

```
#include <syshead.h>
#include "userhead.h"
```

The following is a list of characteristics and rules that apply to the `#include` directive:

- The angle brackets surrounding the file name cause the search to begin in any directories that were specified by using a `-I` option and then continue by looking through the standard set of system directories.

- A pair of quotes surrounding the file name causes the search to begin in the current working directory (the one containing the source file being processed) and then continue with the directories that would normally be searched by a directive with the angle brackets.

- On a UNIX system, the standard set of system directories is as follows:

```
/usr/local/include
/usr/lib/gcc-lib/target/version/include
/usr/target/include
/usr/include
```

- Two separate lists of directories are searched to locate header files. The standard system header files are in the second list. The `-I` command-line option adds directories to the list that is searched first. The options `-prefix`, `-withprefix`, and `-idirafter` all manipulate the directory names in the second list searched.

- If GCC is compiling a C++ program, the directory /usr/include/g++v3 is searched by the preprocessor before any of the other standard system directories.

- A relative path name can be used as the name of the file. For example, if you specify #include <sys/time.h>, the file time.h will be sought in a subdirectory named sys of all the standard directories.

- The slash character is always interpreted as a path separator, even on systems that use a different character (such as a backslash) as the path separator. This way, it is always portable to use a slash for the path names.

- The file name is taken literally. No macros are expanded and no characters have special meanings. If the name specified contains an asterisk or backslash character, the name of the file must contain a literal asterisk or backslash character.

- A #define directive can be used to specify the name of a header file, as in the following example:

```
#define BOGHEADER "bog_3.h"
#include BOGHEADER
```

- It is an error to have anything other than a comment on the same line as the #include directive.

- For the purposes of searching for files, the #line directive does not change the current working directory.

- The -I- option can be used to modify how the -I options specify which directories are to be searched. See Appendix D for more information.

#include_next

The #include_next directive is used only for special situations. It is used inside one header file to include another one, and it causes the search for the new header file to begin in the directory following the one in which the current header was found.

For example, if the normal search for a header file is to look in directories A, B, C, D, and E, and if the current header file has been found in directory B, an #include_next directive in the current header file will cause a search for the newly named header file in directories C, D, and E.

This directive can be used to add or modify definitions to system header files without making modifications to the files themselves. For example, the system header file /usr/include/stdio.h contains a macro definition named getc that reads a single character from an input stream. To change this one macro definition to a dummy that always returns the same character, but leave the rest of the header as it is, you can create your own version of the stdio.h header file containing the following:

```
#include_next "stdio.h"
#undef getc
#define getc(fp) ((int)'x')
```

Using this header will cause the system version of `stdio.h` to be included and then have the `getc` macro redefined.

#line

Debuggers need to be able to associate file names and line numbers with data items and executable code, so the preprocessor inserts this information into its output to the compiler. It is necessary to track the original names and numbers this way because the preprocessor combines several files into one. The compiler uses these numbers when it builds the tables it inserts into the object code.

Normally, allowing the preprocessor to determine the line numbers by counting them is exactly what needs to happen, but it is also possible that some other processing can cause these line numbers to be off. For example, a common method of implementing SQL statements is to write them as macros and a have a special processor expand the macros into the detailed SQL function calls. This expansion can run to several lines and cause the line count to be different. The SQL process will correct this by inserting `#line` directives in its output so that the preprocessor will follow the line numbering of the original source code.

The following is a list of characteristics and rules that apply to the `#line` directive:

- Specifying the `#line` directive with a number causes the preprocessor to replace its current line count with the specified number. For example, the following directive sets the current line number to 137:

  `#line 137`

- Specifying `#line` directive with both a number and a file name instructs the preprocessor to change both the line number and the name of the current file. For example, the following directive will set the current position to the first line of a file named `muggles.h`:

  `#line 1 "muggles.h"`

- The `#line` directive modifies the content of the predefined macros `__LINE__` and `__FILE__`.

- The `#line` directive has no effect on the file names or directories searched by the `#include` directive.

#pragma and _Pragma

The #pragma directive provides a standard method of specifying information that may be specific to the compiler. According to the standard, a compiler may attach any meaning it wishes to a #pragma directive.

All the GCC pragmas are defined as two words—the first being GCC and the second being the name of the specific pragma.

#pragma GCC dependency

The dependency pragma tests the timestamp of the current file against the timestamp of another named file. If the other file is newer, a warning message is issued. For example, the following pragma tests the timestamp of a file named lexgen.tbl:

```
#pragma GCC dependency "lexgen.tbl"
```

If lexgen.tbl is newer than the current file, a message like the following is produced by the preprocessor:

```
warning: current file is older than "lexgen.tbl"
```

Other text can be added to the pragma directive and it will be included as part of the warning message, as in the following example:

```
#pragma GCC dependency "lexgen.tbl" Header lex.h needs to be updated
```

This would create the following warning messages:

```
show.c:26: warning: current file is older than "lexgen.tbl"
show.c:26: warning: Header lex.h needs to be updated
```

#pragma GCC poison

The poison pragma can be used to cause a message to be issued whenever a specified name is used. You can use this, for example, to guarantee that certain function calls are never made. The following pragma will issue a warning whenever either of the memory-to-memory copy functions is called:

```
#pragma GCC poison memcpy memmove
memcpy(target,source,size);
```

This code will produce the following warning message from the preprocessor:

```
show.c:38:9: attempt to use poisoned "memcpy"
```

#pragma GCC system_header

The code beginning with the system_header pragma and continuing to the end of the file is treated as if it were the code in a system header. System header code is compiled slightly differently because runtime libraries cannot be written so they are strictly C standard conforming. All warnings (except on the #warnings directive) are suppressed. In particular, certain macro definitions and expansions are immune to warning messages.

_Pragma

A normal #pragma directive cannot be included as part of a macro expansion, so the _Pragma operator was devised to generate #pragma directives inside macros. To create a poison pragma inside a macro, write it this way:

```
_Pragma("GCC poison printf")
```

The backslash character is used as the escape character, so a quoted string can be inserted to create a dependency pragma this way:

```
_Pragma("GCC dependency \"lexgen.tbl\"")
```

#undef

The #undef directive is used to remove the definition of a macro previously created by a #define directive. This can be done if the macro definition is no longer needed, or if it needs to be redefined with a new value.

##

The concatenation directive can be used inside a macro to join two source code tokens into one. This can be used to construct names that would otherwise be misinterpreted by the parser. For example, the following two macros will perform concatenation:

```
#define PASTE1(a) a##house
#define PASTE2(a,b) a##b
result = PASTE1(farm);
result = PASTE1(ranch);
result = PASTE2(front,back);
```

The following is the code resulting from preprocessing these five lines:

```
result = farmhouse;
result = ranchhouse;
result = frontback;
```

Predefined Macros

The GCC compiler predefines a large number of macros. Exactly which ones are defined, and what values they contain, depends on the language being compiled, the command-line options specified, the platform being used, the target platform, which version of the compiler is running, and what environment variables have been set. You can use the -dM option on the preprocessor to view the entire list by entering a command like the following:

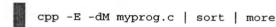

```
cpp -E -dM myprog.c | sort | more
```

The list output by this command contains #define directives for every macro that became defined in the preprocessor after processing the specified input source file and all the headers it included.

Table 3-2 lists the macros that are almost always defined, along with a description of the contents of each one.

Macro	Description
__BASE_FILE__	A quoted string containing the full path name of the source file specified on the command line (not necessarily the file in which the macro is used). Also see __FILE__.
__CHAR_UNSIGNED__	This macro is defined to indicate that the char data type is unsigned on the target machine. This is used by limits.h to determine the values of CHAR_MIN and CHAR_MAX.
__cplusplus	Defined only when the source code is a C++ program. It is defined as 1 if the compiler does not fully conform to a standard; otherwise, it is defined with the month and year of the standard in the same manner as __STDC_VERSION__ for C.
__DATE__	An 11-character quoted string containing the date the program was compiled. It has the form "May 3 2002".

Table 3-2.   *The Basic Set of Predefined Macros*

Macro	Description
__FILE__	A quoted string containing the name of the source file in which the macro is used. Also see __BASE_FILE__.
__func__	The same as __FUNCTION__.
__FUNCTION__	A quoted string containing the name of the current function.
__GNUC__	This macro is always defined as the major version number of the compiler. For example, if the compiler version number is 3.1.2, this macro is defined as 3.
__GNUC_MINOR__	This macro is always defined as the minor version number of the compiler. For example, if the compiler version number is 3.1.2, this macro is defined as 1.
__GNUC_PATCHLEVEL__	This macro is always defined as the revision level of the compiler. For example, if the compiler version number is 3.1.2, this macro is defined as 2.
__GNUG__	Defined by the C++ compiler. This macro is defined whenever both __cplusplus and __GNUC__ are also defined.
__INCLUDE_LEVEL__	An integer value specifying the current depth level of the include file. The value at the base file (the one specified on the command line) is 0 and is increased by 1 inside each file input by an #include directive.
__LINE__	The line number of the file in which the macro is used.
__NO_INLINE__	This macro is defined as 1 when no functions are to be expanded inline, either because there is no optimization or inlining has been specifically disabled.
__OBJC__	This macro is defined as 1 if the program is being compiled as Objective-C.

Table 3-2.   *The Basic Set of Predefined Macros* (continued)

Macro	Description
__OPTIMIZE__	This macro is defined as 1 whenever any level of optimization has been specified.
__OPTIMIZE_SIZE__	This macro is defined as 1 if optimization is set for size instead of speed.
__REGISTER_PREFIX__	This macro is a token (not a string) that is the prefix for register names. It can be used to write assembly language that's portable to more than one environment.
__STDC__	Defined as 1 to indicate that the compiler is conforming to standard C. This macro is not defined when compiling C++ or Objective-C, and it is also not defined when the -traditional option is specified.
__STDC_HOSTED__	Defined as 1 to signify a "hosted" environment (one that has the complete standard C library available).
__STDC_VERSION__	A long integer specifying the standards version number in terms of its year and month. For example, the 1999 revision of the standard is the value 199901L. This macro is not defined when compiling C++ or Objective-C, and it is also not defined when the -traditional option is specified.
__STRICT_ANSI__	Defined if and only if either -ansi or -std has been specified on the command line. It is used in the GNU header files to restrict the definitions to those defined in the standard.
__TIME__	A seven-character quoted string containing the time the program was compiled. It has the form "18:10:34".
__USER_LABEL_PREFIX__	This macro is a token (not a string) that is used as the prefix on symbols in assembly language. The token varies depending on the platform, but it's usually an underscore character.

Table 3-2.   *The Basic Set of Predefined Macros* (continued)

Macro	Description
__USING_SJLJ_EXCEPTIONS__	This macro is defined as 1 if the mechanism for handling exceptions is setjmp and longjmp.
__VERSION__	The complete version number. There is no specific format for this information, but it will at least include the major and minor release numbers.

Table 3-2. *The Basic Set of Predefined Macros* (continued)

Table 3-3 lists a collection of C++ keywords that can be used as the names of operators normally written with punctuation characters. They are treated by the preprocessor as if they were macros created by the #define directive. If you want to have these same operators available in C or Objective-C, they are defined in the header file iso646.h.

Operator Name	Equivalent Punctuation Form
and	&&
and_eq	&=
bitand	&
bitor	|
compl	~
not	!
not_eq	!=
or	||
or_eq	|=
xor	^
xor_eq	^=

Table 3-3. *The Named Form of the Logical Operators*

Including a Header File Only Once

Because header files will include other header files, it is very easy to have a program that includes the same header file more than once. This can lead to error messages because items that have already been defined are being defined again. To prevent this from happening, a header file can be written to detect whether it has already been included. The following is an example of how this can be done:

```
/* myheader.h */
#ifndef MYHEADER_H
#define MYHEADER_H
    /* The body of the header file */
#endif    /* MYHEADER_H */
```

In this example, the header file is named myheader.h. The first line tests whether MYHEADER_H has been defined. If it has, the entire header file is skipped. If MYHEADER_H has not been defined, it is immediately defined and the header file is processed.

The system header files all use this technique. The names defined in them all begin with an underscore character to prevent them from interfering with any names you define. The convention is for the defined name to be in all uppercase and to contain the name of the file.

The GNU preprocessor recognizes this construction and keeps track of the header files that use it. This way, it can optimize processing the headers by recognizing the file name and not even reading header files that have already been included.

Including Location Information in Error Messages

The predefined macros can be used to automate the construction of error messages that contain detailed information about the location at which the error occurred. The predefined macros __FILE__, __LINE__, and __func__ contain the information, but they must be used at the point the message is created. Therefore, if you write a function that contains them all, error messages will be reported as happening in that function.

The perfect solution is to define a macro that contains them. That way, when the preprocessor expands the macros, they will all be in the correct place and have the correct information. The following is an example of an error macro that writes messages to standard error:

```
#define msg(str) \
    fprintf(stderr,"File: %s  Line: %d  Function: %s\n%s\n", \
        __FILE__,__LINE__,__func__,str);
```

To invoke this macro from any place in the code, it is only necessary to specify a string describing the error:

```
msg("There is an error here.");
```

Another advantage of doing it this way is that your method for handling error conditions can be changed by simply changing the macro. It could be converted to throw exceptions or log the error messages to a file. The message produced from this example will look something like the following:

```
File: hamlink.c  Line: 822   Function: hashDown
There is an error here
```

Removing Source Code in Place

During software development, it often becomes necessary to remove blocks of code in such a way that they can be restored later, if needed. The code can be surrounded by comments, but this can cause problems because comments in C don't nest inside one another, and there could be a number of comments included in the code that is to be removed. A clean and safe way to omit the code is by using the preprocessor's #if directive as follows:

```
#if 0
    /* The code being removed */
#endif
```

Not only will this cleanly handle the comments, it is quite obvious that the code was intentionally removed.

Producing Makefiles

The preprocessor can be used to read a source file and produce the dependency line that goes in a makefile. For example, the following command uses the -E to instruct the compiler to invoke the preprocessor and then halt without compiling or linking. The -M option instructs the preprocessor to output a complete dependency line:

```
gcc -E -M trick.c
```

The source file trick.c contains include statements for the system file <stdio.h> and the local file "barrow.h", but the dependency list includes not only these files but every file they cause to be included. The resulting dependency line looks like the following:

```
trick.o: trick.c /usr/include/stdio.h /usr/include/features.h \
    /usr/include/sys/cdefs.h /usr/include/gnu/stubs.h \
    /usr/lib/gcc-lib/i386-redhat-linux/2.96/include/stddef.h \
    /usr/include/bits/types.h /usr/include/bits/pthreadtypes.h \
```

```
/usr/include/bits/sched.h /usr/include/libio.h /usr/include/_G_config.h \
/usr/include/wchar.h /usr/include/bits/wchar.h /usr/include/gconv.h \
/usr/lib/gcc-lib/i386-redhat-linux/2.96/include/stdarg.h \
/usr/include/bits/stdio_lim.h barrow.h
```

As described in Appendix D, the options –MD, –MMD, –MF, –MG, –MP, –MQ, and –MT can be used to create dependencies in different ways and in different formats than –M. Examples of using these options to create makefiles can be found in Chapter 14.

Command-Line Options and Environment Variables

A number of command-line options can be used to specify the way the preprocessor operates. These options are listed here and described in detail in Appendix D.

-A	--include-with-prefix-after
-A-	--include-with-prefix-before
--assert	-iprefix
-C	-isystem
-D	-iwithprefix
--define-macro	-iwithprefixbefore
--dependencies	-M
-fident	-MD
-fpreprocessed	-MF
-H	-MG
-I	-MM
-I-	-MMD
-idirafter	-MP
-imacros	-MQ
-include	-MT
--include-barrier	—no-line-commands
--include-directory	--no-standard-includes
--include-directory-after	-nostdinc
--include-prefix	-nostdinc++
--include-with-prefix	-P

```
--preprocess                          --user-dependencies
--print-missing-file-dependencies     -Wp
-remap                                --write-dependencies
--trace-includes                      --write-user-dependencies
-trigraphs                            -Wsystem-headers
-U                                    -Wundef
-undef                                -Wunknown-pragmas
--undefine-macro
```

The following is a list of the environment variables that can be set to pass instructions to the preprocessor. The environment variables are described in Appendix B.

```
C_INCLUDE_PATH, CPATH, CPLUS_INCLUDE_PATH, DEPENDENCIES_OUTPUT,
OBJC_INCLUDE_PATH, SUNPRO_DEPENDENCIES
```

The
Complete
Reference

Chapter 4

Compiling C

67

This chapter describes the commands and options that can be used to compile C programs into object files, executable programs, and libraries. The chapter includes a general description of the various C standards supported by GCC along with a description of each of the C language extensions that are unique to GCC.

The original C compiler on UNIX is named CC (*C Compiler*). From this, the original GNU C compiler was named GCC (*GNU C Compiler*). The acronym has remained the same, but its meaning has been changed to *GNU Compiler Collection* because the compiler has grown to encompass a number of languages. However, the basic underlying structure of GCC is still the C programming language. Fortunately, the structure of the C language lends itself to representing very low-level hardware-like operations which makes it possible to build other language compilers on top of the code generating software of the C language base.

Fundamental Compiling

Table 4-1 lists the file name suffixes that have to do with compiling and linking C programs. A table listing all the suffixes recognized by GCC can be found in Appendix D.

Suffix	File Contains
.a	Static object library (archive).
.c	C source code that is to be preprocessed.
.h	C source code header file.
.i	C source code that is not to be preprocessed. This type of file is produced as an intermediate step in compilation.
.o	An object file in a format appropriate to be supplied to the linker. This type of file is produced as an intermediate step in compilation.
.s	Assembly language code. This type of file is produced as an intermediate step in compilation.
.so	Shared object library.

Table 4-1. *File Name Suffixes in C Programming*

Single Source to Executable

The following is the source code of a very simple "hello, world" program:

```
/* helloworld.c */
#include <stdio.h>
int main(int argc,char *argv[])
{
    printf("hello, world\n");
    return(0);
}
```

The simplest and most straightforward way to compile this program into an executable is to store the source code in a file named helloworld.c and enter the following command:

```
$ gcc helloworld.c
```

The compiler determines that the file named on the command line is a C source file by examining the suffix of the file name. The default action of GCC is to compile the source file into an object file, link the object into an executable, and then delete the object file. The command does not specify the name of the resulting executable file, so the compiler uses the default name a.out in the current directory. Entering the name of the program from the command line will cause it to run and display its output:

```
$ a.out
hello, world
```

The -o option can be used to specify the name of the executable program output from the compiler. The following command will produce an executable program named howdy:

```
$ gcc helloworld.c -o howdy
```

Entering the name of the program on the command line will run it, as shown here:

```
$ howdy
hello, world
```

Source File to Object File

The –c option instructs GCC to compile the source code but not to leave the object file on disk and skip the step that links the object into an executable. In this case, the default output file name is the same as the input source file name, but with the .o suffix. For example, the following command will produce an object file named helloworld.o:

```
$ gcc -c helloworld.c
```

The –o option can be used to override the name of the object file produced. The following command will produce an object file named harumph.o:

```
$ gcc -c helloworld.c -o harumph.o
```

In the construction of object libraries, or just for the creation of a collection of object files to be linked later, a single command can be used to create object files from several source files. The following command will produce object files named arglist.o, ponder.o, and listsort.o:

```
$ gcc -c arglist.c ponder.c listsort.c
```

Multiple Source Files to Executable

The GCC compiler handles linking automatically, even if more than one source file is being compiled. For example, the following source is stored in a file named hellomain.c and calls a function named sayhello():

```c
/* hellomain.c */
void sayhello(void);
int main(int argc,char *argv[])
{
    sayhello();
    return(0);
}
```

The following source is stored in a file named sayhello.c and defines the sayhello() function:

```c
/* sayhello.c */
#include <stdio.h>
void sayhello()
```

```
{
    printf("hello, world\n");
}
```

The following command compiles the two programs into object files, links them into an executable program named `hello`, and deletes the object files:

```
$ gcc hellomain.c sayhello.c -o hello
```

Preprocessing

The `-E` option instructs the compiler to run only the preprocessor. The following command will preprocess the `helloworld.c` source file and list it to the standard output:

```
$ gcc -E helloworld.c
```

The `-o` option can be used to direct the preprocessed code to a file. As shown earlier in Table 4-1, C source code that does not need to be processed is stored in a file with a `.i` extension, which can be achieved this way:

```
$ gcc -E helloworld.c -o helloworld.i
```

Generating Assembly Language

The `-S` option instructs the compiler to generate assembly language and then stop. The following command will create an assembly language file named `helloworld.s` from the C source file `helloworld.c`:

```
$ gcc -S helloworld.c
```

The form of the assembly language depends on the target platform of the compiler. If multiple source files are compiled, an assembly language module is produced for each one of them.

Creating a Static Library

A static library is a collection of .o files produced by the compiler in the usual way. Linking a program with the object files in the library is the same as linking it with the object files in a directory. Another name for a static library is an *archive*, and the utility that manages the content of such an archive is named `ar`.

To construct a library, it is first necessary to compile object modules that go into it. For example, the following two source files are named `hellofirst.c` and `hellosecond.c`:

```
/* hellofirst.c */
#include <stdio.h>
void hellofirst()
{
    printf("The first hello\n");
}
/* hellosecond.c */
#include <stdio.h>
void hellosecond()
{
    printf("The second hello\n");
}
```

These two source files can be compiled into object files with the following command:

```
$ gcc -c hellofirst.c hellosecond.c
```

The `ar` utility can be used with the `-r` option to create a new library and insert the object files into it. The `-r` option will create the library, if it does not exist, and will add (by replacing, if necessary) the named object modules to the archive. The following command creates a library named `libhello.a` that contains the two object modules of this example:

```
$ ar -r libhello.a hellofirst.o hellosecond.o
```

The library is now complete and ready to be used. The following program, named `twohellos.c`, calls both of the functions in the new library:

```
/* twohellos.c */
void hellofirst(void);
void hellosecond(void);
int main(int argc,char *argv[])
{
    hellofirst();
    hellosecond();
    return(0);
}
```

The `twohellos` program can be compiled and linked in a single command by specifying the library on the command line as follows:

```
$ gcc twohellos.c libhello.a -o twohellos
```

The naming convention for static libraries is to begin the name with the three letters *lib* and end the name with the suffix .a. All the system libraries use this naming convention, and it allows a sort of shorthand form of the library names on the command line by using the -l (ell) option. The following command line differs from the previous one only in the location gcc expects to find the library:

```
$ gcc twohellos.c -lhello -o twohellos
```

Specifying the full path name causes the compiler to look for the library in the named directory. The library name can be specified as either an absolute path (such as /usr/worklibs/libhello.a) or a path relative to the current directory (such as ../lib/libhello.a) The -l option does not provide the capability of specifying a path, but instead instructs the compiler to look for the library among the system libraries.

Creating a Shared Library

A shared library is a collection of object files produced by the compiler in a special way. All the addresses (variable references and function calls) inside each of the object modules are relative instead of absolute, which allows the shared modules to be dynamically loaded and executed while the program is running.

To construct a shared library, it is first necessary to compile the object modules that go into it. For example, the following two source files are named `shellofirst.c` and `shellosecond.c`:

```
/* shellofirst.c */
#include <stdio.h>
void shellofirst()
{
    printf("The first hello from a shared library\n");
}
/* shellosecond.c */
#include <stdio.h>
void shellosecond()
{
    printf("The second hello from a shared library\n");
}
```

These two source files can be compiled into object files with the following command:

```
$ gcc -c -fpic shellofirst.c shellosecond.c
```

The −c option is specified to instruct the compiler to produce .o object files. The −fpic option causes the output object modules to be generated using relocatable addressing. The acronym pic stands for *position independent code*.

The following gcc command uses the object files to construct the shared library named hello.so:

```
$ gcc -shared shellofirst.o shellosecond.o -o hello.so
```

The −o option names the output file, and the .so suffix on the file name tells GCC that the object files are to be linked into a shared library. Normally the linker locates and uses the main() function as the entry point of a program, but this output module has no such entry point, and the −shared option is necessary to prevent an error message.

The compiler recognizes that a file with the .c suffix is the C source code of program, and it knows how to compile it into an object file. Because of this, the two previous commands can be combined into one, and the modules can be compiled and stored directly into the shared library with the following command:

```
$ gcc -fpic -shared shellofirst.c shellosecond.c -o hello.so
```

The following program, in the file named stwohellos.c, is the mainline of a program that calls the two functions in the shared library:

```
/* stwohellos.c */
void shellofirst(void);
void shellosecond(void);
int main(int argc,char *argv[])
{
    shellofirst();
    shellosecond();
    return(0);
}
```

This program can be compiled and linked to the shared library with the following command:

```
$ gcc stwohellos.c hello.so -o stwohellos
```

The program `stwohellos` is now ready to run, but to do so it must be able to locate the shared library `hello.so`, because the routines stored in the library must be loaded at runtime. Information on the location of shared libraries can be found in Chapter 12.

Overriding the Naming Convention

If circumstances require that you name your C source file using something other than with a .c suffix, you can override the default by using the `-x` option to specify the language. For example, the following command will compile the C source code from the file `helloworld.jxj` and create an executable program named `helloworld`:

```
$ gcc -xc helloworld.jxj -o helloworld
```

Normally, without the `-x` option, any source files with unknown extensions are assumed to be known to the linker, and the names are passed to it unchanged. The `-x` option applies to unknown extensions for all files following it on the command line. For example, the following command assumes that both `align.zzz` and `types.xxx` are C source files:

```
$ gcc -c -xc align.zzz types.xxx
```

Standards

By using command-line options, you can compile any C program from the original syntax (now often referred to as *traditional*) to the latest standard language with GNU extensions. By default, GCC compiles the source using the rules of the latest standard, and it has all GNU extensions enabled. The available options are listed in Table 4-2. Appendix D contains a more detailed description of each of these options.

The most fundamental difference between a standards compliant and noncompliant C program is the form of the arguments on a function call and the presence or absence of function prototypes. To help in overcoming this problem, the GCC compiler has the `-aux-info` option, which can be used to automatically generate prototypes for the functions. For example, the following command will create a header file named `slmwrk.h` that contains the prototypes for all the functions defined in a source file named `slmwrk.c`:

```
$ gcc slmwrk.c -aux-info slmwrk.h
```

The following command can be used to create a header file named `prototypes.h` that contains prototypes for the functions of the C source files in an entire directory:

```
$ gcc *.c -aux-info prototypes.h
```

Option	Description
-ansi	Compiles programs that are standards compliant as well as the GNU extensions
-pedantic	Issues warnings required by strict standards compliance
-std=c89	The ISO C89 standard
-std=C99	The ISO C99 standard
-std=gnu89	The ISO C89 standard with GNU extensions and some C99 features
-traditional	Compiles with the original C syntax

Table 4-2. *Options Controlling the C Language Version*

The functions of a C program can be converted to ANSI standard form by using the protoize utility, which is described in Chapter 14.

C Language Extensions

The C compiler can be set to compile according to the rules of one of the C standards by using options such as -ansi and -std, but several extensions can also be used. Many of the GCC extensions in past versions have been specified as part of the new C standards, but the list of extensions described in the following sections are only those that are not part of any C standard. Except for a few special cases, they are unique to GCC.

Specifying the -pedantic option (as well as some other options) will cause warning messages to be issued when using a C language extension, but you can suppress the warning messages by preceding the extended expression with the keyword __extension__.

Because of the internal structure of GCC, many of the extensions described here apply to both C++ and Objective-C as well as C. The C++ and Objective-C compilers use parts of the C compiler, so making an addition to C or the preprocessor will, in some cases, make the same additions to the other languages. However, some of the extensions conflict with fundamental language definitions, so they are disabled or take some other form in C++ or Objective-C.

Alignment

The __alignof__ operator returns the boundary alignment of a data type or a specific data item. The following program displays the alignments of each of the data types:

```
/* align.c */
#include <stdio.h>
typedef struct {
    double dvalue;
    int ivalue;
} showal;

int main(int argc,char *argv[])
{
    printf("__alignof__(char)=%d\n",__alignof__(char));
    printf("__alignof__(short)=%d\n",__alignof__(short));
    printf("__alignof__(int)=%d\n",__alignof__(int));
    printf("__alignof__(long)=%d\n",__alignof__(long));
    printf("__alignof__(long long)=%d\n",__alignof__(long long));
    printf("__alignof__(float)=%d\n",__alignof__(float));
    printf("__alignof__(double)=%d\n",__alignof__(double));
    printf("__alignof__(showal)=%d\n",__alignof__(showal));
    return(0);
}
```

The actual alignments vary from one hardware system to the next, because it is the machine that sets the requirements. The alignment can either be an absolute hardware requirement or a boundary suggestion to make data access more efficient.

Anonymous Unions

Within a struct, a union can be declared without a name, making it possible to address the union members directly, just as if they were members of the struct. The following example provides two names and two data types for the same four bytes:

```
struct {
    char code;
    union {
        char chid[4];
        int numid;
    };
    char *name;
} morx;
```

The members of this struct can be addressed as morx.code, morx.chid, morx.numid, and morx.name.

Arrays of Variable Length

An array can be declared in such a way that its size is determined at runtime. This is achieved by using an expression as the declaring subscript. For example, the following function accepts two strings and combines them into a single string with a space inserted between them:

```
void combine(char *str1,char *str2)
{
    char outstr[strlen(str1) + strlen(str2) + 2];

    strcpy(outstr,str1);
    strcat(outstr," ");
    strcat(outstr,str2);
    printf("%s\n",outstr);
}
```

An array of variable length can be passed in as an argument, as in the following example:

```
void fillarray(int length,char letters[length])
{
    int i;
    char character = 'A';

    for(i=0; i<length; i++)
        letters[i] = character++;
}
```

The order of the arguments can be reversed by making a forward declaration so that the type of length is known at the time the letters array is read, as in the following:

```
void fillarray(int length; char letters[length], int length)
```

You can have as many of these forward declarations as you need (separated by commas or semicolons), as long as the last one is followed by a semicolon.

Arrays of Zero Length

GNU C allows the declaration of arrays of zero length to facilitate the creation of variable-length structures. This only makes sense if the zero-length array is the last member of a struct. The size of the array can be specified by simply being allocated the amount of space necessary. The following program demonstrates the technique:

```
/* zarray.c */
#include <stdio.h>
typedef struct {
    int size;
    char string[0];
} vlen;

int main(int argc,char *argv[])
{
    int i;
    int count = 22;
    char letter = 'a';

    vlen *line = (vlen *)malloc(sizeof(vlen) + count);
    line->size = count;
    for(i=0; i<count; i++)
        line->string[i] = letter++;

    printf("sizeof(vlen)=%d\n",sizeof(vlen));

    for(i=0; i<line->size; i++)
        printf("%c ",line->string[i]);
    printf("\n");

    return(0);
}
```

The printf() statement in this example prints the value 4 because the sizeof operator can only detect the size of the int value in the struct. The output from the zarray program looks like the following:

```
sizeof(vlen)=4
a b c d e f g h i j k l m n o p q r s t u v
```

The same thing can be achieved by defining the array as an incomplete type. This approach not only has the advantage being standard C, but can also be used in exactly the same way as the previous example. As an added benefit the size of the array can be specified in the initializers, as in the following example where the size of the array is set to four characters:

```
/* incarray.c */
#include <stdio.h>
typedef struct {
```

```
        int size;
        char string[];
    } vlen;

    vlen initvlen = { 4, { 'a', 'b', 'c', 'd' } };

    int main(int argc,char *argv[])
    {
        int i;

        printf("sizeof(vlen)=%d\n",sizeof(vlen));
        printf("sizeof(initvlen)=%d\n",sizeof(initvlen));

        for(i=0; i<initvlen.size; i++)
            printf("%c ",initvlen.string[i]);
        printf("\n");

        return(0);
    }
```

The output from this example is as follows:

```
sizeof(vlen)=4
sizeof(initvlen)=4
a b c d
```

Attributes

The __attribute__ keyword can be used to assign an attribute to a function or data declaration. The primary purpose of assigning an attribute to a function is to make it possible for the compiler to perform optimization. The attribute is assigned to a function in the declaration of the function prototype, as in the following example:

```
void fatal_error() __attribute__ ((noreturn));
    . . .
void fatal_error(char *message)
{
    fprintf(stderr,"FATAL ERROR: %s\n",message);
    exit(1);
}
```

In this example, the noreturn attribute tells the compiler that this function does not return to its caller, so any code that would normally be executed on the function's return can be omitted by the optimizer.

Multiple attributes can be assigned in the same declaration by including them in a comma-separated list. For example, the following declaration assigns attributes to assure the compiler that it does not modify global variables and that the function must never be expanded inline:

```
int getlim() __attribute__ ((pure,noinline));
```

Attributes can be assigned to variables and to members of structs. For example, to guarantee that a field has a specific alignment within a struct, it could be declared as follows:

```
struct mong {
    char id;
    int code __attribute__ ((align(4)));
};
```

Table 4-3 lists the set of function attributes, Table 4-4 lists the attributes available for data declarations, and Table 4-5 lists the attributes that can be assigned to data type declarations.

Attribute	Description
alias	A function definition with this attribute causes the definition to become a weak alias of another function. It can be used in combination with the weak attribute to define a weak alias, as in the following example, where centon() is created as a weak alias for __centon(): int __centon() { return(100); } void centon() __attribute__ ((weak,alias("__centon"))); In C++ the mangled name of the target must be specified. This attribute is not supported on all machines.
always_inline	A function that's declared as being inline, and has this attribute, will always be expanded as inline code, even when no optimization has been specified. Normally functions are only inlined during optimization. The following is an example of the prototype of a function that will always be expanded inline: inline void infn() __attribute__ ((always_inline));

Table 4-3.   *Attributes That Can Be Used in Function Declarations*

Attribute	Description
const	A function with this attribute is the same as pure, but it also does not read any values from global memory. This gives the optimizer more freedom than pure because there is no need to make certain that all global values are updated before the function is called.
constructor	A function with this attribute is called automatically before the call is made to main(). Also see the destructor attribute.
deprecated	A function with this attribute will cause the compiler to issue a warning message whenever it is called. The warning message includes the location of the deprecated function to guide the user to more information about it.
destructor	A function with this attribute is called automatically after main() has returned or exit() has been called. Also see the constructor attribute.

format	A function with this attribute has one argument that is a format string and a variable number of arguments for the values to be formatted. This makes it possible for the compiler to check the format content against the list of arguments to verify that the types match the formatting. There are different types of formatting, so it is also necessary to specify whether validation is to be for the printf, scanf, strftime, or strfmon style. For example, the following attribute specifies that the second argument passed to the function is the formatting string, the formatting string is expected to be of the printf type, and the variable-length argument list begins with the third argument:
	`int logprintf(void *log, char *fmt, ...)`
	`        __attribute__ ((format(printf,2,3)));`
	Warning messages are issued when a format string is found to be invalid only if the -Wformat option is specified.

format_arg	A function with this attribute accepts a formatting string as one of its arguments and makes a modification to the string so that the result can be passed on to a printf(), scanf(), strftime(), or strfmon() type function. This attribute will suppress warning messages issued when the option -Wformat-nonliteral is set to detect nonconstant formatting strings. The following example demonstrates the setting of this attribute for a function that has such a format string as its second argument:
	`void fedit(int ndx, const char *fmt)`
	`        __attribute__ ((format_arg(2)));`

Table 4-3. *Attributes That Can Be Used in Function Declarations* (continued)

Attribute	Description
malloc	A function with this attribute informs the compiler that it can be treated as if it were the malloc() function. For purposes of optimization, the compiler is to assume the returned pointer cannot alias anything.
no_instrument_ function	A function with this attribute will not be instrumented and will not have profiling code inserted into it by the compiler, even if the -finstrument-functions option is set.
noinline	A function with this attribute will never be expanded as inline code.
noreturn	A function with this attribute does not return to its caller.
pure	A function with this attribute has no side effects whatsoever, except with respect to its return value. That is, there will be no changes to global values, locations addressed by arguments, or the contents of files. Unlike the const attribute, this function may read global values. This makes it possible for the compiler to perform common subexpression optimization because all the values are guaranteed to be stable.
section	A function with this attribute will have its assembly language code placed into the named section instead of the default text section. The following is an example of a function being put into a section named specials: void mspec(void) __attribute__((section("specials"))); This attribute will be ignored on systems that do not support sectioning. Also see -ffunction-sections in Appendix D.
used	A function with this attribute causes the compiler to generate code for the function body, even if the compiler determines the function is not being used. This can be useful for functions that are called only from inline assembly.
weak	A function with this attribute has its name emitted as a weak symbol instead of a global name. This is primarily for the naming of library routines that can be overridden by user code.

Table 4-3. *Attributes That Can Be Used in Function Declarations* (continued)

Attribute	Description

aligned	A variable with this attribute is aligned on a memory address that is an even multiple of the number specified for the alignment. For example, the following declaration will align `alivalue` at a 32-bit address:
	`int alivalue __attribute__ ((aligned(32)));`
	Alignment can be convenient on some systems to accommodate certain assembly language instructions. It can also be useful with fields in a struct that need to accommodate the data format found in a file. If no alignment number is specified, the compiler will align the item to the largest alignment used for any data item for the hardware, as in the following example:
	`short shlist[312] __attribute__ ((align));`

deprecated	A variable with this attribute will cause the compiler to issue a warning every place it is referenced.
mode	A variable with this attribute is sized to match the size of the specified mode. The mode can be set to byte, word, or pointer. The mode attribute determines the data type. For example, the following creates an int that is the size of a single byte: `int x __attribute__ ((mode(byte)));`
nocommon	A variable with this attribute is not allocated as common but is instead allocated its own space. The variable is provided with an initial value of all zeroes. Specifying the command-line option `-fno-common` will cause this attribute to be applied to all variables.

packed	A variable with this attribute has the smallest possible alignment. A variable will be separated no more than one byte from its predecessor field. In a struct, a field with this attribute will be allocated with no space between it and the field before it. For example, in the following struct, the start of the array named zar is aligned exactly one byte from the top of the struct:
	`struct zrecord {`
	`char id;`
	`int zar[32] __attribute__ ((packed));`
	`};`
	Also see the options `-fpack-struct` and `-Wpacked` in Appendix D.

section	A variable with this attribute will be placed into the named section instead of the default data or bss section. The following is an example of a function being put into a section named domx:
	`struct domx __attribute__ ((section("domx"))) = { 0 };`
	`int trigger __attribute__ ((section("MONLOG"))) = 0;`
	Because of the way the linker handles data, data declared in its own section must have initial values. This attribute will be ignored on systems that do not support sectioning. Variable initialization can be forced by the command-line option `-fno-common`.

Table 4-4. *Attributes That Can Be Used in Data Declarations*

Attribute	Description
unused	A variable with this attribute tells the compiler that the variable may not be used, and no warning should be issued.
vector_size	A variable with this attribute is allocated the total amount of space specified as the size of the vector. For example, the following declares a vector of float data types: `float fvec __attribute__ ((vector_size(32));` Assuming a float data type is 4 bytes long, this declaration creates a block containing 8 float variables for a total size of 32 bytes. This attribute is only valid for integer and real scalars.
weak	A variable with this attribute has its name emitted as a weak symbol instead of as a global name. This is primarily for the naming of library variables that can be overridden by user code.

Table 4-4. *Attributes That Can Be Used in Data Declarations* (continued)

Attribute	Description

aligned	A type declared with this attribute is aligned on a memory address that is an even multiple of the number specified for the alignment. For example, instances of the following struct will be aligned at a 32-bit address boundary:
	`struct blockm {`
	`    char j[3];`
	`} __attribute__ ((aligned(32)));`
	It is possible to affect this same alignment by applying the `aligned` attribute to the first member of the struct. The `aligned` attribute can only be used to increase the alignment, not reduce it. Some linkers may force the compiler to limit the maximum alignment value.
	This attribute can also be applied to types created by `typedef`:
	`typedef int alint __attribute__ ((aligned(8)));`
	If no alignment number is specified, the compiler will align the item to the largest alignment that is used for any data item for the hardware, as in the following example:
	`typedef short alshort __attribute__ ((align));`

deprecated	A type declared with this attribute causes a warning message to be issued each time the type is used in a declaration. The message includes location information for the type declaration.
packed	A struct or union declared with this attribute will take up the minimum amount of space possible. This is equivalent to specifying the `packed` attribute for each member of the struct or union. This attribute can be specified following the closing brace on an `enum` declaration. The command-line option `-fshort-enum` is the same as using the `packed` attribute on all `enum` declarations.

Table 4-5. *Attributes That Can Be Used in Data Type Definitions*

Attribute	Description
transparent_union	A union declared with this attribute and used as the data type of a parameter on a function declaration will enable that function to accept, as an argument, any of the types defined in the union. The following example uses a transparent union to demonstrate calling the same function with three different argument types:

```
/* transp.c */
#include <stdio.h>
typedef union {
    float *f;
    int *i;
} fourbytes __attribute__ ((transparent_union));

void showboth(fourbytes fb);

int main(int argc, char *argv[])
{
    int ivalue = 2562;
    float fvalue = 898.44;
    fourbytes fb;
    fb.i = &ivalue;

    showboth(&ivalue);
    showboth(&fvalue);
      showboth(fb);

    return(0);
}

void showboth(fourbytes fb)
{
    printf("The int value: %d\n",*fb.i);
    printf("The float value: %f\n",*fb.f);
}
```

Attribute	Description
	The function showboth() is declared as requiring the union fourbytes as an argument, but because the union has been declared with the attribute transparent_union, any of the types declared in the union can also be passed to the function. This example contains calls to the function passing the address of a float, the address of an int, and the address of the union itself.
unused	A type declared with this attribute causes any of the data items of that type to appear to be unused, so no warning messages will be issued for them.

Table 4-5. *Attributes That Can Be Used in Data Type Definitions* (continued)

Compound Statements Returning a Value

A compound statement is a block of statements enclosed in braces. A compound statement has its own scope level and can declare its own local variables, as in the following example:

```
{
    int a = 5;
    int b;
    b = a + 5;
}
```

In GNU C, by surrounding a compound statement with parentheses, it produces a return value, as in the following example, which returns the value 8:

```
rslt =  ({
            int a = 5;
            int b;
            b = a + 3;
        });
```

The return value is the result type and value of the last statement in the block.

This construct can be useful when writing macros. A problem occurs with a macro when the expression provided as an argument is calculated more than once. For example, the following macro returns an even number equal to or larger than the one specified, incrementing the value only if necessary:

```
#define even(x) (2*(x / 2) == x ? x : x + 1)
```

This will work unless there is a side effect to evaluating the expression *x*. For example, the following statement would produce an undefined result:

```
int nexteven = even(value++);
```

The following macro performs the same function, but it does so by only evaluating the expression once and storing the result in a local variable:

```
#define evenint(x) \
    ({ int y = x; \
       (2*(y / 2) == y ? y : y + 1); \
    })
```

It should be noted that this extension does not work well with C++, so it could cause problems if you use it in header files that are to be included in C++ programs. The problem comes from the destructors for the temporaries inside the macro being run earlier than they would be for an inline function.

Conditional Operand Omission

In a conditional expression, the true or false condition is determined by the result of an expression being zero or nonzero, so it can happen that the test value and the resulting value are the same. For example, in the following statement, x will be assigned the value of y only if y is something other than zero:

```
x = y ? y : z;
```

The expression y will be evaluated a second time if it is determined to be nonzero the first time it is evaluated. This second evaluation can be omitted by forming the expression as follows:

```
x = y ? : z;
```

This becomes especially useful if the expression y has side effects and should not be evaluated more than once.

Enum Incomplete Types

An enum tag can be declared without specifying its list of values, in the same way that the name of a struct can be declared without specifying its content. An incomplete enum can be used in function prototypes and to declare pointers.

The following is an example of the declaration of an incomplete enum followed by the actual declaration:

```
enum color_list;
. . .
enum color_list { BLACK, WHITE, BLUE };
```

Function Argument Construction

The following three built-in functions can be used to pass the arguments of the current function directly through to another function and then return the results to the original caller. It is not necessary for the function the arguments are being passed through to know anything about the arguments.

The following function retrieves and records the argument's descriptive information:

```
void *__builtin_apply_args(void);
```

Once the argument information is recorded, the following function can be used to construct the stack information required for the call and to make the call to the function:

```
void *__builtin_apply(void (*func)(),void *arguments,int size);
```

The first argument is the address of the function passed as the address of a function that has no arguments and does not return a value. The second argument is the result of the recording process performed by __builtin_apply_args(). The size argument is the number of bytes to be copied from the current stack frame into the new stack frame, and it must be large enough to include all the arguments being passed along with the return address.

After the function has been called by __builtin_apply(), the return value of the called function is positioned on the stack. The following function adjusts the stack frame and returns to the original caller:

```
__builtin_return(void *result);
```

The following example program calls the function passthrough(), which uses the built-in functions to call the average() function and return the value from it:

```c
/* args.c */
#include <stdio.h>
int passthrough();
int average();

int main(int argc,char *argv[])
{
    int result;

    result = passthrough(1,7,10);
    printf("result=%d\n",result);
    return(0);
}

int passthrough(int a,int b,int c)
{
    void *record;
    void *playback;
    void (* fn)() = (void (*)())average;

    record = __builtin_apply_args();
```

USING THE COMPILER COLLECTION

```
        playback = __builtin_apply(fn,record,128);
        __builtin_return(playback);
}

int average(int a,int b,int c) {
    return((a + b + c) / 3);
}
```

Notice that the function passthrough() only has knowledge of the arguments and return value because they are the ones it uses itself. The passthrough() function could be converted to a wrapper around a generalized function call if an ellipsis were used to create a variable-length argument list and the return value were a void pointer. The passthrough() function could then be used to pass an arbitrary set of arguments to a function known only by its address, and the return value could be of any type.

To write a generalized wrapper, it will be necessary to ensure that the value of size passed to __builtin_apply() is large enough to contain all the arguments actually passed.

Function Inlining

A function can be declared inline, and its code will be expanded much like a macro at the point it is called. A function can be declared as an inline function by using the inline keyword, as follows:

```
inline int halve(double x)
{
    return(x / 2.0);
}
```

The following is a list of rules and characteristics having to do with function inlining:

- No functions are actually expanded inline unless you use -O to specify some level of optimization. It is done this way to simplify the use of a debugger. A function can be forced to be expanded inline by assigning it the always_inline attribute.

- The result of declaring a function inline could make the code either larger or smaller, depending on the size of the function, the complexity of setting up the call frame, and the number of times the function is called.

- Certain functions cannot be expanded inline. Among these are functions that use a variable number of arguments, alloca, variable-size arrays, a non-local goto, or a nested function. Problems also arise when a function is recursive or there is a reference to its address. The command-line option -Winline will issue a warning when a function declared as inline cannot be expanded inline.

- In the ISO C program you can use the __inline__ keyword in place of the inline keyword.

- The -finline-functions command-line option can be used to instruct the compiler to automatically select functions that are appropriate for being expanded inline.

- If an inline function is not declared as static, its body must also be generated by the compiler because it could be called from another module. Declaring a function as both inline and static will cause all occurrences of the function to be expanded inline, and the code for the function itself is never generated. The command-line option -fkeep-inline-functions will override this behavior and cause the function body to always be created.

- Defining a function in a header file as both extern and inline is almost the same as declaring a macro. Another copy of the function, without extern and inline, can be compiled and stored in a library so that non-inline references to it can be resolved.

Function Name

The identifier __FUNCTION__ holds the name of the function in which it appears. It is in the form of a string literal and can be concatenated with other string literals, in the same way as __FILE__ and __LINE__. The following example constructs a single line of text containing all three location macros:

```
char *here = "Line " __LINE__ " of " __FILE__ " in " __FUNCTION__;
```

Defined in the ISO C99 standard, the identifier __func__ contains the name of the current function, but instead of a character literal it is in the form of a char array.

> **Note**
>
> *The semantics of __FUNCTION__ is deprecated and is to be modified to match the semantics of __func__.*

The identifier __PRETTY_FUNCTION__ holds the same name as __FUNCTION__ in C, but the two contain the name in different forms in C++.

Function Nesting

Functions can be nested inside one another. The inner function can only be called from inside its parent function. The following function contains a nested function named randint() that returns a pseudo-random int value within a specified range:

```
void rangers()
{
    int randint(int low,int high) {
```

```
        return(((int)random() % (high-low+1)) + low);
    }

    printf("0 to 100: %d\n",randint(0,100));
    printf("5 to 10: %d\n",randint(5,10));
    printf("-1 to 1: %d\n",randint(-1,1));
}
```

The following is a list of rules and characteristics having to do with nesting functions:

- A nested function is created on the stack in much the same way as variables, so it can be declared in a block before the first executable statement of the block—in the same location local variables are declared.

- The address of a nested function cannot be returned to the caller because, just as any other local variable, it disappears when the parent function returns.

- A nested function cannot be declared extern.

- It is possible to pass the address of a nested function to other functions and have it called from there, just as it is possible to pass the address of other local variables.

- A nested function has direct access to all the same variables as the parent functions, but local variables can only be accessed if they are declared before the nested function.

- A nested function can use the goto statement to jump to a label outside itself but in its parent function.

- The prototype of a nested function can be declared by declaring it as auto, as in the following example:

```
void right()
{
    auto double hypotenuse();
    double a = 3.0;
    double b = 4.0;

    double hypotenuse(double x,double y) {
        return(sqrt(x * x + y * y));
    }

    printf("Long side of %lf and %lf is %lf\n",
            a,b,hypotenuse(a,b));
}
```

Function Prototypes

A new style function prototype will override the definition of a function with the old style argument list declaration, if the promotion of the old style argument is matched by the prototype. For example, the following is a valid prototype for the function because the short argument is automatically promoted to an int in the function call:

```
int trigzed(int zvalue);
     . . .
int trigzed(zvalue)
short zvalue;
{
     return(zvalue == 0);
}
```

If the function had been declared with the new syntax of int trigzed(short zvalue), the compiler would have generated an error message because of the conflict between the int and the short.

Function Return Addresses and Stack Frames

The following built-in function retrieves the address to be used by a function to return to its caller:

```
void *__builtin_return_address(unsigned int level);
```

Specifying a level value of 0 retrieves the return address to be used by the current function. A level value of 1 retrieves the return address to be used by the function that called the current one, a level value of 2 retrieves the address from the previous function, and so on, until the call stack is exhausted. The function __builtin_frame_address() can be used to determine when the top of the stack is reached. Also, level must be specified as a constant, not a variable.

On some systems, it is not possible to retrieve the return address of any function other than the current one. On such a system, the retrieved value is either zero or a random value (depending on the platform).

The following function retrieves the address of the function's stack frame:

```
void *__builtin_frame_address(unsigned int level);
```

Specifying a level value of 0 retrieves the address of the stack frame of the current function. A level value of 1 retrieves the address of the stack frame of the function that called the current one, a level value of 2 retrieves the address from the previous function, and so on, until the call stack is exhausted. The function `__builtin_frame_address()` can be used to determine when the top of the stack is reached.

The stack frame is a block of memory that contains the registers saved by the calling function as well as the values of the arguments that were passed in the call. The exact format will vary, depending on the calling convention and the platform.

On some systems, it is not possible to retrieve the stack frame address of any function other than the current one. On such a system, the retrieved value is zero. A return value of zero also occurs if the list of stack frames has been exhausted.

Identifiers

Identifiers may contain dollar signs. This is for compatibility with many traditional C compilers and a large body of C programs that have dollar signs in variable and function names. Dollar signs are not valid for all systems because some assemblers don't accept them.

Integers

The C99 standard defines integer data types that are up to 64 bits long. As an extension, GCC supports them in earlier versions of C and in C++. Examples of the declarations are as follows:

```
long long int a; // Signed 64-bit integer
unsigned long long int b; //Unsigned 64-bit integer
```

Constants can be declared for each of these types, as follows:

```
a = 855LL; // Signed 64-bit constant
b = 855ULL; // Unsigned 64-bit constant
```

The arithmetic operations of addition, subtraction, and the bitwise boolean operations can be performed on these types on all machines. Multiplication, division, and shifts are not supported by all hardware and may require the use of special library routines.

If you are going to use these data types as function arguments, it is important that you use prototypes to define the argument types. Without a function prototype, the size and position of the variables in the calling stack frame could be wrong.

Keyword Alternates

The command-line options `-std` and `-ansi` disable the keywords `asm`, `typeof`, and `inline`, but the alternate forms `__asm__`, `__typeof__`, and `__inline__` can be used in their place.

Label Addresses

It is possible to take the address of a label, store it in a pointer, and then use the goto statement to branch to it. The address is retrieved by using the && operator and is stored in a void pointer. The goto statement will branch to any address resulting from an expression producing a void pointer.

The following simple example demonstrates how this can be done:

```c
/* gotoaddr.c */
#include <stdio.h>
#include <time.h>
int main(int argc,char *argv[])
{
    void *target;
    time_t now;

    now = time((time_t *)NULL);
    if(now & 0x0001)
        target = &&oddtag;
    else
        target = &&eventag;

    goto *target;

  eventag:
    printf("The time value %ld is even\n",now);
    return(0);
  oddtag:
    printf("The time value %ld is odd\n",now);
    return(0);
}
```

The current time is used as a pseudo-random number to determine which label address is stored in target. The goto statement then accepts the address in the void pointer as a valid destination for a jump. It is not valid to branch into another function.

Because any expression resulting in a void pointer can be used by the goto statement, it is possible to create an array of label addresses and branch to them according to an index, as follows:

```c
void *loc[] = { &&label1, &&label2, &&label3, &&label4 };
    . . .
goto *loc[i];
```

Labels Declared Locally

It is possible to declare a label in such a way that it is only defined within a specific scope. The __label__ keyword is used at the top of the scope to declare that the label is to be local, and the label can then be declared and used within the scope. The following program demonstrates the declaration of the use of two labels within a scope:

```
/* loclabel.c */
#include <stdio.h>
int main(int argc,char *argv[])
{
    int count = 0;

    {
        __label__ restart;
        __label__ finished;
    restart:
        printf("count=%d\n",count);
        if(count > 5)
            goto finished;
        count++;
        goto restart;
    finished:
        count += 10;
    }
    return(0);
}
```

The labels can be declared one to a line, as in this example, or more than one can be declared on a line by using commas, as follows:

```
    __label__ restart, finished;
```

Labels of this sort can be useful inside code that is expanded from macros because, by adding braces to create scoping, the same label can be used more than once within a function.

Lvalue Expressions

A compound expression can be used on the left side of an assignment operator (that is, an *lvalue*). This is true as long as the result of the compound expression is something that can have its address taken. The usual form of an lvalue is the name of a specific variable, as in the following example, where the variable a is the name of a location in memory where the value 5 is stored:

```
a = 5;
```

Another form of lvalue actually appears on the right side of a statement, but it is an lvalue because it is the address of a location instead of its value. In the following example, the variable a is used as an lvalue:

```
ptr = &a;
```

Under certain specific circumstances a compound expression can be used as an lvalue. The following is a list of rules and characteristics for creating lvalue expressions:

- A compound expression serves as an lvalue if the last member of the compound expression can have its address taken. For example, the two following statements are identical:

  ```
  (fn(), b) = 10;
  fn(), (b = 10);
  ```

- A compound statement can have its address taken. The address will be that of the last member of the compound statement. In the following statement, the address of b (that is, the lvalue of b) is stored in ptr:

  ```
  ptr = &(fn(), b);
  ```

- A conditional expression can be used as an lvalue provided that both the true and false selections are valid for use as an lvalue. For example, the following statement assigns the value of 100 to b if a is greater than 5; otherwise, 100 is assigned to c:

  ```
  ((a > 5) ? b : c) = 100;
  ```

- An lvalue can be cast to another type. In the following example, the char pointer chptr is cast to an int value to have the absolute address 894 stored in it:

  ```
  char *chptr;
  (int)chptr = 894;
  ```

Macros with Variable Arguments

Two techniques exist for creating macros with a variable number of arguments because GCC implemented one technique as an extension and the ISO standard of 1999 specified a slightly different technique. GCC supports both. The two techniques are actually the same, but the syntax is slightly different.

The following is an example of the ISO standard method for creating a macro with a variable number of arguments:

```
#define errout(fmt,...) fprintf(stderr,fmt,__VA_ARGS__)
```

Any list of arguments specified after fmt will be substituted for __VA_ARGS__ wherever it appears in the macro body. Using the GNU syntax, the same macro can be defined as follows:

```
#define errout(fmt,args...) fprintf(stderr,fmt,args)
```

You will find more information on macros and macro expansion in Chapter 3.

Strings

Newline characters can be embedded in a string without using the \n escape character. They can be included literally in the source code. The following two strings are equivalent:

```
char *str1 = "A string on\ntwo lines"
char *str2 = "A string on
two lines"
```

The '\e' character is the ASCII ESC character. The sequence \e can also be used in strings.

As always, the backslash character at the end of a line will join the two lines into one, as in the following example:

```
char *str3 = "This string will \
be joined into one line.";
```

This is standard C. The GNU extension is a relaxing of the rule that the newline character must follow immediately behind the backslash escape character. With GCC any number of spaces are allowed following the backslash; the extra spaces are removed and the two lines are joined into one, but a warning message is issued from the preprocessor.

Pointer Arithmetic

Addition and subtraction is supported for void and function pointers. A pointer is incremented or decremented by the size of the item it points to, and GCC void and function pointers are incremented or decremented by 1. The consequence of this is that the sizeof operator on a void or function pointer has a value of 1.

The -Wpointer-arith option can be used to issue a warning if this extension is used.

Switch/Case

A range of values can be specified on a `case` statement by using ellipses. The following is the standard way of selecting four values for a single case:

```
case 8:
case 9:
case 10:
case 11:
```

The same thing can be written by using a three-dot ellipsis, this way:

```
case 8 ... 10:
```

It is important that the three dots be surrounded by spaces to prevent the parser from confusing the ellipsis with decimal points on the constants. Just as with single constant values, duplicate values are detected by the compiler—the following two conflicting `case` statements will produce an error message:

```
case 8 ... 15:
   . . .
case 12 ... 32:    // Error
```

This technique is especially useful for ranges of character constants:

```
case 'a' ... 'm':
```

Typedef Name Creation

The `typedef` keyword can be used to create a name for the data type of an expression. The defined name can be used to declare or cast variables of the same type as the expression. The new type name is defined as follows:

```
typedef name = expression;
```

For example, the following statements define `smallreal` as the float type and `largereal` as the double type:

```
typedef smallreal=0.0f;
typedef largereal=0.0;
```

These new names can be used to declare variables of the types they represent. The following statements declare real1 as float and real2 as double:

```
smallreal real1;
largereal real2;
```

One place this can be useful is inside a macro definition to make it possible to apply the macro to multiple data types. The following macro makes no prior assumption about the types of its arguments, other than that they are the same types and can have their values swapped:

```
#define swap(a,b)        \
    ({  typedef _tp=a;   \
        _tp temp = a;    \
        a = b;           \
        b = temp; })
```

The data type of the first argument is used to define _tp as a new local type that is the same as the first argument. A local variable named temp is constructed as the temporary holding location, making it possible to swap the two values regardless of their type.

Typeof References

The typeof keyword results in the type of an expression. It is used like sizeof, but the result is a type instead of a size, as in the following example:

```
char *chptr; // A char pointer
typeof (*chptr) ch; // A char
typeof (ch) *chptr2; // A char pointer
typeof (chptr) chparray[10]; // Ten char pointers
typeof (*chptr) charray[10]; // Ten chars
typeof (ch) charray2[10]; // Ten chars
```

In this example, chptr is declared as a char pointer. Using typeof to determine the type pointed to by chptr, ch is declared as a char data type. In turn, using the data type of ch, chptr2 is declared as a pointer to a char type. The variable chparray is declared as an array of ten pointers to type char. The array charray is based on the type pointed to by chptr, which is the declaration of an array of ten char types. Another array of ten char types is based on ch.

The following declares a variable that is the type returned from a function:

```
char func();
typeof (func) retval;
```

The function `func()` returns a char, so the `typeof` expression declares `retval` as type char.

You can use a type name directly in a `typeof` expression. For example, the following two statements are equivalent:

```
char *charptr;
typeof (char *) charptr;
```

Using `typeof` makes it possible to create macros that can be used to declare variables. The following example defines a macro and then uses it to create arrays of ten double and ten float variables:

```
#define array(type,size) typeof(type[size])
array(double,10) dblarray;
array(float,10) fltarray;
```

Union Casting

A data item that is the same type as the member of a union can be cast to the union. For example, the following program casts a double data item to a union that contains a double and then accesses each byte through a union reference:

```
/* unioncast.c */
#include <stdio.h>
union dparts {
    unsigned char byte[8];
    double dbl;
};

int main(int argc,char *argv[])
{
    int i;
    double value = 3.14159;

    for(i =0; i<8; i++) {
        printf("%02X ",((union dparts)value).byte[i]);
    }
    printf("\n");

    return(0);
}
```

A union cast can also be used as an argument in a function call, as follows:

```
void procun(union dparts);
   . . .
procun((union dparts)value);
```

A cast to a union is a bit different from other casts. It is actually a constructor, so it does not create an lvalue. This makes the following statement invalid:

```
(union dparts)value.dbl = 1.2;    // Error
```

The
Complete
Reference

Chapter 5

Compiling C++

The GNU C++ compiler is a fully functional compiler that generates executable object code as its output. The original C++ compiler from AT&T was named cfront and was actually a translator of C++ code into C code, and there are still some compilers that work this way. The GCC compiler was originally a C compiler, and C++ was added as an optional mode of compilation.

Fundamental Compiling

Table 5-1 lists the file name suffixes that are involved in compiling and linking C++ programs. A complete list of all the file suffix names can be found in Appendix D.

Single Source File to Executable

The following is the source code of a simple C++ program stored in a file named helloworld.cpp:

```
/* helloworld.cpp */
#include <iostream>
int main(int argc,char *argv[])
{
    std::cout << "hello, world\n";
    return(0);
}
```

This program uses cout, defined in the header file iostream, to write a simple string to the standard output. This program can be compiled into an executable with the following command:

```
$ g++ helloworld.cpp
```

The g++ compiler recognizes the file by the suffix on its name as being a C++ source file. The default action is to compile the source into an object file, link the object file with the necessary routines from the library libstdc++, and produce an executable program file. The object file is then deleted. No output file name was specified on the command line, so the default name a.out is used. The program can be run as follows:

```
$ a.out
hello, world
```

It is more common to specify the name of the executable file with the -o command. The following command will produce an executable named helloworld:

```
$ g++ helloworld.cpp -o helloworld
```

Suffix	File Contains
.a	Static object library (archive file).
.C, .c++, .cc, .cp, .cpp, .cxx	C++ source code that is to be preprocessed.
.h	C or C++ header file.
.ii	C++ source code that is not to be preprocessed. This type of file is produced as an intermediate step in compilation.
.o	An object file in a format appropriate to be supplied to the linker. This type of file is produced as an intermediate step in compilation.
.s	Assembly language source code. This type of file is produced as an intermediate step in compilation.
<none>	The standard C++ system header files have no suffix.

Table 5-1. *File Name Suffixes in C++ Programming*

Entering the program name on the command line will execute it:

```
$ helloworld
hello, world
```

The g++ program is a special version of gcc that sets the default language to C++, causing it to automatically link using the standard C++ library instead of defaulting to the standard C library. By following the source file naming convention and specifying the name of the library, it is possible to compile and link C++ programs using gcc, as in the following example:

```
$ gcc helloworld.cpp -lstdc++  -o helloworld
```

The -l (ell) option alters the name following it by tacking on the prefix lib and the suffix .a, making the library named libstdc++.a. It then looks for the library in the standard places. The compilation process and the output file from gcc is identical to g++.

On most systems, the installation of GCC installs a program named c++. If installed, the program is identical with g++ and can be used the same way, as in the following example:

```
$ c++ helloworld.cpp -o helloworld
```

Multiple Source Files to Executable

If more than one source file is listed on the g++ command, they are all compiled and linked together into a single executable. The following is a header file, named speak.h, containing a class definition that contains only one function:

```
/* speak.h */
#include <iostream>
class Speak
{
public:
    void sayHello(const char *);
};
```

The following is a listing of the file speak.cpp, which contains the body of the sayHello() function:

```
/* speak.cpp */
#include "speak.h"
void Speak::sayHello(const char *str)
{
    std::cout << "Hello " << str << "\n";
}
```

The file hellospeak.cpp contains a program that uses the Speak class:

```
/* hellospeak.cpp */
#include "speak.h"
int main(int argc,char *argv[])
{
    Speak speak;
    speak.sayHello("world");
    return(0);
}
```

A single command can be used to compile and link both of these source files into a single executable:

```
$ g++ hellospeak.cpp speak.cpp -o hellospeak
```

Source File to Object File

The -c option can be used to compile the source code but suppress the linker and output an object file instead. The default name is the same as the base name of the source file with the suffix changed to .o. For example, the following command will compile the source file hellospeak.cpp and produce the object file hellospeak.o:

```
$ g++ -c hellospeak.cpp
```

The g++ command also recognizes the .o files as input files to be fed to the linker. The following sequence of commands will compile the two source files into object files and then link the two object files into a single executable:

```
$ g++ -c hellospeak.cpp
$ g++ -c speak.cpp
$ g++ hellospeak.o speak.o -o hellospeak
```

The -o option is not just for naming executables. It can also be used to name the other files output by the compiler. For example, the following series of commands produces the same executable as the previous series, except the intermediate object files have different names:

```
$ g++ -c hellospeak.cpp -o hspk1.o
$ g++ -c speak.cpp -o hspk2.o
$ g++ hspk1.o hspk2.o -o hellospeak
```

Preprocessing

Specifying the -E option instructs g++ to pass the source code through the preprocessor and take no further action. The following command preprocesses the helloworld.cpp source code and writes the results to standard output:

```
$ g++ -E helloworld.cpp
```

The source code for helloworld.cpp, listed earlier in this chapter, is only six lines long and does nothing other than display a line of text, but the preprocessed version is over 1,200 lines long. This is largely because the iostream header file is included, and it includes several other header files as well as defines several large classes that deal with input and output.

The GCC suffix for preprocessed C++ code is .ii, which can be produced by using the -o option, as follows:

```
$ gcc -E helloworld.cpp -o helloworld.ii
```

Generating Assembly Language

The -S option instructs the compiler to compile the program into assembly language, output the assembly language source, and then stop. The following command produces the assembly language file named helloworld.s from the C++ source file:

```
$ g++ -S helloworld.cpp
```

The assembly language generated depends on the target platform of the compiler, but if you examine it, you will see not only the executable code and data storage declarations but also the tables of addresses necessary for inheritance and linkage in a C++ program.

Creating a Static Library

A static library is an archive file containing a collection of object files produced by the compiler. The members of the library can contain regular functions, class definitions, and objects that are instances of class definitions. Anything, in fact, that can be stored in a .o object file can also be stored in a library.

The following example creates two object modules and uses them to create a static library. A header file contains the information necessary for a program to use the function, class definition, and object stored in the library.

The header file say.h contains the prototype of the function sayHello() and the definition of a class named Say:

```
/* say.h */
#include <iostream>
void sayhello(void);
class Say {
private:
    char *string;
public:
    Say(char *str)
    {
        string = str;
    }
    void sayThis(const char *str)
    {
```

```
        std::cout << str << " from a static library\n";
    }
    void sayString(void);
};
```

The following source file is named `say.cpp` and is the source of one of the two object files to be inserted into the library. It contains the definition of the body of the `sayString()` function of the `Say` class. It also contains the declaration of `librarysay`, which is an instance of the `Say` class:

```
/* say.cpp */
#include "say.h"
void Say::sayString()
{
    std::cout << string << "\n";
}

Say librarysay("Library instance of Say");
```

The source file `sayhello.cpp` is the source code of the second module that is to be included in the library. It contains the definition of the function `sayhello()`, which follows:

```
/* sayhello.cpp */
#include "say.h"
void sayhello()
{
    std::cout << "hello from a static library\n";
}
```

The following sequence of commands compiles the two source files into object files, and the `ar` command stores them into a library:

```
$ g++ -c sayhello.cpp
$ g++ -c say.cpp
$ ar -r libsay.a sayhello.o say.o
```

The `ar` utility used with the `-r` option will create a new library named `libsay.a` and insert the listed object files into it. Used this way, `ar` will create a new library if one does not exist or, if the library does exist, it will replace any existing object modules with the new version.

The following is the mainline of a program named `saymain.cpp` that uses the code stored in `libsay.a`:

```
/* saymain.cpp */
#include "say.h"
int main(int argc,char *argv[])
{
    extern Say librarysay;
    Say localsay = Say("Local instance of Say");

    sayhello();
    librarysay.sayThis("howdy");
    librarysay.sayString();
    localsay.sayString();

    return(0);
}
```

This program is compiled and linked with the following command, where `g++` resolves any references made in `saymain.cpp` by looking in the library `libsay.a`:

```
$ g++ saymain.cpp libsay.a -o saymain
```

The external reference to `librarysay` is a reference to the object declared in `say.cpp` and stored in the library. Both `librarysay.sayThis()` and `librarysay.sayString()` are calls to the methods of the object in the library. Also, `sayhello()` is a call to the function in `sayhello.o`, which is also stored in the library. When the program is run, it produces the following output:

```
hello from a static library
howdy from a static library
Library instance of Say
Local instance of Say
```

Creating a Shared Library

A shared library is an archive that contains a collection of object files, but the object files must use relative addressing so the code can be loaded anywhere in memory and run from there without an extensive relocation process. This allows the code to be loaded from the shared library while the program is running instead of being directly attached to the executable by a linker.

The following header file, named `average.h`, defines the class to be stored in the shared library:

```
/* average.h */
class Average {
private:
    int count;
    double total;
public:
    Average(void) {
        count = 0;
        total = 0.0;
    }
    void insertValue(double value);
    int getCount(void);
    double getTotal(void);
    double getAverage(void);
};
```

The source file to be compiled and stored in the shared library contains the bodies of the functions defined in the class:

```
/* average.cpp */
#include "average.h"
void Average::insertValue(double value)
{
    count++;
    total += value;
}
int Average::getCount()
{
    return(count);
}
double Average::getTotal()
{
    return(total);
}
double Average::getAverage()
{
    return(total / (double)count);
}
```

The following two commands first compile the source into an object file and then use it to create a library:

```
$ g++ -c -fpic average.cpp
$ gcc -shared average.o -o average.so
```

The first command uses the -c option so that the compiler will produce the object file average.o without trying to link it into an executable. The option -fpic (position independent code) instructs the compiler to produce code suitable for inclusion in a shared library—code that calculates its internal addresses in relation to the point the code is loaded into memory. The second command uses the -shared option to cause the creation of a shared library that, by being specified on the -o option, is named average.so. The second command could just has well have been g++ in place of gcc because there is nothing specific to C++ about creating a shared library. Creating a shared library containing more than one object module is simply a matter of listing all the object files on the same command line.

The two previous commands can be combined into a single command that compiles the source into object files and uses them to create a shared library:

```
$ g++ -fpic -shared average.cpp -o average.so
```

The following program uses the class definition stored in the shared library to instantiate an object that is used to keep a running total of four values and return their average:

```cpp
/* showaverage.cpp */
#include <iostream>
#include "average.h"
int main(int argc,char *argv[])
{
    Average avg;

    avg.insertValue(30.2);
    avg.insertValue(88.8);
    avg.insertValue(3.002);
    avg.insertValue(11.0);
    std::cout << "Average=" << avg.getAverage() << "\n";
    return(0);
}
```

The following command compiles and links the program with the shared library, producing an executable named showaverage:

```
$ g++ showaverage.cpp average.so -o showaverage
```

To run this program, the shared library must be installed in a directory that will be found at execution time, as described in Chapter 12.

Extensions to the C++ Language

This section describes some GNU-specific extensions to the C++ language. The C++ compiler is very complicated, and the standard definition document is quite large, so there are certainly more extensions and differences from the standard than the ones listed here. Also, because the C++ compiler shares much of its code with the C compiler, many of the extensions listed in Chapter 4 for the C compiler will also apply to C++.

Attributes

Chapter 4 describes a list of attributes that can be used in C. While those attributes can also be used in C++ programs, there are some attributes that apply only to C++. An attribute is applied by using the __attribute__ keyword and enclosing the name of the attribute in parentheses. Table 5-2 contains the attributes designed specifically for use with C++.

Attribute	Description
init_priority	Standard C++ specifies that objects be initialized in the order in which they appear within a compilation unit, but there is no specification for the order across compilation units. The init_priority attribute makes it possible to specify the order of object initialization within a given namespace by assigning priority numbers to the object declarations.The priorities are assigned numerically, with the smaller numbers having priority over larger numbers. For example, the following three objects will be initialized in the order B, then C, then A, no matter what source modules they are found in: SpoClass A __attribute__ ((init_priority(680))); SpoClass B __attribute__ ((init_priority(220))); SpoClass C __attribute__ ((init_priority(400))); The values used have no particular meaning, except in the way they relate to one another.
java_interface	This attribute specifies that the class is to be defined as a Java interface. It can only be applied to classes defined inside an extern "Java" block. Calls to methods of a class defined this way use the GCJ interface table instead of the C++ virtual table.

Table 5-2. *The Attributes Defined for the C++ Language*

Header Files

All system header files are, by default, included as if they were enclosed in an extern "C" { . . . } block. This can cause problems where C++ code exists in a system header file, but the problem can be solved with the following pragma:

```
#pragma cplusplus
```

When this pragma is found in a header file, the rest of the code in the file is compiled as if it were included in an extern "C++" { . . . } block.

Using this pragma inside an explicit extern "C" { . . . } block is an error.

Function Name

The identifier __FUNCTION__ holds the name of the current function in both C and C++. In C++ the identifier __PRETTY_FUNCTION__ also contains the function name, but in a form that carries a bit more information. The following example shows the use of these identifiers as well as the __func__ identifier specified in the C standard:

```cpp
/* showfuncname.cpp */
#include <iostream>
class Xyz
{
public:
    void NameShow(int i,double d)
    {
        std::cout << "__FUNCTION__\n     "
                  << __FUNCTION__ << "\n";
        std::cout << "__PRETTY_FUNCTION__\n      "
                  << __PRETTY_FUNCTION__ << "\n";
        std::cout << "__func__\n      "
                  << __func__ << "\n";
    }
};

int main(int argc,char *argv[])
{
    Xyz xyz;
    xyz.NameShow(5,5.0);
    return(0);
}
```

The output from running this program looks like the following:

```
__FUNCTION__
     NameShow
__PRETTY_FUNCTION__
     void Xyz::NameShow (int, double)
__func__
     NameShow
```

The identifiers __FUNCTION__ and __func__ are both defined as strings that contain the simple name of the current function. The identifier __PRETTY_FUCNTION__ contains the complete function name, including the return type, the name of the class, and a list of parameter types.

Interface and Implementation

The interface and the implementation of a class can be combined into one. That is, there is no need to maintain a separate prototype definition of a class because the code that completely implements a class can also be used as the interface definition.

This is achieved by using #pragma interface to specify that the class definition is to be used as an interface definition only and by using #pragma implementation to instruct GCC to compile the class functions and data into object code.

Note *This is a very convenient feature, but it is subject to change. A future version of GCC is likely to do away with this pair of pragmas and use some other mechanism to achieve the same result.*

To implement this pair of pragmas, you can take the following steps:

1. Create a header file that contains the complete class implementation. For example, the header file for a class named MaxHolder could be called maxholder.h.

2. Inside the header file, and before the class definition, insert the following line:

   ```
   #pragma interface
   ```

3. In any source file that refers to the MaxHolder class, include the header as normal.

4. In one source file (usually the mainline of the program), insert the following #pragma directive before the #include directive:

   ```
   #pragma implementation "maxholder.h"
   #include "maxholder.h"
   ```

The files that include the header file in the normal way will only be including the interface definition for the class, while the one source file with the `#pragma implemention` directive will be including the complete class definition to be compiled into object code. This means that there will be only one copy of the backup copies of inline functions, debugging information, and the internal tables that implement virtual functions.

- If the header file has the same base name as the implementation file, there is no need to specify the file name on the pragma. For example, if the file named `maxholder.cpp` includes the header file named `maxholder.h`, the pragma can be written as simply `#pragma implementation`.

- If a header file includes header files from another directory, they can be named on the interface pragma as `#pragma interface "subdirectory/filename.h"`. If this is done, the same file name must appear on the implementation pragma.

- An `#include` statement must always be used to include the header files because they are not included by the pragma.

- The effect of the interface pragma on functions in the class is that they are all declared as `extern`. The only time the body of a function is used is when the code is expanded inline.

- Use of `#pragma implementation` causes all inline functions to have non-inline versions compiled in case some of the function calls were not inlined in other modules. This action can be suppressed with the command-line option `-fno-implement-inlines`.

Operators <? and >?

Special operators are available to return the minimum value of two arguments. The following expression results in the minimum value of a and b:

```
minvalue = a <? b;
```

Similarly, the following expression results in the maximum of the two values:

```
maxvalue = a >? b;
```

- The operators are primitives in the language, so they can be used without any side effects. The following statement results in the minimum value of x and y and then increments each one of them only once:

```
int minvalue = x++ <? y++;
```

- The >? and <? operators can be overloaded to operate on classes, as demonstrated by the following example, which defines the `Iholder` class

with the >? operator used to return a copy of the object containing the largest int value. The Iholder class also uses the >? operator internally to compare the two int values:

```
/* minmax.cpp */
#include <iostream>
class Iholder
{
    friend Iholder operator>?(Iholder&,Iholder&);
protected:
    int value;
public:
    Iholder(int v)
    {
        value = v;
    }
    int getValue(void)
    {
        return(value);
    }
};

Iholder operator>?(Iholder& ih1,Iholder& ih2)
{
    return(Iholder(ih1.getValue() >? ih2.getValue()));
}

int main(int argc,char *argv[])
{
    Iholder ih1 = Iholder(44);
    Iholder ih2 = Iholder(34);
    Iholder imax = ih1 >? ih2;
    std::cout << "The maximum is " << imax.getValue() << "\n";
    return(0);
}
```

Restrict

The restrict keyword of standard C99 for the C language was rejected by the standards committee for C++, but GCC has implemented it as the keyword __restrict__. Any pointer declared __restrict__ is guaranteed to have exclusive access to the location in memory to which it points. The fact that the compiler can be assured that there are no alias references to a memory location means that more efficient code can be generated.

The __restrict__ keyword can be used as a qualifier like const or volatile, as in the following example:

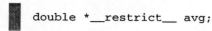

```
double *__restrict__ avg;
```

- The __restrict__ keyword is only valid for pointers and references. Unlike const or volatile, the __restrict__ qualifier applies only to a pointer and never to the data being addressed.

- Function pointer arguments can be qualified as restricted. In the following example, the function is assured that pointers bp1 and bp2 do not overlap:

```
void copy(char *__restrict__ bp1,
          char *__restrict__ bp2, int size) {
    for(int i=0; i<size; i++)
        bp1[i] = bp2[i];
}
```

- Function reference arguments can be restricted using the same syntax that is used for pointers, as in this example:

```
void icopy(int &__restrict__ ip1,
           int &__restrict__ ip2) {
    ip1 = ip2;
}
```

- The __restrict__ keyword is ignored in function matching, so the __restrict__ keyword is unnecessary in the prototype.

- The this pointer can be restricted by using the __restrict__ keyword on the member function declaration, as follows:

```
void T::fnctn() __restrict__ { ... }
```

Compiler Operation

This section describes some of the internal operations of the C++ compiler that you may need to be aware of in special circumstances. Usually you will only need to use the g++ command to compile and link your C++ programs, but there are some internal operations that you should be aware of so you can handle special situations.

Libraries

The standard C++ library is named libstdc++.a, and it contains all the standard C++ routines. The library is quite large and, although this usually doesn't matter, a statically linked C++ program can include many routines that are not actually used. This is a consequence of the fact that if you need a single routine that is part of an object file in the library, the entire object file is linked as part of your program.

If you need to statically link a program and you are not using library routines, you can link with `libsupc++.a` instead and include only routines that are part of the fundamental language definition. To make the change, it is only necessary to specify the library name on the g++ command line as `-lsupc`.

Mangling Names

Both C++ member functions and Java methods can be overloaded by specifying different data types in the parameter list. For example, the following three lines are prototypes for entirely different functions:

```
int *cold(long);
int *cold(struct schold *);
int *cold(long, char *);
```

The compiler has no problem determining which one you call because the argument types are distinct. The only problem that arises is from the linker, because linkers blindly match the names referenced in one module with the names defined in another module without regard to their type. The solution is to have the compiler change the names in such a way that the argument information is not lost and the linker is able to match them up. The process of changing the names is called *mangling*.

A mangled name is made up from the following pieces of information, in this order:

1. The base name of the function

2. A pair of underscore characters

3. A possibly zero-length list of codes indicating any function qualifiers, such as `const`

4. The number of characters in the name of the class of which the function is a member

5. The name of the class

6. A list of codes indicating the data types of the parameters

For example, the function `void cname::fname(void)` is encoded as `fname__5cname`. The function `int cname::stname(long frim) const` is encoded as `stname__C5cname1`, where `C` indicates the function is `const` and the trailing 1 (ell) indicates a single parameter of type `long`. A constructor is encoded by omitting the function name. For example, the constructor `cname::cname(signed char)` is encoded as `__5cnameSc`, where the `Sc` pair indicates a `signed char` parameter.

The codes for the various types and qualifiers are listed in Table 5-3. The meanings of some of the codes depend on how and where they are used in the encoding string, but with the entries in the table and a little practice you will be able to demangle the names in object files well enough to match the names with the source.

Code Letter	Meaning
`<number>`	The number of characters in a custom data type name. For example, the function `Mph::pdq(char, drip, double)` encodes as `pdq__3Mphc4dripd`. Optionally, the number can be preceded by the letter G—that is, `pdq__3Mph4drip` is equivalent to `pdq_3MphG4drip`.
A	An array. In C++ the arrays always decay to pointers, so this type is never actually seen. In Java, an array is encoded as a pointer to a `JArray` type.
b	A C++ `bool` data type or a Java `boolean` data type.
c	The C++ `char` data type or the Java `byte` data type.
C	A modifier indicating a `const` parameter type or member function.
d	The `double` data type.
e	Extra arguments of unknown types. For example, the function `Mph::pdq(int,...)` encodes as `pdq__3Mphie`.
f	The `float` data type.
G	See `<number>`.
H	A template function.
i	The `int` data type.
I	A special integer data type containing a nonstandard number of bits. For example, the function `Mph::pdq(int, int60_t, char)` with a 60-bit integer type as its second argument will be encoded as `pdq__3MphiI_3C_c`. A hexadecimal number surrounded by underscore characters is used to specify the number of bits in the integer. The hexadecimal number may not be delimited by underscore characters if the surrounding characters are not ambiguous.
J	The C++ `complex` data type.
l (ell)	The C++ `long` data type.
L	The name of a local class.

Table 5-3. *Code Letters Used in Name Mangling*

Code Letter	Meaning
p	A pointer. It is always followed by an indicator of the pointer type. Same as P.
P	A pointer. It is always followed by an indicator of the pointer type. Same as p.
Q	A qualified name, such as arises from a nested class.
r	The C++ long double data type.
R	A C++ reference. It is always followed by an indicator of the type being referenced. For example, the function Mph::pdq(ostream&) is encoded as pdq__3MphR7ostream.
s	The short data type.
S	If S is used to precede the name of a class, it implies static. For example, Mph::pdq(void) static is encoded pdq__S3Mph. If S is used to precede a char data type indicator, it implies signed. For example, the function Mph::pdq(signed char) is encoded pdq__3MphSc.
t	A C++ template instantiation.
T	A back reference to a previously seen parameter type.
u	The type qualifier for a restricted pointer.
U	A modifier indicating an unsigned integer data type. It is also used as a modifier for a class or namespace name to indicate Unicode encoding.
v	The void data type.
V	A modifier indicating a volatile data type.
w	The C++ whcar_t data type or the Java char data type.
x	The C++ long long data type or the Java long data type.
X	A template type parameter.
Y	A template constant parameter.

Table 5-3.   *Code Letters Used in Name Mangling* (continued)

A demangler named c++filt is part of the binutils package. You can enter a mangled name on the command line, and it will present you with a demangled version of the name, as shown in the following example:

```
$ c++filt pdq__3MphiUsJde
Mph::pdq(int, unsigned short, __complex double, ...)
```

The c++filt utility is capable of demangling more that one scheme. The scheme will vary from one platform to another and from one language to another. Among the options that can be set by using the -s option are lucid, arm, hp, and edg. Two of the language -s options are java for Java and gnat for Ada.

Note   *The mangling schemes used by GCC for C++ and Java, while compatible with one another, are not compatible with other compilers. Each compiler uses its own mangling scheme, but this is not altogether bad. Each compiler also uses its own scheme for laying out classes, implementing multiple inheritance, and in the technique for handling virtual functions. If a compatible mangling scheme were used, it would be possible to link your GCC object with modules and libraries produced by other compilers, but the programs still would not run.*

Linkage

Some things appear in the object file that are not strictly a part of the executable code, but they can be important for certain optimizations and for resolving references. Some of this type of information are categorized as *vague linkage* because they are something other than the normal (and simpler) process of associating a specific name with a specific address. The following is a description of the C++ vague linkage items.

Virtual Function Table

A virtual table is a list of the addresses of the virtual functions in a class. If class A contains a virtual function, and the function is overridden by the subclass B, then the address of the new function replaces the address of the original function in the virtual function table, or *vtable*. This is done because of the requirements of polymorphism—if an object of class B has been cast as being an object of class A, then a call to the virtual function uses the table and will actually be a call to the function in B, not the one in A.

Runtime Type Identification

In C++ each object contains identity information for the implementation of dynamic_cast, typeid, and exception handling. For classes with virtual functions, the information is included along with the vtable so that the type can be determined at runtime by dynamic_cast. If there is no vtable (that is, the class is not polymorphic), the information is only included in the object code where it is actually used (on a typeid statement or where an exception is thrown).

COMDAT

A declaration in a header file can cause a copy of the generated code to be included as part of the object file of every compilation unit that includes the header file. This involves such things as global data declarations and member functions with bodies declared as part of the class definition. On systems that support it (the GNU linker on an ELF system, such as Linux or Solaris, and on Microsoft Windows and others), the linker will discard all but one copy of the code to be placed in the final executable.

In the documentation of linkers, you will see this referred to as *folding, comdat folding, identical comdat folding, comdat discarding,* or even *transitive comdat elimination.*

Inline Functions

An inline function is generally declared in a header file that is included by every module that needs to call the function. Even though it may be declared as `inline`, an instance of the function itself is also created in case it is needed in a situation where it cannot be expanded inline, such as when its address is taken.

Compiling Template Instantiations

Including a template definition in a header file and including the header file in multiple modules creates multiple copies of the compiled template. This approach will work, but, in a large program with a large number of templates, a compiled copy of every template is included in every object file. This can make the compile time very long and can create very large object files. Here are some alternatives:

- The `#pragma interface` and `#pragma implementation` directives can be used in the source files (as described earlier in this chapter), which causes the creation of only one version of the compiled template.

- An approach similar to using the two pragmas is to use the command-line option `-falt-external-templates` to compile all the source. This instructs the compiler to include a compiled template instance only if the module actually uses it. One important characteristic of this approach is that the header file must be identical for each module using it.

- Compile the code using the `-frepo` command-line option. This causes the creation of files with the suffix .rpo, each listing the template instantiations to be found in its corresponding object file. The link wrapper utility, named `collect2`, will then be invoked to update the .rpo files with instructions to the linker as to the placement of the template instances in the final program. The only difficulty with this approach has to do with libraries—unless the associated `.rpo` files are also present, linking template instantiations stored in a library will fail.

- Compile the code using `-fno-implicit-templates`, which disables implicit template instantiation and explicitly instantiates the ones you want. This approach requires that you know exactly which template instantiations you are using, but it does cause the source code to be more explicit and clear.

Chapter 6

Compiling Objective-C

bjective-C is C with classes added to it. Another way of looking at it is that
Objective-C is the result of mixing C and Smalltalk. It is a much simpler
language than C++. Objective-C, as implemented by GCC, is the same as
standard C with the added ability to define classes, to use the classes to instantiate objects,
and to send messages (call functions) of the objects. Messages are sent to objects using
syntax very similar to Smalltalk.

Unlike the other languages compiled by GCC, Objective-C has no standard definition.
The GCC implementation of Objective-C is quite similar to the one developed for and
used in the NeXTStep system.

Fundamental Compiling

Table 6-1 lists the file name suffixes that have to do with compiling and linking
Objective-C programs. A table listing all the suffixes recognized by GCC can be
found in Appendix D.

Single Source to Executable

An Objective-C program can be written, in every way, exactly like a C program. That is,
you can write Objective-C without objects and it will have the same syntax and form as
a C program. The following is an example of a simple program that can be compiled
and run as Objective-C:

```
/* helloworld.m */
#import <stdio.h>
int main(int argc,char *argv[])
{
    printf("hello, world\n");
    return(0);
}
```

This program is identical to a C program in every way, except the preprocessor
directive #import is used in place of #include. The two directives achieve the same
purpose, with the added benefit that a header file specified on an #import directive
will not be included more than once in the same compilation unit. The same thing is
usually achieved for files read by the #include directives by using conditional
compilation inside the header files, as described in Chapter 3. You can use whichever
technique you would like.

This program can be compiled into an executable with the following command:

```
$ gcc -Wno-import helloworld.m -lobjc -o helloworld
```

Suffix	File Contains
.a	A library (archive file) containing object files for static linking
.h	A header file
.m	An Objective-C source file that is to be preprocessed
.mi	An Objective-C source file that is not to be preprocessed
.o	An object file in a format appropriate to be supplied to the linker
.so	A library containing object files for dynamic linking

Table 6-1.   *File Name Suffixes in Objective-C Programming*

The option -Wno-import is needed to suppress a warning message stating that the program uses #import instead of #include for the header files. Because you have the source of GCC, you can change the default setting of the command-line option in the file cppinit.c by removing the following line:

```
CPP_OPTION (pfile, warn_import) = 1;
```

The -lobjc option specifies that the library libobjc.a (the Objective-C object library) is to be used, but it is not really necessary because there are no objects included in the code of this simple program. The compiler recognizes the source file as being Objective-C because of the .m suffix on the file name, and the -o option specifies the name of the output file. The default name of the output file is a.out.

Compiling an Object

A class definition is made up of two source files. The Objective-C language is designed for a .h header file to contain the interface definition of the class and a .m source file to contain the implementation of the methods of the class. In the following example, the header file Speak.h specifies the interface of a class named Speak that is capable of storing a character string internally and then displaying it to standard output on request:

```
/* Speak.h */
#import <objc/Object.h>
@interface Speak : Object
{
    char *string;
```

```
}
- setString: (char *) str;
- say;
- free;
@end
```

The `#import` directive is used to read the header file named `Object.h`, which contains the definition of the `Object` class. The `Object` class is the super class of all Objective-C classes. The definition of the `Speak` class is surrounded by the compiler directives `@interface` and `@end`. Inside the definition is a block set off with braces where the data definitions are stored (in this example, the only data is the pointer to the string). The data block is followed by the list of methods defined for the class. Each method is specified by a minus sign, the name of the method, and the list of the types of arguments passed to it (if any).

The actual method bodies of the `Speak` class are defined in file `Speak.m`, as follows:

```
/* Speak.m */
#import "Speak.h"
@implementation Speak

+ new
{
    self = [super new];
    [self setString: ""];
    return self;
}
- setString: (char *)str
{
    string = str;
    return self;
}
- say
{
    printf("%s\n",string);
    return self;
}
- free
{
    return [super free];
}
```

The `Speak.h` header file is imported so that the definitions of all the data and methods are available. The `@implementation` compiler directive specifies that this source file contains the implementation of the methods of the `Speak` class. Method body definitions preceded by a minus sign are instance methods and can only be called after an object already exists, and those preceded by a plus sign are class variables and can be called any time.

The form of declaration of a method matches the one in the header file, with the addition of a method body inside a pair of braces. Unless some specific data type is being returned by a method, the return type is always assumed to be an `id` (the data type that represents a generic Objective-C object). Because of this, the methods mostly return `self`, which is the way an object refers to itself.

The following program uses a `Speak` object to write the `"hello, world"` string to the standard output:

```
/* helloobject.m */
#import <objc/Object.h>
#import "Speak.h"

main()
{
    id speak;

    speak = [Speak new];
    [speak setString: "hello, world"];
    [speak say];
    [speak free];
}
```

This program can be compiled by compiling each of the source files into object files and then linking them together, as follows:

```
$ gcc -Wno-import -c helloobject.m -o helloobject.o
$ gcc -Wno-import -c Speak.m -o Speak.o
$ gcc -helloobject.o Speak.o -lobjc -o helloobject
```

Alternatively, all three steps can be performed in a single command, as follows:

```
$ gcc -Wno-import helloobject.m Speak.m -lobjc -o helloobject
```

Creating a Static Library

A collection of `.o` object files produced from compiling Objective-C can be stored in a library (archive) of object files. The following example creates a library named `libcat.a` containing the implementation code of a class named `Cat`. The class has methods that will accept a sequence of character strings and concatenate them into a single string.

The file Cat.h is the header file defining the interface of the Cat class:

```
/* Cat.h */
#import <objc/Object.h>
@interface Cat : Object
{
    char *string;
}
- add: (char *) str;
- (char *) get;
- init;
- free;
@end
```

The file Cat.m contains the implementation of the Cat class. The add method is used to add characters onto the end of the string, and get retrieves the current concatenated string. The init method is meant to be called just once when a new Cat object is created.

```
/* Cat.m */
#import "Cat.h"
@implementation Cat

+ new
{
    self = [super new];
    [self init];
    return self;
}
- init
{
    string = NULL;
    return self;
}
- add: (char *)str
{
    int length;
    char *newstring;
    if(string == NULL) {
        length = strlen(str) + 1;
        string = (char *)malloc(length);
        strcpy(string,str);
```

```
    } else {
        length = strlen(str) + strlen(string) + 1;
        newstring = (char *)malloc(length);
        strcpy(newstring,string);
        strcat(newstring,str);
        free(string);
        string = newstring;
    }
    return self;
}
- (char *) get
{
    return string;
}
- free
{
    if(string != NULL)
        free(string);
    return [super free];
}
```

The `Cat.m` file is compiled into the object file `Cat.o` with the following command:

```
$ gcc -c -Wno-import Cat.m -o Cat.o
```

The object file is then used to construct a library with the following command:

```
$ ar -r libcat.a Cat.o
```

The `-r` option replaces any existing version of the named object files with the newer version, or it will create a completely new library file if none already exists.

The following is a sample program that uses the `Cat` class to concatenate two strings into one, then extracts the result and displays it:

```
/* docat.m */
#import <objc/Object.h>
#import "Cat.h"

main()
{
```

```
        id cat;
        char *line;

        cat = [Cat new];
        [cat add: "Part one"];
        [cat add: " and part two"];
        line = [cat get];
        printf("%s\n",line);
}
```

This program is compiled into an executable named docat with the following command:

```
$ gcc -Wno-import docat.m libcat.a -libobjc -o docat
```

Creating a Shared Library

Object files produced by compiling Objective-C can be stored in a shared library. To construct a shared library it is necessary to compile the source into a form of object code that can be loaded into any location in memory and executed from there. To do this, it is necessary to specify the -fpic (position-independent code) option on the command line. The following line will create such an object file from the class defined in Cat.m:

```
$ gcc -fpic -Wno-import -c Cat.m -o Cat.o
```

The following command line will use the object file to create a shared library:

```
$ gcc -shared Cat.o -o cat.so
```

The two command lines can be combined and the shared library can be produced directly from source, as follows:

```
$ gcc -Wno-import -fpic -shared Cat.m -o cat.so
```

The following program uses an instance of the Cat class to combine three strings into one and then display the result:

```
/* showcat.m */
#import <objc/Object.h>
```

```
#import "Cat.h"
main()
{
    id cat;
    char *line;

    cat = [Cat new];
    [cat add: "The beginning"];
    [cat add: ", the middle"];
    [cat add: ", and the end."];
    line = [cat get];
    printf("%s\n",line);
}
```

The following command will compile the showcat.m program and link it so that it will run using the shared library:

```
$ gcc -Wno-import showcat.m cat.so -lobjc -o showcat
```

To be able to execute an application that relies on a shared library, it is necessary for the program to locate the library, as discussed in Chapter 12.

General Objective-C Notes

Objective-C has no standard that specifies what it should not contain. When you write Objective-C code, don't expect it to be portable to another compiler. The items mentioned in this section are peculiar to the GCC version of Objective-C and may not pertain to any other version. Because the GCC Objective-C compiler is built in with a complete and standard C compiler, you can generally count on all the standard C and preprocessor facilities being available.

Predefined Types

Table 6-2 lists the data types that are defined in the header file Object.h. These same types exist in most Objective-C compilers, but the names may be different.

Creating an Interface Declaration

The gcc option -gen-decl can be used to facilitate the update of an interface for the class found in the source file. This can be useful to make certain that the header file (the interface definition) and the class source file (the implementation) stay the same. If a new method is added to the implementation, or if an existing method has its calling sequence

Type	Description
BOOL	A Boolean data type that can only assume the value of YES or NO. The fundamental data type will vary depending on the platform, but NO is zero and YES is nonzero, so a BOOL type will work as expected in a C style conditional statement.
id	A pointer to any type of Objective-C object.
IMP	A reference to the method of an object by address.
nil, Nil	A null pointer to an Objective-C object.
SEL	A reference to the method of an object by name. The name SEL is short for *selector*, because it is a variable that can be used to select a method.
STR	A typedef of a char *.

Table 6-2.   *The Predefined Types of Objective-C*

changed, the GCC can be run with the -gen-decl option to produce a correct insert to replace the method definitions in the existing interface.

For example, the class named Speak from the previous examples can have a new interface definition generated with the following command:

```
$ gcc -Wno-import -gen-decls -c Speak.m
```

The -gen-decls option does not keep the compiler from attempting to compile and link. It is necessary to use the -c option to prevent gcc from attempting to link the newly compiled class definition. The result is a file named w.decl with the following contents:

```
@interface Speak : Object
- free;
- say;
- setString:(char *)str;
+ new;

@end
```

Naming and Mangling

Method definitions in Objective-C are designated either by a plus (+) or minus (–) sign as being a class method or an instance method, respectively. For example, the following class interface definition contains the class methods new and copy along with the instance methods reset and sort:

```
@interface TinyList : Object
+ new;
+ copy;
- reset;
- sort;
@end
```

For purposes of debugging, you may need to be able to recognize the names in their mangled form in the object code. A class method is preceded by the letter c and the name of the class, with underscoring used to separate the parts of the name. An instance method is preceded by the letter i and follows the same format. The four methods of the previous example would be named as follows:

```
_c_TinyList__new
_c_TinyList__copy
_i_TinyList__reset
_i_TinyList__sort
```

A method that accepts more than one parameter can have more than one name. For example, the following method accepts two char pointers—one named string and the other named desc—and the method has the two names accept and as:

```
- accept: (char *) string as: (char *) desc
```

The following is an example of calling this method of a class named Lister in an instance named lister:

```
[lister accept: "Herbert" as: "name"]
```

In the object code, the mangled name of this instance method is as follows:

```
_i_Lister__accept_as
```

The Complete Reference

Chapter 7

Compiling Fortran

ortran is renowned for its ability to handle intricate mathematical computations. This has caused it to remain an important language in the scientific community. In some scientific circles, such as physics, Fortran is the predominant language. The GNU Fortran compiler is primarily based on the ANSI standard definition of Fortran 77, but it is by no means limited to that. It contains many (but not all) features and characteristics defined in the Fortran 90 and Fortran 95 standards documents. The Fortran language is as much a tradition as it is a standard, and the standards documents themselves leave a lot in the hands of the implementers of the compilers. Every Fortran compiler works primarily the same way, but each supports its own dialect of the language.

Fundamental Compiling

Table 7-1 lists the file name suffixes that are involved with compiling and linking Fortran programs. A table listing all the suffixes recognized by GCC can be found in Appendix D.

Single Source to Executable

A traditional Fortran program is written using all uppercase, and the first six character positions of each line are reserved for special purposes. The first column is reserved for the character C to indicate that the entire line is a comment. The second through sixth columns are reserved for labels. The code begins in the seventh column. The following example is a program formatted in the traditional Fortran format:

```
C   helloworld.f
C
      PROGRAM HELLOWORLD
      WRITE(*,10)
   10 FORMAT('hello, world')
      END PROGRAM HELLOWORLD
```

The GCC compiler does not require that the source be all uppercase, but, unless specified otherwise, the fixed format is required. The following command will compile the program into an executable:

```
$ g77 helloworld.f -o helloworld
```

The g77 command is a front end for gcc and sets up the basic environment requirements of a Fortran program. The same result can be achieved by using a gcc command as follows:

```
$ gcc helloworld.f -lfrtbegin -lg2c -lm -shared-libgcc -o helloworld
```

Suffix	File Contains
.a	Static object library (archive)
.f, .for, .FOR	Fortran source code that is not to be preprocessed
.F, .fpp, .FPP	Fortran source code that is to be preprocessed
.o	An object file in a format appropriate to be fed to the linker
.r	Fortran source code to be preprocessed by Ratfor
.so	Shared object library

Table 7-1.   *File Name Suffixes in Fortran Programming*

The library `libfrtbegin.a` (invoked by the command line option `-lfrtbegin`) contains the startup and exit code necessary to start a Fortran program running and to terminate it cleanly. The library `libg2c.a` contains the necessary Fortran runtime routines for such fundamental capabilities as input and output. The library `libm.a` is the system math library. The `-shared-libgcc` option specifies that the shared version of the standard library `libgcc` be used.

GCC also allows Fortran code to be compiled in a free form format. Comments are formed beginning with an exclamation point (`!`) character and continuing to the end of the line. A free-form version of the previous program can have the statements, and labels, begin in any column, as follows:

```
!  helloworldff.f
!
Program Helloworld
write(*,10)
10 format('hello, world')
      end Program Helloworld
```

This program can be compiled the same as the previous one by adding the `-ffree-form` option to the command line, as follows:

```
$ g77 -ffree-form helloworldff.f -o helloworldff
```

Because of some of the fundamental differences between the two syntactic forms, programs are written in either free form or fixed form format—it is difficult to write a program that will compile in either form because of differences in the syntax of the comments and the general layout rules.

USING THE COMPILER COLLECTION

Multiple Source Files to Executable

The g77 command is capable of compiling and linking multiple Fortran source files into a single executable. The following listing is the mainline of a simple program, stored in a file named caller.f, that makes a single function call and displays the result:

```
C   caller.f
C
      PROGRAM CALLER
      I = Iaverageof(10,20,83)
      WRITE(*,10) 'Average=', I
  10 FORMAT(A,I5)
      END PROGRAM CALLER
```

The function named Iaverage is defined in a separate source file named called.f, as follows:

```
C   called.f
C
      INTEGER FUNCTION Iaverageof(i,j,k)
      Iaverageof = (i + j + k) / 3
      RETURN
      END FUNCTION Iaverageof
```

These two source files can be compiled and linked into an executable named caller with the following statement:

```
$ g77 caller.f called.f -o caller
```

The same result can be achieved in three separate steps by first creating an object file for each of the source files and then linking the object files into an executable, as follows:

```
$ g77 -c caller.f -o caller.o
$ g77 -c called.f -o called.o
$ g77 caller.o called.o -o caller
```

Generating Assembly Language

The -S option instructs g77 to generate assembly language from the source code and then stop. To generate assembly language of the helloworld.f example used earlier in this chapter, enter the following command:

```
$ g77 -S helloworld.f
```

The resulting assembly language file is named `helloworld.s`. The exact form of the assembly language depends on the target platform.

Preprocessing

Compiling a Fortran program with a file suffix of `.F`, `.fpp`, or `.FPP` will cause the source to be preprocessed before it is compiled. This is the preprocessor, described in Chapter 3, originally designed to work with the C programming language. The following example is a Fortran free form program that uses the preprocessor to include a function into the main program:

```
!   evenup.F
!
#define ROUNDUP
#include "iruefunc.h"
!
program evenup
do 300 i=11,22
    j = irue(i)
    write(*,10) i,j
300 continue
 10 format(I5,I5)
end program evenup
```

The source code of the function `irue()` is in the file named `iruefunc.h`, and it will compile differently depending on whether the macro ROUNDUP has been defined. The function will round any odd number to an even number. By default, it will round down, but if ROUNDUP has been defined, the function will round up to get an even number. The body of the `irue()` function is as follows:

```
integer function irue(i)
k = i / 2
k = k * 2
if (i .EQ. k) then
    irue = i
else
#ifdef ROUNDUP
    irue = i + 1
#else
    irue = i - 1
```

```
#endif
end if
end function irue
```

The following command line will compile this program into an executable:

```
$ g77 -ffree-form evenup.F -o evenup
```

It is not necessary to write a program in free form format to be able to use the preprocessor. Because the preprocessor discards the directives and passes only the resulting code to the compiler, the following program is also valid:

```
C  adder.F
C
#define SEVEN 7
#define NINE 9
C
      program adder
      isum = SEVEN + NINE
      write(*,10) isum
   10 format(I5)
      end program adder
```

Creating a Static Library

A library of object modules can be created by compiling Fortran source code into .o files and then using the `ar` utility to store the object files into an *archive* file, which is another name for a static library.

The following example demonstrates the creation of a library containing a pair of simple functions that are both called from the same mainline program. The first function is named `imaximum()` and returns the largest of the three integers passed to it:

```
C  imaximum.f
C
      INTEGER FUNCTION imaximum(i,j,k)
      iret = i
      IF (j .gt. iret) iret = j
      IF (k .gt. iret) iret = k
      imaximum = iret
      RETURN
      END FUNCTION imaximum
```

The second function is very much like the first, except that it returns the smallest of the three integers passed to it:

```
C   iminimum.f
C
      INTEGER FUNCTION iminimum(i,j,k)
      iret = i
      IF (j .lt. iret) iret = j
      IF (k .lt. iret) iret = k
      iminimum = iret
      RETURN
      END FUNCTION iminimum
```

The following three commands compile these two functions and store them in the library:

```
$ g77 -c iminimum.f -o iminimum.o
$ g77 -c imaximum.f -o imaximum.o
$ ar -r libmima.a imaximum.o iminimum.o
```

The -c option on g77 instructs the compiler to compile the source into an object file but not to invoke the linker. The ar utility with an -r option will create a library named libmima.a if it does not already exist. If the library does exist, any object files inside it will be replaced by the ones named on the command line.

The following program calls the two functions stored in the library and displays the result:

```
C   minmax.f
C
      PROGRAM MINMAX
      WRITE(*,10) 'Maximum=', imaximum(10,20,30)
      WRITE(*,10) 'Minimum=', iminimum(10,20,30)
   10 FORMAT(A,I5)
      END PROGRAM MINMAX
```

This program can be compiled and linked to the functions stored in the library with the following command:

```
$ g77 minmax.f libmima.a -o minmax
```

The compiler recognizes minmax.f as Fortran source, so it compiles the source into an object file and then links the program into an executable by passing the name of the library libmima.a to the linker.

Creating a Shared Library

The creation of a shared library is much the same as the creation of a static library, but object files to be stored in the library must be compiled with either the -fpic or -fPIC option so that the code can be loaded into memory and executed while the program is running. (PIC stands for *position independent code*.)

Using the same source code as used in the static library example, the two object files and the shared library can be created with the following commands:

```
$ g77 -c -fpic iminimum.f -o iminimum.o
$ g77 -c -fpic imaximum.f -o imaximum.o
$ g77 -shared iminimum.o imaximum.o -o libmima.so
```

The -c option is necessary to instruct the compiler to produce .o object files, and -fpic is required to have the object files produced in the correct format for being loaded from a shared library at runtime. The -shared option combines all the object files on the command line into a shared library named libmima.so. For the library to be used by an application, it is necessary for the program to locate the library when it starts running, as described in Chapter 12.

To compile and link the program to use the shared library, it is only a matter of including the name of the shared library on the command line as the program is linked:

```
$ g77 minmax.f -lmima -o minmax
```

The -l option specifies the library name as mima, which the compiler expands to libmima.so and searches for a library by that name in the places the system is configured to look for all shared libraries.

Ratfor

Ratfor is an acronym for Rational Fortran. It is a publicly available preprocessor of source code that allows Fortran to be written with C-like syntax and then be converted into standard Fortran to be compiled.

The original Ratfor translator was implemented by Kernighan and Plauger in 1976. Since its inception at AT&T, there have been a number of versions of Ratfor. The two latest ones can be freely downloaded from a number of locations, including http://sepwww.stanford.edu/software/ratfor.html for ratfor77 and http://sepwww. standord.edu/software/ratfor90.html for ratfor90. The downloads are very small, and installation is quite simple. The installation procedure that comes with them will install the executable as either ratfor77 (which is a C program that compiles into a binary executable) or ratfor90 (a Perl script). Either of these can be used to generate Fortran code for input into the GCC compiler.

The two versions of Ratfor are different enough that you will need to select one and stay with it. Ratfor90 is not a direct extension of Ratfor77. It is very easy to write simple programs that will compile with one but will not compile with the other.

The source code of a Ratfor program is Fortran and can be written as pure Fortran, but there are many C constructs available. The following simple example demonstrates the form and appearance of a Ratfor program:

```
#  ratdemo.r
program ratdemo {
    integer i;
    integer counter;

    counter = 10;
    for(i=0; i<10; i=i+1) {
        counter = counter + 5;
        write(*,10) i, counter;
    }
  10 format(I5,I5);
}
end program ratdemo
```

This code can be processed through `ratfor77` and compiled into an executable with the following two commands:

```
$ ratfor77 <ratdemo.r >ratdemo.f
$ g77 ratdemo.f -o ratdemo
```

The file `ratdemo.f`, output from the Ratfor translator, is Fortran and looks like the following:

```
C Output from Public domain Ratfor, version 1.0
      program ratdemo
      integer i
      integer counter
      counter = 10
      i=0
23000 if(.not.(i.lt.10))goto 23002
      counter = counter + 5
      write(*,10) i, counter
23001 i=i+1
      goto 23000
23002 continue
10    format(i5,i5)
      end program ratdemo
```

GNU Fortran Extensions and Variations

The GCC compiler supports the ANSI Fortran 77 standard, along with some special GNU extensions. It supports some, but not all, of the features defined in Fortran 90.

Intrinsics

The GNU Fortran compiler includes hundreds of intrinsic functions. They are all documented on the GNU website and include implementations not only of a large set of GNU specific intrinsics, but also intrinsics defined in other places.

The ANSI FORTRAN 77 language specification defines a set of both generic and specific intrinsics that are included. A *specific* intrinsic is one that has a specific return data type defined for it. A *generic* intrinsic's return type will vary depending on how it is used—usually the return type is determined by the type of one of its argument values.

The GCC Fortran compiler is more restrictive than some other compilers in the requirements for arguments passed to intrinsic functions, so you may find a program that compiles and runs with another compiler, but g77 balks and refuses to compile it. For example, if the variable X is declared as INTEGER*8, the ABS() intrinsic may not accept it because it is written to accept INTEGER*4 and will refuse to discard the extra precision. It will be necessary to make an adjustment to the source, which could be to simply force the conversion.

GCC Fortran supports the MIL-STD 1753 intrinsics BTEST, IAND, IBCLR, IBITS, IEOR, IOR, ISHIFT, ISBFTC, MVBITS, and NOT.

The intrinsics found in both f77 and f2c are available in g77. These include the bit-manipulation intrinsics AND, LSHIFT, OR, RSHIFT, and XOR. Among the other intrinsics supported are CDABS, CDCOS, CDEXP, CDLOG, CDSIN, CDSQRT, DCMPLX, DCONJG, DFLOAT, DIMAG, DREAL, IMAG, ZABS, ZCOS, ZEXP, ZLOG, ZSIN, and ZSQRT.

In all, there are 402 documented Fortran intrinsics supported by GCC.

Source Code Form

As shown in the examples earlier in this chapter, GNU Fortran accepts source in ANSI Fortran 77 format and in a free form format. The free form format is very much like the Fortran 90 format, but GNU Fortran is a bit more forgiving with things such as tabs. The following list summarizes the special situations of both the free form and fixed form formats:

- **Carriage returns**   Any carriage return characters in the source are ignored.
- **Tabs**   Each tab is expanded into the appropriate number of spaces to expand to an eight-character boundary.
- **Ampersands**   An ampersand in column 1 of the fixed form format designates that the line is a continuation of the previous line.

- **Short lines** The line length has no meaning in the free form format, but fixed form lines are all 72 characters long. A line shorter than 72 characters is automatically padded with spaces on the right to fit the 72-character requirement. This can only have an effect on continued characters and Hollerith constants. This fixed line requirement can be modified or eliminated by using the command-line option `-ffixed-line-length`.

- **Long lines** Lines longer than the designated length are truncated without warning. This is mostly to accommodate legacy Fortran code that may have other information in columns 73 through 80 (usually source code sequence numbers). The fixed-line requirement can be modified or eliminated by using the command-line option `-ffixed-line-length`.

Comments

The characters `/*` and `*/` can be used to create a comment block only if the code is to be preprocessed, because the preprocessor will remove the comment block so it will not be seen by the compiler. The form `//` cannot be used to specify a comment line because these characters already have meaning (concatenation) in the Fortran language. In GNU Fortran, the `!` character can be used to designate the rest of the current line as being a comment, whether or not the code is being preprocessed. Of course, in fixed format, the letter `c` or `C` in the first column designates the rest of the line as being a comment.

Dollar Signs

You can use dollar signs in names as long as one is not the leading character of the name and the option `-fdollar-ok` is specified on the command line.

Case Sensitivity

A large number of option combinations are available to be used to specify the rules to be followed for upper- and lowercase letters. By default, there are no case restrictions on the input source code—both upper and lower case letters are accepted and are treated as if they are the same case. Setting any of the options to limit or adjust the case has no effect on comments, character constants, or Hollerith fields.

Table 7-2 lists the options that can be used to set the requirements for the cases of the input source. There are separate settings for the Fortran keywords, the intrinsics, and the symbols defined in the program. Table 7-3 describes each of the four options (`any`, `upper`, `lower`, and `initcap`) shown in Table 7-2.

Three settings can be used to determine the case of the output of symbols written to the assembly language, as shown in Table 7-4. Care must be taken when setting these options because external references must match up properly with library routines.

Keyword	Intrinsic	Symbol
-fmatch-case-any	-fintrin-case-any	-fsymbol-case-any
-fmatch-case-upper	-fintrin-case-upper	-fsymbol-case-upper
-fmatch-case-lower	-fintrin-case-lower	-fsymbol-case-lower
-fmatch-case-initcap	-fintrin-case-initcap	-f symbol-case-initcap

Table 7-2. *Options Used to Specify Upper and Lower Case Requirements*

Option	Description
any	There is no restriction on specifying case, and all combinations will match. For example, Function, FUNCTION, function, and FuncTion are all the same.
upper	All characters must be uppercase.
lower	All characters must be lowercase.
initcap	The initial letter must be uppercase and all other letters must be lowercase. For example, Maximum, Function, Do, and Return.

Table 7-3. *The Four Possible Case Requirements*

Option	Description
-fsource-case-preserve	The output in the assembly language is in the same case as the input to the compiler.
-fsource-case-upper	All symbols output in the assembly language are converted to uppercase.
-fsource-case-lower	All symbols output in the assembly language are converted to lower case.

Table 7-4. *Control of Case Output to the Assembler*

Certain combinations of the options in Tables 7-2 and 7-4 are common and can be specified as one of the single options listed in Table 7-5.

Option	Description
-fcase-initcap	This option requires that everything begin with initial capital letters, except comments and character constants. This is the same as specifying all three initcap options from Table 7-2 and also specifying -fsource-case-preserve.
-fcase-lower	This is the "canonical" UNIX model where all source is translated to lowercase. This is the same as specifying all three any options from Table 7-2 and also specifying -fsource-case-lower.
-fcase-preserve	This option allows any case input pattern, and the input case is preserved in the output assembly language. This is the same as specifying all three any options from Table 7-2 and also specifying -fsource-case-preserve.
-fcase-strict-upper	This is the "strict" ANSI FORTRAN 77 requirement that everything be in uppercase, except comments and character constants. This is the same as specifying all three upper options from Table 7-2 and also specifying -fsource-case-preserve.
-fcase-strict-upper	This option requires that everything be in lowercase except comments and character constants. This is the same as specifying all three lower options from Table 7-2 and also specifying -fsource-case-preserve.
-fcase-upper	This is the "classic" ANSI FORTRAN 77 model where all source is translated to uppercase. This is the same as specifying all three any options from Table 7-2 and also specifying -fsource-case-upper.

Table 7-5. *Single Options That Specify Input and Output Case Combinations*

Specific Fortran 90 Features

This section contains brief descriptions of some of the more useful Fortran 90 features supported by g77. The list is almost certainly not complete because the language specifications are large and complex, but the following features exist in g77 and can be used without any special flags or settings.

Character Strings

Character string constants may be surrounded by double quotes as well as single quotes. That is, the string "hello world" is the same as 'hello world'. Inside a string defined with double quotes, a single double-quote character is defined by a pair of double-quote characters.

A character constant may be zero length (contain no characters). Also, it is possible to declare a substring in the form 'hello world' (7:4), which as the value 'worl'.

Construct Name

A *construct name* can be used to specify the block of executable statements controlled by an IF, DO, or SELECT CASE statement. The following example uses the construct name cname as an identifier at the top and bottom of an IF block:

```
C   conname.f
C
      PROGRAM conname
      key = 12
      cname: IF(key .gt. 10) THEN
          key = key - 1
          WRITE(*,10) key
      END IF cname
10    FORMAT('Key=',I5)
      END PROGRAM conname
```

CYCLE and EXIT

An EXIT statement can be used to immediately abandon the execution of a loop and jump to the statement following it. That is, executing an EXIT statement inside a loop is the same as executing a GOTO statement that jumps to the statement immediately following the loop. (If you are familiar with C syntax, EXIT is to Fortran what break is to C.)

A CYCLE statement can be used to immediately abandon the execution of a loop and jump to the bottom of the loop to start another iteration. That is, executing a CYCLE statement inside a loop is the same as executing a GOTO statement that jumps to a CONTINUE statement that is the last statement of the loop. (If you are familiar with C syntax, CYCLE is to Fortran what continue is to C.)

The following example demonstrates both the EXIT and CYCLE statements:

```
C  cycle.f
      PROGRAM cycle
      DO 10 i=1,3
          IF (i .EQ. 2) CYCLE
          WRITE(*,30) i
 10    CONTINUE
      DO 20 i=1,3
          IF (i .EQ. 2) EXIT
          WRITE(*,30) i
 20    CONTINUE
 30    FORMAT('i=',I5)
      END PROGRAM cycle
```

The following is the output from this program:

```
i=     1
i=     3
i=     1
```

The first loop writes the number 1 on its first iteration, skips the WRITE statement (by skipping to the bottom of the loop) on the second iteration, and writes 3 on the third iteration. The second loop writes the number 1 on its first iteration and then abandons the loop while in its second iteration.

DO WHILE

The DO WHILE statement can be used with a logical expression and terminated by an END DO to form a loop, as in the following example:

```
C  dowhile.f
      PROGRAM dowhile
      k = 5
      DO WHILE ( k .gt. 0)
          WRITE(*,20) k
          k = k - 1
      END DO
 20    FORMAT('k=',I5)
      END PROGRAM dowhile
```

DO Forever

By using a DO statement with nothing else on the line, a loop is constructed that will continue to iterate until the program is terminated or a specific exit is made from the loop. The following example iterates until the value of the counter reaches 8 and the GOTO statement jumps out of the loop:

```
C   doforever.f
      PROGRAM doforever
      k = 0
      DO
          WRITE(*,20) k
          if ( k .ge. 8 ) GOTO 100
          k = k + 1
      END DO
 20   FORMAT('k=',I5)
100   CONTINUE
      END PROGRAM doforever
```

IMPLICIT NONE

The IMPLICIT NONE statement will prevent the automatic declaration of variables and require that each one be explicitly declared as to type. For example, the following program automatically defines and assumes the type of the loop counter:

```
      PROGRAM imp
      DO 10 k=1,5
          PRINT *,k
 10   CONTINUE
      END PROGRAM imp
```

Adding an IMPLICIT NONE statement at the top of the program requires that everything be declared before it is used, including the loop counter, as in the following example:

```
      PROGRAM imp
      IMPLICIT NONE
      INTEGER k
      DO 10 k=1,5
          PRINT *,k
 10   CONTINUE
      END PROGRAM imp
```

INCLUDE

The INCLUDE directive is defined in the standard as having the following syntax:

```
INCLUDE filename
```

The meaning of *filename* is left to the implementation. The GNU compiler interprets *filename* as the name of a file either in the current directory or in any directory named by an -I option on the command line. Therefore, the INCLUDE directive works the same as the #include preprocessor directive described earlier in this chapter, except there is no preprocessing required for the INCLUDE directive.

Integer Constants

Integer constant values can be expressed in base 2, 8, 10, or 16. The following example declares the same value in each of these bases. A base 2 (binary) number is preceded with the letter *B*. A base 8 (octal) constant is preceded by the letter *O*. A base 16 (hexadecimal) constant is preceded by either the letter *X* or the letter *Z*, and each hexadecimal digit can be in either upper- or lowercase.

The following example demonstrates the syntax of a constant being declared in each of the bases by having the same value declared in each one:

```
C   bases.f
C
      PROGRAM bases
      M = 18987
      PRINT *,M
      M = X'4A2b'
      PRINT *,M
      M = Z'4A2b'
      PRINT *,M
      M = O'45053'
      PRINT *,M
      M = B'0100101000101011'
      PRINT *,M
      END PROGRAM bases
```

Comparison Operators

Table 7-6 lists the characters that can be used in place of the traditional comparison operators.

Original	Alternative	Means
.GT.	>	Greater than
.LT.	<	Less than
.GE.	>=	Greater than or equal to
.LE.	<=	Less than or equal to
.NE.	/=	Not equal to
.EQ.	==	Equal to

Table 7-6. *Alternative Characters for the Original Comparison Operators*

Kinds of Data

A special notation has been devised that allows for making modifications to the fundamental variable types. For example, the syntax for defining an INTEGER value of KIND 3 is as follows:

```
INTEGER(KIND=3)
```

The possible values for KIND are 0, 1, 3, 5, and 7. The syntax is valid for all the generic types (INTEGER, REAL, COMPLEX, LOGICAL, and CHARACTER), although not all values are valid for all types. Table 7-7 describes each value along with how (and whether) it applies to each of the data types for GCC. The exact meaning of the KIND value will vary from one platform to the next because of differences in hardware, as do the sizes and ranges of the default types.

KIND Value	Description
0	This value currently has no effect but is reserved for future use. There are plans to have the resulting type be context sensitive and adjust its semantics depending on how it is used.
1	This is the default setting. The result is the same as if no KIND value had been specified. This is typically REAL*4, INTEGER*4, LOGICAL*4, and COMPLEX*8.
2	These types occupy twice the space of the default. In GNU, variables of this KIND are equivalent to the Fortran 90 standard for double precision. That is, REAL(KIND=2) is equivalent to DOUBLE PRECISION, which, in turn, is typically REAL*8. Also, COMPLEX(KIND=2) is equivalent to DOUBLE COMPLEX, which, in turn, is typically COMPLEX*16. INTEGER(KIND=2) and LOGICAL(KIND=2) are not supported on every GNU implementation.
3	These types occupy as much space as a single CHARACTER(KIND=1) type. These are typically INTEGER*1 and LOGICAL*1. This KIND is not necessarily implemented for all types on all GNU implementations.
5	These types occupy half as much space as the default type (as specified by KIND=1). These are typically INTEGER*2 and LOGICAL*2. This KIND is not necessarily implemented for all types on all GNU implementations.
7	This is valid only for INTEGER(KIND=7) and is the same size as the smallest possible pointer that can hold a unique address of a CHARACTER*1 variable. On a 32-bit system, this is equivalent to INTEGER*4, while on a 64-bit system it is equivalent to INTEGER*8.

Table 7-7.   *The Numbers Defined for the KIND Notation*

Chapter 8

Compiling Java

Although there is no standard definition of the Java language in the same way that an official standards body has published a document for C, C++, and Ada, there is a single and very clear definition of the Java language. Sun Microsystems has complete control of the language definition and has assumed the responsibility of maintaining and extending the language. The syntax and fundamental operation of the language itself has changed very little, but the API (the system classes) has been updated regularly and has grown to several times its original size.

As far as the compiler is concerned, Java is a bit different from the other languages because it has two distinct forms of object code for each platform. Just as with C, C++, or any other compiled language, the compiler can be used to generate binary executable object files that can be run natively on the target machine. The Java compiler is also capable of producing an object file in the Java bytecode format that can be executed by any Java Virtual Machine (JVM). The Java compiler is also capable of using Java bytecode as input to produce a native executable object.

Fundamental Compiling

Table 8-1 lists the file name suffixes that have to do with compiling and linking Java programs. A table listing all the suffixes recognized by GCC can be found in Appendix D.

Single Source to Binary Executable

For a Java class to be executable, it must be `public` and it must contain a public method named `main()`, as in the following example:

```
/* HelloWorld.java */
public class HelloWorld {
    public static void main(String arg[]) {
        System.out.println("hello, world");
    }
}
```

To compile a Java program, it is necessary to use the `gcj` command, which is the Java front end to the `gcc` compiler. The Java language allows every class to have its own `main()` method and thus be executable. This works fine for the Java interpreter, where the class name is specified on the command line when you run the program, but when dealing with an executable program, there must be a single starting point specified. The following command compiles and links `HelloWorld.java` into a native executable program. The --main option specifies that the program should use the `main()` method of the `HelloWorld` class as the starting point of the program:

```
$ gcj --main=HelloWorld -Wall HelloWorld.java -o HelloWorld
```

Suffix	File Contains
.a	A library (archive file) containing object files for static linking
.class	An object file containing bytecodes in a format that can be executed by a Java Virtual Machine
.java	Java source code
.o	A binary object file in a format appropriate to be supplied to a linker
.s	Assembly language source code
.so	A shared library containing object files for dynamic linking

Table 8-1.   *File Name Suffixes in Java Programming*

The -o option is used to name the executable HelloWorld, which would otherwise default to being named a.out. To execute this program, simply enter its name from the command line, as follows:

```
$ HelloWorld
```

Because this file is a binary executable, it is free from the naming restrictions required of the interpreted Java class files. The executable can be named anything you would like, as in the following example, which compiles the same HelloWorld.java into an executable file named howdy:

```
$ gcj --main=HelloWorld -Wall HelloWorld.java -o howdy
```

But this relaxation only applies to the binary executable file. The source file of a public class must be the same name as the file that contains it. That is, a public class by the name of HelloWorld must be defined in a source file named HelloWorld.java.

Single Source to Class File

The GNU compiler can be used to produce a Java .class file that can be executed by a Java Virtual Machine. The following command uses the -C option to create the file HelloWorld.class from the source file HelloWorld.java:

```
$ gcj -C -Wall HelloWorld.java
```

The –o option is not available in combination with the –C option, so the output .class file will always have the same base name as the input .java file. The class HelloWorld contains the required public static void main() method, so it can be executed by the Java Virtual Machine from the command line as follows:

```
$ gij HelloWorld
```

The class file is compatible with other Java interpreters. The same program can be executed by Sun's Java Virtual Machine as follows:

```
$ java HelloWorld
```

Single Source to Binary Object File

The following command uses the –c option to suppress linking and produce a binary object file that can be either linked into an executable or stored in a static library to be linked later:

```
$ gcj -c HelloWorld.java
```

This command will produce an object file named HelloWorld.o. Optionally, the name of the object file can be specified by using the –o option, as in the following example:

```
$ gcj -c HelloWorld.java -o hello.o
```

The gcj command can be used to link the hello.o file into an executable. The hello.o file contains the definition of the class named HelloWorld, and that class contains the static main() method that is to be used as the entry point of the program, so it must be specified on the command line as follows:

```
$ gcj --main=HelloWorld hello.o -o hello
```

There is seldom a need to change the names of the object files this way. It was done in this example to point out the fact that the --main option requires the name of a class, not the name of a file.

Class File to Native Executable

The gcj command can be used to compile Java bytecodes directly into a native binary executable. The file with the .class suffix is treated on the command line just as if it were a source file with the .java suffix. In the following example, the first command compiles the source into a class file, and the second command compiles the class file into an executable:

```
$ gcj -C HelloWorld.java
$ gcj HelloWorld.class -o HelloWorld
```

Multiple Source Files to Binary Executable

Compiling a collection of Java source files into a single executable is a matter of compiling the individual source files and then linking them into a single executable while specifying the one that contains the main() method. The following simple example has a mainline that uses another class to construct a string and yet another class to display the string. The SayHello class contains the mainline:

```java
/* SayHello.java */
public class SayHello {
    public static void main(String arg[]) {
        WordCat cat = new WordCat();
        cat.add("Hello");
        cat.add("cruel");
        cat.add("world");
        Say say = new Say(cat.toString());
        say.speak();
    }
}
```

The add() method of the WordCat class accepts one word, which it appends to its internal string. The toString() method of WordCat returns the resulting string, which is passed to the speak() method of an object of the Say class, causing the string to be displayed. The following is the WordCat class, which builds strings one word at a time:

```java
/* WordCat */
public class WordCat {
    private String string = "";
    public void add(String newWord) {
        if(string.length() > 0)
            string += " ";
        string += newWord;
    }
    public String toString() {
        return(string);
    }
}
```

The Say class is constructed containing a character string and has the speak() method, which can be used to display the string:

```java
/* Say.java */
public class Say {
    private String string;
    Say(String str) {
        string = str;
    }
    public void speak() {
        System.out.println(string);
    }
}
```

These three classes can be compiled into a native executable in several ways. The most straightforward is to do it in a single command line, as follows:

```
$ gcj --main=SayHello Say.java SayHello.java WordCat.java -o SayHello
```

This command will compile all three source files into object files and link the object files into a single executable named SayHello (establishing the main() method of SayHello as the program's entry point). The same result can be achieved by using a sequence of commands to compile the individual object files and then linking them together into an executable:

```
$ gcj -c SayHello.java
$ gcj -c Say.java
$ gcj -c WordCat.java
$ gcj --main=SayHello Say.o SayHello.o WordCat.o -o SayHello
```

It is possible to first compile the source files into class files and then compile and link them into an executable, as described in the next section.

Multiple Input Files to Executables

Using the same source code examples as in the previous section, the following command can be used to compile three source files into three class files:

```
$ gcj -C SayHello.java Say.java WordCat.java
```

The result is a set of class files that can be executed by using the Java Virtual Machine, as follows:

```
$ java SayHello
```

All the Java source code in the current directory can be compiled into class files with the following single command:

```
$ gcj -C *.java
```

Java class files can be treated as if they were source code files that can be compiled and linked into a native executable. In the following example, the first command compiles the source into a collection of class files, and the second command compiles the class files into a native executable program:

```
$ gcj -C SayHello.java Say.java WordCat.java
$ gcj --main=SayHello Say.class WordCat.class SayHello.class -o SayHello
```

The gcj command determines what to do with an input file named on the command line by looking at the file name suffix. If the suffix is .java, the compiler knows that it is a Java source code file that must be compiled. If the suffix is .class, the file is assumed to be Java bytecodes that are to be compiled. The .o suffix indicates a native object file that can be linked directly into the native executable. Because of this, it is possible to mix the input and have a program compiled and linked from a combination of source, class, and object files, as in the following example:

```
$ gcj -c SayHello.java -o SayHello.o
$ gcj -C WordCat.java
$ gcj --main=SayHello SayHello.o Say.java WordCat.class -o SayHello
```

Generating Assembly Language

The following class, when executed, creates an instance of itself that it uses to display a string on standard output:

```
/* Jasm.java */
public class Jasm {
    public static void main(String arg[]) {
        Jasm jsm = new Jasm();
        jsm.speak();
    }
    public void speak() {
        System.out.println("Jasm speaks");
    }
}
```

This class is a complete application and can be compiled and run. It can also be compiled into native assembly language with the following command:

```
$ gcj -S Jasm.java
```

The output from this command is a file named Jasm.s with the assembler code that can be used to create an executable.

An alternate method of producing an assembly language file is to use a class file as input. The two following commands create a class file from Jasm.java and use it to generate an assembly language file:

```
$ gcj -C Jasm.java
$ gcj -S Jasm.class
```

The output files from these commands are named Jasm.class and Jasm.s.

Creating a Static Library

A static library is a collection of .o files stored in a single file, called a *static library* or an *archive file*. Linking a program with the contents of the library is the same as linking a program with the individual object files.

Using the example source files from earlier in this chapter, the following command will create the object files WordCat.o and Say.o to be stored in a library:

```
$ gcj -c WordCat.java Say.java
```

The ar utility is used to construct and maintain static libraries. Using ar with the -r option will cause the named library file to be created from the named object files, or if the library already exists, the -r option will update the library with newer versions of the object files. The following command creates a library named libsay.a that contains the two object files:

```
$ ar -r libsay.a WordCat.o Say.o
```

To use the object files stored in the library, it is only necessary to include the name of the library on the gcj command line, as in the following example, which produces an executable program named libhello:

```
$ gcj --main=SayHello SayHello.java libsay.a -o libhello
```

Specifying the library name on the command line this way requires that the library be in the current directory. If the library is in a directory that gcj searches to find libraries, you can use the -l option for specifying the library name, as in the following example:

```
$ gcj --main=SayHello SayHello.java -lsay -o libhello
```

More information on the location of libraries can be found in Chapter 12.

Creating a Shared Library

A shared library is a collection of object files stored inside a single file, in much the same way as a static library, with two main differences. First, the object files inside the shared (also called *dynamic*) library are loaded and linked to the program at the time the program starts running. Second, the object files must be compiled in a special way so they can be executed without modification wherever they happen to be loaded into memory. The following example uses the source files described earlier in this chapter.

To create the object files to be stored in the shared library, they must be compiled with the -fpic option to produce *position independent code*. This is code that uses only relative addressing for internal references and branching, which precludes the necessity of an extensive relocation process every time the code is loaded into memory. The following command will produce object files in the desired format:

```
$ gcj -fpic -c WordCat.java Say.java
```

The gcj command is used with the -shared option to link the object files into a new shared library named libsay.so, as follows:

```
$ gcj -shared WordCat.o Say.o -o libsay.so
```

The source file SayHello.java can be compiled into an executable program named shlibhello that uses the object files stored in the library by including the library name on the command line as follows:

```
$ gcj --main=SayHello SayHello.java libsay.so -o shlibhello
```

The actual content of libsay.so is not included inside the shlibhello executable. What is included in the executable are the instructions necessary to load the required object modules from a shared library with the correct name. For this to happen, the executable must be able to locate the library whenever it is run. Information on the location of shared libraries can be found in Chapter 12.

Creating a Jar File

The Java language has a special kind of archive file that contains class files. The Java archive file is known as a *jar* file. The format of a jar file is the same as a zip file, but a jar file also contains a special *manifest* that contains descriptive information. All external references in Java are based on class names, so it is only necessary for a Java program to locate the correct jar file (or files), and it will search through the manifest to find any class it needs. The following example uses the sample source files found earlier in this chapter.

To create a jar file, it is first necessary to compile the source into class files, as in the following example:

```
$ gcj -C WordCat.java Say.java
```

The jar utility with the c option will create a jar file. The f option indicates that the name of the jar file is the next argument on the command line. The rest of the command line is made up of the names of the class files to be stored in the jar file. The following command creates a jar file named libsay.jar containing the two class files and a manifest:

```
$ jar cf libsay.jar WordCat.class Say.class
```

The class files stored in a jar file can be compiled and linked directly into an executable program, the same as jar files stored in a directory. The following command compiles the Java mainline class SayHello.java into an executable named jarlibhello by compiling it and linking it with the classes in the jar file libsay.jar:

```
$ gcj --main=SayHello libsay.jar SayHello.java -o jarlibhello
```

The Java Utilities

Besides the gcj compiler, the GCC distribution includes a number of utility programs for dealing with Java source and object files.

gij

The gij utility is a Java Virtual Machine that interprets and executes the bytecodes found in Java class files. The command line contains the name of either the class file or the jar file to be executed. For example, the following Java program echoes whatever it finds on the command line:

```
/* ListOptions.java */
public class ListOptions {
    public static void main(String arg[]) {
        for(int i=0; i<arg.length; i++) {
            System.out.println(arg[i]);
        }
    }
}
```

The program can be compiled into a class file and the class file can be executed with the following commands:

```
$ gcj -C ListOptions.java
$ gij ListOptions
```

Any arguments appearing on the command line following the name of the class are passed to the program being run. The ListOptions class echoes the options to standard output, so executing the class file from the command line results in the following:

```
$ gij ListOptions apple butter --help
apple
butter
--help
```

Table 8-2 lists the options that can be used on the command line of gij. Any options that appear on the command line before the class name or jar file name are assumed to be for gij.

The -jar option makes it possible to execute a class stored in a jar file. The jar file must be constructed to contain a manifest file specifying the attribute Main-Class as the name of the class to be executed. For example, in the jar file sayhello.jar, if the class file SayHello.class is the one with the main() method to be the entry point of the program, the manifest file must contain the following line:

```
Main-Class: SayHello
```

The following command will execute the jar file:

```
$ gij -jar sayhello.jar
```

Option	Description
-D*name*[=*value*]	The name becomes a defined system property name with the specified value. If the value is omitted, the name is defined with a value of a zero-length string.
--help	Prints this list of options and quits.
-jar	The name on the command line is interpreted as the name of a jar file instead of a class file.
-ms=*number*	The number is the initial size of the heap.
-mx=*number*	The number is the maximum size of the heap.
--version	Prints the version number of gij and quits.

Table 8-2. *The Command-Line Options Available for gij*

jar

A jar (Java archive) file contains a collection of Java class files, and possibly other files, in a form that can be read and executed directly by a Java Virtual Machine. The jar utility can be used to create jar files, as well as view and modify their contents. Table 8-3 lists the command-line options of jar.

Option	Description
-@	Reads the list of files named from standard input.
-c	Creates a new jar file.
-C *dir file*	Retrieves the file named *file* from the directory named *dir*.
-E *dir*	Specifies that no files from the directory named *dir* are to be included.
-f *file*	The named file is the jar file.
--help	Prints this list of options and some other brief help information.
-m *file*	The named file is a file containing manifest information to be included.

Table 8-3. *The Command-Line Options of jar*

Option	Description
-M	Specifies that no manifest file is to be created.
-0	Stores the files in the jar file without using compression.
-t	Lists the contents of the jar file.
-u	Updates an existing jar file.
-v	Displays verbose output to standard output describing the actions being taken.
-V	Same as --version.
--version	Displays the version number of the jar utility.
-x	Extracts files from a jar file.

Table 8-3.   *The Command-Line Options of* `jar` *(continued)*

The command-line options of `jar` are very similar to those of the UNIX `tar` utility. The option letters can be specified at the beginning of the command line without a preceding hyphen. For example, the following command creates a jar file named `sayhello.jar` containing all the class files in the current directory:

```
$ jar cvf sayhello.jar *.class
```

To create the same jar file and also specify that the manifest file include the information from the text file `hello.manifest`, use the following command:

```
$ jar cvfm sayhello.jar hello.manifest *.class
```

The name of the jar file and the name of the manifest file must come in the same order as the f and m options. The following command is the same as the previous one, except the file names are reversed on the command line:

```
$ jar cvmf hello.manifest sayhello.jar *.class
```

The same result can be achieved by using hyphens in front of the option letters, as in the following example:

```
$ jar -c -v -f sayhello.jar -m hello.manifest
```

The following command will list the contents of the jar file sayhello.jar:

```
$ jar tvf sayhello.jar
```

The contents of a jar file can be simply files, but it can also be an entire directory tree. The manifest file is always named MANIFEST.MF and stored in the jar file in a sub-directory named META-INF.

gcjh

Native methods for Java can be written in either CNI (a C++ interface) or JNI (a C interface). The gcjh utility reads Java class files and generates CNI and JNI header files and stub files used to implement native methods. A CNI header file is for inclusion in a C++ program, and a JNI file is valid for inclusion in a C program. The -stubs option can be used to generate starter C and C++ files to be used for implementing native methods using JNI or CNI. Table 8-4 lists the options available on the command line of gcjh.

Option	Description
-add *text*	Inserts the specified text into the C++ class body. This option is ignored if -jni is specified.
-append *text*	Inserts the specified text into the header file following the C++ class declaration. This option is ignored if -jni is specified.
--bootclasspath=*path*	Overrides the built-in classpath.
--classpath=*path*	Specifies the path to be used to locate class files.
--CLASSPATH=*path*	Specifies the path to be used to locate class files.
-d *directory*	Specifies the output directory name.
-friend *text*	Inserts the specified text into the C++ class definition as a friend declaration. This option is ignored if -jni is specified.
--help	Lists the options in this table to standard output.
-I*directory*	Appends the specified directory onto the end of the classpath.

Table 8-4. *The Command-Line Options of* gcjh

Option	Description
-M	Suppresses normal output and prints all dependencies to standard output.
-MD	Prints all dependencies to standard output.
-MM	Suppresses normal output and prints non-system dependencies to standard output.
-MMD	Prints non-system dependencies to standard output.
-o *file*	Specifies the name of the output file. This option will produce an error if more than one file is to be output.
-prepend *text*	Inserts the specified text into the header file before the C++ class declaration. This option is ignored if -jni is specified.
-stubs	Stub files are generated instead of header files. The stub file has the same base name as the class but with the file suffix .cc. If -jni is also specified, the suffix is .c.
-td *directory*	The name of the directory to use for temporary files.
-v	Prints extra information during processing. Same as --verbose.
--verbose	Prints extra information during processing. Same as -v.
--version	Prints the version number and exits.

Table 8-4. *The Command-Line Options of gcjh* (continued)

The input to gcjh is one or more Java class files. For example, the following command will read the class file named Spangler.class and create a header file named Spangler.h that is suitable for implementing native C++ methods for the class:

```
$ gcjh Spangler
```

The following command will read the file Spangler.class and produce the file Spangler.cc, which can be edited and used as the C++ code that interfaces with the Java class:

 $ gcjh -stub Spangler

The following command will read Spangler.class and produce the file Spangler.h, which is a header file suitable for implementing native methods in C:

 $ gcjh -jni Spangler

The following command will read the file Spangler.class and produce the file Spangler.c, which can be edited and used as the C code that interfaces with the Java class:

$ gcjh -jni -stub Spangler

Chapter 10 contains examples of using gcjh to mix C and C++ with Java.

jcf-dump

The jcf-dump utility lists information about the contents of a class file. Included with this information is a complete list of the values in the pool of constants, the superclasses, and interfaces, fields, and methods. Table 8-5 lists the options available for the jcf-dump utility.

Option	Description
--bootclasspath=*path*	Overrides the built-in classpath setting.
-c	Disassembles the bytecodes of the method bodies.
--classpath=*path*	Specifies the path to be used to locate class files.
--CLASSPATH=*path*	Specifies the path to be used to locate class files.
--help	Prints this list of options and exits.
-I*directory*	Appends the specified directory onto the end of the classpath.

Table 8-5. *The Command-Line Options for* jcf-dump

Option	Description
--javap	Generates the output in the same format as javap. The program javap is provided as part of the standard Sun Microsystems Java distribution.
-o file	Directs the output to the named file instead of to standard output.
-v	Prints extra information during processing. Same as --verbose.
--verbose	Prints extra information during processing. Same as -v.
--version	Prints the version number and exits.

Table 8-5. *The Command-Line Options for jcf-dump* (continued)

For example, the following command will dump to the internal information of the class file SwmpMilin.class to the file sm.dump:

```
$ jcf-dump SwmpMilin.class -o sm.dump
```

jv-scan

The jv-scan utility reads and analyzes the contents of one or more Java source files and then prints information about them. Table 8-6 lists the command-line options available for jv-scan.

Option	Description
--complexity	Prints the cyclomatic complexity value of each class. The number is calculated by analyzing the control flow as a directed graph and counting the nodes, edges, and the number of connected components.
--encoding=name	Specifies the encoding name of the particular character set to be used when reading the source. If a locale name is set, it is used; otherwise, UTF-8 is assumed.

Table 8-6. *The Command-Line Options for jv-scan*

Option	Description
`--help`	Prints this list of options and exits.
`--list-class`	Prints the names of the classes found in all the files on the command line.
`--list-filename`	When used in conjunction with `--list-class`, the file name containing each class is also listed.
`-o file`	The output is directed to the named file instead of to standard output.
`--print-main`	Prints the names of the classes containing a `public static void main()` method.
`--version`	Prints the version number and exits.

Table 8-6. *The Command-Line Options for `jv-scan`* (continued)

jv-convert

The `jv-convert` utility converts from one form of character encoding to another. The input defaults to being standard input but can also be the first file name listed on the command line or the file named with the `-i` option. The output defaults to standard output but can also be the second file named on the command line or the file named with the `-o` option. Table 8-7 lists the command-line options. For example, the following command will convert the contents of a file named `PierNun.uni` containing the Unicode 8-bit encoding format to a file named `PierNun.java` in the format of Java source code with Unicode characters using \u escape sequences:

```
$ jv-convert --from UTF8 --to JavaSrc PierNun.uni PierNun.java
```

The command-line options for `jv-convert` are listed in Table 8-7, and the types of encoding available are listed in Table 8-8.

There is no command that can be used to list the available conversion options. Table 8-8 contains the encoding options that existed at the time of this writing, but more are almost certain to be added over time. To find out which ones are available for your compiler, look at the source code directory tree `gcc/libjava/gnu/gcj/convert` for files with names of the form `Input_*.c` and `Ouput_*.c`, where the asterisk is the name of an encoding scheme that can be used as input or output, respectively. The conversion process uses Unicode as an internal, intermediate form, so any input/output pairs can be used together. Some conversions are platform dependent.

Option	Description
--encoding *name*	The name of the encoding scheme of the input data. The default is the local computer's locale encoding. Same as --from.
--from *name*	The name of the encoding scheme of the input data. The default is the local computer's locale encoding. Same as --encoding.
--help	Prints this list of options.
-i *file*	The name of the input file.
-o file	The name of the output file.
--reverse	Reverses the specified --from and --to encodings.
-to *name*	The name of the encoding scheme of the output data. The default is JavaSrc, which is ASCII text with Java \uXXXX hexadecimal encoding for non-ASCII characters.
--version	Prints the version number of jv-convert.

Table 8-7.   *Command-Line Options for* `jv-convert`

Encoding Name	Description
8859_1	ISO-Latin-1 (8851-1) text.
ASCII	The standard ASCII character set.
EUCJIS	Extended UNIX Code for Japan.
JavaSrc	The standard ASCII character set with embedded Java hexadecimal \uXXXX encoding for Unicode characters.
SJIS	Shift JIS, which is used on Japanese Microsoft Windows.
UTF8	A form of encoding Unicode characters that preserves ASCII characters as 8-bit entities.

Table 8-8.   *Character Encodings Known to* `jv-convert`

grepjar

The grepjar utility searches through the contents of a jar file to attempt to find a match on a regular expression, and it prints the names of the files along with the actual string that matched the regular expression. All files in the jar file are searched, including the manifest. For example, the following command will list all the classes in the jar file sayhello.jar that have a main() method:

```
$ grepjar main sayhello.jar
```

The following command will list the class specified as the Main-Class in the manifest file:

```
$ grepjar Main-Class sayhello.jar
```

Table 8-9 lists the grepjar command-line options.

Option	Description
-b	Prints the byte offset into the file of the match.
-c	Prints the number of matches found instead of printing each individual match.
-e	This option can be used to specify the pattern to be matched, if the position on the command line does not make it clear.
--help	Prints this list of options.
-i	Ignores case when determining a match.
-n	Prints the line number in the file for each match.
-s	Suppresses the printing of error messages.
--version	Prints the version number of grepjar.
-w	Specifies that the regular expression pattern only match full words.

Table 8-9. *Command-Line Options for grepjar*

RMI

The Remote Method Invocation (RMI) facility allows a Java object executing in one virtual machine to make a call to a method of an object in another virtual machine. The two virtual machines may be on the same computer or on separate computers. Arguments are serialized (a process known as *marshaling*) so they can be transmitted from the call to the called method, and the return value is serialized to be transmitted back to the caller.

A central registry contains the name and location of the active methods that can be called. The object making the call need not be aware of the fact that the method is remote. The calling object calls the method by its name, and the local method called is known as a *stub*. It is the stub that locates the actual method in the registry, marshals the arguments, and transmits the arguments (along with the return address) to the *skeleton* method at the other location. The transport uses TCP/IP, so the remote virtual machine can be located anywhere. On the remote machine, the skeleton method unmarshals the arguments and calls the actual method. The method returns the resulting value to its skeleton caller, which marshals the result and transmits it back to the stub. The stub unmarshals the return value and returns it to the original caller.

The virtual machine making the call is the client. The virtual machine receiving the call is the server. Some special situations must be considered when handling remote method calls:

- Because, during the remote calling process, objects can be created, marshaled, and unmarshaled, it is necessary to handle automatic garbage collection on a distributed system. The RMI uses a counter that increases with each reference and decreases when a reference is dropped. It gets complicated because, for one thing, remote objects returned to the caller can contain references to other remote objects.

- The client virtual machine keeps a local count of the active references to each remote object. A "referenced" message is sent to the remote virtual machine. The count is incremented and decremented as references come and go, and each change is sent to the remote virtual machine. When the count becomes zero, the object can be garbage collected by the server.

- The server virtual machine keeps a list of all the client virtual machines and the active object references for each one. If an object no longer has any remote references, it can be removed. Also, a timer for each remote reference gets reset each time the object is referenced, and if the timer expires, the reference counts from that machine are set to zero.

rmic

The `rmic` utility is the RMI stub and skeleton compiler. The input to the compiler is a compiled class file that implements the `java.rmi.Remote` interface, and the output is the Java stub and skeleton source files and compiled class files.

For example, the following is a very simple class that implements the `Remote` interface:

```
/* HelloRemote.java */
public class HelloRemote implements java.rmi.Remote {
    public void speak() {
        System.out.println("hello from remote");
    }
}
```

The following commands will produce the stubs and skeletons:

```
$ gcj -C HelloRemote.java
$ rmic HelloRemote
```

The output resulting from the first command is HelloRemote.class. The output from the second command is `HelloRemote_Stub.java`, `HelloRemote_Skel.java`, `HelloRemote_Stub.class`, and `HelloRemote_Skel.class`. The `rmic` compiler invokes `gcj` to compile the stub and skeleton. Table 8-10 lists the command-line options

Option	Description
`-classpath` *path*	The classpath to use for locating referenced classes.
`-d` *directory*	The name of the directory to contain the generated stub and skeleton files.
`-depend`	Checks dependencies and recompiles any files that are out of date.
`-g`	Includes debugging information in the generated files.
`-help`	Prints this list of options.
`-J` *flag*	Passes the specified flag to the Java compiler for compilation of the stub and skeleton classes.
`-keep`	Retains the intermediate files instead of deleting them. Same as `-keepgenerated`.

Table 8-10. *Command-Line Options for* `rmic`

Option	Description
-keepgenerated	Retains the intermediate files instead of deleting them. Same as -keep.
-nocompile	Specifies not to compile the generated stub and skeleton source files into class files.
-nowarn	Suppresses warning messages.
-v1.1	Generates stubs for Java 1.1.
-v1.2	Generates stubs for Java 1.2.
-vcompan	Generates stubs for both Java 1.1 and Java 1.2.
-verbose	Prints descriptions of the steps taken to produce the stub and skeleton files.
-version	Prints the version number of the rmic compiler.

Table 8-10. *Command-Line Options for rmic (continued)*

for rmic. The options all use the single hyphen form, as shown in the table, but they can also be written with a double hyphen.

rmiregistry

The rmiregistry is a daemon program that maintains a list of methods inside the virtual machine available for remote invocation. It listens on a port (by default, port number 1099) for incoming messages. If a port number other than the default is desired, this can be entered on the command line. The only other options are those shown in Table 8-11.

Option	Description
--help	Prints this list of options and exits.
--version	Prints the current version number of rmiregistry and exits.

Table 8-11. *Command-Line Options for rmiregistry*

Properties

Java has a set of predefined system properties that can be accessed from inside a program. Each property consists of a key and a value, both of which are character strings. To retrieve the value of a property, it is only necessary to know the key. For example, the following method call can be used to determine the name of the user running the program:

```
String username = System.getProperty("user.name");
```

The following program lists all the system properties:

```java
/* AllProps.java */
import java.util.Properties;
public class AllProps {
    public static void main(String arg[]) {
        Properties properties = System.getProperties();
        properties.list(System.out);
    }
}
```

More than 30 properties are predefined. The list includes the name of the operating system, the version of the Java compiler, the version of the operating system, the name of the user, the path- and line-separator characters, and so on. In addition, you can define properties of your own from either inside the program or on the command line.

The following program displays the values of three standard system properties named java.vm.version, java.vm.vendor, and java.vm.name. The program also displays the value of magic, if it is defined:

```java
/* ShowProps.java */
public class ShowProps {
    public static void main(String arg[]) {
        System.out.println(
            "vm.version="+System.getProperty("java.vm.version"));
        System.out.println(
            "vm.vendor="+System.getProperty("java.vm.vendor"));
        System.out.println(
            "vm.name="+System.getProperty("java.vm.name"));
        String magic = System.getProperty("magic");
        if(magic == null)
            System.out.println("There is no magic");
        else
```

```
        System.out.println("magic=" + magic);
    }
}
```

The property `magic` can be defined on the command line with the –D option when compiling the program into a binary executable, as follows:

```
$ gcj --main=ShowProps -Dmagic=xyzzy ShowProps.java -o showprops
```

Running the program results in a display that looks like the following:

```
$ showprops
vm.version=3.2 20020412 (experimental)
vm.vendor=Free Software Foundation, Inc.
vm.name=GNU libgcj
magic=xyzzy
```

The situation is different when compiling and running the program as a class file. The property is defined when the program is run, not when it is compiled. For example, the source file can be compiled into a class file with the following command:

```
$ gcj -C ShowProps.java
```

The following command will execute the class file with the property defined:

```
$ gij -Dmagic=xyzzy ShowProps
```

The output from executing the program as a class is the same as executing it as a binary executable.

Chapter 9

Compiling Ada

G NAT, which stands for GNU NYU Ada95 Translator or for simply GNU Ada Translator, is the Ada compiler that has been integrated into, and is now a part of, the GNU Compiler Collection.

Ada 95 is the latest Ada language standard, and the GCC compiler fully supports this standard. It includes object oriented programming, inheritance, polymorphism, and dynamic dispatching, along with the strong typing from Ada 83. The language standard itself includes definitions for interfacing with programs written in C and Fortran.

Ada as a language, and as a compiler, has some unique requirements. Most notably, the Ada object files can be traced back and verified against the source files that produced them. Not only is this verification a normal part of the compiling and linking process, but a number of utility programs can also be used from the command line to make these comparisons and validations. Unlike the other GCC languages, Ada is written in Ada, so there is a bit of bootstrapping that must take place to install it on your system.

Installation

The Ada front end is the newest addition to GCC. With the release of GCC 3.1, it has been integrated into the compiler family well enough to produce executable code for several platforms, but it is not easily ported to new systems. The Ada front end is written in Ada, which is a perfectly reasonable way to do things, just as the C front end of GCC is written in C, but this has made the porting situation for Ada different from the other languages. Hopefully, over time the Ada language will be made as portable as the other GCC languages, but for now it is necessary to have a minimal Ada compiler installed on your system before you can compile the GCC Ada compiler.

To install the latest Ada compiler on your system, you will need to first install a bootstrap Ada compiler. You can then use the regular GCC source code to compile newer versions of your Ada compiler. The process for doing this is certainly going to become simpler with time, and eventually the Ada compiler will be ported to as many systems as the C compiler, but for now the following steps will work to get Ada installed on any system to which it has been ported:

1. Download a binary executable copy of an Ada compiler to use as the bootstrap compiler. Here are some places to look for a version for your computer:

   ■ http://www.gnuada.org

   ■ ftp://cs.nyu.edu/pub/gnat

   ■ http://www.gnat.com

   Alternatively, if you already have an Ada compiler installed, you will only need to set the ADAC environment variable to its name and make sure that the program by that name is somewhere on the PATH setting.

2. Follow the installation instructions that come with the download and install the compiler on your computer. The exact installation procedure will vary depending on the platform. The installation has two steps. First, the doconfig script explains the installation procedure, asks questions about the style and location of the installation, and constructs the actual installation script, named doinstall. Second, executing the doinstall script will complete the installation.

3. Modify the PATH variable so the newly installed gcc will execute when entered on the command line. If you already have a version of gcc installed, it is important that this new directory (with the Ada compiler) come before the previously installed version of gcc in the list of path directories. At this point, you have a fully functional Ada compiler that can be used to write programs so, if you wish, you can stop after this step and begin writing Ada programs. However, if you want to be able to build your own Ada compiler from GNU source, continue with the next step.

4. Execute the configure script as described in Chapter 2. The Ada and C languages should both be specifically enabled. Even if you will be including other languages later, it is best to start by including only these two, because the compile times are very long, and if your experience is like mine, you may need to restart more than once. The following is an example series of commands that will work from the parent directory of the gcc source directory and will set up the build configuration in a directory named mybuild. Because of the setting of the --prefix option, this configuration will ultimately install the compiler's parts in the directories /usr/gnat/bin, /usr/include, /usr/info, /usr/gnat/lib, /usr/man, and /usr/share:

```
$ DIR='pwd'
$ mkdir $DIR/mybuild
$ cd $DIR/mybuild
$ $DIR/gcc/configure --prefix=/usr --enable-languages=c,ada
```

You will probably find it to your advantage to put this series of commands in a script. Also, no matter what you are doing, you always need to enable the C language, because if you build a compiler without C enabled, you cannot compile a new version of the compiler.

5. Force certain files in the source directory to be up to date to guarantee that the bootstrap programs for Ada will be compiled. After the configuration script has been executed, the touch command will update the date and time of the files so they are guaranteed to be newer than other files they are compared to. Again, it would probably be best to put this into a script:

```
$ cd $DIR/gcc/gcc/ada
$ touch treeprs.ada
$ touch einfo.h
$ touch sinfo.h
```

```
$ touch nmake.adb
$ touch nmake.ads
```

6. Compile the programs you will need to help you bootstrap your compiler:

```
$ cd $DIR/mybuild
$ make bootstrap
```

7. It may be necessary to compile gnatlib separately. If not, it won't hurt anything to enter the command. The following commands will compile gnatlib:

```
$ cd $DIR/mybuild/gcc
$ make gnatlib
```

8. If everything has gone well up to now, you are ready to install Ada with one final make command. Because this installation requires modification to some system directories, you will likely need to have super user permissions:

```
$ su
Password: ******
$ cd $DIR/mybuild
$ make install
$ exit
```

If you explore the installation directories, you may find that some of the GCC files are duplicated by the Ada installation. This is normal, and future releases will certainly clear this up, but for now it is necessary.

9. Finally, restore the PATH variable. First, remove the temporary setting that you put in place to compile the bootstrap and the other Ada components, and then add the new bin directory:

```
$ PATH=$PATH:/usr/gnat/bin
```

Fundamental Compiling

Table 9-1 lists the file name suffixes that have to do with compiling and linking Ada programs. A table listing all the suffixes recognized by GCC can be found in Appendix D.

Suffix	File Contains
.a	A library (archive file) containing object files for static linking.
.adb	An Ada *body* file, which is source code containing a library unit body.

Table 9-1. *File Name Suffixes in Ada Programming*

Suffix	File Contains
.adc	A GNAT configuration file for dead code elimination.
.ads	An Ada *spec* file, which is source code containing a library unit declaration or a library unit renaming a declaration.
.adt	A GNAT tree file for dead code elimination.
.ali	An intermediate file that is produced by the compiler to contain information necessary for consistency checks and for linking.
.atb	A file containing a representation of the internal tree used by the compiler to represent the content of an .adb file.
.ats	A file containing a representation of the internal tree used by the compiler to represent the content of an .ads file.
.o	An object file in a format appropriate to be supplied to the linker.
.s	Assembly language code. This type of file is produced as in intermediate step in creating the object file.
.so	A library containing object files for dynamic linking.

Table 9-1. *File Name Suffixes in Ada Programming* (continued)

Single Source to Executable

The following three steps are required to create an executable program from an Ada source file:

1. The Ada source file is compiled into an object file.
2. The object file (or files) must be processed by the Ada binder.
3. The object file (or files) is linked with the appropriate libraries to create an executable.

The first and third steps in this sequence are the same as the ones performed when compiling other languages, but the second step is unique to Ada. The binder examines the object files and does the following:

- Checks for consistencies among the object files for such things as compatibilities among the option settings and versions of the compiler used.
- Verifies that there is a valid order of elaboration for the program.

■ Generates a mainline program based on the determined order of elaboration. This is a small C program that calls the elaboration functions in the correct order and then calls the main program.

■ Determines the complete set of object files that make up the program and includes the information in the generated C program. This makes the information available to gnatlink, which is used to link the program into an executable.

The following is the source code of a simple program that writes a line of text on the display:

```
with Text_IO; use text_IO;
procedure HelloWorld is
begin
    Put_Line("hello world");
end HelloWorld;
```

This program is stored in a file named helloworld.adb and is compiled into an object file with the following command:

```
$ gcc -c helloworld.adb
```

The -c option specifies that the program is to be compiled into an object file but not linked into an executable. The -c option is required for Ada because the linking process is different from that for other languages. The next step is to use the gnatbind utility to do the binding:

```
$ gnatbind helloworld.ali
```

The result of the command is a pair of temporary work files named b~helloworld.adb and b~helloworld.ads. The file helloworld.ali is unchanged, as is the original source file, helloworld.adb, so now there are a total of four files on disk.

The final step is to invoke gnatlink as follows:

```
$ gnatlink helloworld.ali
```

The result is an executable program named helloworld. Also left on disk is the original source file helloworld.adb, along with the helloworld.ali file and an object file named helloworld.o.

Ada programs can be compiled and linked in another way. The utility `gnatmake` uses criteria similar to that of `make` to determine which files need to be compiled; then it invokes the compiler, `gnatbind`, and `gnatlink` to produce the same results as you would get issuing the three separate commands. The following single command will result in the same four files as the previous three-command combination:

```
$ gnatmake helloworld.adb
```

To make it even simpler, if no file suffix is provided, the `gnatmake` utility will automatically append an `.adb` suffix, so the same command can be entered as follows:

```
$ gnatmake helloworld
```

Multiple Source to Executable

A collection of procedures can be defined as a package. The file howdy.abs contains the specification of a package named Howdy that contains the procedures Hello and Goodbye:

```
package Howdy is
    procedure Hello;
    procedure Goodbye;
end Howdy;
```

The procedure bodies themselves are defined in a file named howdy.adb as follows:

```
with Text_IO; use Text_IO;
package body Howdy is
    procedure Hello is
    begin
        Put_Line("Howdy from package");
    end Hello;
    procedure Goodbye is
    begin
        Put_Line("Goodbye from package");
    end Goodbye;
end Howdy;
```

A program that uses the procedures of the Howdy package to display text is stored in a file named howdymain.adb:

```
with Howdy;
procedure HowdyMain is
begin
    Howdy.hello;
    Howdy.goodbye;
end HowdyMain;
```

The gnatmake utility understands this organization and will compile the source files necessary to complete a program. The following command will produce an executable from the source:

```
$ gnatmake howdymain
```

This is exactly the same as entering the following sequence of commands:

```
$ gcc -c howdymain.adb
$ gcc -c howdy.adb
$ gnatbind -x howdymain.ali
$ gnatlink howdymain.ali
```

The result is the creation of new files named howdy.ali, howdymain.ali, howdy.o, howdymain.o, and the executable program named howdymain. Executing the program howdymain results in the following output:

```
Howdy from package
Goodbye from package
```

Source to Assembly Language

The -S option instructs gcc to generate assembly language from the source code and then stop. The following command will produce an assembly language file named helloworld.s from the Ada source file helloworld.adb:

```
$ gcc -S helloworld.adb
```

The content of the assembly language file depends on the platform targeted by the compiler. If more than one source file is included on the command line, a separate assembly language file is produced.

Options

All the command-line options are listed in Appendix D, but there are a few that have special meaning to Ada. Table 9-2 lists the command-line options that affect any language being compiled but have a special meaning for Ada.

In addition to the general command-line options in Table 9-2 and the many other options listed in Appendix D, Table 9-3 lists another set of options that apply only to Ada. These Ada-specific options all begin with the five character sequence -gnat.

Option	Description
-c	Specifies to compile the source into an object but not to link to an executable. This option is required when compiling Ada because gcc does not invoke gnatbind and gnatlink.
-fno-linline	Suppresses all function inlining, no matter what level of optimization is set.
-g	Includes debugging information in the object file, which is copied by the linker into the executable and is made available to the debugger.
-Idirectory	Adds the named directory to the list of those that are searched for source files of programs required by the program being compiled.
-I-	Specifies to not look for other source files in the same directory as the source file named on the command line to be compiled.
-O[n]	The optimization levels for Ada are the same as for other languages, as described in Appendix D, including *n=3*, which enables automatic inlining.
-S	Generates assembly language output.
-v	Displays the current version of GCC and displays all the commands generated by the gcc driver.
-Vversion	Executes the named version of the gcc compiler.
-Wuninitialized	Generates a warning message for each uninitialized variable. This only works if -O is also specified.

Table 9-2.   *General Command-Line Options That Pertain to Ada*

Option	Description
-gnat83	Specifies that the program is to be compiled to the Ada 83 standard. The primary use of this option is in the porting of source code to an Ada 83 compiler. The default is -gnat95.
-gnat95	Compiles the source code according to the Ada 95 standard. This is the default mode.
-gnata	Enables pragma Assert and pragma Debug. If this option is not specified, any of these pragma settings encountered in the source files are ignored.
-gnatb	Any errors will cause the brief form of the error message to be sent to standard output as well as the verbose error messages included in the listing.
-gnatc	The compiler runs detailed semantics checks but generates no output files, other than possible error and warning messages.
-gnatd*xx*	This option can be used to extract information about the compilation process for debugging the compiler itself. The value *xx* is a combination of one or more letters or digits that specifies the type of debugging information to be extracted. There are 65 available codes (the uppercase letters, lowercase letters, and the digits 1 through 9). These are seldom used, and descriptions for them can be found in the comments of the source file debug.adb, which is part of the compiler.
-gnate	Error messages are generated as they are encountered instead of being saved up until the end and reported at the conclusion of compilation. This can cause error messages to appear out of sequence, but it does allow messages to be reported that would otherwise be lost if the compiler crashes.
-gnatE	Enables dynamic access checking before the elaboration of subprogram calls and generic instantiations.

Table 9-3. *Command-Line Options Specific to Ada*

Option	Description
-gnatf	The compiler issues error messages that could be redundant. For example, an error message is normally only generated once when a variable is found to be undefined, but this option will cause the generation of a message every time the variable is referenced.
-gnatg	Enforces the styles defined by the routines in the source file (part of the compiler) named style.adb. The elements of the style enforced are documented as comments in the file. Normally this option is used only for compiling units of the compiler itself.
-gnati*ch*	The value of *ch* is a single character indicating the character set recognized by the compiler. All characters from the chosen character set may be used in character literals and in identifiers. The value of *ch* may be any one of the following: 1: Latin-1 character set. The character values 0 through 127 are the standard ASCII characters. The values 128 through 255 represent additional European alphabetic characters, such as the German vowels with umlauts and the Swedish A-ring. This is the default. 2: Latin-2 character set. 3: Latin-3 character set. 4: Latin-4 character set. P: The IBM PC (code page 437) character set. This is similar to the Latin-1 character set, but the encodings of the values 128 through 255 are different. 8: The IBM PC (code page 850) character set. This is a modification of code page 437 extended to include all the Latin-1 letters, but not with the usual Latin-1 encoding. F: Any character code in the range 128 through 255 is valid, and each of the values is considered distinct. This makes custom character sets possible (it is typically used to represent Chinese characters). H: None of the character values 128 through 255 are valid. This is an Ada 83 compatible format.

Table 9-3.   *Command-Line Options Specific to Ada* (continued)

Option	Description
-gnatj*ch*	The value of *ch* is a single character indicating the format of wide characters appearing in string literals and in identifiers. The value of *ch* may be any one of the following: N: No wide character format is specified. This is the default. H: Hex encoding. Each wide character is represented by a five-character sequence. The first character is ESC, and the next four are uppercase hexadecimal digits representing the 16-bit character code value. U: Upper half encoding. The first bit set to 1 indicates that it is the first byte of a 16-bit-wide character value. The wide characters, then, are the hexadecimal values 16#8000# through 16#FFFF#. Note that this prevents the use of the upper half of the Latin-1 character set. S: Shift JIS encoding. Similar to upper half encoding, except each wide character is written as two separate characters. The first value has its upper bit set, so it is in the range 16#80# through 16#FF#, and the second is in the range 16#00# through 16#FF#. Note that this prevents the use of the upper half of the Latin-1 character set. E: EUC encoding. Similar to upper half encoding, except each wide character is written as two separate characters, and both values have their upper bits set. The first and second values are both in the range 16#80# through 16#FF#. Note that this prevents the use of the upper half of the Latin-1 character set.
-gnatk*n*	The value of *n* is a number in the range of 1 through 999 and specifies the maximum allowable length of a file name (not including the .ads or .adb extension).
-gnatl	The entire source file is listed, with line numbers, and with any error messages included within it in the format specified by the -gnatv option.
-gnatm*n*	Specifies the maximum number of error messages to be output from the compiler. The value of *n* is in the range 1 to 999. For example, -gnatm3 will allow three error messages to be output before abandoning the compile. The default is an unlimited number of messages.

Table 9-3.   *Command-Line Options Specific to Ada* (continued)

Option	Description
-gnatn	Enables inlining within the same unit and across compilation units where pragma inline is specified. This has an effect only if the -O optimization flag is also specified.
-gnatN	The same as -gnatn, except that pragma inline is assumed for every source file.
-gnato	Enables runtime checking for overflow on integer operations. The code is larger and slower because of the insertion of a test for every integer overflow condition as well as division by zero.
-gnatp	Suppresses the creation of the runtime checks just as though pragma Suppress(all_checks) had been included in the source. Improves performance at the expense of protection from invalid data.
-gnatq	This option forces the compiler to attempt to generate output even in the presence of syntax errors in the source code. This may lead to the exposure of more errors, but it can also crash the compiler or generate code with undefined behavior.
-gnatr	This option verifies that the layout of the source code matches the source code layout conventions specified in the Ada language reference manual. Violations of the conventions are considered syntax errors.
-gnats	Runs syntax checking on the source and then halts. No output is generated. When this option is used, it is valid to specify more than one source file on the command line (although it is still necessary to specify the -c flag).
-gnatt	The compiler will write the internal tree to a file. The file bears the same base name as the source and has the extension .atb for a body source file and .ats for a spec source file.
-gnatu	The compiler prints, to standard output, a list of all units on which the current compilation unit is dependent, either directly or indirectly.

Table 9-3.   *Command-Line Options Specific to Ada* (continued)

Option	Description

-gnatv	The error messages are formatted to contain more information. The default format contains the file name, line number, column number, and a descriptive message, as follows:
	`hlowrld.adb:2:01: incorrect spelling of the keyword "procedure"`
	With the -gnatv option, the format is more like the following:
	`Compiling hlowrld.adb (source file time stamp 2002-05-13 20:00:29)`
	`2. proccedure HelloWorld is`
	`     |`
	`>>> incorrect spelling of keyword "procedure"`

-gnatwe	All warning messages are treated as errors. The message issued does not change, but any warning will suppress the generation of an object file.
-gnatwl	Issues warning messages relating to the order of elaboration.
-gnatws	Suppresses the output of all warning messages.
-gnatwu	Issues warning messages for entities that are defined but never referenced. A warning is issued if no members of a package are referenced. Warnings are also issued for anything on a with statement that is never referenced.
-gnatx	Suppress the cross-reference information normally included in the .ali file. Some space is saved, but the tools that need the information, such as gnatfind and gnatxref, cannot be used.

Table 9-3. *Command-Line Options Specific to Ada* (continued)

Each option is defined by one or two characters and can be specified separately, as in the following example, which specifies both verbose mode and the enabling of dynamic checks:

```
$ gcc -gnatv -gnatE -c helloworld.adb
```

The same pair of options can be specified in combination, as follows:

```
$ gcc -gnatvE -c helloworld.adb
```

Ada Utilities

A number of utility progams are included along with the Ada compiler. Some are required for development, such as `gnatbind` and `gnatlink`, and others are needed only for special circumstances. These utilities provide a variety of ways you can analyze your Ada source code. These types of tools are particularly important when working on large projects or exploring code written by someone else.

gnatbind

The `gnatbind` utility performs the Ada binding action, which consists of the following:

1. Checks for program consistency and will issue error messages for any inconsistencies among the various modules.

2. Determines whether there is a consistent order of elaboration available and issues an error message if no such order is found.

3. Generates a small C program to be used as the mainline of the finally linked executable. This program first calls the elaboration routines that initialize the packages and then calls the mainline of the Ada program.

4. Determines the list of object files that are to be combined into the final executable. This list is inserted into the generated C program so that it becomes available to `gnatlink`.

The `gnatbind` utility requires as input an `.ali` file, which is the product of the compiler. The other `.ali` files, and source files, are scanned by `gnatbind` to verify consistency throughout. If the source code of any of the files the program depends on has been modified without having been compiled, the `gnatbind` utility will detect and report the situation.

The result of binding all the modules of a program together results in the output of the source code of the entire program. The default name of the program is the same as that of the original input `.ali` file, except the two new Ada files begin with b~ and one has an `.ads` suffix and the other has an `.adb` suffix. Alternatively, the –C option can be used to cause the generation of a C source code file with a `.c` suffix.

Table 9-4 lists the command-line options available for `gnatbind`.

For gnatbind to perform its validation task, it must be able to locate all the source and .ali files that make up the program. The search for each file is made in the following order:

- The directory of the `.ali` file named on the command line. This may or may not be the current directory. If `-I-` is specified, this directory is skipped.

- All directories named on any `-I` options specified on the command line.

- For source files only (not `.ali` files), each directory listed in the environment variable `ADA_INCLUDE_PATH`. This is a path of colon-separated directory names (the same format as the `PATH` environment variable).

- For .ali files only (not source files), each directory listed in the environment variable ADA_OBJECTS_PATH. This is a path of colon-separated directory names (the same format as the PATH environment variable).
- The default installation directory of the Ada compiler, which was determined at the time the compiler was installed.

Option	Description
-aI directory	Specifies the name of the directory to be searched for the source file.
-aO directory	Specifies the name of the directory to be searched for .ali files.
-b	Produces a brief error message to standard error, even when the -v flag is set to redirect error messages to standard output.
-c	No output file is produced, but the input files are processed and all error messages are produced.
-C	The output file is a C source file instead of an Ada source file.
-e	Prints a complete list, to standard output, of the elaboration order dependencies, including the reason for each dependency.
-E	Stores trace-back information in occurrences of Exception objects.
-h	Prints a brief description of this list to standard output.
-I directory	Specifies the name of the directory to be searched for both source and .ali files.
-I-	Specifies to not look in the current directory for source files and not to look for other .ali files in the directory containing the .ali file named on the command line.
-K	Prints to standard output the list of options that are to be passed to the linker. This is the same list of options that appears as part of the generated .adb file.
-l	Prints the chosen elaboration order to standard output.
-Lxxx	For a library build (an Ada program without a mainline), the programs named adainit and adafinal are changed to xxxinit and xxxfinal.

Table 9-4.   *Command-Line Options for the gnatbind Utility*

Option	Description
-mnumber	Limits the maximum number of error messages reported to the specified *number*. The value of *number* can range from 1 to 999. Once this number is reached, gnatbind quits processing.
-Mxxx	Renames the generated main program from main to *xxx*.
-n	There is no main program. (That is, the main program is not written in Ada.)
-nostdinc	Specifies to not look for source files in the system default directory.
-nostdlib	Specifies to not look for library files in the system default directory.
-o filename	Specifies the name of the output file instead of allowing it to default to b_*name*.c, where *name* is the base name of the input file.
-O	Prints a list of the objects required to complete the link.
-p	Specifies to use the pessimistic (worst-case) elaboration order.
-r	Prints to standard output a list of additional pragma restrictions being applied.
--RTS=*dir*	Specifies *dir* as the directory to be used as the default for searching for source and object files.
-s	All source files must be present and are checked for consistency. Normally gnatbind will ignore any missing source files, but this option requires the presence of source files on which the main compilation unit is dependent.
-S*xx*	Specifies the way that scalar values are to be initialized. Specifying *xx* as in will initialize them to values invalid for the type. Specifying lo will initialize them to the lowest value, and hi will initialize them to the highest value. Any other pair of characters is interpreted as hexadecimal digits to specify the per-byte initial value.
-shared	Specifies to link using the shared runtime libraries.
-static	Specifies to link using the static runtime libraries.

Table 9-4. *Command-Line Options for the gnatbind Utility* (continued)

Option	Description
-t	Timestamp error messages are treated as warnings. In effect, the file consistency checks are disabled.
-Tnnn	Sets the time slice value to *nnn* microseconds, where *nnn* is an integer value greater than zero.
-v	Produces verbose error messages and redirects them to standard output instead of the default, standard error.
-we	Treats all warning messages as fatal errors.
-ws	Suppresses all warning messages.
-x	No source files are checked. Only the .ali files are checked for consistency with one another. This runs faster, but it is possible that a change to a source file could slip by undetected. This is reasonable to use inside a makefile because there should be no change to the source between the compilation and the running of gnatbind. The gnatmake utility uses this option to invoke gnatbind.
-z	There is no main subprogram.

Table 9-4. *Command-Line Options for the gnatbind Utility* (continued)

gnatlink

The gnatlink utility links Ada object files into executable programs. This program is a front end for invoking the linker via the gcc program, providing it with the correct list of object files and libraries. It uses the file output from gnatbind to determine how the link is to proceed.

Most of the information required by gnatlink is stored in the output file from gantbind, so there are very few command-line options, as shown in Table 9-5. The order of appearance of the various elements on the gnatlink command line can be important. The following is the general layout of the command line:

```
$ gnatlink [options] mainprog.ali [non-ada object] [linker options]
```

The gnatlink options come first, followed by the name of the .ali file of the mainline of the program. This is followed by any object files produced from a language other than Ada that are to be included as part of the final executable. Any command-line options after this are passed directly to the linker as it constructs the final executable.

Option	Description
-A	The gnatbind-generated intermediate source file is expected to be an Ada program. This is the default.
-b target	The source from gnatbind is to be compiled to run on the specified target.
-B directory	Loads the executables for compiling and linking from the specified directory.
-C	The gnatbind-generated intermediate source file is expected to be a C program.
-f	Prints a list of the object files being linked.
-g	This option includes debugging information and does not delete the temporary work files produced by gnatbind.
--GCC=name	Specifies the name of the front end for compiling. The default is gcc.
--LINK=name	Specifies the name of the front end for linking. The default is gcc.
-n	Specifies to not compile the files produced by gnatbind.
-o	The name of the executable file produced from the link.
-v	Verbose mode. This option can be specified twice for an even more verbose mode.

Table 9-5.   *The Command-Line Options of gnatlink*

gnatmake

The gnatmake utility is a program designed to work something like the standard make utility but is customized for Ada and its special requirements. With gnatmake, you can enter a single command naming the source file of the mainline of your program, and the entire program will be compiled and linked into an executable. The source files are all examined to determine which other source and object files are needed, and each object file is checked against its source file to determine whether it also needs to be compiled.

The gnatmake utility has a large number of options, as shown in Table 9-6. Some of these are used by gnatmake, but the majority of them are passed through to gcc, gnatbind, or gnatlink. Note that the options -P, -vPx, and -Xnm refer to a *project*

Option	Description
-a	Considers all files for input, including any read-only .ali files. By default, an .ali file that is write-protected is not checked by gnatmake.
-aIdirectory	The named directory is included in the list of those searched for source files.
-aLdirectory	The .ali files in the named directory are presumed to be supplied from another source, and gnatmake does not attempt to validate or compile them. This has the same effect as having the .ali files write-protected.
-aOdirectory	The named directory is included in the list of those searched for library and object files.
-Adirectory	The same as specifying both -aLdirectory and -aIdirectory.
-bargs list	The options following -bargs on the command line are passed to gnatbind. These can be any of the options listed in Table 9-4.
-c	Specifies to compile only. Does not invoke gnatbind and gnatlink. This is the default if the source file specified on the command line is not a mainline.
-cargs list	The options following -cargs on the command line are passed to the compiler. These can be any of the Ada-specific options listed in Table 9-2 and any of the general-purpose options described in Appendix D.
-f	Forces all source files to be recompiled with regard to the timestamps on the object files.
--GCC=name	Uses name as the front end for the compiler. The default is gcc.
--GNATBIND=name	Uses name as the binder command. The default is gnatbind.
--GNATLINK=name	Uses name as the linker command. The default is gnatlink.

Table 9-6. *The Command-Line Options for gnatmake*

Option	Description
`-i`	Specifies that all compilations are to be done in place, replacing any existing `.ali` file. If no `.ali` file exists, one will be created in the same directory as the source file. The default is to create new files only in the current directory.
`-Idirectory`	The same as specifying `-aIdirectory` and `-aOdirectory`.
`-I-`	Specifies to not look for other source files in the directory containing the source file named on the command line.
`-jnumber`	Uses up to *number* processes to carry out compilations and recompilations. Messages from the various compilations may become intertwined.
`-k`	Specifies to continue compiling after error conditions. An attempt will be made to compile all source files, and a list summarizing those that failed is output before `gnatmake` terminates.
`-largs list`	The options following `-largs` on the command line are passed to `gnatlink`. These can be any of the options listed in Table 9-5.
`-Ldirectory`	Adds the named directory to the list of those searched for libraries.
`-m`	Keeps the number of recompilations to a minimum. This option ignores timestamp differences if the only modifications made were to comments or text formatting.
`-M`	Prints the file dependencies to standard output in a form suitable for insertion into a makefile. Each file is listed by an absolute or relative path name unless the `-q` option is also specified. System dependencies are omitted unless the `-a` option is also specified. Dependencies on external libraries are not included.
`-n`	Suppresses the compile, bind, and link steps. This option only makes checks to determine whether all object files are up to date. If they are not up to date, the name of the first file needing compilation will be listed.

Table 9-6.   *The Command-Line Options for* `gnatmake` (continued)

Option	Description
-nostdinc	Specifies to not look for source files in the system default directory.
-nostdlib	Specifies to not look for library files in the system default directory.
-o name	Specifies the name of the executable file. The default is to use the name of the input file.
-P name	Uses the named project file.
-q	Proceeds in quiet/terse mode. The commands issued by gnatmake are not displayed.
-s	Recompiles all files for which the compiler option settings have been changed.
-u	Compiles only the named file, ignoring any dependencies that may be out of date.
-v	Proceeds in verbose mode. Displays the reasons why all compilations or recompilations are necessary.
-vPx	Proceeds in verbose mode when using a project file to control compilation.
-Xnm=*value*	For this option, *value* is an external reference to be used by the project file.
-z	There is no main subprogram, so it is not possible to link the object files into a final executable file.

Table 9-6. *The Command-Line Options for gnatmake* (continued)

file, which is a special feature of the Emacs editor (version 20.2 or later) that enables the editing and maintaining of these project files to configure and control compilation.

Because the options -cargs, -bargs, and -largs can be followed by any number of options associated with them, these must appear as the last members of the command line. The general syntax of the gnatmake command line is as follows:

```
$ gnatmake [options] filename [-cargs ...] [-bargs ...] [-largs ...]
```

The file name on the command line can be specified with or without the .abs suffix.

Following the -cargs option is a list of any number of options to be passed to the compiler. The list is terminated by the -bargs option, the -largs option, or the end of the command line. These three can be in any order. The options following -bargs are all passed to the binder, and the -largs options are all passed to the linker.

gnatchop

The gnatchop utility reads source files and writes each one to one or more new source files that follow the strict GNAT Ada file naming convention. The compiler requires that a file contain only one compilation unit, and there must be a strict correspondence between the compilation unit name and the file name. The gnatchop utility allows you to convert all your source files at once. Alternatively, you can set up a list of compilation commands (as in a makefile) to make the file name conversions each time you compile your program.

The command line for gnatchop has the following basic format:

```
$ gnatchop [options] file [file ...] [directory]
```

With the command, the named file (or files) is chopped and the resulting new file (or files) is placed in the current directory, or in the named directory if one is specified. The options are listed in Table 9-7.

gnatxref

The gnatxref utility reads and displays the information stored by the compiler in the .ali file. The command-line syntax of gnatxref is as follows:

```
$ gnatxref [options] file [file ...]
```

Option	Description
-c	Invokes compilation mode, and the configuration pragmas in the chopped are configured to conform to the rules of the Ada 95 standard.
-gnat*xxx*	Any specified -gnat option is passed on to the parser.
-k[number]	The generated file names are to be no longer than *number* characters. If *number* is not specified, it defaults to 8.

Table 9-7.   *Command-Line Options for* gnatchop

Option	Description
-q	Quiet mode suppresses the normal listing of the input and output file names.
-r	Includes Source_Reference pragmas in the output files. This option can be used if the output files are temporary work files—the compiler will use the pragma information in the text of error and warning messages to refer to the original source file instead of the chopped file. Debugging information inserted into the object file with the -g option will also refer to the original file.
-v	Verbose mode, where all generated commands are echoed to standard output.
-w	Overwrites existing files if necessary to produce the output. Normally gnatchop will not replace a file if it already exists.
-x	Specifies to exit immediately on any error.

Table 9-7. *Command-Line Options for gnatchop* (continued)

Each file name in the list is an .ali file, and the output is an alphabetical listing of each package and procedure, along with the location of its declaration, body, and all references to it. The options are listed in Table 9-8.

Option	Description
-a	Considers all files. Normally, the content from read-only .ali files is not included.
-aIdirectory	Includes the named directory in the list of those searched for input source files.
-aOdirectory	Includes the named directory in the list of those searched for input library and object files.

Table 9-8. *Command-Line Options for gnatxref*

Option	Description
-d	Includes derived type information as part of the cross reference.
-f	The files listed in the cross reference are shown with their complete path names, instead of the default of displaying the simple file names.
-g	Limits the symbols in the cross reference to only library-level entities. Local entities are omitted.
-Idirectory	The same as specifying both -aI*directory* and -aO*directory*.
-pfilename	The named file is used as the project file. By default, gnatxref will try to locate a project file in the current directory.
-u	Includes only unused symbols in the output.
-v	Instead of a cross reference, the text of the output is in the form of a tags file that can be used with the vi editor.

Table 9-8.   *Command-Line Options for gnatxref* (continued)

gnatfind

The gnatfind utility reads the information in the .ali files and locates the item specified on the command line. The output is a list of every location in which the specified item is found. The syntax of the command line is as follows:

```
$ gnatfind [options] pattern[:filename[:line[:column]]] [file ...]
```

The specified pattern is a subset of the regular expression available in the grep utility. It can include an asterisk (*) to represent any group of characters, a question mark (?) to represent any single character, and the standard [. . .] bracket construct to specify a match on any one of a specific set of characters. Also, as you can see from the command-line syntax, you can restrict the search to one specific file, and even to a specific line and column number. If one or more file names are listed on the command line, they will be the only ones searched.

The command-line options are listed in Table 9-9.

Option	Description
-a	Considers all files. Normally, the content from read-only .ali files is not included.
-aIdirectory	Includes the named directory in the list of those searched for input source files.
-aOdirectory	Includes the named directory in the list of those searched for input library and object files.
-d	Includes derived type information as part of the output.
-e	Accepts the full regular expression syntax beyond simply the asterisk, question mark, and pair of brackets. The full regular expression syntax includes the following character set as the set of available operators: [ ] . * + ? ^
-f	The files listed in the output are shown with their complete path names, instead of the default of displaying the simple names.
-g	Limits the symbols in the output to only library-level entities. Local entities are omitted.
-Idirectory	The same as specifying both -aI*directory* and -aO*directory*.
-pfilename	The named file is used as the project file. By default, gnatxref will try to locate a project file in the current directory.
-r	Locates and lists all references. The default is to list only the declarations.
-s	Prints the entire source line in which the item is found instead of simply listing its location.
-t	Prints the type hierarchy of each item found.

Table 9-9.   *Command-Line Options for* gnatfind

gnatkr

Given an Ada name, the gnatkr utility will produce a shortened form of the name. Although a specific set of rules is followed by gnatkr to reduce the name, the shortened names are not guaranteed to be unique. The default length of the shortened file name is eight characters, but it is possible to specify another length, as shown by the following command syntax:

```
$ gnatkr name [length]
```

The name shortening is done by breaking the name into parts using hyphens and underscores and then shortening each piece, in turn, until the desired length is reached. Some examples follow:

```
$ gnatkr longer-names-can-be-crunched
lncabecr
$ gnatkr The_Ada_Names_Are_Long
tanaarlo
$ gnatkr The_Ada_Names_Are_Long 5
tanal
```

gnatprep

The gnatprep utility can be used as a simple preprocessor of Ada source code. The command line requires that both the input and output file names be specified on the command line, and all the preprocessing definitions must be defined in a third file or specified on the command line. The syntax of the command is as follows:

```
$ gnatprep inputfile outputfile [definitionsfile] [options]
```

Both inputfile and outputfile are required, and the full file names (including suffixes) must be specified. Because outputfile is usually the one that is going to be compiled, it will normally have a suffix of .adb or .ads. The command-line options are listed in Table 9-10. The optional definitionsfile should contain one or more symbol definitions in the following form:

```
symbol := value
```

The value in the definition can be blank, a quoted string, or any set of valid Ada characters. Unlike the C preprocessor, gnatprep does not substitute every match it finds. The symbols to be substituted must be specifically marked with a dollar symbol. For example, suppose the definitions file contains the following line:

```
bracklin := thermolimit
```

Option	Description
-b	Replaces each preprocessor line with a blank line. The default is to remove the line.
-c	Retains the preprocessor lines as comments in the output source file. Each of these lines is marked with the string " - ! ".
-Dsymbol=value	Defines symbol as the specified value, just as if it had been included in a definitions file as symbol := value.
-r	Generates a Source_Reference pragma so that all error messages and debugging information will refer back to the original file. Unless -c is also specified, this option implies -b to keep the line numbers consistent.
-s	Prints a sorted list of the defined symbol names and their values.
-u	On an #if directive, this option treats an undefined symbol as if it had been defined as false.

Table 9-10.   *The Command-Line Options for gnatprep*

This will cause thermolimit to replace every occurrence of the string $bracklin found in the input source. Also, the directives #if, #elsif, and #end if; can be used to control conditional compilation by testing symbols that are defined as either true or false, as follows:

```
#if condrep then
    Put_Line("condrep is defined as true");
#else
    Put_Line("condrep is defined as false");
#end if;
```

The logic of the previous statement can be reversed by the not operator, as follows:

```
#if not condrep then
    Put_Line("condrep is defined as false");
#else
```

```
      Put_Line("condrep is defined as true");
#end if;
```

gnatls

The `gnatls` utility is a library browser that can be used to extract and display information about compiled units. It displays the relationships among objects, unit names, and source files. It can also be used to determine the source code dependencies of a compilation unit. The input files can be either `.ali` or `.o` files produced by the compiler.

The default format of the output consists of four columns. The first column is the name of the object file being analyzed, the second is the name of the principal unit of the object file, the third is the status of the source file, and the fourth is the name of the source file. The possible source file status values are listed in Table 9-11.

The command-line options for `gnatls`, shown in Table 9-12, allow you to customize the content and form of the output, as well as specify the search paths.

gnatpsys and gnatpsta

The output from `gnatpsys` is the source code of an Ada package that contains all the system-dependent sizes and characteristics of the system on which it is run. It includes the system definitions of such things as the maximum and minimum values contained in an integer, the number of digits of accuracy of a floating-point number, the default

Status	Definition
???	The source file was not found.
DIF	At least one matching source code file was found, but no version of source could be found that matches the object file.
HID	A version of the source exactly matches the object, but at least one other version of the source (found first) does not match. The matching source file is effectively hidden.
MOK	The source code has been slightly modified since the object file was produced, but not in such a way that requires it to be recompiled. The modifications could have been in the formatting or in the comments.
OK	The object file is up-to-date and completely matches the source file.

Table 9-11. *The Status Codes* `gnatls` *Assigns to the Source Files*

integer size of the hardware, the maximum size of addressable memory, and whether the hardware is big endian or little endian.

The output from gnatpsta is the source code of an Ada package that contains the values assigned to definitions that are implementation dependent. This includes the maximum and minimum floating-point numeric values, the entire character set recognized by the compiler, and the method used to represent wide characters.

No command-line options exist for either of these programs. It is simply a matter of running each program, which dynamically determines the values for its output.

Option	Description
-a	Adds to the output information about relevant predefined units. All units are listed, including those in the predefined Ada library.
-aIdirectory	The named directory is added to those included in the source file search path.
-aOdirectory	The named directory is added to those included in the object file search path.
-d	Includes in the output list of file names the source files on which the files specified on the command line have compilation dependencies.
-h	Prints this list of command-line options.
-Idirectory	The same as specifying both -aIdirectory and -aOdirectory.
-I-	Specifies to not look for source or object files in the system default directory.
-nostdinc	Specifies to not look for source files in the system default directory.
-o	Limits the output to information about object files.
-Pname	Uses the named project file.
-s	Limits the output to information about source files.
-u	Limits the output to information about compilation units.

Table 9-12.   *Command-Line Options for* gnatls

Option	Description
`-v`	Generates verbose output, including the complete path to source and object files. Also, descriptive terms are attached to the listed files, as follows: `Elaborate_Body`: The unit contains the pragma `Elaborate_Body`. `No_Elab_Code`: No elaboration code has been generated by the compiler for this unit. `Predefined`: The unit is part of the predefined environment and cannot be modified by the user. `Preelaborable`: The unit is preelaborable, as defined by the Ada 95 standard. `Pure`: The unit is pure, as defined by the Ada 95 standard. `Remote_Call_Interface`: The unit contains the pragma `Remote_Call_Interface`. `Remote_Type`: The unit contains the pragma `Remote_Type`. `Shared_Passive`: The unit contains the pragma `Shared_Passive`.
`-vPnumber`	Sets the level of verbosity for reporting from the project file to 0, 1, or 2.
`-Xsymbol=value`	Specifies an external value.

Table 9-12.   *Command-Line Options for* `gnatls` (continued)

Chapter 10

Mixing Languages

215

Circumstances arise that call for portions of a program to be written in a different language. This usually happens because an existing body of software in one language needs to be made compatible with another body of software. This can be the result of the merging of projects, departments, or even companies. Probably the most common reason for combining languages is to have the capabilities of one language available to another—quite often a higher level language will find it convenient to have access to the system-level facilities of C. Another cause of the use of two languages in the same program is plain old politics.

This chapter discusses mixing languages inside the GCC family. It is possible, but more difficult, to mix languages by producing object code from different compilers, but the solution to that problem lies in the peculiarities of the compilers involved. The complexities of such a mixture can lead to an unstable situation. GCC, by using the same back end to produce the object code for all its languages, makes it possible to mix languages in such a way that even an upgrade to the compiler should not disturb the proper operation of the resulting program. There is no guarantee along this line, of course, because a compiler is a complicated thing, and a minor tweak can cause a major problem with language mixing.

When mixing languages, some tricky situations can arise. There is more to it than fitting the fundamental structure of one language up against the fundamental structure of another. The programmer must be ready to deal with global naming conventions, name mangling, argument passing, data type conversion, error handling, and mixing the standard runtime libraries from two languages.

Mixing C++ and C

The C and C++ languages mix naturally because C++ was designed as an extension to C, so the calling conventions are the same and the data types are fundamentally the same. The only difference is in the names of the functions—the C language uses simple function names without regard to the number or types of parameters, whereas the name of a C++ function always includes the list of parameter types as part of the function name. However, C++ provides a special facility for making declarations of C functions, which means a C++ program can declare and call a C function directly.

Calling C from C++

The following example is a C++ program that calls a C function named `csayhello()`. This call can be made directly because the function is declared in the C++ program as `extern "C"`:

```
/* cpp2c.cpp */
#include <iostream>

extern "C" void csayhello(char *str);

int main(int argc,char *argv[])
{
    csayhello("Hello from cpp to c");
    return(0);
}
```

The C function requires no special declaration and appears as follows:

```
/* csayhello.c */
#include <stdio.h>
void csayhello(char *str)
{
    printf("%s\n",str);
}
```

The following three commands compile the two programs and link them into an executable. The flexibility of g++ and gcc allow this to be done in different ways, but this set of commands is probably the most straightforward:

```
$ g++ -c cpp2c.cpp -o cpp2c.o
$ gcc -c csayhello.c -o csayhello.o
$ gcc cpp2c.o csayhello.o -lstdc++ -o cpp2c
```

Notice that it is necessary to specify the standard C++ library in the final link because the gcc command is used to invoke the linker instead of the g++ command. If g++ had been used, the C++ library would have been implied.

It is most common to have the function declarations in a header file and to have the entire contents of the header file included as the extern "C" declaration. The syntax for this is standard C++ and looks like the following:

```
extern "C" {
    int mlimitav(int lowend, int highend);
    void updatedesc(char *newdesc);
    double getpct(char *name);
};
```

Calling C++ from C

For a C program to call a function in a C++ program, it is necessary for the C++ program to provide a function that uses the C calling sequence. The following example demonstrates the syntax for creating a C function inside a C++ program:

```
/* cppsayhello.cpp */
#include <iostream>

extern "C" void cppsayhello(char *str);

void cppsayhello(char *str)
{
    std::cout << str << "\n";
}
```

Although the function cppsayhello() is declared by extern "C" as being a C function, the fact that it is part of the source code of a C++ program means that the code inside the body of the function is actually C++ code. You can freely create and destroy objects within this function. Also, if you were to call a C function from inside cppsayhello(), it would be necessary to declare it as extern "C". Otherwise, the compiler would assume a C++ function and change the function name accordingly.

The following is a C program that calls the C++ cppsayhello() function:

```
/* c2cpp.c */
int main(int argc,char *argv[])
{
    cppsayhello("Hello from C to C++");
    return(0);
}
```

The following commands compile and link the c2cpp program:

```
$ g++ -c cppsayhello.cpp -o cppsayhello.o
$ gcc -c c2cpp.c -o c2cpp.o
$ gcc cppsayhello.o c2cpp.o -lstdc++ -o c2cpp
```

Mixing Objective-C and C

Because the Objective-C language is nothing other than C with the addition of some syntax that allows for the declaration of classes, it is very simple to mix modules from the two languages. The calling sequences are the same for both, so there is nothing to be done but call the function.

Calling C from Objective-C

The following Objective-C program passes the address of a character string to a C function named `csayhello()`:

```
/* objc2c.m */
#import <stdio.h>
int main(int argc,char *argv[])
{
    csayhello("Hello from Objective-C to C");
    return(0);
}
```

The `csayhello()` function displays the string to standard output, as follows:

```
/* csayhello.c */
#include <stdio.h>
void csayhello(char *str)
{
    printf("%s\n",str);
}
```

The following three statements compile and link the program into an executable. When linking the program, it is necessary to specify `-lobjc` to include the runtime library for Objective-C:

```
$ gcc -Wno-import -c objc2c.m -o objc2c.o
$ gcc -c csayhello.c -o csayhello.o
$ gcc objc2c.o csayhnello.o -lobjc -o objc2c
```

Calling Objective-C from C

The following is a C program that calls an Objective-C function named `objcsayhello()`:

```
/* c2objc.c */
int main(int argc,char *argv[])
{
```

```
        objcsayhello("Hello from C to Objective-C");
    return(0);
}
```

The source code of the Objective-C function being called is as follows:

```
/* objcsayhello.m */
#import <objc/Object.h>
#import "SpeakLine.h"
void objcsayhello(char *str)
{
    id speak;

    speak = [SpeakLine new];
    [speak setString: str];
    [speak say];
    [speak free];
}
```

The function `objcsayhello` creates a `SpeakLine` object, stores the line of text into it, and then uses the Say method to display the string. The `SpeakLine` header file and implementation file are as follows:

```
/* SpeakLine.h */
#import <objc/Object.h>
@interface SpeakLine : Object
{
    char *string;
}
- setString: (char *) str;
- say;
- free;
@end
/* SpeakLine.m */
#import "SpeakLine.h"
@implementation SpeakLine

+ new
{
```

```
        self = [super new];
        return self;
}
- setString: (char *)str
{
        string = str;
        return self;
}
- say
{
        printf("%s\n",string);
        return self;
}
- free
{
        return [super free];
}
```

The following four commands compile each of the source files into object files and then link the two object files into an executable program:

```
$ gcc -Wno-import -c objcsayhello.m -o objcsayhello.o
$ gcc -Wno-import -c SpeakLine.m -o SpeakLine.o
$ gcc -c c2objc.c -o c2objc.o
$ gcc c2objc.o objcsayhello.o SpeakLine.o -lobjc -o c2objc
```

Mixing Java and C++

The Cygnus Native Interface (CNI) can be used to access Java classes from C++. The two languages are quite different, but have certain fundamental similarities:

- Classes are declared by name as inheriting characteristics of other classes.
- Classes contain member functions that can be overloaded by parameter matching.
- Data types and expressions are patterned after the ones in C.

Because GCC compiles both Java and C++ classes in a similar manner, it is only necessary for the most fundamental language incompatibilities to be avoided, or adjusted, so that classes written in Java can be made available.

Creating a Java String and Calling a Static Method

The following example program creates an object of the Java class java.lang.String and passes it to the method java.lang.System.out() to be displayed:

```
/* cnistrout.cpp */
#include <gcj/cni.h>
#include <java/lang/System.h>
#include <java/io/PrintStream.h>

int main(int argc, char *argv)
{
    java::lang::String *str;

    JvCreateJavaVM(NULL);
    JvAttachCurrentThread(NULL,NULL);

    str = JvNewStringLatin1("Hello from C++ to Java");
    java::lang::System::out->println(str);

    JvDetachCurrentThread();
}
```

This program can be compiled and linked with the following command:

```
$ g++ cnistrout.cpp -lgcj -o cniexception
```

The header file cni.h contains the prototypes of the function calls required to activate the CNI interface. Also, there are include statements for C header files for both the java.lang.System and java.io.PrintStream classes. It would not hurt to include the header file for java.lang.String, but it and a few other system-level headers are always included in cni.h.

Java uses pointers (called *references*) to keep track of its classes, so a pointer to a java.lang.String object is declared to hold the address of the object. The full name includes the C++ syntax of pairs of colons to fully qualify the name of the Java class. This naming convention is required for every reference to a Java class name unless a namespace is specified. For example, the String and System classes could have been declared and used as follows:

```
using namespace java::lang;
String *str;
 . . .
System.out->println(str);
```

The call to the function JvCreateJavaVM() initializes the Java runtime. This includes setting up the Java threading interface, garbage collecting, and exception handling. This function must be called once in the application before any Java classes are created or Java methods are called.

The call to the function JvAttachCurrentThread() registers the thread of this program with the previously initialized Java runtime. This function also must be called once before any Java classes are created or Java methods are called, but it can only be called after the call to JvCreateJavaVM().

At the end of the program, the call to the function JvDetachCurrentThread() drops the registration with the Java runtime that was made by the earlier calls to JvCreateJavaVM() and JvAttachCurrentThread(). This call guarantees the clean release of any resources being held by the application.

In the CNI interface, Java String objects are always constructed by calling one of the following functions:

- JvNewString(const char *chars, jsize length)   A String object of the specified length is returned, containing the characters found in the chars string.

- JvNewStringLatin1(const char *bytes, jsize length)   A String object of the specified length is returned, containing the values from the bytes array.

- JvNewStringLatin1(const char *bytes)   A String object is returned, containing the values from the bytes array up to, but not including, the first byte of value zero.

- JvNewStringUTF(const char *bytes)   A String object is returned, containing the UTF-encoded values from the bytes array up to, but not including, the first byte of value zero.

Loading and Instantiating a Java Class

Using CNI makes it possible to freely mix C++ and Java classes in the same program. The following example is made up of a simple C++ mainline program and a single Java class that is loaded, instantiated into an object, and used to store and display a string of characters.

The Java class is named Speak and is designed to contain and display a simple string:

```
/* Speak.java */
public class Speak {
    String string;
    Speak() {
        string = "Uninitialized";
    }
    public void setString(String str) {
        string = str;
```

```
    }
    public void showString() {
        System.out.println(string);
    }
}
```

The constructor of the Speak class initializes the internal string with a default setting, but this can be overwritten with a call to setString(). The showString() method can be called to display the current string to standard output. This class must be compiled into a Java .class file, which can be achieved with any standard Java compiler or with the GCC compiler using a command like the following:

```
$ gcj -C Speak.java
```

The next step is to use the gcjh command and the Speak.class file to produce the CNI header file named Speak.h, as follows:

```
$ gcjh Speak
```

The gcjh command can produce both JNI and CNI header files, but the default is to produce a CNI header file, so no command-line options are necessary. The header file output from the command is named Speak.h and looks like the following:

```
// DO NOT EDIT THIS FILE - it is machine generated -*- c++ -*-

#ifndef __Speak__
#define __Speak__

#pragma interface

#include <java/lang/Object.h>

extern "Java"
{
  class Speak;
};

class ::Speak : public ::java::lang::Object
{
public: // actually package-private
  Speak ();
public:
```

```
   virtual void setString (::java::lang::String *);
   virtual void showString ();
public: // actually package-private
   ::java::lang::String *string;
public:

   static ::java::lang::Class class$;
};

#endif /* __Speak__ */
```

As you can see, the Speak.h header file defines the Speak class in terms of C++, so the header file can be included directly into a C++ program, as in the following example:

```cpp
/* cnispeak.cpp */
#include <gcj/cni.h>
#include "Speak.h"

int main(int argc, char *argv)
{
    java::lang::String *str;

    JvCreateJavaVM(NULL);
    JvAttachCurrentThread(NULL,NULL);

    Speak *speak = new Speak();
    speak->setString(JvNewStringLatin1("Hello from CNI to Java"));
    speak->showString();

    JvDetachCurrentThread();
}
```

This program is fundamentally the same as the previous example, named cnistrout.cpp. The CNI header file gcj/cni.h is included, followed by the header files for any Java classes to be used. Once the Java Virtual Machine has been created and this thread has been attached to it, Java classes can be loaded and executed. The keyword new is used to invoke the constructor of the Speak class and return the address of a new Speak object. The method setString() is called to store a new String object in Speak; then the showString() method is called to display the string.

The following command will compile and link the program:

```
$ g++ cnispeak.cpp Speak.class -lgcj -o cnispeak
```

Exceptions

Exceptions can be thrown from Java classes and caught in a C++ program, as demonstrated in the following example:

```
/* cniexception.cpp */
#include <gcj/cni.h>
#include <java/lang/System.h>
#include <java/io/PrintStream.h>
#include <java/lang/Exception.h>

using namespace java::lang;

int main(int argc, char *argv)
{
    JvCreateJavaVM(NULL);
    JvAttachCurrentThread(NULL, NULL);
    try {
        String *message = JvNewStringLatin1("Hello from CNI");
        System::out->println(message);
    } catch(Exception *e) {
        e->printStackTrace();
    }
    JvDetachCurrentThread();
}
```

This example is the same as the other CNI examples in that it begins by initializing a Java Virtual Machine and finishes by detaching the current thread from it. A using statement is included to specify the java::lang namespace so references to the class names String, System, and Exception will be automatically resolved without the need of being fully qualified.

The try and catch blocks are written exactly as they would be in a Java class, with a collection of statements inside the try block. If an Exception object is thrown by a statement in the try block, it will be caught by the catch statement, and a stack trace will be printed that describes the location from which the exception originated.

Data Types of CNI

The data types of C++ and Java are similar, but not exactly the same. Because the Java data types are very specifically defined, it is possible to use the C++ typedef command to declare types that exactly match the Java types. The defined types are listed in Table 10-1.

Java Type	C++ Type Name	Description
char	Jchar	16-bit Unicode character
boolean	Jboolean	Logical value of either true or false
byte	Jbyte	8-bit signed integer
short	Jshort	16-bit signed integer
int	Jint	32-bit signed integer
long	Jlong	64-bit signed integer
float	Jfloat	32-bit IEEE floating-point number
double	Jdouble	64-bit IEEE floating-point number
void	Void	No value

Table 10-1.   *The Java Primitive Types Defined for C++*

Mixing Java and C

The Java Native Interface (JNI) can be used to communicate between Java classes running in a Java Virtual Machine and native executable modules written in C, C++, or assembly language. This interface was designed for, and is most useful for, Java programs that need access to some facility that is platform specific and therefore cannot be included as part of Java because of its portability requirements. However, using the JNI interface retains the portability of the Java code but can require the new C functions to be written for different platforms.

A Java Class with a Native Method

One common method of blending Java and C is to create Java classes that contain methods that are implemented in C. The same thing can be done with C++ and with assembly language, but the most common approach is to use C. This example creates a simple Java class that contains only one method, but that method is implemented in C.

The following class, named `HelloNative`, contains a `main()` method that uses a native method to display a string of characters. The native method is declared as part of the class, but its body is not included because the body is to be written in another language. The class also contains a static initializer that uses the system method `loadLibrary()` to load a shared library. It is this library that contains the body of the native method.

```
/* HelloNative.java */
public class HelloNative {
    static {
        System.loadLibrary("libspeak.so");
    }
    public static void main(String arg[]) {
        HelloNative hn = new HelloNative();
        hn.sayHello();
    }
    public native void sayHello();
}
```

The following command is used to compile `HelloNative.java` into the class file `HelloNative.class`:

```
$ gcj -C HelloNative.java
```

A header file containing the prototype of the native function is created from the `HelloNative.class` file by using the `gcjh` command with the `-jni` options as follows:

```
$ gcjh -jni HelloNative
```

The result of this command is a file named `HelloNative.h` that contains the following:

```
/* DO NOT EDIT THIS FILE - it is machine generated */

#ifndef __HelloNative__
#define __HelloNative__

#include <jni.h>

#ifdef __cplusplus
extern "C"
{
#endif

extern void Java_HelloNative_sayHello (JNIEnv *env, jobject);
```

Chapter 10: Mixing Languages **229**

```
#ifdef __cplusplus
}
#endif

#endif /* __HelloNative__ */
```

The name of the native function is constructed from the name of the class and the name of the Java method. The name always begins with Java and an underscore character, followed by the fully qualified class name, and ends with the method name preceded by another underscore character. Therefore, the name of the C function is written as Java_HelloNative_sayHello().

Two parameters appear on the prototype for the new function, even though there were no parameters defined for it in Java. These two parameters are required for every function to be called as a native method. The first parameter is the pointer to the interface used in the body of the method to access any arguments passed to the method, and the second parameter is a reference to the calling object (it is the this variable from the HelloNative object).

The function is written according to the prototype found in the header file HelloNative.h, as follows:

```
/* HelloNative.c */
#include <jni.h>
#include "HelloNative.h"

void Java_HelloNative_sayHello(JNIEnv *env,jobject this)
{
    printf("A native JNI hello\n");
}
```

The JNI header file jni.h is included as well as the HelloNative.h header file, which contains the prototype of the function. The function is implemented with exactly the same name and parameters as specified in the prototype. The following two commands compile a version of the function suitable for insertion into a shared library and then use the object file to create a shared library:

```
$ gcc -fpic -c HelloNative.c -o HelloNative.o
$ gcc -shared HelloNative.c -o libspeak.so
```

The final step is to place the library libspeak.so somewhere on the search path for shared libraries and to invoke the mainline program with the following command:

```
$ gij HelloNative
```

Passing Arguments to Native Methods

Just as with any other Java method, it is possible to pass arguments to a native method, and it is also possible for the caller to retrieve a return value. The data types for a C or C++ program are the same as those for the CNI interface, which were listed earlier in Table 10-1.

The following example is a class with a native method named sum() that accepts four int values as arguments and returns an int value that is the sum of the four:

```
/* AddFour.java */
public class AddFour {
    static {
        System.loadLibrary("libaddfour.so");
    }
    public static void main(String arg[]) {
        AddFour af = new AddFour();
        int value = af.sum(1,2,3,4);
        System.out.println("The sum of four is " + value);
    }
    public native int sum(int a,int b,int c,int d);
}
```

The implementation of the native method is as follows:

```
/* AddFour.c */
#include <jni.h>
#include "AddFour.h"

jint Java_AddFour_sum(JNIEnv *env,jobject this,
        jint a,jint b,jint c,jint d)
{
    jint total = a + b + c + d;
    return(total);
}
```

The four new parameters are added to the end of the pair of default arguments. The Java int data type is defined in the jni.h header file as jint and is used to define all the parameter types as well as the type of the function and the value returned.

The following four commands compile and link the two source files into a form that can be executed. The first command creates the file AddFour.class, which is the mainline of the program. The second command creates the header file AddFour.h containing the native method prototype. The third command compiles the native method using the -fpic option, which makes it possible to insert the object file into a shared library. The last statement creates the shared library named libaddfour.so.

```
$ gcj -C AddFour.java
$ gcjh -jni AddFour
$ gcc -fpic -c AddFour.c -o AddFour.o
$ gcc -shared AddFour.o -o libaddfour.so
```

All that is left to do is to place the library in a location that will be found by the loader and to execute the program with the following command:

```
$ gij AddFour
```

Calling Java Class Methods from C

It is possible for a native method to make a call back to the Java object by directly calling a Java method. The following example, named EchoKeystroke, is a Java class with one native method and one callback method. The native method, named getKeystrokes(), reads characters from the keyboard and makes a callback to characterCallback() with each character input:

```java
/* EchoKeystrokes.java */
public class EchoKeystrokes {
    static {
        System.loadLibrary("libgetkeys.so");
    }
    public static void main(String arg[]) {
        EchoKeystrokes ek = new EchoKeystrokes();
        ek.getKeystrokes();
    }
    public native void getKeystrokes();
    public void characterCallback(char character) {
        System.out.println(character);
    }
}
```

The native method uses the two arguments automatically passed to every native method to get the information required to make the callback. The function GetObjectClass() is called to return a Class object representing the class of the object containing the method to be called. The function GetMethodID() is called to retrieve a unique identifier of the method to be called. The method can then be called repeatedly using the function CallVoidMethod(), as follows:

```c
/* getkeystrokes.c */
#include <jni.h>
#include <stdio.h>
```

```
#include "EchoKeystrokes.h"

void Java_EchoKeystrokes_getKeystrokes(JNIEnv *env,jobject obj)
{
    jchar character = ' ';
    jclass class = (*env)->GetObjectClass(env,obj);
    jmethodID id = (*env)->GetMethodID(env,class,
            "characterCallback","(C)V");

    if(id != 0) {
        while(character != '.') {
            character = getchar();
            (*env)->CallVoidMethod(env,obj,id,character);
        }
    }
}
```

The call to getMethodID() requires the name of the method, the return type,
and the list of parameter types so it can uniquely identify the method. The return and
parameter values are identified by a character string in the following format:

```
"(argument type list)return type"
```

The type indicators included in the string are shown in Table 10-2.

For example, if a method is passed one int and one double value, and it returns
a double, the specifier string would look like the following:

```
"(ID)D"
```

If the first parameter is an array of bytes and the second is a string, and the return is
void, the specifier string looks like the following:

```
"([BLjava/lang/String;)V"
```

The following sequence of commands will compile EchoKeystrokes.java
into the class file EchoKeystrokes.class, use the gcjh utility to read the
EchoKeystrokes.class file and produce the EchoKeystrokes.h header file
containing the prototype of the native method, compile getkeystrokes.c into the

Indicator	Java Data Type
Z	boolean
B	byte
C	char
S	short
I	int
J	long
F	float
D	double
V	void
Lclassname;	An object of the specified class
[type	An array of the specified type
(arg type list) return type	A method with the specified argument and return types

Table 10-2. *Return and Parameter Types for Callback Methods*

positional independent object file `getkeystrokes.o`, and use `getkeystrokes.o` to construct the shared library `libgetkeys.so`:

```
$ gcj -C EchoKeystrokes.java
$ gcjh -jni EchoKeystrokes
$ gcc -fpic -c getkeystrokes.c -o getkeystrokes.o
$ gcc -shared getkeystrokes.o -o libgetkeys.so
```

Mixing Fortran and C

The GNU Fortran and C languages can be used together quite easily because either one can make a direct function call to the other. As long as you are careful to make sure the arguments passed during the call are of the correct type, functions from the two languages can call back and forth, just as if they were from the same language.

Table 10-3 lists the Fortran data types and their C counterparts. This table works for most platforms, but there are possible exceptions. It would be prudent to create a small

C Type	Fortran Type	Description
signed char	INTEGER*1	An 8-bit signed integer
short	INTEGER*2	A 16-bit signed integer
int	INTEGER	A 32-bit signed integer
float	REAL	A 32-bit floating point number
double	DOUBLE PRECISION	A 64-bit floating point number
SUBROUTINE SUB()	void sub_()	A void C function is the equivalent of a Fortran subroutine.
REAL FUNCTION FUN()	float fun_()	A non-void C function is the equivalent of a Fortran function.

Table 10-3.   *Compatible Data Types Between C and Fortran*

test program (from the examples in this section) and test any data types you intend to pass to make certain they are compatible.

Because Fortran always passes arguments by reference and C always passes arrays by address, the passing of arrays is straightforward and requires no modification. However, for arrays of more than one dimension, the subscript used in the different languages will need to be reversed, because Fortran arrays are organized in column-major order and C arrays are organized in row-major order.

Calling C from Fortran

The following Fortran program calls a C function, passing it a character string and a floating-point number:

```
C   f772c.f
C
      PROGRAM F772C
C
      CHARACTER*32 HELLO
      REAL PI
C
      HELLO = "Hello C from Fortran"
      HELLO(21:21) = CHAR(0)
```

```
      PI = 3.14159
      CALL SHOWHIPI(HELLO,PI)
      END PROGRAM F772C
```

The CHARACTER data type named HELLO, which is large enough to hold 32 characters, has a 21-character string stored into it, causing the remainder of the string to be filled with spaces. To format the string so it will be in the standard form used by C, it is necessary to insert a zero byte as a string terminator following the last byte of the actual string. The REAL data type named PI is in the same format as a C float data type, so it can be passed directly to the function.

It is important to note that Fortran arguments are passed by reference, so the C function will always receive the address of the value being passed, as opposed to the value itself. The following C function displays the string and the real number passed to it from the Fortran program:

```
/* showhipi.c */
#include <stdio.h>
void showhipi_(char *string,float *pi)
{
    printf("%s\nPI=%f\n",string,*pi);
}
```

There will be some variation from one platform to the next in the naming convention and in the data type compatibility between the two languages. As you can see in this example, it was necessary to append an underscore character to the end of the function name, but the data passed to the function is in the correct format.

The following command will compile the two source files and link them into a single executable:

```
$ g77 -c f772c.f -o f772c.o
$ gcc -c showhipi.c -o showhipi.o
$ g77 c2f77.o showhipi.o -o f772c
```

Calling Fortran from C

When calling a Fortran subroutine from a C program, it is necessary to pass the addresses of the arguments as well as to format strings properly for Fortran. The following example passes a character string and a floating-point value to a Fortran subroutine:

```
/* c2f77.c */
int main(int argc,char *argv[])
```

```
{
    int i;
    float e = 2.71828;
    char hello[32];
    int length = sizeof(hello);

    strcpy(hello,"Hello Fortran from C");
    for(i=strlen(hello); i<length; i++)
        hello[i] = ' ';
    showhie_(hello,&length,&e);
    return(0);
}
```

In C, the length of strings is determined by the position of a null character, but in Fortran all strings are a fixed length. Because there is no way for Fortran to determine the length of the string passed to it, it is also necessary to include the actual length of the string as an argument. In this example, the entire array is blank-filled, and the size of the array is passed as the second argument. Notice that all three arguments are passed as pointers to the actual data—this is because Fortran always expects addresses instead of the actual data. It is usually necessary to add an underscore to the name of the subroutine being called.

The following is the source code of the Fortran subroutine being called:

```
C   showhie.f
C
      SUBROUTINE SHOWHIE(HELLO,LENGTH,E)
      CHARACTER*(*) HELLO
      INTEGER LENGTH
      REAL E
C
      WRITE(*,100) HELLO(1:LENGTH),LENGTH,E
  100 FORMAT(3X,A,2X,I3,4X,F6.4)
      RETURN
      END SUBROUTINE SHOWHIE
```

The following three commands compile the two source files into object files and link them together into an executable:

```
$ g77 -c showhie.f -o showhie.o
$ gcc -c c2f77.c -o c2f77.o
$ gcc c2f77.o showhie.o -lfrtbegin -lg2c -lm -o c2f77
```

The third command requires the presence of the Fortran libraries because the gcc command was specified. The libraries are included automatically in the case of the g77 command, so the last command could be shortened to the following:

```
$ g77 c2f77.o showhie.o -o c2f77
```

Mixing Ada and C

The Ada language contains the facilities necessary to call C and Fortran functions. This is done by declaring the body of an Ada procedure using pragma import to specify the external language and the name of the code that is the body of the function.

The data types used by Ada and C are quite compatible with one another, especially when GCC is used to generate object code for both languages. Table 10-4 lists the data types that are the same in both languages.

Calling C from Ada

This simple example demonstrates how the body of a procedure in an Ada package can be implemented in C. The following is the mainline of the Ada program, which calls the procedures hello and goodbye in the Howdy package:

```
-- ada2c.adb
with Howdy;
procedure Ada2C is
begin
    Howdy.hello;
    Howdy.goodbye;
end Ada2C;
```

The hello and goodbye procedures both display a line of text, but where goodbye is written in Ada, the hello procedure is written in C. The members of the Howdy package are specified in the file howdy.ads as follows:

```
-- howdy.ads
package Howdy is
    procedure Hello;
    procedure Goodbye;
end Howdy;
```

Ada Type	C Type
Float	float
Integer	int
Long_Float	double
Long_Integer	long
Long_Long_Integer	long long
Short_Float	float
Short_Integer	short
Short_Short_Integer	signed char

Table 10-4. *Ada Data Types and the Corresponding C Data Types*

The implementation of the bodies of the procedures is in the file howdy.adb, which contains the actual code for goodbye and declares an external reference for hello:

```
-- howdy.adb
with Text_IO; use Text_IO;
with Interfaces.C;
package body Howdy is
    procedure Hello is
        procedure sayhello;
        pragma Import(C,sayhello);
    begin
        sayhello;
    end Hello;
    procedure Goodbye is
    begin
        Put_Line("Goodbye");
    end Goodbye;
end Howdy;
```

The with Interfaces.C statement is used to set off the definitions for data types that are compatible between C and Ada, but it is not strictly required here because there are no parameters or return values on the C function being called. The procedure named hello calls the C function sayhello, so the procedure and pragma Import statements are necessary to specify that sayhello is an external C function.

The first argument to the `Import` pragma is the name of the language in which the external procedure is written. The Ada standard states that the known languages are C, C++, Fortran, and COBOL. The second argument is the name of the function as it will be used locally in this program. If the actual function name is of a form that is not valid for Ada, a third argument can be used to specify the actual external name. For example, if you wish to call the remote function `_stprob()`, the leading underscore is not valid for Ada, so you could specify the pragma as follows:

```
pragma Import(C,stprob,"_stprob")
```

This way, you can use the internal name `stprob` to refer to the external name `_stprob`.

In this example, the C function being called is very simple and looks like the following:

```
/* sayhello.c */
#include <stdio.h>
void sayhello()
{
    printf("Hello C from Ada\n");
}
```

The following command sequence will compile the Ada and C source files and link the object files into an executable:

```
$ gcc -c sayhello.c -o sayhello.o
$ gcc -c howdy.adb
$ gcc -c ada2c.adb
$ gnatbind ada2c.ali
$ gnatlink ada2c.ali sayhello.o
```

Calling C from Ada with Arguments

This example is much like the previous one, except arguments are passed to the C functions that also return values. This example uses the UNIX system calls to start a process running in the background and then stop it. The file `adaspawn.adb` contains the mainline of the program:

```
-- adaspawn.adb
with Spawn;
procedure AdaSpawn is
pid : Integer;
```

```
status : Integer;
begin
    pid := Spawn.startProcess("flex");
    status := Spawn.stopProcess(pid);
end AdaSpawn;
```

In the mainline, a call is made to startProcess() with the name of the program to be executed. The return value is the process ID number, which is used in the call to stopProcess() to halt the running program. The two functions are defined as members of the Spawn package in the file spawn.ads:

```
-- spawn.ads
package Spawn is
    function startProcess(name : String) return Integer;
    function stopProcess(pid : Integer) return Integer;
end Spawn;
```

The data passed into and out of the Spawn functions are all Ada types. Inside these functions, calls are made to the C functions, so there needs to be some data conversion to guarantee compatibility. The body of the functions are defined in the file spawn.adb:

```
-- spawn.adb
with Interfaces.C;
package body Spawn is
    function startProcess(name : String) return Integer is
        function start(name : String) return Interfaces.C.int;
        pragma Import(C,start);
    begin
        return Integer(start(name));
    end startProcess;
    function stopProcess(pid : Integer) return Integer is
        function stop(pid : Integer) return Interfaces.C.int;
        pragma Import(C,stop);
    begin
        return Integer(stop(pid));
    end stopProcess;
end Spawn;
```

The Ada functions startProcess() and stopProcess() act as wrappers around the C functions start() and stop(). Some minor data conversion takes place. Both start() and stop() return the C data type Interface.C.int, which is converted to the Ada type Integer to make it possible to return the values from startProcess() and stopProcess().

All that is left are the C functions themselves, which are stored in a file named startstop.c, as follows:

```c
#include <unistd.h>
#include <signal.h>
#include <errno.h>

int start(char *name)
{
    int pid;
    char *argv[4];

    pid = fork();
    if(pid == -1)
        return(-1);
    if(pid == 0) {
        argv[0] = "sh";
        argv[1] = "-c";
        argv[2] = name;
        argv[3] = 0;
        execve("/bin/sh",argv,0);
        exit(-1);
    } else {
        return(pid);
    }
}
int stop(int pid)
{
    if(kill(pid,SIGTERM) < 0)
        return(errno);
    return(0);
}
```

The `start()` function calls the `fork()` system call, which clones the current process. The return value from `fork()` informs the process whether it is the original or the clone, and the clone converts itself into a different process by calling `execve()`. The system call `execve()` does not return because it immediately replaces itself with a new process by having the shell start a program from the beginning. Only the original program returns from `start()`, and it returns the PID of the newly started process.

This overall organization provides a wrapper of Ada functions around the C functions, and the C functions make the actual system calls. This type of organization was used in these examples to make each step as clear as possible, but it is not absolutely necessary to do it this way. There is nothing to prevent you from making a direct call to `execve()`, `kill()`, or any other system call from your Ada code in the same way the calls were made to `startProcess()` and `stopProcess()`.

The
Complete
Reference

Chapter 11

Internationalization

Every program, including the GCC compiler itself, if written properly, can be run in such a way that it adapts its interface to the local language and conditions.

Internationalization is the inclusion of the ability to support multiple languages within a program or set of programs acting as a package. These programs are written using only one language, but the code inside the programs is organized in such a way that the character strings in the programs can be dynamically replaced by strings in another language.

Localization is the operation of using the facilities built into a program, or a set of programs, to convert all its user-readable text to a different language. This is known as *setting the locale*, which is done through system settings that are read and acted upon by the programs when they are loaded.

Native language support (NLS) is the term used when referring to the overall operation of internationalization and localization.

You will often see the term *internationalization* abbreviated as i18n. This is derived from the fact *internationalization* begins with the letter *i*, followed by 18 letters, and ends with the letter *n*. Using the same scheme, the term *localization* is sometime written as l10n.

In general, i18n is managed by programmers, whereas l10n is managed by translators and users.

The examples and explanations in this chapter are in terms of the C language, but the same process can be used with C++, Objective-C, Python, Lisp, EmacsLisp, Java, and awk.

A Translatable Example

The following program contains the code necessary to have its strings translated:

```
/* starter.c */
#include <locale.h>
#include <libintl.h>

#define PACKAGE "starter"
#define LOCALEDIR "/usr/share/locale"

int main(int argc,char *argv[])
{
    setlocale(LC_ALL,"");
    bindtextdomain(PACKAGE,LOCALEDIR);
    textdomain(PACKAGE);

    printf("%s\n",gettext("This string will translate."));
}
```

The header file `locale.h` contains some of the fundamental macro definitions that are used to indicate the type of data that is to be localized as well as the data structures involved with monetary conversions. The header file `libintl.h` contains the prototypes of the functions required to configure and activate the internationalization process.

In the `main()` function, a call is made to `setlocale()` to specify which items are to be internationalized. Specifying `LC_ALL` indicates that everything is to be internationalized, but it may be that you wish to have only certain items internationalized. Instead of a single call to `setlocale()` using `LC_ALL`, a program can make several calls to `setlocale()` specifying the individual items listed in Table 11-1. The string returned from `setlocale()` is the identity of the current locale setting.

Locale Category	Description
LC_ADDRESS	The layout of the standard parts of an address, including firm name, building name, department name, c/o address, house number, postal code, country designation, and so on.
LC_ALL	This is the same as specifying all the members of this list.
LC_COLLATE	Regular expression matching. Determines the meaning and range of expression characters.
LC_CTYPE	Regular expression matching. Determines character classification, conversion, case-sensitive comparison, and the wide character functions.
LC_IDENTIFICATION	Formatting of information such as name, address, telephone, e-mail address, fax number, and so on.
LC_MEASUREMENT	Localizes the units of measure to metric or the English system.
LC_MESSAGES	Localizes the text natural language messages.
LC_MONETARY	Formatting of monetary display strings.
LC_NAME	Formats the presentation of a person's name, including the initial, salutation, salutation abbreviation, and the position of the first and last names.
LC_NUMERIC	Formatting of numeric values containing decimal points and thousands separators.
LC_PAPER	The standard paper size used for printing.
LC_TELEPHONE	Formatting of telephone numbers, including prefixes and country codes.
LC_TIME	Formatting of time and date strings.

Table 11-1. *Categories of Locales Known to* `setlocale()`

In this example the name of the package containing the program and the name of the directory containing the locale directories are specified on a pair of #define directive statements inside the program, but it is more normal for these to be named in a config.h file or by a -D option in the command line generated by the makefile.

To translate a string from one language to another, a call is made to the function gettext(). There is actually a family of gettext() functions, as described in the next section, any one of which will trigger the xgettext utility, described later, to extract a string. The original string (the one shown in the program listing) is used as a key to locate the translation for the current locale. If no match is found, the original string is used. The return value from the gettext() function is a character string. Therefore, in the example, the printf() statement simply displays whatever string returns from the call to gettext() without knowing whether an actual translation has taken place.

For convenience in programming and in converting existing programs, it is not uncommon to use a short macro in place of the name gettext(). For example, the function call can be shortened to a single underscore character using the following macro definition:

```
#define _(a) gettext(a)
```

Using the macro, the printf() statement in the example becomes the following:

```
printf("%s\n",_("This string will translate"));
```

Using this technique, the call to the translating function is reduced to consuming a total of three characters (the underscore and the two parentheses).

Creating a New .po File

Once all the strings that need to be translated in the text have been appropriately marked by being included on calls to the gettext() function, it is necessary to begin the construction of the file that uses the strings and keywords and supplies the translations for each target locale. The project is begun by using the utility xgettext to extract the lines of text and organize them in a new .po file. The following command will extract the appropriate strings from starter.c and create a file named messages.po:

```
$ xgettext starter.c
```

The file messages.po contains some standard header information, and contains the following:

```
msgid "This string will translate."
msgstr ""
```

For the file to be completed, it is only necessary for a translator to edit the .po file and enter the translation in place of the empty string to the right of the msgstr tag. If the program has a number of strings to be translated, they will all appear in this same file.

The xgettext utility can be used with a number of programming languages and will combine the strings from all the input source files into a single .po file to be used for the entire package. The command-line options for xgettext are listed in Table 11-2.

The following is a command that will generate a file named messages.po containing the string or strings designated by calls to gettext() in the source file named starter.c:

```
$ xgettext starter.c
```

Option	Description
-	Instead of reading a file, the source is read from standard input.
-a	If the language is C or C++, this option extracts all strings.
--add-comments=*tag*	Same as -c.
--add-location	Same as -n.
-C	Shorthand for --language=C.
-c *tag*	Used to place a comment block with the specified *tag* in the output file.
--c++	Shorthand for --language=C++.
--copyright-holder=*str*	The *str* is the name of the copyright holder of the package and therefore of the extracted strings. If this is not specified, the default is the Free Software Foundation.
-d *name*	The output file is named *name*.po (instead of the default, messages.po). Also see -o.
-D*directory*	Adds the named *directory* to the list of those sought for named source files.
--default-domain=*name*	Same as -d.
--directory=*directory*	Same as -D.
--exclude-file=*file*	Same as -x.
--extract-all	Same as -a.

Table 11-2.   *Command-Line Options for xgettext*

Option	Description
-F	Sorts output by file location.
-f *file*	The input file names are read from file instead of from the command line.
--files-from=*file*	Same as -f.
--force-po	Produces an output file even if no translatable strings are found.
--foreign-user	Omits the default output from --copyright-holder.
-h	Displays this list of options and exits.
--help	Displays this list of options and exits.
-i	Uses indention when writing the .po file.
--indent	Same as -i.
-j	Joins the messages with those in an existing output file.
--join-existing	Same as -j.
-k *keywordspec*	If the language is C or C++, the *keywordspec* is an additional keyword that will trigger the extraction of a string. The format of *keywordspec* is *named:num,* where *num* is the argument number for the string. The default keywords are gettext, dgettext:2, dcgettext:2, ngettext:1, dngettext:2,3, dcngettext, and gettext_noop. If no *keywordspec* is specified, the default keywords are not used.
-keyword=*keywordspec*	Same as -k.
-L *name*	The name of the language of the input files. It can be C, C++, ObjectiveC, PO, Python, Lisp, EmacsLisp, librep, Java, awk, YCP, Tcl, RST, or Glade.
--language=*name*	Same as -L.
-m [*string*]	Uses the specified *string* (or uses "" if no *string* is specified) as the prefix for all msgstr entries in the output file. Also see -M.
-M [*string*]	Uses the specified *string* (or uses "" if no *string* is specified) as the suffix for all msgstr entries in the output file. Also see -m.
--msgstr-prefix[=*string*]	Same as -m.

Table 11-2. *Command-Line Options for* xgettext (continued)

Option	Description
-msgstr-suffix[=*string*]	Same as -M.
-n	Includes the comment lines indicating the source of the string. This is the default.
--no-location	Specifies to not include the comment lines indicating the source of the string.
--no-wrap	Long message lines are not to be split in the output file.
-o *file*	The output file is named *file* (instead of the default, messages.po). Also see -d.
--omit-header	Omits the header, which is normally tagged with a msgid "" entry.
--output-dir=*directory*	Same as -p.
--output-file=*file*	Same as -o.
-p *directory*	The output file will be placed in the named *directory*.
-s	Generates the output in sorted order instead of the order in which the strings are encountered in the source.
--sort-by-file	Same as -F.
--sort-output	Same as -s.
--strict	Writes the .po file in strict Uniforum format. This format does not support GNU extensions.
-T	If the language is C, trigraphs will be recognized.
--trigraphs	Same as -T.
-v	Displays version information and exits.
--version	Displays version information and exits.
-w *number*	Specifies the output page width. Lines longer than this width will be broken.
--width=*number*	Same as -w.
-x *file*	Entries from the named .po or .pot file are not extracted.

Table 11-2. *Command-Line Options for xgettext* (continued)

One of the most important options for xgettext is the -j option, which will generate a new messages.po file from the source, but will also read an older version of messages.po and retain any translations that have been inserted into the file by a translator. This is very important because it automates the updating of the messages file without throwing out any work that has already been done. For example, the following command will read the file named starter.po and merge the translations that are still valid with any new strings and then create a new version of starter.po:

```
$ xgettext -j -d starter starter.c
```

Use of the gettext() Functions

The simplest form of marking a string for translation is to use the string as an argument to a call to gettext(). Situations exist where it is necessary to use a slightly different approach, and other functions can be used to solve certain problems.

Static Strings

The following example shows how a string can be declared as the initial value of a global variable and still be dynamically translated when the program runs:

```
/* statictrans.c */
#include <locale.h>
#include <libintl.h>

#define PACKAGE "starter"
#define LOCALEDIR "/usr/share/locale"

#define gettext_noop(a) (a)

char *glbl = gettext_noop("This is a global static string.");

int main(int argc,char *argv[])
{
    setlocale(LC_ALL,"");
    bindtextdomain(PACKAGE,LOCALEDIR);
    textdomain(PACKAGE);

    printf("%s\n",gettext(glbl));
}
```

The function name gettext_noop() is declared as a do-nothing macro that simply results in the string itself, which will cause xgettext to see the name of the dummy function and cause it to skip the string. The later call to gettext() is passed the address of the actual string, so the translation will take place at the point the string is used. The result is the same as if the string had been declared as a constant argument passed to gettext(). If you use the global string in more that one place in the program, it will be translated at each point of reference.

Translation from Another Domain

If you need to retrieve the translation of a string from another package, you can do so by calling the function dgettext() and specifying the name of the other package. For example, if there is a package named hrdomain and the key string "Daily average catch" has been translated in that domain, you can specify that the translation of the other domain be retrieved at runtime by using dgettext() this way:

```
dgettext("hrdomain","Daily average catch");
```

Executing xgettext will not extract this particular string because you have specified that it has a translation in another location.

Translation from Another Domain in a Specified Category

Like dgettext(), the function dcgettext() makes it possible to retrieve a translation string from another domain. It also makes it possible for you to select a category for the translation. The category is one of the constant values defined in Table 11-1. For example, the following can be used to translate a date according to the rules of a domain named hrdomain:

```
dcgettext("hrdomain","12/04/03",LC_TIME);
```

Plurality

The ngettext() method takes plurality into consideration when translating the string. Both the singular and plural forms of the original string are passed to the function, along with the degree of plurality. Some languages have a singular form for one, a dual form for two, and the plural form only applies to three or more. For example, the following call would be made to translate the word "image" when it is a reference to two images:

```
ngettext("picture","pictures",2L);
```

In this example, the automatic translation process will need to select the target language's correct form of plurality to indicate two pictures.

Plurality from Another Domain

The function dngettext() works the same as ngettext(), except it will look for the translation in another domain. The following example looks in the domain hrdomain for the correct plural form to indicate a pair of images:

```
dngettext("hrdomain","picture","pictures",2L);
```

Plurality from Another Domain Within a Category

The function dcngettext() works the same as dngettext(), except it will look for the translation according to the definitions of the specified category. The category is one of the categories specified in Table 11-1. The following example looks in the domain hrdomain for the correct plural form to indicate a pair of images:

```
dcngettext("hrdomain","Mr. Garcia","Messrs. Garcia",2L,LC_NAME);
```

In this example, the correct translation will be chosen, according to rules that are applicable to formatting names, for two gentlemen with the last name Garcia.

Merging Two .po Files

Even though it is possible to use xgettext to simultaneously generate new translation tables that are automatically merged with those in an existing .po file, you may find yourself in the situation (or prefer to operate) with two separate .po files—an older, existing .po file containing translations for a previous version of the program and a new file containing entries generated for the newer version of the software. If this is the case, the two can be merged by using the msgmerge utility as follows:

```
$ msgmerge oldfile.po newfile.po
```

In this example, oldfile.po contains all the existing translations, and they will all be carried over to the newly created file as long as the strings also exist in newfile.po. In addition, all the new strings in newfile.po that are not found in oldfile.po are added to the output. The new data is written to standard output unless an output file is specified as one of the command-line options. The options for msgmerge are listed in Table 11-3.

Option	Description
--add-location	Includes the comment lines specifying the location of each string in the original source. This is the default. See --no-location.
-D directory	The named directory is added to the list of those searched for the named input files.
--directory=directory	The same as -D.
-e	Specifies to not used C language escape sequences in the text of the output. This is the default.
-E	Uses C language escape sequences in the output text.
--escape	Same as -E.
--force-po	Writes the output file even if it is empty.
-h	Displays this list of options and exits.
--help	Same as -h.
-i	Generates the output with indented text.
--indent	Same as -i.
--no-location	Suppresses the comment lines specifying the location of each string in the original source. See --add-location.
-o file	The output is written to the named file. The default is to write the output to standard out.
--output-file=file	Same as -o.
--strict	Produces strict Uniforum output style, which omits GNU extensions.
-v	Produces more verbose output describing the processing.
-V	Displays the version number and quits.
--verbose	Same as -v.
--version	Same as -V.
-w number	The number is the maximum width. Lines longer than number will be broken.
-width=number	Same as -w.

Table 11-3. *Command-Line Options for* msgmerge

USING THE COMPILER COLLECTION

Producing a Binary .mo File from a .po File

Once the translation text has been added to the .po file, the next step is to create the .mo file. This binary file is used by the programs to make translations. The binary file is created using the .po file as input to the msgfmt utility, as follows:

```
$ msgfmt starter.po
```

This command produces a binary file named starter. Recall from the beginning of this chapter that the program starter.c begins with the following three function calls:

```
setlocale(LC_ALL,"");
bindtextdomain(PACKAGE,LOCALEDIR);
textdomain(PACKAGE);
```

The macro PACKAGE is defined as "starter" and LOCALEDIR is defined as "/usr/share/locale". For the program to find the translation tables for, say, Canadian English, it is only necessary to copy the binary file to /usr/share/locale/en_CA/starter. Whenever the current local is set to en_CA, the program will look for, and find, the appropriate translation tables. To create translations for other languages, it is only necessary to edit a copy of starter.po to insert the appropriate translation strings, create another binary file, and copy it to the appropriate subdirectory.

The utility msgfmt has a few command-line options, which are listed in Table 11-4.

Option	Description
-a *number*	Aligns strings to the specified number of bytes. The default is 1.
--alignment=*number*	Same as -a.
-c	Performs language-dependent checks on the strings. This includes checking for the validity of % formatting sequences in C strings and the correctness of the information being inserted in the header. It also checks that there are no conflicts in the domain name and --output-file option.
--check	Same as -c.

Table 11-4. *Command-Line Options for* msgfmt

Option	Description
-D *directory*	Adds the named directory to the list of those to be searched for input files.
--directory=*directory*	Same as -D.
-f	Uses fuzzy entries on input.
-h	Displays this list of options and exits.
--help	Same as -h.
--no-hash	The binary output file will not include the hash table.
-o *file*	Specifies the name of the output file as *file*. The default is to use the base name of the input file without an extension.
--output-file *file*	Same as -o.
--statistics	Displays statistical information on the translation tables.
--strict	Enables the strict Uniforum mode.
--use-fuzzy	Same as -f.
-v	Lists any anomalies found in the input.
-V	Displays version information and quits.
--verbose	Same as -v.
--version	Same as -V.

Table 11-4.   *Command-Line Options for* msgfmt (continued)

The Complete Reference

Part III

Peripherals and Internals

The Complete Reference

Chapter 12

Linking and Libraries

The compiler produces object files that contain executable code, but in virtually every case the object file produced by the compiler is incomplete and needs to be combined with other object modules to produce an executable program. Even a simple "hello world" program employs a function from another object file to do the actual work of displaying the string of characters.

This chapter discusses linking and the utilities that can be used to examine and manipulate object files. An object file is the .o file produced by the compiler. Many of the utilities described in this chapter can work with more than one object file, whether they are stored in a directory as discrete files, in a static library (also known as an *archive*), or in a shared library (also known as a *dynamic library*). Also, some of the utilities operate on fully linked executable files.

Object Files and Libraries

When combining object modules together to create a single executable, the linker can find the object modules as separate files in a directory, as object modules stored in a static library, or as object modules stored in a shared library. A single link operation can, and often does, involve object files from all three locations.

Object Files in a Directory

The simplest form of linking is to compile a collection of object files into a directory, or set of directories, and then name them on the command line for the linker. This works out quite well for object modules that are to be linked into only one or two programs. For example, a C program consists of the source files main.c, inlet.c, outlet.c and genspru.c. The following sequence of commands will compile them all into object files and link them into an executable program named spinout:

```
$ gcc -c main.c -o main.o
$ gcc -c inlet.c -o inlet.o
$ gcc -c outlet.c -o outlet.o
$ gcc -c genspru.c -o genspru.o
$ gcc main.o inlet.o outlet.o genspru.o -o spinout
```

After this series of commands has been successfully executed, the disk contains the four object files and one executable file. A simpler way to achieve the same thing is to let the compiler manage the entire process with a command like the following:

```
$ gcc main.c inlet.c outlet.c genspru.c -o spinout
```

In either case, the final executable contains all the code from all four of the object files, along with other code from the system that the linker determines to be necessary.

Object Files in a Static Library

Object files can be stored in a static library and linked from there in much the same way as they can be linked from separate files, except the linker will automatically search through the contents of the library and include only the object files that are necessary. If nothing in an object file is referenced from inside the program, it is not included as part of the executable.

A static library containing object files is known as an *archive* file, and it's constructed and maintained by a utility named ar. The name of an archive file normally has a prefix of lib and a suffix of .a. The following sequence of commands compiles three object files and stores a copy of them in a library named libspin.a. Then the linker uses the object file named main.o and the contents of the library to construct an executable program named spinner:

```
$ gcc -c inlet.c outlet.c genspru.c
$ ar -r libspin.a  inlet.o outlet.o genspru.o
$ gcc main.c libspin.a -o spinner
```

The first gcc command produces the three object files that are inserted into the static library by the ar command. The last command compiles main.c into main.o and then invokes the linker, which reads the contents of libspin.a to try to resolve external function and data references made in main.o. A module stored in libspin.a is included as part of the final executable file only if it contains a function or data item referred to from a module that has already been included as part of the executable. Because unnecessary object modules are not included, linking from a library can produce smaller executable files than the ones produced by linking from a collection of object files in a directory (which always includes all named files).

Inside the static library, along with the object modules, is an index that lists all the names of global data and functions defined in the library. The linker uses this index to determine which modules to include and which ones to ignore. Normally, this index is created by the ar utility when the library is created or updated, but options are available on the ar utility that can suppress the creation of the index. This can be useful when maintaining a large library—multiple changes can be made without bothering to update the index until the modifications have been completed. To create an index or to update an existing index, you can use the ranlib utility. For example, the following pair of commands use the -q option of ar to quickly append files to an existing archive without updating the index, and then it uses ranlib to update the index to reflect the current status of the archive:

```
$ ar -q libspin.a mongul.o strop.o klbrgr.o
$ ranlib libspin.a
```

The order of appearance of the modules in the library can make a difference. If the same symbol is defined in more than one module, then the linker will find and include the first module if it is looking for that symbol. Further, different versions of the same module can be stored in the same archive and, again, the linker will be satisfied with finding the first one. Options on the `ar` utility can be used to add new modules in specific positions and to change the order of the ones already in the archive.

The syntax of the `ar` command is as follows:

```
ar [options] [positionname] [count] archive objectfile [objectfile
...]
```

The `ar` command is one of the older UNIX utilities, and its syntax is similar to some of the other older utilities, such as `tar`, in that all the option flags come first, the option letters are all included in a group without spaces between them, and the options can be expressed with or without the leading hyphen. The optional command-line entries `positionname` and `count` can be present only if options that require them are also present. The options on the `ar` command fall into two categories: the command options tell `ar` what action is to be taken (there is only one of these options on a valid command line), and the modifier options specify how the command option is to perform. The list of command options for `ar` can be found in Table 12-1, and the modifier options are listed in Table 12-2.

Option	Description
d	Deletes from the archive the modules named as `objectfiles`. With the v modifier, each module is listed as it is deleted.
m	Moves modules inside an archive. By default, any members listed as `objectfiles` will be moved to the end of the archive. The modifiers a, b, and i can be used to move the named modules to other locations.
p	Prints the binary content of named `objectfiles` to standard output. If no `objectfiles` are specified, they are all printed. The v modifier will cause the name of each one to be listed before its content is printed.
q	Quickly appends the named `objectfiles` to the end of the archive without checking for replacement possibilities. The index is not updated, so `ranlib` must be used before the library can be linked.

Table 12-1.   *The ar Options That Specify the Action to Be Taken*

Option	Description
r	Inserts the named objectfiles into the archive. If any of the named objectfiles are already in the archive, the old ones are replaced by the new ones. If the named archive does not exist, it is created. By default, new modules are appended to the end of the file, but the a, b, or i modifier can be used to position the new modules.
t	Displays a listing of the contents of the archive file. The v modifier causes the list to include the timestamp, owner, group, and size of each module. If no objectfiles are named, the entire archive is listed.
x	Extracts the named objectfiles to regular disk files. If no objectfiles are named, all files are extracted.

Table 12-1.   *The ar Options That Specify the Action to Be Taken* (continued)

Option	Description
a	Adds any new files immediately after the file named on the command line as positionname.
b	Adds any new files immediately before the file named on the command line as positionname. This is the same as i.
c	Creates the archive if necessary. A new archive is always created if need be, but using this option suppresses the warning message.
f	Truncates the file names inside the archive. Normally, ar allows file names to be of any length, which may cause the creation of archives that are not compatible with some systems.
i	Adds any new files immediately before the file named on the command line as positionname. This is the same as b.
N	Uses the count parameter as a selector of the named objectfile when there is more than one of that name in the archive.
o	When files are being extracted from an archive, the original dates are preserved.

Table 12-2.   *The ar Options That Modify the Action to Be Taken*

Option	Description
s	Creates a new archive index even if no other change is made to the archive. This modifier can be used alone as in ar s, which has the same result as using ranlib.
u	When files are being added to an archive, this option will cause only files to be added that are newer than the ones already in the archive. This modifier is only valid with the r option.
v	Runs in verbose mode to display additional information as the process runs.
V	Displays the version information and quits.

Table 12-2. *The ar Options That Modify the Action to Be Taken* (continued)

Object Files in a Dynamic Library

A dynamic library contains object files that are loaded into memory and linked with a program only when the program starts to run. The two advantages of this are that the program's executable file is much smaller, and two or more programs are able to share object modules loaded from the same dynamic library (which is the reason dynamic libraries are also called *shared libraries*).

The object files stored in a dynamic library have a slightly different form than regular object files that are intended for static linking. They are the same except for the way internal addressing is handled inside the code generated from the compiler.

A Front End for the Linker

In an object oriented language such as C++, it is necessary for a program to have the ability to execute static constructors before the mainline of the program begins execution. Not all linkers have the capability of setting things up to do this, so it became necessary to add a front end named collect2 to the linking process.

On almost every system, gcc invokes a utility program named collect2 that assumes the responsibility of linking. The collect2 process detects static constructors that must be executed before the mainline of the program begins. To make certain these static constructors are executed, collect2 generates a special table of the constructors in a temporary .c source file, compiles it, and includes it as part of the linked executable. At the beginning of the main() function is a call to __main() to execute the static constructors.

The collect2 program can be executed just as if it were the linker ld. It takes the same set of arguments and passes the arguments on to ld to do the actual linking. In fact, it may need to link the program twice—once to determine the names of the static constructors (which will be found in the linker's output) and again to produce the final executable file.

Not only does `collect2` invoke `ld` the linker, it also uses nm to demangle and extract names from object files, and it uses `strip` to remove symbols from the object files.

Locating the Libraries

For a program to link properly, the linker must be able to locate the libraries required to resolve the external references. For a statically linked program where all the object files are gathered together and stored in a single executable file, the executable is entirely portable and can be executed on any compatible system, even if the original library no longer exists. On the other hand, a shared library must be available at the time the program is linked and again every time the program is run.

Locating Libraries at Link Time

Whenever the linker needs to find a library, it looks for it in a specific list of directories. Which directories are included in the search path depends on which emulation mode `ld` is using, how `ld` was configured when it was compiled, and which directories are specified on the command line. Most often the system libraries are stored in the directories `/lib` and `/usr/lib`, so these two directories are automatically searched. You can specify other directories to be searched by using one or more `-L` options. For example, the following command instructs the linker to look in both the current directory and the directory named `/home/fred/lib` for any libraries that are not found on the default search path:

```
$ gcc -L. -L/home/fred/lib prog.o
```

The linker searches for shared libraries before searching for static libraries. The following command will search each directory for a library named `libmilt.so` and then for `libmilt.a`:

```
$ gcc -lmilt prog.o
```

All the searching can be eliminated by specifying the exact name of the libraries on the command line. The following example will use the library named `libjj.a` in the current directory and the library named libmilt.so in the directory named `/home/fred/lib`:

```
$ gcc libjj.a /home/fred/lib/libmilt.so prog.o
```

Locating Libraries at Runtime

Once a program has been linked to use shared libraries, it must be able to find the shared library when it runs. The libraries are located by name, not by directory, so it is possible to link the program against one copy of the library and run it using another. This can, of course, cause problems if you switch from one version of the library to another without updating the program—which is the reason most libraries include a version number as part of the name (for example, `libm.so.6` or `libutil-2.2.4.so`).

Whenever a program loads and prepares to run, the shared libraries it needs are sought in the following places:

- Each of the directories listed in the colon-separated list in the environment variable `LD_LIBRARY_PATH`
- The list of libraries found in the file `/etc/ld.so.cache`, which is maintained by the `ldconfig` utility
- The directory `/lib`
- The directory `/usr/lib`

If you want to find out which libraries are being loaded and used by a specific application, you can use the `ldd` utility described later in this chapter.

Another environment variable, `LD_PRELOAD`, can contain a list of shared library names (separated by spaces, tabs, or newlines) that will be preloaded before any other library searching takes place. In this way, you can override the functions that would normally be loaded from a shared library. For security reasons, some limitations are imposed on this technique for `setuid` programs.

Loading Functions from a Shared Library

Functions in a shared library can be loaded and executed without ever having been linked to the program. It is only necessary to load the shared library into memory and then call the desired function or functions by name. The following example consists of two simple functions stored in a shared library, and then a program dynamically loads and executes each one.

The two functions in the library display strings to standard output to demonstrate that they are actually being called. The first one, named `sayhello`, displays its own internally declared string, as follows:

```
/* sayhello.c */
#include <stdio.h>
void sayhello()
{
    printf("Hello from a loaded function\n");
}
```

The second function, named saysomething, requires a string be passed to it:

```
/* saysomething.c */
#include <stdio.h>
void saysomething(char *string)
{
    printf("%s\n",string);
}
```

These two functions are compiled as position-independent code and used to create a shared library named libsayfn.so with the following command:

```
$ gcc -fpic -shared sayhello.c saysomething.c -o libsayfn.so
```

A program that will dynamically load these functions can be written using four fundamental functions. A call to dlopen() loads the shared library into memory (if it is not already there) and returns a handle that can be used to address it. Calls to dlsym() return the addresses of the functions. A call can be made to dlcose() that detaches the current program from the shared library. If no other programs are attached to it, the dynamic library is unloaded from memory. The function dlerror() returns a descriptive string describing the error that occurred on the most recent call to any one of the other functions. The dlerror() function returns NULL if no error occurred.

The following program loads the shared library libsayfn.so and executes the two functions it contains:

```
/* say.c */
#include <dlfcn.h>
#include <stdio.h>

int main(int argc,char *argv[])
{
    void *handle;
    char *error;
    void (*sayhello)(void);
    void (*saysomething)(char *);

    handle = dlopen("libsayfn.so",RTLD_LAZY);
    if(error = dlerror()) {
        printf("%s\n",error);
        exit(1);
    }
```

```
        sayhello = dlsym(handle,"sayhello");
        if(error = dlerror()) {
            printf("%s\n",error);
            exit(1);
        }

        saysomething = dlsym(handle,"saysomething");
        if(error = dlerror()) {
            printf("%s\n",error);
            exit(1);
        }

        sayhello();
        saysomething("This is something");

        dlclose(handle);
    }
```

The header file dlfcn.h is included because it contains the function prototypes and some other definitions. At the top of the main() function are declarations for the handle to be used to address the shared library, a string pointer to contain the address of any error messages, and pointers to each of the functions that are to be found in the library.

The command line to compile this example requires the inclusion of the library containing the functions, as follows:

```
$ gcc say.c -ldl -o say
```

The call to dlopen() requires the name of the library to be loaded and a flag value to indicate how the functions are to be loaded. The call to dlopen() searches for the named library in the following places:

- If the name of the library begins with a slash (/) character, it is assumed that the address is an absolute path name, so the name must be an exact match. If the name does not begin with a slash, the search continues with the other locations in this list.

- Each of the directories listed in the colon-separated list in the environment variable LD_LIBRARY_PATH.

- The list of libraries found in the file /etc/ld.so.cache, which is maintained through the ldconfig utility.

- The directory /usr/lib.
- The directory /lib.
- The current directory.

The flag used as the second argument on the call to dlopen() can be RTLD_NOW, which causes all the functions in the library to be loaded into memory and become immediately available. The other option is to specify RTLD_LAZY, which will delay the actual loading of each function until it is referenced on a call to dlsym(). Either of these flags can be OR'ed with RTLD_GLOBAL, which allows any external references in this library to be resolved by calling functions found in other (also loaded) dynamic libraries.

The calls to dlsym() in the example, with the handle returned from dlopen() and the name of a function, return the address of a function in the loaded library. Once the function address is returned and stored in the appropriate pointer, it can be called directly.

After the calls to dlopen() and dlsym(), calls to dlerror() are made so the program will detect and report any error condition.

Utility Programs to Use with Object Files and Libraries

Managing libraries and the object files stored in them can become quite a chore, depending on the naming conventions and level of organization of your system. Even with the object- and library-management capabilities of gcc and ar, there are times when you need to examine the contents of binary files and reorganize things based on what you find.

Configuring the Search for Shared Libraries

The ldconfig utility performs two fundamental functions dealing with shared libraries. First, it creates links so that references to shared libraries are always to the latest version. Second, it stores a complete list of the available shared libraries in the file /etc/ld.so.cache.

The ldconfig utility reads the file /etc/ld.so.conf, which is a list of directories containing shared libraries, and uses these directory names (along with the directories /lib and /usr/lib) to locate the libraries to be linked and listed in /etc/ld.so.cache. The directory names in the file /etc/ld.so.conf can be separated by newlines, colons, tabs, or spaces. The contents of /etc/ld.so.cache is not text and not intended to be edited.

Before constructing the /etc/ld.so.cache file, ldconfig analyzes the name and content of the libraries and creates dynamic links so that the latest version of the libraries will be loaded. For example, a program loading `libdl.so.2` may actually be loading, through a link, the library named `libdl-2.2.4.so`. When a new bug-fix version of the library is released (for example `libdl-2.2.5.so` or `libdl-2.3.0.so`), the `ldconfig` utility will update the link `libld.so.2` to point to the new version. However, if a major new release is made that could possibly break old programs, and it is named `libdl-3.0.0.so`, the old link will be undisturbed and a new link named `libdl.so.3` will be created. This naming convention makes it possible for programs using either the old or new version of the shared library to run in the same environment.

Because of the privileged accesses required, it is necessary to log in as root to run `ldconfig`. The following command will create all the new links necessary and generate a new version of the file `/etc/ld.so.cache`:

```
% ldconfig -v
```

The `-v` option generates a list of all the links and other information about the processing that takes place. The complete option list is described in Table 12-3.

Option	Description
`-?`	Displays this option list and quits.
`-C filename`	Uses the named file to hold the cache instead of the default, `/etc/ld.so.cache`.
`-c fmt`	Same as `--format`.
`-f filename`	Uses the named file as the input configuration file instead of the default, `/etc/ld.so.conf`.
`--format=fmt`	Specifies the format of the content of /etc/ld.so.cache. The available selections are `old`, `new`, and `compat`. The default is `compat`.
`--help`	Displays this option list and quits.
`-n`	Links the libraries in the directories specified on the command line and does not produce the cache file.

Table 12-3. *Command-Line Options for* `ldconfig`

Option	Description
-N	Specifies to not rebuild the cache file.
-p	Same as --print-cache.
--print-cache	Displays an alphabetic listing of all the libraries in the cache file, along with the full path name of the library to which they are linked.
-r *directory*	Changes to and uses the named directory as the root directory.
--usage	Displays the syntax of the command line and quits.
-v	Produces a verbose listing of the actions taken.
-V	Displays the version information.
--verbose	Produces a verbose listing of the actions taken.
--version	Displays the version information.
-X	Specifies to not create the library name links.

Table 12-3. *Command-Line Options for ldconfig* (continued)

Listing Symbols Names in Object Files

The nm utility can be used to list all the symbols defined in (or referenced from) an object file, a static archive library, or a shared library. If no file is named on the command line, the file name a.out is assumed. Using the command-line options, the symbols can be organized according their address, size, or name, and the output can be formatted in a number of ways. The symbols can also be demangled and presented in the same form as they appear in the original source code.

As an example, the following command will list the names of the object modules along with all the symbols defined and referenced in the library named libc.a:

```
$ nm libc.a
```

Table 12-4 lists the command-line options of the nm command.

Option	Description
-A	Same as --print-file-name.
-a	Same as --debug-syms.
-B	Same as --format=bsd. This is the default.
-C [type]	Same as --demangle.
-D	Same as --dynamic.
--debug-syms	Displays the symbols intended for use by the debugger. Normally these do not display.
--demangle[=type]	Demangles the symbol names back into the user-level names found in the source code. If the type is specified, it is one of the following: auto, gnu, lucid, arm, hp, edg, gnu-v3, java, gnat, or compaq.
--dynamic	For dynamic objects, such as shared libraries, this option displays the dynamic symbols instead of the normal symbols.
--extern-only	Displays only symbols that have been defined as being external.
-f fmt	Same as --format.
--format=fmt	Uses the specified output format to display the symbols. The choices are bsd, sysv, and posix, with bsd as the default.
-g	Same as --extern-only.
-h	Displays this list of options and quits.
--help	Displays this list of options and quits.
-l	Same as --line-numbers.
--line-numbers	Uses the debugging information stored in the file to determine the file name and line number for each symbol.
-n	Same as --numeric-sort.
--no-sort	Specifies to not sort the symbols.
--numeric-sort	Sorts the symbols numerically by their addresses.

Table 12-4. *Command-Line Options of the nm Utility*

Option	Description
`-o`	Same as `--print-file-name`.
`-p`	Same as `--no-sort`.
`-P`	Same as `--format=posix`.
`--portability`	Same as `--format=posix`.
`--print-armap`	When listing the symbols from members of a static library, this option includes the index information along with the other information about the module containing the symbols.
`--print-file-name`	Tags each symbol with the name of its source file rather than naming the source file only once at the top.
`-r`	Same as `--reverse-sort`.
`--radix=`*base*	Specifies the numeric base for printing symbol values. The selection can be d for decimal, o for octal, or x for hexadecimal.
`--reverse-sort`	Reverses the sort, whether alphabetic or numeric.
`-s`	Same as `--print-armap`.
`--size-sort`	Sorts the symbols by size. The size is computed as the difference between the address of the symbol with the next highest address and the address of this symbol. The size is listed in the output instead of the usual address.
`-t` *base*	Same as `--radix`.
`--target=`*bfdname*	The *bfdname* is the name of an object file format that is something other than the format for the current machine. To get a list of the known format names, enter the command `objdump -i`.
`-u`	Same as `--undefined-only`.
`--undefined-only`	Displays only the symbols that are referenced but not defined in this file.
`-V`	Same as `--version`.
`--version`	Displays the version information and quits.

Table 12-4. *Command-Line Options of the nm Utility* (continued)

PERIPHERALS AND
INTERNALS

Removing Unused Information from Object Files

The `strip` utility removes the debugging symbol table information from the object file or files named on the command line. The object file can be a static library, a shared library, or a `.o` file produced by the compiler. Depending on how much debugging information has been included in the file, stripping can dramatically reduce the size of the file. As an example, the following command will strip all debugging information from the object file `main.o` and all the object files in the library `libglom.a`:

```
$ strip main.o libglom.a
```

The `strip` utility replaces the existing file with the stripped version, so if you want to be able to restore the original unstripped versions, you will need to save the files before stripping them or use the `-o` option to produce the output in a different file.

The command-line options for `strip` are listed in Table 12-5. Several of the options in the table refer to *bfdname*. This is the name of the format of the object file to be stripped, and it will be necessary if the file is something other than the native format for the current machine. To get a list of the available bfdnames, enter the command `objdump -i`.

Option	Description
`--discard-all`	Removes all nonglobal symbols.
`--discard-locals`	Removes the local symbols that were generated by the compiler. These usually start with the letter L or a period.
`-F` *bfdname*	Same as `--target`.
`-g`	Same as `--strip-debug`.
`-h`	Displays this list of options and quits.
`--help`	Displays this list of options and quits.
`-I` *bfdname*	Same as `--input-target`.
`--input-target=`*bfdname*	Treats the input object files as files in the format of the named *bfdname*. Also see `--output-target` and `--target`.

Table 12-5. *The Command-Line Options for* `strip`

Option	Description
`-K name`	Same as `--keep-symbol`.
`--keep-symbol=name`	Copies only the named symbols to the output file. This option can be used more than once to retain more than one name.
`-N name`	Same as `--strip-symbol`.
`-O bfdname`	Same as `--output-target`.
`-o filename`	Instead of overwriting the original file, the output is written to a new file named `filename`. Using this option limits the command to operate on a single file.
`--output-target= bfdname`	Replaces the original file with a stripped file in the format specified as `bfdname`. Also see `--input-target` and `--target`.
`-p`	Same as `--preserve-dates`.
`--preserve-dates`	The newly stripped file will have the same access times as the original input file.
`-R name`	Same as `--remove-section`.
`--remove-section=name`	Removes the named section from the object file. This option may be used more than once to remove more than one section.
`-s`	Same as `--strip-all`.
`-S`	Same as `--strip-debug`.
`--strip-all`	Removes all symbols, including the relocation information necessary for linking.
`--strip-debug`	Removes only the symbols necessary for debugging.
`--strip-symbol=name`	Removes the named symbol. This option may be used more than once and can be used along with other strip options.

Table 12-5. *The Command-Line Options for* `strip` (continued)

PERIPHERALS AND INTERNALS

Option	Description
`--strip-unneeded`	Removes all symbols that are not necessary to relocate the code.
`--target=bfdname`	Sets both the input format and output format to the specified *bfdname*. Also see `--input-target` and `--output-target`.
`-v`	Same as `--verbose`.
`--verbose`	Produces a more verbose output by listing all the files stripped.
`-x`	Same as `--discard-all`.
`-X`	Same as `--discard-locals`.

Table 12-5. *The Command-Line Options for* `strip` (continued)

Listing Shared Library Dependencies

The `ldd` utility reads through the object files in the binary executable or shared library named on the command line and lists all the shared library dependencies. For example, the following command lists the shared libraries used by the bash shell program on a Linux system:

```
$ ldd /bin/bash
    libtermcap.so.2 => /lib/libtermcap.so.2 (0x40027000)
    libdl.so.2 => /lib/libdl.so.2 (0x4002b000)
    libc.so.6 => /lib/libc.so.6 (0x4002f000)
    /lib/ld-linux.so.2 => /lib/ld-linux.so.2 (0x40000000)
```

The first name listed on each line is the name of a shared library as it appears inside the program, and the second is the path name of the actual library as it was found on the disk. The address at which the library has been loaded into memory appears at the end of the line. The bash shell uses the functions in `libtermcap` to display text on the screen, and it uses `libdl` to load and execute functions in a shared library. The library `libc` is the standard C function library. The file named `ld-linux.so` is the program `ld.so`, which is the helper program for shared libraries and does the actual job of loading and executing shared libraries.

It is convenient to use `ldd` to determine exactly which version of a shared library is being used by a program. Another reason for using `ldd` is to determine any unresolved references to shared libraries. For example, if the program `stwohellos` from Chapter 4 were to compile correctly, but the shared library compiled with it was not installed properly, the output from `ldd` would look like the following:

```
$ ldd stwohellos
    shello.so => not found
    libc.so.6 => /lib/libc.so.6 (0x40027000)
    libgcc_s.so.1 => /usr/lib/libgcc_s.so.1 (0x4015d000)
    /lib/ld-linux.so.2 => /lib/ld-linux.so.2 (0x40000000)
```

Displaying the Internals of an Object File

The `objdump` utility can be used to extract information from object files, static libraries, and shared libraries and then list this information in a human-readable form. It can be used to dump the information from several different formats of object files. To determine the object file formats recognized by `objdump`, enter the following command:

```
$ objdump -i
```

When executing `objdump` to extract information from a file, you must use one or more of the options from Table 12-6 (each of which has both a short and long form) to specify what information is to be extracted. Table 12-7 lists additional options that can be used to refine the selection of incoming data or to format the output. For example, to list both the file header and the section headers from the object file named `helloworld.o`, and to assume the input code is big endian, enter the following command:

```
$ objdump -f -h -EB helloworld.o
```

Short	Long	Displays
-a	--archive-headers	Archive header information
-d	--disassemble	Assembly language of the executable code
-D	--disassemble-all	Assembly language of the executable code and data
-f	--file-headers	Contents of the overall file headers
-g	--debugging	Debugging information

Table 12-6. *Short and Long Forms of Dump Selection Options for* `objdump`

Short	Long	Displays
-G	--stabs	Raw form of any STABS information
-h	--section-headers	Contents of the section headers
-H	--help	This list of options
-i	--info	A list of object formats and architectures supported
-p	--private-headers	File header contents that are specific to the object format
-r	--reloc	Relocation information
-R	--dynamic-reloc	Dynamic relocation information
-S	--source	Assembly language of the executable with source code intermixed
-s	--full-contents	Assembly languages of all code with source code intermixed
-t	--syms	Contents of the symbol table
-T	--dynamic-syms	Contents of the dynamic symbol table
-V	--version	Version information
-x	--all-headers	Contents of all headers

Table 12-6. *Short and Long Forms of Dump Selection Options for* objdump *(continued)*

Option	Description
--adjust-vma=*offset*	Adds the specified *offset* value to all the displayed section addresses.
--architecture=*machine*	Specifies the format of the input object file in terms of the hardware. To determine the architecture types available, enter objdump -i.
-b *bfdname*	Same as --target.
-C *type*	Same as --demangle.

Table 12-7. *Modifier Command-Line Options for* objdump

Option	Description
`--demangle=type`	The symbols are assumed to be of the specified type and demangled back to the form they appeared in the source code. The valid types are `auto`, `gnu`, `lucid`, `arm`, `hp`, `edg`, `gnu-v3`, `java`, `gnat`, and `compaq`.
`--disassembler-options=op`	The specified *op* is one or more options to be passed to the disassembler.
`--disassemble-zeroes`	Specifies to not skip blocks of zeroes when disassembling code.
`-EB`	Same as `--endian=big`.
`-EL`	Same as `--endian=little`.
`--endian=which`	Specifies whether the input object file is big endian or little endian. The word `little` specifies little endian and `big` specifies big endian.
`--file-start-context`	When the `-S` option is used, this option will include the context information from the start of the file.
`-j name`	Same as `--section`.
`-l`	Same as `--line-numbers`.
`--line-numbers`	Includes the line numbers and file names in the output.
`-M`	Same as `-disassembler-options`.
`-m machine`	Same as `-architecture`.
`--prefix-addresses`	Prints the entire address information adjacent to each disassembled instruction.
`--section=name`	Limits the displayed information to the named section of the object file.
`--show-raw-insn`	Displays hexadecimal opcodes along with the mnemonic assembly language instructions.
`--start-address=address`	Only processes data with an address greater than the specified *address* value.

Table 12-7. *Modifier Command-Line Options for* `objdump` (continued)

Option	Description
`--stop-address=address`	Only processes data with an address less than the specified *address* value.
`--target bfdname`	Specifies the format of the input object file. To determine the formats available, enter the command `objdump -i`.
`-w`	Same as `--wide`.
`--wide`	Formats the output for more than 80 columns.
`-z`	Same as `--disassemble-zeroes`.

Table 12-7. *Modifier Command-Line Options for `objdump` (continued)*

The Complete
Reference

Chapter 13

Using the
GNU Debugger

The utility program gdb is the GNU debugger. It is a command-line debugger that can be used to completely control and examine a running process.

Any program will respond to the commands issued to it from gdb, but only those that have been compiled and linked with the appropriate options to contain information relating to the original source code can provide you with the information you need to trace the flow of execution. Probably the simplest way of starting an interactive debug session is to name the program on the command line as gdb is started, although the same result can be achieved by starting the debugger and loading the program later. The debugger can also be instructed to attach itself to a running program, making it possible to examine the processing inside a program that does strange things only after it has been running for a time. A third use of gdb is to perform a postmortem on a program that has crashed and determine the cause of the crash.

Debugging Information Formats

To be able to debug a program, it is necessary that information about the program be included in the object file. Using this information, the debugger can relate the executable code to the source code and deliver information about the program in a form that you can read to determine exactly what the program is doing. Without this information, all the debugger knows is the absolute binary addresses and the machine language opcodes that are being executed—it is very difficult for you to relate this to the source code of your program.

More than one format exists for storing this information in an object file. For a debugger to be able to work, it must understand the format of the debugging data. Fortunately the gdb debugger understands more that one of these formats, and it also understands some special extensions that can be inserted into the code by gcc.

STABS

The STABS format for debugging information was originally devised for use by a Pascal language debugger, but the format has proven to be quite useful and has become fairly widespread.

The gcc compiler adds STABS (symbol table) debugging information to the assembly language code it generates, and this information is then included with the object code produced by the assembler. The assembler adds the STABS information to the symbol table and string table appended to the end of each .o file. The linker combines the .o files into an executable file, combining the tables into a single symbol table, which is used by the debugger to identify sections of executable code.

The three assembler directives used to create the symbol tables take the following forms:

```
.stabs "name:symdesc=typeinfo",type,other,description,value
.stabn type,other,description,value
.stabd type,other,description
```

Each directive has a `type` field that provides basic information (such as whether this directive is a new definition or a reference to an existing definition). The `type` field also indicates the meaning of the content of the `other` and `description` fields. The `value` field is the value assigned to the definition.

The `.stabs` directive defines a character string that goes in the symbol table. Inside the quotes, `name` is the name by which the symbol is inserted into the table. The `symdesc` is a single character (such as `F` for a global function, `G` for a global variable, or `t` for a type name) and a type number (which can actually be two numbers) that either define the symbol as a new type or refer to a previously defined type number. The `typeinfo` provides further information about the type, such as numeric ranges or size.

The `.stabn` directive defines a numeric value.

The `.stabd` directive defines a tag for the current address (the address at the location of the directive). It has no value specified for it because that can be derived from the location of the directive.

You can view a document describing the entire STABS format at http://sources.redhat.com/gdb/onlinedocs/stabs.html.

DWARF

The DWARF format of debugging information is well into its second generation, called DWARF2, and work is proceeding on the DWARF3 standard. Some encoding differences exist among the versions such that they are not compatible with one another, but the `gdb` debugger recognizes and reads both the original DWARF and DWARF2.

The debug information is generated in the assembly language in special sections of code with names such as `.debug_pubnames`, `.debug_aranges`, `.debug_info`, or just `.debug`. These special sections contain data and executable code that can be used to identify and extract information from a running program. The linker groups the ones with the same section names into single blocks in the object code, which can be used to identify the location of items and establish relationships between object code addresses and lines of source code.

You can view the DWARF2 specification at http://services.worldnet.fr/~stcarrez/dwarf2.pdf.

COFF

The Common Object File Format (COFF), sometimes called the *a.out* format, is a standard format of object files on UNIX System V and many of its derivative systems. This is the object file format adopted by Microsoft for DOS and Windows. The Linux variant of this format is called ELF.

The COFF format doesn't contain information specifically designed for debugging—the information is primarily for linking—but it does contain much of the information required by a debugger. The symbol table contains every relocatable symbol, and the relocation table contains references to the symbol table entries and information on the data types. It also contains line number information that can be used to associate the binary code with the original source code. The symbol table contains a full description of each symbol, along with size and descriptive information.

The COFF format divides the object into sections. The `.text` section contains executable code, the `.data` section contains variables with initial values, and the `.bss` section contains uninitialized data. The fundamental reason for this division is that if more than one instance of a program is running, they can share the same `.text` section in memory, the `.data` section can be loaded into memory as a single block to set all initial values, and the `.bss` section can exist in the file as only a single number (the size) and can be expanded to the correct size when the program is loaded.

The information contained in this format is not as extensive as that contained in STABS or DWARF, so you will often see a basic COFF file with STABS or DWARF information inserted into it to allow for more extensive debugging.

XCOFF

The XCOFF object file format is an extension of the basic COFF format. The XCOFF format provides tables and references appropriate for dynamic linking. Also, XCOFF can contain object code for either the 32-bit or 64-bit model.

The fundamental format is the same as COFF, but the XCOFF format also includes STABS strings stored in a `.debug` section rather than the COFF approach of storing them in a string table. That is, the XCOFF format is a blend of COFF and STABS, with some of the COFF pieces left out so there is no duplication of data, as is required when STABS is inserted into the COFF format.

Compiling a Program for Debugging

For the debugger to be able to associate the binary executable code with the source code—which is a requirement for displaying information in a human-readable form—the compiler must be instructed to include information in the object code. You can do this by setting command-line options to specify the amount and type of information to be included.

The amount of included information is controlled by a level number, as shown in Table 13-1. The level number is set in conjunction with the option flags, as shown in Table 13-2.

The format of the debugging information in the object file varies with the native format of the object code for each platform. The gdb debugger recognizes and can work with several different formats. Systems that use the STABS format generally contain extra debugging information that is recognized only by gdb.

Table 13-2 lists the gcc command-line options that can be used to instruct the compiler to insert debugging information in the object code. It is possible to use the -O optimization option along with a debugging option, but you should be aware that optimization can rearrange (and even remove) code, causing it to be difficult to follow the logic flow of

Level	Description
1	This level inserts the minimum amount of information into the object code. There is enough information to trace function calls and examine global variables, but there is no information relating executable code to source code, nor is there sufficient information to examine local variables.
2	This is the default level. This level includes all of the level 1 information, and it adds the information necessary to relate source code lines to the executable code as well as the names and locations of local variables.
3	This level includes all the level 1 and level 2 information, and it adds extra information, including the preprocessor macro definitions.

Table 13-1.   *The Three Levels of Debugging Information in an Object File*

Option	Description
-g[level]	Produces debugging information in a format that is native for the system. The GNU debugger can work with this format, as can other debuggers. On systems that use the STABS format, this option will produce extra information that can only be used by gdb and could possibly cause other debuggers to fail. The optional-level number defaults to 2.
-ggdb[level]	Produces debugging information in the default format and includes the gdb extensions if possible. The information is produced in the best format available—the native format is used if neither STABS nor DWARF2 is available.
-gstabs[level]	Produces debugging information in the STABS format (if available).
-gstabs+	Produces debugging information in the STABS format (if available) and adds the extensions understood only by the gdb debugger. These extensions may cause other debuggers to fail.

Table 13-2.   *The List of gcc Options Used to Insert Debugging Information*

Option	Description
-gcoff[level]	Produces object code and debugging information in the COFF format (if available). This format is used most often on System V prior to Release 4.
-gxcoff[level]	Produces object code and debugging information in the XCOFF format (if available).
-gxcoff+	Produces object code and debugging information in the XCOFF format (if available) and adds the extensions understood only by the gdb debugger. This format may cause non-GNU debuggers and linkers to fail.
-gdwarf	Produces debugging information in the DWARF version 1 format (if available). This is the format used on most System V Release 4 systems.
-gdwarf+	Produces debugging information in the DWARF version 1 format (if available) and adds the extensions understood only by the gdb debugger. This format may cause non-GNU debuggers and linkers to fail.
-gdwarf-2	Produces debugging information in the DWARF version 2 format (if available).
-gvms[level]	Produces debugging information in the VMS debug format (if available). This is the format used on DEC VMS systems.

Table 13-2. *The List of* gcc *Options Used to Insert Debugging Information* (continued)

your program. However, situations can arise where it is appropriate to debug an optimized version of the program.

Some of the command-line options in Table 13-2 allow you to add a level number, and some don't. For the ones that don't, you can still specify the level by using a separate -g option. For example, to specify -gstabs+ and set the level to 3, use the following sequence of options:

```
$ gcc -g3 -gstabs+ ...
```

Loading a Program into the Debugger

Naming a program on the gdb command line is sufficient for the program to be loaded into memory and prepared for debugging. The program is loaded but does not start running until you command it to do so. This pause gives you the opportunity to set up some breakpoints (places at which the running program will halt) and make other preparations, such as specifying variables that are to have their values displayed as you step through the program.

The following is an example of running a program with the debugger that demonstrates how the interface works as well as how a set of basic commands can be used to monitor the running of a program. The C program named fibonacci.c displays the first 20 terms of the Fibonacci sequence:

```c
/* fibonacci.c */

int current;
int next;
int nextnext;

void calcnext();
void setstart();

int main(int argc,char *argv[])
{
    int i;

    setstart();
    for(i=0; i<20; i++) {
        printf("%2d: %d\n",i+1,current);
        calcnext();
    }
    return(0);
}
void setstart()
{
    current = 0;
    next = 1;
}
void calcnext()
{
    nextnext = current + next;
    current = next;
    next = nextnext;
}
```

To compile the program so it will include debugging information, it is only necessary to use the -g option, as follows:

```
$ gcc -g fibonacci.c -o fibonacci
```

It is not necessary for gdb to have access to the source file to be able to produce diagnostic information because everything needed is included as part of the object file. However, if the source is found when the debugger starts, checks are made to verify that the source file correctly matches the object file. If a mismatch is suspected, a warning message is displayed.

The following simple debug session loads the program, sets a breakpoint at the entry to the function main(), and sets up the continuous display of two variables. The program is then started running, which it does until it reaches the breakpoint, where the step and next commands are used to execute the program one line at a time:

```
$ gdb fibonacci
(gdb) break main
Breakpoint 1 at 0x80483a0: file fibonacci.c, line 14.
(gdb) display current
(gdb) display next
(gdb) run
Starting program: /home/fred/progs/fibonacci

Breakpoint 1, main (argc=1, argv=0xbffffa9c) at fibonacci.c:14
14          setstart();
2: next = 0
1: current = 0
(gdb) step
setstart () at fibonacci.c:23
23          current = 0;
2: next = 0
1: current = 0
(gdb) step
24          next = 1;
2: next = 0
1: current = 0
(gdb) step
25  }
2: next = 1
1: current = 0
(gdb) step
main (argc=1, argv=0xbffffa9c) at fibonacci.c:15
```

```
15        for(i=0; i<20; i++) {
2: next = 1
1: current = 0
(gdb) step
16            printf("%2d: %d\n",i+1,current);
2: next = 1
1: current = 0
(gdb) next
17            calcnext();
2: next = 1
1: current = 0
(gdb) step
calcnext () at fibonacci.c:28
28      nextnext = current + next;
2: next = 1
1: current = 0
(gdb) step
29      current = next;
2: next = 1
1: current = 0
(gdb) step
30      next = nextnext;
2: next = 1
1: current = 1
(gdb) step
31  }
2: next = 1
1: current = 1
(gdb) bt
#0  calcnext () at fibonacci.c:31
#1  0x080483d4 in main (argc=1, argv=0xbffffa9c) at fibonacci.c:17
#2  0x40042316 in __libc_start_main (main=0x8048390 <main>, argc=1,
    ubp_av=0xbffffa9c, init=0x8048230 <_init>, fini=0x8048460
<_fini>,
    rtld_fini=0x4000d2fc <_dl_fini>, stack_end=0xbffffa8c)
    at ../sysdeps/generic/libc-start.c:129
(gdb) quit
The program is running.  Exit anyway? (y or n) y
$
```

The first action performed by gdb is the loading of the executable program. The debugger then halts and waits for you to enter a command. The loaded program is not running. At the time the program is loaded, gdb extracts the debugging information and builds its own set of internal tables, which means the debugger knows the name and location of everything (assuming it was compiled and linked with one of the -g options) and is ready for analysis.

Before the program is started running, the display command is used to instruct the debugger to display the names and values of the variables named current and next. These variables will be displayed automatically each time the program stops.

If you were to start the program running at this point, the program would simply run to its conclusion and halt without you being able to intervene. The purpose of a debugger is to examine the execution, which means it is necessary to pick a point at which you would like to halt the program so you can look around and step through instructions. In this example the command break main sets a breakpoint at the entry point of the function named main(). The debugger acknowledges the command by listing the address and line number at which the breakpoint has been set. The source code of line 14 is displayed, which is the call to the function setstart() used to set the two initial values of the Fibonacci sequence.

The run command starts the program. Execution begins with the initialization code inserted into every program by gcc. The initilization code runs until it eventually calls main(). As soon as the code corresponding with line 14 of the source code is reached, the program is frozen, the two values are displayed, and gdb issues a prompt for a new command.

The step command executes one line of source code. At the assembly language level this is often more than one instruction, but gdb executes as many instructions as necessary to complete all the instructions created from a single line of source. In this example, the first step command executes the call to the function setstart() and then stops on the first line of code in the function, which is line 23 in the source file. The following two step commands execute the two statements inside the function, which sets current and next to the initial values of 1 and 0, respectively. The next step command executes the return from the function and stops at the top of the for loop.

Once the step statement enters the top of the loop, the program is halted on the call to the printf() function. If another step statement were used at this point, execution would enter the printf() function, which is probably not what you intend to have happen. Unless you have gone to the special effort required to compiled the printf() function with one of the -g options, there will be no debugging information included and, although the debugger can step through the function, there is no possibility of displaying values or the source code. Instead of using step, the command next is used to execute the entire function call as a single line of code and stop on the line following the call.

A series of step statements is used to execute the statements through iterations of the loop. This procedure can be continued while you examine the actions of the program to try to discover places where calculations go amiss. You can interactively verify that things are being done the way you envisioned them when you wrote the program.

In this example, the `bt` command is used to generate a backtrace of function calls, which lists the execution path followed by the program to get to the current location. The information found in the backtrace includes not only the names of the functions, but the names and values of the arguments passed to each one and the source code file in which each one is found.

Performing a Postmortem

On a UNIX system, a program that crashes will trigger a function of the operating system that dumps a copy of the program's image in memory to a file named `core`. If the program has been compiled with the `-g` option, it is a relatively simple matter to determine exactly where in the code the crash occurred.

The following program will crash every time it runs because it attempts to store information at the address zero in memory, which is a forbidden area to any program:

```
/* falldown.c */

char **nowhere;
void setbad();

int main(int argc,char *argv[])
{
    setbad();
    printf("%s\n",*nowhere);
}
void setbad()
{
    nowhere = 0;
    *nowhere = "This is a string\n";
}
```

The program can be compiled and run with the following commands, producing a core file containing an image of the running program:

```
$ gcc -g falldown.c -o falldown
$ falldown
Segmentation fault (core dumped)
```

To instruct gdb to load both the program and the core file it dumped, enter the following command:

```
$ gdb falldown core
```

In most cases, this command will provide you with all the information you need because it immediately lists the line of code being executed at the point at which the program died. The following debug session demonstrates the information displayed by gdb as well as how you can use other commands to extract more information if you need it:

```
$ gdb falldown core
Core was generated by `falldown'.
Program terminated with signal 11, Segmentation fault.
Reading symbols from /lib/libc.so.6...done.
Loaded symbols for /lib/libc.so.6
Reading symbols from /lib/ld-linux.so.2...done.
Loaded symbols for /lib/ld-linux.so.2
#0  0x080483d0 in setbad () at falldown.c:14
14        *nowhere = "This is a string\n";
(gdb) print nowhere
$1 = (char **) 0x0
(gdb) bt
#0  0x080483d0 in setbad () at falldown.c:14
#1  0x080483a5 in main (argc=1, argv=0xbffffa8c) at falldown.c:8
#2  0x40042316 in __libc_start_main (main=0x8048390 <main>, argc=1,
    ubp_av=0xbffffa8c, init=0x8048230 <_init>, fini=0x8048410
<_fini>,
    rtld_fini=0x4000d2fc <_dl_fini>, stack_end=0xbffffa7c)
    at ../sysdeps/generic/libc-start.c:129
(gdb) quit
$
```

In this example, the offending line of code (the one where the address of a string is stored into the absolute address zero), including the name of the function and the source file it is found in, is printed out. The print command is used to verify that the pointer nowhere is set to an invalid address, and the bt command is used to generate a backtrace to demonstrate how the program got itself into this situation. A number of other commands are available that can be used to examine the contents of variables, but you will usually find that you have enough information to fix the problem immediately.

Attaching the Debugger to a Running Program

The ability to attach the debugger to a running process can be very useful. If, for example, a program goes into an unresponsive loop after running for some period of time, you can attach gdb to it and find out exactly where the program is looping. Another situation is an interactive program that suddenly starts doing things it shouldn't do—you can attach the debugger and trace the cause of the strange actions.

There are two prerequisites for attaching the debugger to a running process. First, the process must have been compiled with some form of the -g option. Second, you must determine the Process ID (PID) number of the running process. If you don't already know the PID, you can use the ps command to discover it. The command-line arguments for the ps command vary from one system to the next because different operating systems provide information about running processes in different forms, but the following form is typical and determines the PID of the process named looper is 29627:

```
$ ps ax | grep looper
29627 pts/4     R        1.58 looper
32298 pts/4     S        0:00 grep looper
```

The output from the ps command also indicates that the looper process is active (R means running). In fact, the program looper.c was written specifically to run in a continuous loop to demonstrate the ability of gdb to attach itself to a process:

```
/* looper.c */
void goaround(int);
int main(int argc,char *argv[])
{
    printf("started\n");
    goaround(20);
    printf("done\n");
}
void goaround(int counter)
{
    int i = 0;

    while(i < counter) {
        if(i++ == 17)
            i = 10;
    }
}
```

The mainline of the program looper calls the function goaround(), which never returns because the value of i never reaches the value of counter. The program can be compiled with debugging information included by using the following command:

```
$ gcc -g looper.c -o looper
```

To start the program running in the background, enter the following command:

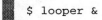

```
$ looper &
```

The shell program used to start the program will usually display the PID number of the new process, but if it does not, you can use ps to determine the number. The following sequence demonstrates how to attach the debugger to the process and use it to discover the problem. The command line specifies the name of the binary file on disk and the PID:

```
$ gdb looper 29627
Attaching to program: /home/fred/looper, process 29627
Reading symbols from /lib/libc.so.6...done.
Loaded symbols for /lib/libc.so.6
Reading symbols from /lib/ld-linux.so.2...done.
Loaded symbols for /lib/ld-linux.so.2
0x080483ea in goaround (counter=20) at looper.c:14
14              if(i++ == 17)
(gdb) display i
1: i = 14
(gdb) step
13      while(i < counter) {
1: i = 15
(gdb) step
14              if(i++ == 17)
1: i = 15
(gdb) step
13      while(i < counter) {
1: i = 16
(gdb) step
14              if(i++ == 17)
1: i = 16
(gdb) step
13      while(i < counter) {
1: i = 17
(gdb) step
14              if(i++ == 17)
1: i = 17
(gdb) step
15                  i = 10;
1: i = 18
(gdb) step
```

```
13        while(i < counter) {
1: i = 10
(gdb) step
14            if(i++ == 17)
1: i = 10
(gdb) step
13        while(i < counter) {
1: i = 11
(gdb) quit
The program is running.  Quit anyway (and detach it)? (y or n) y
Detaching from program: /home/fred/looper, process 29627
$
```

At the beginning, the debugger reads the binary file from disk and loads the symbol table information from the program and, as indicated by the first few lines of output, the symbol table from the libraries used by the program. If any of the libraries have been compiled with debugging information included, it would be possible to trace through them if necessary, but this simple demonstration only traces the loop in the goaround() function.

The gdb debugger then attaches itself to the process and freezes at its current location, displaying the source code text and line number. At this point you are free to set breakpoints, examine variables, or perform any other normal debugging activity. In this example a display command is used to instruct gdb to display the value of i with the execution of each instruction. A series of step commands is used to track the value through a few iterations of the loop, exposing the fact that the value of i is reset in such a way that the loop will never exit.

At the end of the session, by using the quit command, the debugger detaches itself from the process and allows the process to keep running. In this example, as soon as gdb detaches itself, the program will continue with its looping until halted in some other way. The process is completely normal again and can be reattached to gdb at any time. The looper process could have been halted by entering a kill command before the quit command.

Command Summary

The gdb debugger has an enormous number of commands available. To see them, you only need to enter help at the gdb prompt. You will be shown a list of categories from which to choose. Some of these categories contain lists of command descriptions, where others contain subcategory names containing further lists.

Table 13-3 lists some of the more useful commands, which are all you will need for most debugging sessions.

Command	Description
awatch	Sets a watch point so that execution will stop whenever the value in the named location is either read from or written to. Also see rwatch and watch.
backtrace	Prints a backtrace of all stack frames showing the function calls and argument values that brought the program to this location. This command has the short form bt.
break	Sets a breakpoint that stops execution at the specified line number or function name.
clear	Clears the breakpoint at the line number or function that was initially set by the break command.
continue	Continues execution of a program that has been halted by the debugger.
Ctrl-C	Interrupts a running program just as if a breakpoint were hit at the current line.
disable	Disables the breakpoints listed by number.
display	Displays the value of the specified expression each time the program is halted.
enable	Enables the breakpoints listed by number.
finish	Continues execution of a program that has been halted by the debugger and continues until the current function returns.
ignore	Sets the ignore count of a breakpoint. For example, the command ignore 4 23 will require that breakpoint number 4 be hit 23 times before it actually breaks.
info breakpoints	Lists the status and description, including the number, of all breakpoints.
info display	Lists the status and description, including the number, of the previously defined display commands.
kill	Kills the running of the current process.

Table 13-3. *Some of the More Useful Commands of* gdb

Command	Description
list	Lists ten lines of code. If no other arguments are on the command line, the ten lines begin with the current location. If a function is named, the ten lines start with the beginning of the function. If a line number is specified, that line number will be the one in the center of the listing.
load	Dynamically loads the named executable file into gdb and prepares it for debugging.
next	Continues execution of a program that has been halted and executes all the instructions corresponding to a single line of source code, but treats a call to a function as one line of code and doesn't stop until it returns.
nexti	Continues execution of a program that has been halted and executes a single assembly language instruction, but treats a call to a function as one instruction and doesn't stop until it returns.
print	Immediately displays the value of the specified expression.
ptype	Prints the type of the named item.
return	Forces an immediate return from the current function.
run	Starts the program into execution from its beginning.
rwatch	Sets a watch point so that execution will stop whenever the value in the named location is read. Also see awatch and watch.
set	Sets the named variable to the expression. For example, set nval=54 will store the value 54 into the memory location named nval.
step	Continues execution of a program that has been halted and executes all the instructions corresponding to a single line of source code. It will step into a called function.

Table 13-3.   *Some of the More Useful Commands of* gdb (continued)

Command	Description
stepi	Continues execution of a program that has been halted and executes a single assembly language statement. It will step into a called function.
txbreak	Sets a temporary breakpoint (works only one time) at the exit point of the current function. Also see xbreak.
undisplay	Deletes the display expression listed by number.
watch	Sets a watch point so that execution will stop whenever the value in the named location is written. Also see rwatch and awatch.
whatis	Prints the data type and the value of the specified expression.
xbreak	Sets a breakpoint at the exit point of the current function. Also see txbreak.

Table 13-3. *Some of the More Useful Commands of* gdb (continued)

The Complete Reference

Chapter 14

Make and Autoconf

This chapter is an introduction to the operation of the make utility, which can be used to manage a software-development project, and Autoconf, which can be used to configure and package open source software for release and distribution. This chapter is not a complete tutorial on all the features of these utilities, but there is enough here to make it fairly easy for a programmer to extrapolate what is needed to complete a development environment. The basic purpose and general operation of each one are exposed.

Make

The make utility is, by far, the most used tool in software development. The fundamental idea behind make is quite simple: examine the source and object files to determine which source files need to be recompiled to create new object files. It is assumed by make that any source file that is newer than the object file produced from it has been modified and needs to be compiled. Everything make does is based on this one fundamental operation. The relationship of an object file to the source file used to produce it is known as a *dependency*. The object file produced by the commands associated with a dependency is known as the *target*.

To determine the dependencies, make reads a script that defines them. The script is normally named makefile or Makefile. The script contains the dependencies along with the commands that will translate source into object files. For example, the following makefile entry specifies that the program named frammis is dependent on the source file frammis.c, and it specifies the exact gcc command used to create the target, frammis:

```
frammis: frammis.c
    gcc frammis.c -o frammis
```

It should be pointed out that make dates from the early days of UNIX, and it retains an arcane quirk about formatting commands that follow a dependency line—the command lines *must* be indented with a tab character. The tab character, even though invisible on the screen or when printed, is part of the syntax of the makefile script. If you fail to use a tab (or use spaces instead), you will get a "missing separator" message, which, fortunately, specifies the line number of the missing tab.

It is common to have one file depend on a file produced from another dependency. For example, the following set of dependencies compiles the program frammis:

```
frammis: frammis.o
    gcc frammis.o -o frammis

frammis.o: frammis.c
    gcc -c frammis.c -o frammis.o
```

In this example, the executable program `frammis` depends on `frammis.o`, which, in turn, is defined as depending on `frammis.c`. When `make` starts running, it begins by reading the entire makefile and constructing an internal tree from the dependency chains, with the first dependency in the file being the root of the tree. In this example, the root is the `frammis` dependency, with the `frammis.o` dependency beneath it in the tree. Once the tree is constructed, the program begins at the root of the tree and descends the tree to the lowest level, then works its way back up, executing the commands that it determines should be executed until it has reached the root of the tree and all dependencies have been satisfied.

It should be pointed out that `make` constructs and executes only one internal tree, so it is possible to have dependencies defined in the file that are never executed because they are not linked, through dependencies, to the first dependency in the file. This is not as much of a limitation as it may seem at first, because you can always insert a special dependency that includes all the other dependencies, as in the following example, where `all` is used as a dummy target:

```
all: frammis cooker

frammis: frammis.c frammis.h
    gcc frammis.c -o frammis

cooker: cooker.c cooker.h
    gcc cooker.c -o cooker
```

The target named `all` depends on `frammis` and `cooker`. Although the `all` target has two dependencies, it has no commands associated with it, but that's okay because the only purpose is to force the dependencies to be satisfied. The internal `make` tree has `all` as its root and `cooker` and `frammis` as the tree nodes beneath it.

Items other than dependencies and their associated commands can be included in a makefile, but they are all there for the sole purpose of defining the dependencies and commands.

A makefile is invoked with the following simple command:

```
$ make
```

By default, `make` looks in the current directory first for a file named `makefile`. Then, if `makefile` is not found, it looks for a file named `Makefile`. If neither of these are found, no action is taken. You can optionally specify the name of the file on the command line as follows:

```
$ make -f mymakefile.text
```

Internal Definitions

For convenience in constructing rules based on targets and dependencies, it is possible to use predefined macros and establish implicit rules that make can use to convert one file type to another.

Macros

A macro can be defined in one of three different ways. The following target in a makefile demonstrates the definition and use of macros:

```
showmacros:
    echo HOME is $(HOME)    # defined as an environment variable
    echo COMPILE.f is $(COMPILE.f) #defined as a makefile default
    echo HERBERT is $(HERBERT)   # defined locally in the makefile
```

While reading a makefile, whenever make encounters a # character, the rest of the line is considered a comment and is ignored.

The target named showmacros will always execute its associated commands because no dependencies are listed for it, and the default is to assume the target must be made. The content of a variable can be extracted and used in statements by preceding it with a dollar ($) character and enclosing it in parentheses. In this example, the value of HOME is taken from the setting of your environment variable, the value of COMPILE.f is a name that is defined by GNU make itself, and HERBERT is defined somewhere in the makefile with a line like the following:

```
HERBERT=Herbivore
```

The output from the makefile looks like this:

```
echo HOME is /home/arthur
HOME is /home/arthur
echo COMPILE.f is f77    -c
COMPILE.f is f77 -c
echo HERBERT is herbivore
HERBERT is herbivore
```

Each of the echo commands is displayed before the output it produces because the default mode of make is to echo each command before it is executed.

Suffix Rules

Rules can be specified to recognize file types by their name suffixes and automatically translate one file type to another. The following example is a makefile that recognizes three suffixes and defines a pair of commands that will translate a file with one suffix into a new file with a target suffix:

```
all: hello.o hello.s

hello.o: hello.c
hello.s: hello.c

.SUFFIXES: .o .c .s

.c.o:
    gcc -c $<

.c.s:
    gcc -S $<
```

This makefile is designed to make two targets: one is hello.o, and the other is hello.s. Because the rules to make these targets have no commands associated with them, the three file suffixes recognized are .c, .o, and .s. The suffix rule named .c.o converts a file with a .c suffix into a file with a .o suffix, and the suffix rule .c.s has a command that will convert a file with a .c suffix into a file with a .s suffix. The special macro $< is a reference to the name of the file being used to construct the target. The result is the same as if the following had been included in the makefile:

```
hello.o: hello.c
    gcc -c hello.c
hello.s: hello.c
    gcc -S hello.c
```

Suffix rules can be, and usually are, a bit more complicated than the ones shown here, but you normally don't have to write them yourself. A large number of suffix rules are built into GNU make—enough that you only need to spell out the commands if you are doing something special.

Viewing the Definitions

Command-line options exist that make it possible for you to see the complete list of macros and suffix definitions that are defined when you run make. The -p option will cause the makefile to be read and executed as normal, but all the rules from the makefile, along with all the macros and suffix rules, are also listed. To see this entire list, enter the following:

```
$ make -p | more
```

To see the same list but prohibit the makefile commands from actually being executed, you can enter the command this way:

```
$ make -p -q | more
```

If you would rather see only the definitions that are built into GNU make without seeing any of the definitions from the local makefile, you can have make read an empty makefile this way:

```
$ make -p -f /dev/null | more
```

How to Write a Makefile

If you are new to writing makefiles, the best thing to do is copy an existing one and modify to it do what you would like it to do. After you do this for your first few makefiles, you begin to get the feel for the general form. If you want to learn enough about how make works to be able to write makefiles from scratch, you are going to need to spend some time researching and experimenting. It isn't that difficult, really, but it is different enough that it can be confusing until you get the hang of it.

You may want to create a skeleton makefile to be used as a starter kit each time you need to create a new makefile, but sadly there is no universal form that fits all occasions. The following is a somewhat generic example of a makefile that compiles two C programs and links them into executables:

```
CC=gcc
PROGS=howdy hello
CFLAGS=-Wall

all: $(PROGS)

howdy: howdy.c

hello: hello.c
    $(CC) $(CFLAGS) hello.c -o hello

clean:
    rm -f *.o
    rm -f *.so
    rm -f *.a
    rm -f $(PROGS)
```

The CC variable is set to gcc, and CFLAGS is set to -Wall. The list of target names is stored in the variable PROGS. This makefile compiles the two programs in exactly the same way, but one of them defaults to using the built-in command while the other uses an explicit command. The output from a successful make looks like the following:

```
gcc -Wall    howdy.c    -o howdy
gcc -Wall hello.c -o hello
```

There is a clean target that can be invoked at any time to remove all files generated by the makefile. The current set of commands doesn't leave any .o, .so, or .a files on disk, so those commands serve no purpose. However, the -f option instructs rm to not complain if the files are not present, and makefiles grow with a project and begin to produce all kinds of intermediate files. The make utility, by default, attempts to build the first target found in the file, but it can be made to build any one of the targets by naming it on the command line, as follows:

```
$ make clean
```

A bit of help is available from the compiler. Chapter 18 contains examples of using the compiler to produce dependency lists that can be inserted into a makefile.

The Options of Make

There are as many versions of make as there are of UNIX. All of them are fundamentally the same, but special features and characteristics have been added here and there. The GNU version of make has the advantage of being freely available in source code form and, although it contains extensions of its own, it is probably the best one to use when working with GCC. In particular, if you are going to be building GCC from source, it would be wise to begin by acquiring the binutils (which includes make and several other utilities) because they are guaranteed to be compatible with GCC. While many of the command-line options are universally recognized in all versions of make, the options known to GNU make are listed in Table 14-1.

Option	Description
--assume-old=*filename*	Specifies to not remake the named file regardless of its age, and not remake any other files based on a dependency on this file.

Table 14-1. *The Command-Line Options of make*

Option	Description
`--assume-new=filename`	Assumes that the specified file name is a new file and that every target depending on it must be rebuilt.
`-C directory`	Changes to the named directory before searching for files to determine dependencies.
`--directory=directory`	Same as `-C`.
`-d`	Same as `--debug=a`.
`--debug[=flags]`	Displays information about processing in a form that can be useful for debugging makefile errors. If no flags are specified, basic debugging information is displayed. The value of `flags` can be any combination of the following letters: a Displays all types of debugging information. This is a very verbose option. b Displays basic information, including a list of out-of-date targets and whether the commands were successful. i Displays information about the search for implicit rules for each target along with the information of the b flag. j Displays information on the invocation of subcommands. m The other options are disabled during the construction of makefiles by this makefile, but this flag enables any other flags during makefile generation. v Displays the information of the b flag and adds information about targets that did not require command execution.
`--dry-run`	Specifies to not execute any commands. Instead, this option lists all the commands that would be executed if this were not a dry run.
`-e`	Same as `--environment-overrides`.
`--environment-overrides`	Environment variables override variables defined inside the makefile.

Table 14-1.   *The Command-Line Options of* `make` (continued)

Option	Description
-f *filename*	Same as --file.
--file=*filename*	Uses the named file as the makefile instead of looking for a file named Makefile or makefile.
-h	Displays this list of options.
--help	Displays this list of options.
-i	Same as --ignore-errors.
-I *directory*	Same as --include-dir.
--ignore-errors	Processing normally stops at the first failure to make a target, but this option instructs make to continue by going to the next target.
--include-dir= *directory*	The named directory is searched for included makefiles.
-j *[number]*	Same as --jobs.
--jobs[=*number*]	Specifies the number of commands that can be executed simultaneously. If no number is specified, make runs as many as possible.
--just-print	Same as --dry-run.
-k	Same as --keep-going.
--keep-going	Specifies to continue to process as many targets as possible after an error. Nothing that depends on a failed target can be made, but the failure of one dependency does not prevent the others from being processed.
-l [*number*]	Same as --max-load.
--load-average[= *number*]	Same as --max-load.
--makefile=*filename*	Same as --file.

Table 14-1.   *The Command-Line Options of make* (continued)

Option	Description
--max-load[=*number*]	No new commands are to be started if there is at least one command running and the system load average is greater than the specified value (a floating-point number). If the number is not specified, no load limit is set.
-n	Same as --dry-run.
--new-file=*filename*	Same as --assume-new.
--no-builtin-rules	Eliminates the built-in rules and suffix definitions, although it is still possible to define your own. Default variable settings remain in effect.
--no-builtin-variables	Eliminates the built-in variables, although it is still possible to define your own. This option implies the --no-builtin-rules option.
--no-keep-going	Same as --stop.
--no-print-directory	Disables the setting of --print-directory.
-o *filename*	Same as --assume-old.
--old-file=*filename*	Same as --assume-old.
-p	Same as --print-data-base.
--print-data-base	Prints the rules and the values of variables. This information is a combination of the predefined values and the contents of the makefile.
--print-directory	Prints a message stating the name of the working directory both before and after executing the makefile. This only has meaning when makefiles are invoking one another.
-q	Specifies to not run any commands or produce any other form of output, except a return status code. A status code of 0 indicates that all targets are up to date and nothing would be compiled if make were run normally. A status code of 1 indicates that one or more of the targets need to be made. A status code of 2 indicates an error.

Table 14-1. *The Command-Line Options of* make (continued)

Option	Description
-quiet	Same as --silent.
-r	Same as --no-builtin-rules.
-R	Same as --no-builtin-variables.
--recon	Same as --dry-run.
-s	Same as --silent.
-S	Same as --stop.
--silent	Suppresses the normal printing of each command as it is executed.
--stop	Cancels the effect of the -keep-going option.
-t	Same as --touch.
--touch	Adjusts the date settings on the target files to bring them up to date, instead of actually executing the commands to create new versions of the files.
-v	Displays the version information and quits.
--version	Displays the version information and quits.
-w	Same as --print-directory.
-W *filename*	Same as --assume-new.
--warn-undefined-variable	Issues a warning for each reference to a variable that has not been defined.
--what-if=*filename*	Same as --assume-new.

Table 14-1.   *The Command-Line Options of make* (continued)

As one of its commands, one make process can invoke another. When this happens, the options that are set in the running of the parent make are passed on to the newly invoked child. Because of this situation, you will find options that restore default settings (which can be included as part of the command invoking the child make process). Another reason for options that restore the default setting is that the defaults can be modified by the MAKEFLAGS environment variable.

Autoconf

Autoconf is a utility that creates installation shell scripts to be included as part of the distributed source code. By default, the installation script is named `configure`. The `configure` script runs independently, so there is no need for Autoconf to be present on the system to be able to configure and install the software.

There is more than one advantage to using Autoconf to package and organize your distribution. The `configure` script will check for the presence or absence of certain system capabilities and will generate makefiles that reflect the current environment, which means your application can be immediately ported to virtually every version of UNIX. The procedure for installing software by using the `configure` script to set up the compilation has become common enough that most people already know the installation procedure. To install software that has been packaged using Autoconf, the procedure usually goes something like this:

```
$ ./configure
$ make
$ make install
```

Autoconf is actually a set of tools, as described in Table 14-2.

Tool	Description
autoconf	Using a template file as input, this tool generates a configuration script that will generate makefiles and installation scripts for the current (or the specified) platform.
autoheader	This program creates a template file containing #include statements to be used by the configure script created by autoconf.
autoreconf	This program updates the configuration scripts by running autoconf only in the directories where the date stamp on the files indicates that an update is necessary.
autoscan	This program scans the source files in the directory tree and generates a preliminary version of the template file that is the input file to autoconf.

Table 14-2.   *The Autoconf Family of Tools*

Tool	Description
autoupdate	This program updates an existing template file to match the syntax of the current version of autoconf.
ifnames	This program scans all the C source files and the names appearing on #if, #elif, #ifdef, and #ifndef preprocessor directives. The list is sorted, and each name includes a list of file names in which it was found.

Table 14-2. *The Autoconf Family of Tools* (continued)

Depending on the complexity of the application and the degree of portability you require, the process of creating the installation scripts can be quite simple or very involved. In any case, the following sequence can be used as a guide to the overall process. Change to the directory in which the source is stored and perform the following steps:

1. **Determine conditional compilation.** It is not uncommon to use preprocessor directives in header files to add to the portability of the software. To gather information on conditional compilation, run the ifnames program on all the source files that will be preprocessed. For example, the following command will process all the C source and header files:

   ```
   $ ifnames *.c *.h
   ```

   The output is a list of the conditionally defined macro names and the files in which they are defined.

2. **Create the configure.in file.** In the directory with the source code, run the autoscan utility with no arguments on the command line, as follows:

   ```
   $ autoscan
   ```

   This will produce a file named configure.scan, which is a skeleton of the file that will be used to construct the final configure script. Copy (or move) configure.scan to configure.in so the appropriate setup lines can be added to it.

3. **Edit the configure.in file.** This is the main part of the task. This file is made up of m4 macro directives to be parsed by Autoconf to generate the final configure script. If your installation becomes more complex than can be handled by the macros, this script can also include shell script fragments that will be copied directly into the final configure script.

The original `configure.in` script contains many of the macros you will need in your final version, and it also contains a number of descriptive comments (which begin with a hash character). It is a good idea to add further comments as you change the information in this file. Table 14-3 contains descriptions of the information you will need to supply for the various macros. Each macro contains a list of comma-separated items in the following format:

```
AC_CHECK_LIB(dl, dlopen, socket)
```

There must be no space between the macro name and the opening parentheses. Arguments may optionally be enclosed in square brackets ([and]) and must be so enclosed if an argument is more than one line long.

Macro	Description
AC_C_CHAR_UNSIGNED	This macro checks the default char data type and defines the macro __CHAR_UNSIGNED__ if it is unsigned.
AC_C_CONST	This macro checks the way the C compiler handles the const keyword and redefines it if necessary.
AC_CHECK_FUNCS	This macro verifies the presence of the functions named in the space-separated list.
AC_CHECK_HEADERS	This macro checks for the presence of one or more header files specified in a space-separated list.
AC_CHECK_LIB	This macro checks for the presence of the named libraries. A library name is specified in its short form, and a function that is a library member must also be specified for testing. For example, the libcfont library must contain the function bdf if AC_CHECK_LIB(cfont, bdf) is specified.
AC_CONFIG_AUX_DIR	This macro specifies the name of the directory that contains install-sh, config.sub, and config.guess. The default is usually correct, but this macro can be used to specify either an absolute or relative path.

Table 14-3.   *The m4 Macros Used in the* `configure.in` *Script*

Macro	Description
AC_CONFIG_HEADER	This macro composes header files containing #define directives. The name of the file to be created is followed by a colon and the name of an input file supplying the directives. For example, config.h is created from the contents of config.in with AC_CONFIG_HEADER(config.h: config.in).
AC_CONFIG_SUBDIRS	This macro specifies a list of directories that are expected to contain configure scripts that are to be run by the one being produced here. The directory names are separated by spaces.
AC_FUNC_MEMCMP	This macro verifies that memcmp() operates correctly on 8-bit boundaries.
AC_FUNC_STRFTIME	This macro checks the correctness of the operation of the strftime() function.
AC_FUNC_VPRINTF	This macro checks for the presence of vprintf().
AC_HEADER_STDC	This macro checks whether the system has the standard C headers.
AC_HEADER_SYS_WAIT	This macro checks for the presence of the POSIX-compliant header sys/wait.h.
AC_HEADER_TIME	This macro verifies that both time.h and sys/time.h can be included in the same compilation unit.
AC_INIT	This macro must come first. It contains the name of a uniquely named file as a safety check to verify that the user is running the script in the correct directory—for example, AC_INIT(hello.c). The only other required macro is AC_OUTPUT.
AC_OUTPUT	This macro is required. It names and outputs the makefile, and possibly some other output files. If you include extra arguments, these are commands that will be added to config.status to be executed after all other commands. It is usually written as AC_OUTPUT(Makefile). The only other required macro is AC_INIT.

Table 14-3.   *The m4 Macros Used in the* `configure.in` *Script* (continued)

Macro	Description
AC_OUTPUT_COMMANDS	This macro specifies extra commands to be run at the end of `config.status`. This macro can be used repeatedly—for example, `AC_OUTPUT_COMMANDS`(echo An extra command).
AC_PREFIX_DEFAULT	This macro sets the installation prefix instead of defaulting to /usr/local—for example, `AC_PREFIX_DEFAULT`(/home/fred/sets).
AC_PREFIX_PROGRAM	If the user does not select a prefix with the --prefix option, this macro will search for the named program, using the PATH variable, and set the prefix to the directory containing the program.
AC_PREREQ	This macro ensures that a sufficiently recent version of Autoconf is being used. For example, this macro will make certain that version 1.8 or later is being used: `AC_PREREQ`(1.8).
AC_PROG_MAKE_SET	This macro predefines the MAKE variable as if the command MAKE=make had been set in the environment.
AC_REVISION	This macro copies the specified revision information into the `configure` script.
AC_TYPE_OFF_T	This macro checks for the presence of certain typedefs and defines them if they are missing.
AC_TYPE_SIZE_T	This macro checks for the presence of certain typedefs and defines them if they are missing.

Table 14-3.   *The m4 Macros Used in the* `configure.in` *Script* (continued)

4. **Create makefile.in.**   To take advantage of the configuration decisions made by Autoconf, you need to modify your makefile (and name it `makefile.in`) to contain the definitions produced by Autoconf. Some of the common definitions are listed in Table 14-4.

Keyword	Description
@CC@	The C compiler.
@CFLAGS@	The set of flags to be passed to the C compiler.
@CPP@	The C preprocessor.
@CPPFLAGS@	Flags to be passed to the C preprocessor.
@CXX@	The C++ compiler.
@CXXFLAGS@	The set of flags to be passed to the C++ compiler.
@DEFS@	This is usually defined as -DHAVE_CONFIG_H if the AC_CONFIG_HEADER macro has been used.
@INSTALL@	The install utility or the install-sh script.
@LDFLAGS@	Flags to be passed to the linker.
@LIBOBJS@	Object files to be included when linking programs.
@LIBS@	Libraries to be included when linking programs.
@RANLIB@	The ranlib utility.
@SET_MAKE@	Usually "MAKE=make".
@srcdir@	The name of the directory containing the source files.

Table 14-4. *Makefile Keywords Defined by Autoconf*

5. **Create config.h.in.** The simplest way to create the header file is to run autoheader and let it create config.h.in, which is used as the input in the creation of config.h. This can be done by entering the command with no arguments, as follows:

```
$ autohead
```

6. **Update your source.** In any of your source files that require portability considerations, you will want to include the header config.h. This makes it possible to conditionally compile according to the installation environment. For

example, if the standard C headers are not present, you may need to change your processing:

```
#ifndef STDC_HEADERS
    /* Compiled only if there are no standard C headers */
#endif
```

7. **Create the installation script.** The `autoconf` utility reads configure.in and produces the `configure` file with the following command:

```
$ autoconf
```

8. **Copy the Autoconf scripts.** The following three scripts should be included as part of your installation package. They are part of your Autoconf installation and can normally be found in a directory named `/usr/lib/autoconf` or `/usr/share/automake`:

```
config.guess
config.sub
install-sh
```

The Complete Reference

GCC

Chapter 15

The GNU Assembler

The GNU assembler is actually a family of assemblers because a different one is required for each platform. This means that, although the assembly language itself will vary, a basic set of directives is common to all of them, and even some of the opcode mnemonics are the same from one platform to the next.

The GNU assembler is primarily designed to assemble the output of the compiler into an object code format that can be fed to the linker. As such, the assembler normally works behind the scenes and is automatically invoked through GCC, but circumstances can arise that could require you to work directly with the assembler.

Assembling from the Command Line

When you are writing in a higher level language, GCC normally invokes the assembler for you, so you seldom need to deal with the command-line options. However, if you decide to write an assembly language module, it is probably for a special purpose, and you may need to use some of the command-line options. The options are listed in Table 15-1.

Option	Description
`-a[opts][=file]`	Turns on the output listing. A combination of one or more of the following letters can be used with this option to specify the format and content of the output listing. The default is `-ahls`. The listing defaults to standard output but can be directed to a file by specifying the file name following an equals sign as part of the option; for example, `-ahls=assembly.list`. c Omits code not assembled because of a false conditional. d Omits any debugging directives found in the source. h Includes the source code from the higher level language. l Includes the assembled code in hexadecimal format. L Includes the line debugging statistics. m Includes macro expansions. n Omits forms processing. s Includes a symbol cross-reference table.

Table 15-1.   *Command-Line Options of the GNU Assembler*

Option	Description
--defsym *symbol=value*	Defines the named symbol and assigns it the specified value.
-f	Skips the preprocessing of whitespace and comments.
--fatal-warnings	Treats warnings as errors.
--gdwarf2	Generates DWARF2 debugging information and includes it in the object file.
--gstabs	Generates STABS debugging information and includes it in the object file.
--help	Displays this list of options and quits.
-I directory	Adds the named *directory* to the list of those searched in response to the .include directive.
-J	Specifies to not issue warnings about signed overflow.
-K	Issues warnings for alteration in the differences table. This table contains absolute values derived by subtraction of a pair of relocatable values and needs to be altered when addresses are adjusted.
--keep-locals	Retains symbol table entries for locally defined symbols, which begin with .L.
-L	Same as --keep-locals.
-M	Same as --mri.
-MD *filename*	Dependency information, formatted for inclusion in a makefile, is written to the named file.
--mri	Compiles in MRI compatible mode. That is, the assembly process assumes syntax compatible with the assembler from Microtec Research.
--no-warn	Suppresses all warning messages. Same as --W.
-o *filename*	The name of the output object file.

Table 15-1. *Command-Line Options of the GNU Assembler* (continued)

Option	Description
-R	Folds the code from the data section into the text section.
--statistics	Displays the total amount of space and execution time taken by the assembler.
--strip-local-absolute	Any symbol that is local to this assembly and has a constant value is removed, and only its value is used.
--traditional-format	Specifies to use the same format for the output file as used by the native assembler.
--target-help	Displays the list of options that are specific to this target and quits.
--version	Displays the version information and quits.
-W	Suppresses all warning messages. Same as --no-warn.

Table 15-1. *Command-Line Options of the GNU Assembler* (continued)

If you find yourself in a situation where you need to write an assembly module, the best way to start is to write a simple program in C that contains all the structural elements you need and then use gcc with the -S option to generate assembly language source. Writing in assembly language is error prone and can be very tedious, so it is best to start with a solid mechanical foundation.

If you don't need much assembly language, it may be easier to insert it as inline assembly, as described later in this chapter.

Absolute, Relative, and Boundaries

Much of the assembly language code has to do with addressing and address calculations. The address of a location is calculated by the assembler for you whenever you simply mention the name of the location. For example, the following jle (jump on less than or equal to) statement branches to the address named .L3:

```
addl    $16,%esp
jle     .L3
```

```
    call    function
.L3:
    movl    $0,%eax
```

The location labeled .L3 is not an absolute number because the linker will change its location when the program is linked into an executable. Until then, it is a relative value, because its value can only be defined as an offset relative to the top of this module. The linker changes the value of all references to relative addresses, such as the reference by the jle statement in this example.

An absolute expression is a constant value that is not altered by the linker. It can be any numeric constant value, or it can be calculated as an expression. It is possible to create an absolute value by performing calculations on relative addresses. For example, the following expression is an absolute value because it is the constant value of the distance between two locations:

```
.L6 - .L3
```

The linker will relocate both .L6 and .L3, but the distance between them will not change. However, not all expressions involving relative addresses result in an absolute value. For example, the following expression is relative to .L44 because all it does is calculate a constant value and add it to the relative address:

```
.L44 + .L6 - .L3
```

Some expressions involving arithmetic on addresses are ill defined. For example, the following expression would result in a meaningless number that is a function of the location chosen by the linker:

```
.L6 + .L3
```

Another important concept is an *address boundary*. If an address is an even multiple of 16, then the address is said to be on a 16-byte boundary. This can be important for certain data structures and instructions. In some cases it is a matter of efficiency, and in some cases it is a matter of necessity because of hardware requirements. Assembler directives such as .org and .align are used to insert filler bytes to force the items that follow them onto a boundary. Of course, for the boundaries to remain correct, it is necessary for the linker to align the beginning of the module such that its internal boundaries are still valid.

PERIPHERALS AND INTERNALS

Inline Assembly

There are a number of reasons for writing code in assembly language, but there are almost none for writing an entire program (or even an entire module) in assembly language. The things that need to be done at the machine level can usually best be done by including a passage of assembly language inside the code of a higher level language. To this end, GCC provides the capability of inserting assembly language commands directly into a C function.

By its very nature, there is nothing portable about assembly language. Code written for any particular platform will almost certainly be wrong for any other platform. However, the basic procedure of writing the code is the same for all platforms. This section describes the procedure of writing code using a syntax compatible with the Intel family of processors.

The asm Construct

The following example program uses asm to insert assembly language into C source code. This example loads the value of a C variable into a register, shifts it one bit to the right to halve the value, and stores the result in another variable:

```
/* half.c */
#include <stdio.h>
int main(int argc,char *argv[])
{
    int a = 40;
    int b;

    asm("movl %1,%%eax; \
         shr  %%eax; \
         movl %%eax,%0;"
           :"=r"(b)
           :"r"(a)
           :"%eax");

    printf("a=%d  b=%d\n",a,b);
    return(0);
}
```

This construct is much more than a simple technique for inserting assembly language code—it makes it possible for you to use C syntax to address your variables and even allows you to specify information to be passed on to the C code generation and optimization stages, so it can generate efficient code in the context of what you are doing. The following is the syntax of the asm construct:

```
asm(assembly language template
    : output operands
    : input operands
    : list of clobbered registers);
```

If you want to prevent the compiler from trying to optimize your assembly language code, you can use the volatile keyword, like the following:

```
asm volatile ( ...
```

Also, if you need to be POSIX compliant, you can use the keywords __asm__ and __volatile__ instead of asm and volatile.

The Assembly Language Template

The assembly language template consists of one or more statements of assembly language and is the actual code to be inserted inline. The opcodes can address immediate (constant) values, the contents of registers, and memory locations. The following is a summary of the syntax rules for addressing values:

- A register name begins with two percent signs, such as %%eax and %%esi. The Intel register names normally begin with a percent sign, and the asm template also requires a percent sign, which is why there must be two.

- A memory location is one of the input or output operands. Each of these is specified by a number according to the order of its declaration following the colons. The first output operand is %0. If there is another output operand, it will be %1, and so on. The numbers continue with the input operands—for example, if there are two output operands, the first input operand will be %2.

- A memory location can also be addressed by having its address stored in a register and enclosing the register name in parentheses. For example, the following will load the byte addressed by the contents of register %%esi into the %%al register:

```
movb    (%%esi),%al
```

- An immediate (constant) value is designated by the dollar ($) character followed by the number itself, as in $86 or $0xF12A.

- All the assembly language is a single-quoted string, and each line of the assembly code requires a terminator. The terminator can be a semicolon or a newline (\n) character. Also, tabs can be inserted to improve readability of assembly language listings.

Input and Output Operands

The input and output operands consists of a list of variable names that you wish to be able to reference in the assembly code. You can use any valid C expression to address memory. For example, the following code is a variation on the preceding example that uses an array to store the input and output values, and doubles the number by shifting it to the left:

```
/* double.c */
#include <stdio.h>
int main(int argc,char *argv[])
{
    int array[2];
    array[0] = 150;
    int i = 0;

    asm("movl %1,%%eax; \
        shl  %%eax; \
        movl %%eax,%0;"
           :"=r"(array[i+1])
           :"r"(array[i])
           :"%eax");

    printf("array[0]=%d  array[1]=%d\n",array[0],array[1]);
    return(0);
}
```

The rules for specifying the input and output variables are as follows:

- The C expression, which results in an address in your program, is enclosed in parentheses.

- If the address is preceded by "r", it applies the constraint that the value must be stored in a register. Input variables will be loaded before your assembly language is executed, and output variables will be stored in memory after your code has executed. The "=r" form should be used for output operands.

- A variable may be constrained to a specific register with one of the following:

```
"a"    %%eax
"b"    %%ebx
"c"    %%ecx
"d"    %%edx
```

```
"S"    %%esi
"D"    %%edi
```

- A variable can be constrained to be addressed in memory instead of being loaded into a register by using the "m" constraint.

- In the case of the same variable being used as both an input and output value, the "=a" constraint is used for its output constraint, and its reference number is used for its input constraint. The following example uses counter for both input and output:

```
asm("incw %0;"
    : "=a"(counter)
    : "0"(counter));
```

- You may use any number of input and output operands by separating them with commas.

- The output and input operands are numbered sequentially beginning with $0 and continuing through $n-1, where n is the total number of both input and output operands. For example, if there is a total of six operands, the last one would be named $5.

List of Clobbered Registers

The list of registers that are clobbered by your code is simply a list of the register names separated by commas, as in the following example:

```
. . .
"%eax", "%esi");
```

This information is passed on to the compiler so it will know not to expect any values to be retained in these registers.

Assembler Directives

The primary purpose of an assembler is to translate mnemonic opcodes into binary opcodes that can be executed by the hardware or used as data storage locations. In addition, the assembler understands and acts on assembler directives, which can be used to align code, define macro expansions, divide the code into named sections, declare named constants, provide conditional assembly, or simply be a shorthand method for defining character data.

The following is a list of the assembler directives for the GNU assembler. In each case, the directive begins with a period. Some directives stand alone, some have arguments that appear on the same line, and some can be several lines long, until another directive acts as a terminator. Some directives—particularly the ones used to insert debugging information—are only valid with one or two object file formats.

Some directives are recognized by the assembler, but they are either deprecated or have no effect. For example, the `.abort` directive still aborts the assembly process but will probably soon disappear. Examples of directives that are often recognized by the assembler but do nothing are `.file`, `.app-file`, `.extern`, `.ident`, and `.lflags`.

You will find some bizarre behavior in some of the directives. It has to do with history. Assemblers have been around for a long time, and some of the very early design decisions are still with us. As the years passed and the hardware changed, the old assembler directives that catered to hardware peculiarities remained intact. The GNU assembler was written to be compatible with the assembler on the host platform, so it adopted the behavior of the existing directives. It isn't that the directives are useless, it's just that some of them operate in a very odd sort of way. For an example of this, see the `.fill` directive in the following list.

Many of these directives use or declare symbols. A symbol is a name with the attributes *value* and *type*. The value can be either an absolute or relative number, and the type specifies both the size of the data and how it should be interpreted.

.align boundary [,filler] [,maximum]   Inserts `filler` at the current location to align the address to a specified boundary. All three values are absolute expressions. If the `filler` value is not specified, the value of the filler defaults to zero for data sections and `noop` opcodes for executable sections. If a `maximum` value is specified, and it would take more than that number of bytes of filler to reach the boundary, no action is taken.

Both `filler` and `maximum` are optional. To specify `maximum` without specifying `filler`, use two commas.

The exact meaning of this directive is inconsistent because the GNU assembler emulates the native assembler on each system. For example, on some systems the alignment to an 8-byte boundary is specified by the address multiple in the form `.align 8`. On other systems the alignment to an 8-byte boundary is specified by `.align 3`, which is the minimum number of zeroes required to end the address value. To have a consistent syntax, you may want to use `.balign` or `.p2align`.

.ascii [string][,string ...]   Assembles zero or more quoted strings into ASCII character data. The strings are not allocated with trailing zeroes appended.

.asciz [string][,string ...]   Assembles zero or more quoted strings into ASCII character data. Each string is allocated with a trailing zero appended to it.

.balign boundary [,filler] [,maximum]   Inserts `filler` bytes at the current location to align the address to a specified boundary. All three values are absolute expressions. If the `filler` value is not specified, it defaults to zero for data sections and `noop` opcodes for executable sections. If a maximum value is specified, and it would take more than that number of bytes to reach the boundary, no action is taken.

Both filler and maximum are optional. To specify maximum without specifying filler, use two commas.

.balignl boundary [,filler] [,maximum]   The same as .balign, except filler is a 32-bit (long) value.

.balignw boundary [,filler] [,maximum]   The same as .balign, except filler is a 16-bit value.

.byte expression [,expression ...]   One byte is allocated for each expression, and the value of the expression is inserted into the allocated byte.

.comm symbol, length   An uninitialized memory location of length bytes is declared and tagged with the name symbol. If more than one module defines the same symbol, they are merged into one. If the declared symbols are not of the same size, the largest one is used.

On ELF systems, there is a third optional argument to specify the alignment. On HPPA, the syntax of this directive is symbol .comm, length.

.data subsection   The statements following the .data directive are to be assembled into the subsection numbered subsection, which is an absolute expression. The default subsection number is zero.

.def name   Begins a block of debugging information, tagged by the symbol name, for insertion into a COFF formatted object. The block continues until an .endef directive terminates it. Also see .dim, .scl, .tag, .type, .val, and .size.

.desc symbol, value   The symbol is defined as having the specified value. The value must be an absolute expression. This directive produces no output for the COFF format.

.dim   This directive can only be used between .def and .endef pairs. It is used by compilers to include auxiliary information for the symbol table. It is only valid for the COFF object format.

.double value [,value ...]   For each value specified, a floating-point number is assembled and stored into memory. The internal representation of floating-point numbers, including size and range, varies depending on the platform. Also see .float.

.eject   Inserts a page break in the listing output from the assembler.

.else   See .if.

.endef   See .def.

.endif   See .if.

.equ symbol, value   This directive defines the symbol as having a value. The value can be either an absolute or relative expression. The .equ directive can be used multiple times on the same symbol, changing the value each time. On HPPA, the syntax for this directive is symbol .equ value. This directive is the same as .set. Also see .equiv.

.equiv symbol, value   This is the same as .equ or .set, except an error message is generated if the symbol has been previously defined.

.err   The .err directive generates an error and, unless the -Z option has been specified, prevents the generation of an object file. It is used inside conditionally assembled code to indicate an error, as in the following example, which causes an error if the symbol BLACKLINE has not been defined:

```
.ifndef BLACKLINE
.err
.endif
```

.fill repeat, size, value   This directive creates multiple blocks of data of up to 8 bytes each. The value of repeat is an absolute expression that specifies the number of blocks to be created. The value of size can be any absolute value, but any value larger than 8 is treated as the value 8 and is the number of bytes in each block.

The value used to fill each block is taken from an 8-byte array. The highest order 4 bytes are always zero. The lowest order 4 bytes are derived from value, rendered as a 32-bit binary integer in the byte order of the native machine. Each block is filled with the number of bytes necessary from the lower order end of the resulting array.

If size is not specified, it defaults to 1. If value is not specified, it defaults to 0. Also see .org and .p2align.

.float value [,value ...]   For each value specified, a floating-point number is assembled and stored into memory. The internal representation of floating-point numbers, including size and range, varies depending on the platform. Also see .double.

.global symbol   The named symbol, which must be defined elsewhere, is made global in the sense that it becomes known to the linker. The symbol could be defined in a separate module, and the references to it can only be resolved by the linker. On HPPA it may be necessary to use the .EXPORT directive to achieve the same thing.

.globl   An alternate spelling of .global.

.hword value   A 16-bit location is created and has the specified value stored in it. This may be the same as `.short` or `.word`, depending on the platform.

.if expression   The code following this directive is assembled only if the expression (which must be absolute) evaluates to a value other than zero. The end of the section of conditionally assembled code is marked with an `.endif` directive. For example, the following two instructions will only be assembled if the value of `topside` and `current` are the same:

```
.if topside - current
    pushl     %ebp
    movl      %esp, %bp
.endif
```

The optional `.else` clause is assembled if the expression is `false`, as in the following example:

```
.if ENTERING
    pushl     %ebp
.else
    popl      %ebp
.endif
```

The alternative forms of `.if` are `.ifdef`, `.ifndef`, and `.ifnotdef`, which test whether a symbol has been defined.

.ifdef symbol   The conditional assembly occurs only if the symbol has been defined. See `.if`.

.ifndef symbol   The conditional assembly occurs only if the symbol has *not* been defined. See `.if`.

.ifnotdef symbol   The conditional assembly occurs only if the symbol has *not* been defined. See `.if`.

.include "filename"   The named file is inserted into this file and assembled at the point of the directive. The `-I` command-line option can be used to specify directories to be searched for the file.

.int value [,value ...]   For each value specified, an integer is assembled and stored into memory. The size and byte order of the integer depends on the platform. Also see `.long`, `.int`, `.short`, and `.word`.

.irp tag,str[,str ...]   The code between the .irp and .endr directives is assembled once for each value listed, with the value inserted for each occurrence of the tag preceded by a backslash. For example, the following specifies three registers:

```
.irp      tag,esp,ebp,eax
subl      $1,%\tag
.endr
```

The code is assembled once for each of the strings, as follows:

```
subl      $1,%esp
subl      $1,%ebp
subl      $1,%eax
```

Also see .macro, .rept, and .irpc.

.irpc tag,charlist   The code between the .irpc and .endr directives is assembled once for each character in charlist, with the character inserted for each occurrence of the tag preceded by a backslash. The following example expands one line of code into three:

```
.irpc     tag,123
addl      $\tag,%esp
.endr
```

The code is assembled once for each character in the string, as follows:

```
addl      $1,%esp
addl      $2,%esp
addl      $3,%esp
```

Also see .macro, .rept, and .irp.

.lcom symbol, length   Reserves the number of bytes specified by length, an absolute expression, as a local block of data in the bss section (causing the block to be initialized to zero when the program is loaded). The symbol is local so it is unknown to the linker.
    The syntax for HPPA is symbol .lcomm, length.

.line number   Changes the current line number of the following line to the absolute expression number. On some systems the synonym .ln must be used.

.linkonce [type]   Marks the current section so it is included by the linker only once, even if the same section appears in multiple modules. The directive must appear once in each instance of the section. The section is selected only by name, so the name must be unique.

The optional `type` argument can be `discard` to have duplicates silently discarded (the default). A type of `one_only` will issue a warning for each duplicate found. A type of `same_size` will issue a warning if any of the duplicates are not the same size. A type of `same_contents` will issue a warning if any of the duplicates do not contain exactly the same data.

.list   This directive increases the output listing counter by one. If the counter is greater than zero, the assembler generates a listing to standard output. The `.nolist` directive can be used to subtract one from the counter. The counter normally defaults to zero but can be set to one by the `-a` option on the command line.

.ln number   A synonym of `.line`.

.long expression   This directive is a synonym of `.int`.

.macro name [tag[=value]] [,tag[=value]]   A recursive macro processor that can be used to assign a name to a block of code, with optional arguments, that can be expanded and assembled in other locations. For example, the following macro is named `saveregs` and will expand to a pair of `pushl` statements wherever it is used:

```
    .macro saveregs
    pushl   %ebp
    pushl   %eax
    .endm
```

To expand the macro, it is a matter of using its name wherever you would normally use an opcode, like the following:

```
main:
    saveregs
    movl    %esp,%ebp
```

The `.macro` directive can be used recursively and can accept arguments. The following macro can be used in the declaration of a block containing a variable number of constants of a selected type:

```
    .macro block type=.int count=1
    .if \count
    \type 0
    block \type,\count-1
```

```
.endif
.endm
```

If no arguments are supplied to the macro, the declaration will consist of one .int. The following statement will generate the declaration of five .long data types:

```
block .long 5
```

It is possible to use .exitm to halt a macro expansion at any point. For example, the following statement will abandon macro expansion if the value of trigger is 12:

```
.if trigger-12
.exitm
.endif
```

Also see .rept, .irp, and .irpc.

.mri expression   If the expression evaluates to a nonzero value, the assembly switches to MRI mode. This is the same as using –M or ––mri on the command line. The mode remains in effect until the end of the file or until there is an .mri directive with an expression value of zero.

.nolist   See .list.

.octa bignum[,bignum ...]   For each bignum entry in the list, a 16-byte number will be declared for it, and the declared value stored in it. This can be treated as eight 16-bit values, thus the name .octa. Also see .quad.

.org address[,filler]   The current address in this section is adjusted forward the location specified by address. The address value is relative to the top of the current section. The address is either an absolute expression or a relative expression based on the address of the current section. This directive can only move the address forward, not backward. The inserted bytes, if any, are initialized to the value of filler. The default filler value is zero.
Also see .fill, .skip, and .p2align.

.p2align zeroes[,filler][,maximum]   The current address is increased, if necessary, until it has the specified number of zeroes as its low order bits. For example, a zeroes value of 3 advances the location counter until there are at least three zero bits as the low order of the address, resulting in the address being on an 8-byte boundary. The absolute value filler is the byte value that is to be stored in the new space. If filler is not specified, the default is zero for data sections or `noop` instructions for code sections. The `maximum` value is the maximum number of bytes to advance the address.

Also see `.org`, `.fill`, `.skip`, `.p2alignl`, and `.p2alignw`.

.p2alignl zeroes[,filler][,maximum]　　The same as `.p2align`, except `filler` is taken to be a 16-bit value.

.p2alignw zeroes[,filler][,maximum]　　The same as `.p2align`, except `filler` is taken to be a 32-bit value.

.psize lines[,columns]　　Specifies the number of lines per page and, optionally, the number of columns of the listing output. The default is 60 lines and 200 columns. If you specify lines as zero, no form feeds are inserted.

.quad bignum[,bignum ...]　　Each `bignum` value is declared as an 8-byte value. Also see `.octa`.

.rept count　　Repeats the code between `.rept` and `.endr` the specified number of times. For example, the following sequence will declared 14 `.int` values, each initialized to 10:

```
.rept 14
.int 10
.endr
```

Also see `.macro`, `.irp`, and `.irpc`.

.sbttl "subtitle"　　Uses the specified subtitle as the subheading on each page of the listing.

.scl class　　This directive can be used inside a `.def` and `.endef` pair to specify the storage class of a symbol.

.section name　　This form of the `.section` directive is valid for any object format that supports arbitrarily named sections. It assembles the following code into a section of the specified name.

.section name[,"flags"]　　This form of the `.section` directive is valid for the COFF object format. Each flag is a single character in the `"flags"` string, as follows:

- b　　A section containing uninitialized data (a `bss` section).
- n　　This section is not loaded when the program is executed.
- w　　This section can be written to during execution.

- d   A data section, as opposed to an executable section.
- r   This section is read-only.
- x   This is an executable section, as opposed to a data section.

If no flags are specified, the default settings depend on the section name. If the section name has no predefined meaning, the default section is loaded and can be written to.

.section name[,"flags"[,type]]   This form of the `.section` directive is valid for the ELF object format. Each flag is a single character in the `"flags"` string, as follows:

- a   The section is allocatable.
- w   The section is writable.
- x   The section is executable.

If a type is specified, it can be one of the following:

- @progbits   The section contains data.
- @nobits   The section does not contain data (it is empty space).

If no flags are specified, the default settings depend on the section name. If the section name has no predefined meaning, the default is for the section to not be allocatable, writable, or executable, and the section will contain data.

.section "name"[,flag ...]   This form of the `.section` directive is valid for the Solaris assembler generating the ELF object format. The optional list of flags can be one or more of the following:

- #alloc   The section is allocatable.
- #write   The section is writable.
- #execinstr   The section consists of executable instructions.

.set symbol, value   This directive defines the symbol as having a value. Here, `value` can be either an absolute or relative expression. The `.set` directive can be used multiple times on the same symbol, changing the value each time. On HPPA, the syntax for this directive is `symbol .set value`. This directive is the same as `.equ`. Also see `.equiv`.

.short value[,value...]   This may be a synonym for `.hword` or `.word`, depending on the platform. Also see `.int`.

.single value[,value]   This is a synonym for `.float`.

.size   This directive can only be used between .def and .endef pairs. It is used by compilers to include auxiliary information for the symbol table. It is only valid for the COFF object format.

.sleb128 value[,value]   This directive is an acronym for "signed little endian base-128." This is a compact variable-length representation of numbers used by DWARF symbolic debugging. Also see .uleb128.

.skip size[,filler]   This directive creates a block made up of size bytes containing the filler value. The default value for filler is zero. Also see .fill, .org, and .p2align.

.stabd type,other,description   See the description of STABS in Chapter 13.

.stabs "name:symdesc=typeinfo",type,other,description,value   See the description of STABS in Chapter 13.

.stabn type,other,description,value   See the description of STABS in Chapter 13.

.string "characters",["characters"]   The character string (or strings) is stored in memory. Each string has a null byte (value of zero) added to the end of it as a terminator. The backslash escape sequences defined for C can be used in the string.

.symver name,name2@nodename   For the ELF object format, this directive binds the symbol to specific version nodes and is used when assembling code with a shared library. The symbol name2@nodename is created by this directive as an alias of name, which has been defined elsewhere in the same source file. The name2 portion of the alias is the actual external reference name to be resolved. The nodename portion is the name of a node supplied to the linker on the command line.

.tag structname   This directive can only be used between .def and .endef pairs. It is used by compilers to include summary debugging information for the symbol table. It is only valid for the COFF object format.

.text [subsection]   The statements following this directive are appended to the end of the text subsection named subsection, which is an absolute expression. If subsection is not specified, it is assumed to be zero.

.title "heading"   The specified string is the title used at the top of the listing pages immediately following the name of the source file and the page number.

.type value   This directive can only be used between .def and .endef pairs. The value is an int to be used as the type value for the symbol table entry. It is only valid for the COFF object format.

.val address   This directive can only be used between .def and .endef pairs. The value is the address to be assigned to the symbol table entry. It is only valid for the COFF object format.

.uleb128 value[,value]   This directive is an acronym for "unsigned little endian base-128." This is a compact variable-length representation of numbers used by DWARF symbolic debugging. Also see .sleb128.

.word value[,value]   This directive declares a numeric value with the size and the byte order depending on the platform. This may be a synonym for .hword or .short, depending on the platform.

Chapter 16

Cross Compiling and the Windows Ports

B y default, the GCC compiler system will generate code for the same machine on which it is running, but it can be installed to generate code for other machines also. You can install the modules necessary to produce code for several targets and select the one you wish to use from the command line.

The Target Machines

To get an updated list of the possible target machines, go to the Web site http:// gcc.gnu.org/install/specific.html. At that site you will find the updated list of target machines and the latest information about porting to each one. Each possible target has a brief description, and you will often find notes about some special requirements for porting. The list of known targets is quite long, and new ports are always in the works. The following is the list of ports at the time this book was written:

```
#s390-*-linux*                    m6811-elf
#s390x-*-linux*                   m6812-elf
*-*-freebsd*                      m68k-att-sysv
*-*-linux-gnu                     m68k-crds-unos
*-*-solaris2*                     m68k-hp-hpux
*-*-sysv*                         m68k-ncr-*
*-ibm-aix*                        m68k-sun
*-lynx-lynxos                     m68k-sun-sunos4.1.1
alpha*-*-*                        Microsoft Windows
alpha*-dec-osf*                   mips-*-*
alphaev5-cray-unicosmk*           mips-sgi-irix5
arc-*-elf                         mips-sgi-irix6
arm*-*-linux-gnu                  Older systems
arm-*-aout                        OS/2
arm-*-elf                         powerpc*-*-*powerpc-*-sysv4
avr                               powerpc-*-darwin*
c4x                               powerpc-*-eabi
DOS                               powerpc-*-eabiaix
dsp16xx                           powerpc-*-eabisim
ELF (SVR4, Solaris 2, etc)        powerpc-*-elf powerpc-*-sysv4
h8300-hms                         powerpc-*-linux-gnu*
hppa*-hp-hpux*                    powerpc-*-netbsd*
hppa*-hp-hpux10                   powerpcle-*-eabi
hppa*-hp-hpux11                   powerpcle-*-eabisim
hppa*-hp-hpux9                    powerpcle-*-elf powerpcle-*-sysv4
```

```
i370-*-*                          powerpcle-*-winnt powerpcle-*-pe
i?86-*-esix                       sparc-*-linux*
i?86-*-linux*                     sparc-sun-solaris2*
i?86-*-linux*aout                 sparc-sun-solaris2.7
i?86-*-sco                        sparc-sun-sunos4*
i?86-*-sco3.2v4                   sparc-unknown-linux-gnulibc1
i?86-*-sco3.2v5*                  sparc64-*-*
i?86-*-udk                        sparcv9-*-solaris2*
ia64-*-linux                      vax-dec-ultrix
m32r-*-elf                        xtensa-*-elf
m68000-hp-bsd                     xtensa-*-linux*
```

Creating a Cross Compiler

A GCC file naming convention enables you to compile and install as many cross compilers as you need on the same machine. To be able to compile and link programs for another computer, you will need the fundamental tools (assembler, linker, and so on) that accept object files and produce executable code in the format for the target. Also, you will need to install a copy of any necessary libraries from the target machine onto your local machine.

The following set of steps can be used as a general guide for establishing a cross-compiler environment, but you need to be aware that it is not out of the ordinary to encounter some situation that requires special handling.

Before you start the procedure, you should review the information about `binutils` and the `configure` script described in Chapter 2. Also, visit the GCC Web site to check for any information about your specific port. It would be a good idea to subscribe to any appropriate mailing lists mentioned in Chapter 1 so you will be able to communicate with others who are doing the same thing you are—discussions about problems with compiling GCC for various platforms are always going on.

Unless you have good reason for wanting to be on the cutting edge, it would be better to use a stable released version of the compiler source rather than the latest CVS snapshot. The snapshot may work as a native compiler on several machines, but there is no need to deal with more unknowns than necessary.

Installing a Native Compiler

Where the cross compiler is to produce object code to be installed on the target machine, the compiler itself, along with the support programs such as the assembler and linker, will actually need to be compiled to run on the local machine. For this, you will need a native compiler so, if you have not already done so, your first job is to install a native version of GCC along with a native version of `binutils`.

It may be possible to build a cross compiler with something other than GCC, but that would be leaving yourself open for some possibly confusing problems. Again, there is no need to deal with more unknowns than necessary.

Building binutils for the Target

The binutils described in Chapter 2 must be compiled for the target machine. Because of the naming convention used by GCC, there will be no conflict in compiling and installing binutils for another machine. The compilation can be based on the same set of source files used to create the native binutils.

For the following example, the binutils source code is located in a subdirectory of the current directory named src. The following four commands in a simple script will create a new directory named sun and configure it for compilation of the source to run on the local machine and produce output for sparc-sun-solaris2.7:

```
DIR=`pwd`
mkdir $DIR/sun
cd $DIR/sun
$DIR/src/configure --prefix=/usr/local \
        --target=sparc-sun-solaris2.7
```

After configuration is complete, the binutils can be compiled by changing to the new sun directory and using make, as follows:

```
$ cd sun
$ make
```

The final step is to change permission settings to the super user and install the new programs with the following command:

```
$ make install
```

This command creates a new set of files in /usr/local/bin, as follows:

```
$ ls /usr/local/bin/sparc-sun-solaris2.7-*
sparc-sun-solaris2.7-addr2line    sparc-sun-solaris2.7-objdump
sparc-sun-solaris2.7-ar           sparc-sun-solaris2.7-ranlib
sparc-sun-solaris2.7-as           sparc-sun-solaris2.7-readelf
sparc-sun-solaris2.7-c++filt      sparc-sun-solaris2.7-size
sparc-sun-solaris2.7-ld           sparc-sun-solaris2.7-strings
sparc-sun-solaris2.7-nm           sparc-sun-solaris2.7-strip
sparc-sun-solaris2.7-objcopy
```

You should also have a new directory with a pair of subdirectories, as follows:

```
$ ls /usr/local/sparc-sun-solaris2.7
bin    lib

$ ls /usr/local/sparc-sun-solaris2.7/bin
ar    as    ld    nm    ranlib    strip
```

Installing Files from the Target Machine

To compile source for the target machine, you must have the system header files that are configured for that machine. Also, to compile and link programs that will run on the target machine, it is necessary to link them with the libraries for that machine. Which ones you will need depends on the purpose of your cross compiler. If you want a general-purpose compiler that compiles complete applications for the target, you will need all the header files and libraries. At the other extreme, if you are creating a cross compiler for an embedded system that does not use the standard libraries and headers, there may be no need to copy any files.

You will need to copy some of the libraries stored on the target machine in the directories /lib and /usr/lib. You will need to store these new files in the file structure started by the earlier installation of binutils. All the libraries you are going to be using should be copied from the target machine to your local directory /usr/local/sparc-sun-solaris2.7/lib. The exact set of libraries you are going to need depends on the target machine and the type of programs you intend to write.

Besides the libraries, you will need the object modules that are linked into the executable programs—modules with names such as crt0.o and crtn.o—and they can be copied into the same directory as the libraries.

The header files from the target machine should be copied into /usr/local/sparc-sun-solaris2.7/include. It is important that the header files be copied to the local machine before the cross compiler is built, because the build process uses them in the construction of libgcc.a.

The Configurable Library libgcc1.a

If GCC is resident on your target machine and you are able to copy libgcc1.a from it, there is no need for you to construct one. If there is no libgcc1.a library for the target machine, it will be necessary for one to be constructed.

This library contains routines that are necessary for performing floating-point math on systems that do not have floating-point hardware. If floating-point emulation is not necessary, it may be sufficient to supply an empty libgcc1.a and let the compiler generate all the code.

Some embedded systems come with the floating-point arithmetic routines required for libgcc1.a.

If your target system has a C compiler but does not have GCC, you can either install GCC to cause the library to be generated or use the native C compiler to construct only the library. To do so, install the GCC source tree on the target machine as you normally would, create a build directory, and execute the `configure` script, specifying both the target and the host machines, where the host is the machine that is to be the host of the cross compiler. Then make the library, as in the following example:

```
$ ./configure --host=host --target=target
$ make libgcc1.a
```

The resulting library should then be included with the other libraries from the target machine.

Building the Cross Compiler

If the proper groundwork has been laid, all that is left is to compile the new compiler. The following script assumes that the source code of GCC is in a subdirectory named gcc. It creates a new directory named sun to contain the configuration and to be used for compilation. Just as was done with `binutils` earlier, the `configure` script is executed, specifying the prefix directory as /usr/local and the target machine as sparc-sun-solaris2.7:

```
DIR=`pwd`
mkdir $DIR/sun
cd $DIR/sun
$DIR/src/configure --prefix=/usr/local \
        --target=sparc-sun-solaris2.7
```

Once the configuration procedure has completed, change to the new directory and compile the cross compiler, as follows:

```
$ cd sun
$ make
```

This is a full compilation of GCC, so it will take quite a while. If everything has been set up properly, there will be no error messages. If the libgcc1.a library is not correct, or if it is missing, the compilation will fail when the first module that needs it is encountered. You may also discover that a header file is missing.

If the compiler is built without error, entering the following command, executed with super user permissions, will install it and prepare it to be run:

```
$ make install
```

Running the Cross Compiler

You can run the cross compiler from the command line by using the `gcc` command and the `-b` option. For example, to compile `helloworld.c` using the compiler constructed in this chapter, enter the following command:

```
$ gcc -b sun-sparc-solaris2.7 helloworld.c -o helloworld
```

Assuming the current version of `gcc` is 3.2, this command will execute the compiler named sun-sparc-solaris2.7-gcc-3.2. If, for some reason, you upgrade your local compiler to a new version but still need to execute version 3.2 of the cross compiler, you can specify the version number as follows:

```
$ gcc -b sun-sparc-solaris2.7 -V 3.2 helloworld.c -o helloworld
```

Using the `-V` option, you can select from a number of versions of installed compilers. The different versions of the compilers are usually stored in directories named in the following way:

```
/usr/local/lib/gcc-lib/machine/version
```

MinGW

On the Windows operating system, two different kinds of programs can be compiled. The simpler of the two—the one that does not use a windowing interface—is referred to as a *console* program. A Windows console program is one that is run from the command line in the usual way and can accept arguments on the command line. A C console program begins execution with a function named `main()` and uses standard input, standard output, and standard error in the normal ways.

A Windows console program can be compiled by using MinGW (Minimalist GNU for Windows), and you can reach the download page through http://www.mingw.org. MinGW comes as a collection of packages, but you can download all of them in a single installation file with a name in one of the following formats:

```
MinGW-<version>[-<stamp>].tar.gz
MinGW-<version>[-<stamp>].zip
```

The `<version>` is the version number, such as 1.0 or 1.1. The optional `<stamp>` is the date, in the form YYYYMMDD, that the various packages were bundled together to create the download file.

To install MinGW, download the file into a working directory and create the directory you would like to use for your installation, such as `c:\mingw`. Extract the contents of the downloaded file into this new directory. The archive includes directories, so make certain that the program you use to extract the files preserves the directory structure defined in the downloaded file—this may require a special command-line option.

All that is left to do is add the new bin directory to your PATH environment variable. Exactly how this is done varies among the different versions of Windows, but the following command will work for most systems:

```
PATH=%PATH%;c:\mingw\bin
```

You can quickly test your installation by entering the following command to display the version information:

```
gcc -v
```

The MinGW gcc and g++ programs have much the same form of command line as the UNIX versions of gcc and g++.

Cygwin

Cygwin is a UNIX environment that is installable on a Windows system. Included with the environment is a port of the binutils package and a DLL named cygwin1.dll, which is an implementation of the UNIX API. The installation of Cygwin is quite simple and can be summed up in the following steps:

1. Create a working directory to contain the downloaded files. This is an intermediate directory, not the one for final installation.

2. Use your Web browser to go to the Web site http://cygwin.com. Select one of the icons on the right that reads, "Install Cygwin now." This will start the download of a file named setup.exe into your working directory.

3. From the command line or from the Run selection on the system menu, execute the program named setup.exe. It will take you through a step-by-step process for downloading and installing the Cygwin system.

Compiling a Simple Cygwin Console Program

The commands for compiling and linking programs are very similar to those you would normally use for GCC, but some of the file-naming conventions vary. All executable files have the suffix .exe, and all shared libraries have the suffix .dll. The following command will compile the simple helloworld.c program into an executable:

```
C:\> gcc helloworld.c -o helloworld.exe
```

Compiling a Cygwin GUI Program

The source code of your Windows applications should compile almost unchanged, but there are a couple of exceptions.

It is necessary to remove the __export attributes. In most cases you can simply remove the __export attributes, but you may want to replace the __export attributed functions with new declarations in the following form:

```
int fn(int) __attribute__ ((__dllexport__));
int fn(int) ...
```

The following conditionally compiled code can be included in the source:

```
#ifdef __CYGWIN__
WinMainCRTStartup() { mainCRTStartup(); }
#endif
```

Without the preceding code included, it will be necessary to specify the linker option -e _mainCRTStartup on the command line.

The following is an excerpt from a makefile that will compile a Windows program into a GUI executable:

```
hellowin.exe: hellowin.o hellowin.res
    gcc -mwindows hellowin.o hellowin.res -o hellowin.exe

hellowin.res: hellowin.rc resource.h
    windres hellowin.rc -O coff hellowin.res
```

The windres utility compiles the hellowin.rc file into a COFF format that includes the icons, bitmaps, and any other resources required by the program. If the -O coff option were not present, the resulting .res file would be in the Windows format and could not be linked using GCC.

The Complete Reference

Compiling software to be installed in an embedded system is fundamentally the same as cross-compiling for another system. That is, a program is compiled on one machine to produce an executable that runs on another. The fundamental difference is that the target operating system is designed for a special purpose and has no software development capabilities of its own.

Normally an embedded system is constrained in the amount of memory available and is generally a much more restricted environment than a desktop system. This means that the compiler of embedded software has to produce not only code that will execute on the CPU of the embedded system but also executables that are as small and efficient as possible.

Setting Up the Compiler and Linker

The fundamental process of preparing GCC to produce code for your embedded system can be found in Chapter 16. GCC is particularly well suited for this kind of configuration because it can be compiled and installed to execute on any one of a number of platforms to produce code that will run on other platforms. One of your tasks is to set up a cross compiler for the target CPU using the libraries and linkable object modules supplied with the target operating system. Another task you have is to download and install the binutils (which include the assembler and linker) so you can produce object modules for your target.

Once you have the cross compiler and linker installed, you can select your language from among the GNU languages (or mix them, if you wish), and you have available all the optimization features built into GCC. Also, inline assembly language is available for those situations where you need to get closer to the hardware.

With all the GCC options available, you can tune the content of the object code to fit with the requirements of the system. By setting up a makefile you can adjust the option settings for each individual module, giving you the power to optimize the result. Pay particular attention to the command-line options that include information in the object files that will pass through the linking process into the final executable program. Some of the information—particularly debugging information—could be incompatible with the object file format of your target system.

For an embedded system you will find that you need to link to a special startup module that fits with your operating system. Often it is a small block of assembly language that you assemble and link directly into your program. Some of these initialization routines can be quite extensive, where others are very simple. The general initialization sequence is fairly standard and follows a procedure that contains all or some of the following steps:

- Disable all hardware interrupts.
- Zero the data area.
- Copy data initialization values into memory from ROM.
- Allocate space for the stack and initialize the stack pointer.

- Allocate space for the heap.
- Enable the appropriate hardware interrupts.
- Call or jump to the main execution loop of the program.

It is possible for some code to be inserted following the call to the main execution loop. It could report some diagnostic information for debugging and then call the main loop again. It could also issue a reset command that starts the entire process over again, or, depending on the purpose of the embedded software, it could simply halt the processor.

The mainline of an embedded system is almost always a continuous loop that calls functions to perform the fundamental tasks of the software. In more complicated systems, the mainline may initiate a collection of threads of execution, each having its own continuous loop performing its own task. In embedded systems, threads are generally referred to as *tasks*.

To be able to use your own startup code, it may be necessary to have the linker ignore instructions it receives from GCC. To this end, the GNU linker has a scripting language, the Linker Command Language, that you can use to provide explicit and tight control over the linking process. The scripting language is robust enough that you may want to skip linking from GCC and specify your own linking—the scripting language is detailed enough that you can describe how the sections of the linked object are to be laid out.

Choosing a Language

Writing code for embedded systems is different from writing it for general purpose computing. Size can be a factor, and speed is almost always a concern. Code that is "correct" for a desktop system can be the source of problems in embedded software. This situation translates into the selection of a language and a compiler.

The question usually arises whether one should write in assembly or in C. Of course, other languages are also available, and often used, but these two choices are by far the most popular. It is always better to work in a higher level language because the code is easier to read, write, and understand. Everything goes faster and with fewer errors if the code is easier to read. The C compiler will generally produce code that, if not quite as tight and efficient as hand crafted assembly language, is very clean and quite usable. Assembly language is certainly not going to go away any time soon, but there is no need to include more of it than is necessary.

If you find yourself in a time critical situation, GCC can provide you with some information you can use to determine whether an assembly language fix is in order. You may want to consider one or more of the following.

- **Optimization** Use the -S option to have assembly language output from the compiler. Do this at various optimization levels and with different optimization flag settings. You may find that the optimizer does everything required.

- **Analyze the instructions** Using the -dp option in conjunction with the -S option causes the assembly language listing to have the length of each instruction in a comment. Along with the length is the number of the tree node and the specific tree instruction that generated the line of assembler code.

- **Analyze the tree** Using the -dP option in conjunction with the -S option produces the same output as the -dp option as well as adds lines of comments containing the intermediate language tree nodes. This option probably has limited value for most people because its content assumes you are familiar with the gcc internal tree structure.

- **Verify the option settings** Specifying the -fverbose-asm option instructs the compiler to include, at the top of the assembly language listing produced by -S, a complete list of all the option settings that were in effect when the program was compiled into assembly language code. It could be that one or more of these settings need to be changed to produce the type of assembly language you are after.

Other information about the produced code is also available, as described in Chapter 18. Most useful are the overall size and allocation numbers.

If you decide that an assembly language solution is what you need, you have more than one option for implementing it. If you just need to make some changes to the code inside the routine you've analyzed, you can simply edit the compiler-generated assembly language module. It already has the interfacing code that can be linked to the rest of the program. Probably a better approach would be to determine what changes you need to make and then use the inline assembler to replace the C code.

GCC Embedding Facilities

The GCC compiler hasn't been designed specifically for the development of embedded software, but it is a very mature compiler that has had so much flexibility added to it over the years that it has just about everything an embedded developer could ask for in a compiler.

Command-Line Options

Several of the command-line options are particularly useful for embedded programming. The level of error checking can be made to be very sensitive to the particular things you want to watch out for. Look through the collection of -W options in Appendix D and set (or unset) the ones that pertain to your particular environment. You might want to start out by using the -Wall option to instruct the compiler to issue a warning about even the smallest of infractions. If it turns out that it is reporting warnings that you would rather suppress, you can use individual option settings to turn off only the ones in which you have no interest.

Optimization can be important to the generated code, and the compiler has a very fine-grained control over optimization settings. See the description of the -O option in Appendix D.

You can use the -ffixed command-line option to prevent the compiler from using a specific register. For example, if your particular CPU has a register named gr4, and that register should not be used by the generated code, then you can use a set of options like the following:

```
$ gcc -c -Wall -ffixed-gr4 mainloop.c -o mainloop.o
```

Diagnostics

The compiler has the ability to format the names of functions, as well as the name of the source file, into a string that you can use to construct diagnostic messages. For example, the following code creates a string that contains the current function name, its source file name, and the date it was compiled:

```
sprintf(msg,"Function %s in file %s compiled %s\n",
    __FUNCTION__,__FILE__,__DATE__);
```

When C++ is the language, the macro __PRETTY_FUNCTION__ will do a better job of formatting a descriptive function name. Using either __FUNCTION__ or __PRETTY_FUNCTION__ will produce the same result for C.

Assembler Code

As described in Chapter 15, it is a relatively straightforward task to link assembler modules with those of a higher level language. Also, assembly language code can be inserted inline and included with your compiled code.

It can happen that you need to link an assembler module as part of your executable, but it hasn't been written with C in mind, and the name doesn't have the requisite leading underscore character. The following statements define C symbols that can be used locally to address global symbols defined in assembler:

```
extern int musref asm("muslimit");
int rebar asm("rebclean");
extern int gribbit(void) asm("asmgribbit");
```

The symbol musref in the C source file will be linked, as a reference to an int, to the globally defined name muslimit. The int variable named rebar is declared in the assembly language code as rebclean, where a normal declaration of rebar would produce the assembly language symbol _rebar. The third line in the example is a function prototype definition that will cause the function declared or referenced as gribbit to actually have the name asmgribbit in the assembly language code.

The GCC __attribute__ keyword can be used to specify a section name into which a function or data item is declared in the assembly language. For example, the following use of __attribute__ will cause the variable named trigmax to be placed in the section named convals:

```
const int trigmax __attribute__ ((section("convals")));
```

The ability to specify the names of sections gives you the capability of using the linker to specify the exact location and order of placement of the object code.

Libraries

Runtime libraries are often provided as part of the embedded operating system software. A good runtime library may provide you with everything you need, so you will only need to write your application code. Once you have compiled and installed the cross compiler, you can compile and/or assemble the runtime library and set up the linker commands to refer to it.

If you have no runtime library provided, you will more than likely need to extract portions of the GNU standard library to use with your application. Unfortunately, if you are going to use very much of the GNU library, this extraction can be a tedious process because of the extensive cross-referencing inside the library. Fortunately, this tedious process can be avoided by the use of the newlib library.

Trimming the Standard Library

Using the complete standard C library can cause the generation of an executable module that is several times larger than it needs to be. Many of the standard C modules are designed for very broad use and are implemented with the idea of being loaded into memory from a shared library and being used by a number of processes. In an embedded system, statically linked modules of this type can be quite expensive because of their size.

One of the most well-known examples is the printf() function. This function has a variable number of arguments—the first argument is a character string and the other arguments are a variable length list of a variety of data types. Because the formatting information is dynamically specified inside the character string, the routines to format any possible data type into any requested form must be included as part of the program. In addition, many of the formatting routines require other library routines. The result is a huge domino effect, causing the inclusion of a large amount of code that is never used for anything.

If you are going to be using the standard library routines that come with GCC, it may be prudent to trim the library to just the modules you actually need and leave the others out entirely. Depending on how much of the library you use, this can be a long and tedious process. You can start by creating a library with only the function calls you know you will need. Then you can add other modules as you need them to satisfy unresolved references.

A Library Designed for Embedded Systems

A standard library is available for linking with embedded systems. The library is licensed as freeware and can be downloaded from the website http://source.redhat.com/newlib/.

The library, called newlib, is a C library designed for use on embedded systems. It is largely made up of a combination of routines gathered from various locations, all of which are licensed as free software. It comes as source, and the code is straightforward enough that it compiles cleanly for a number of processors. One great advantage of newlib is the fact that is has been devised and written specifically for embedded systems.

The library is downloaded and installed much the same as GCC and binutils. Once you have downloaded the source, it should be installed in the newlib working directory. The newlib directory should be a sibling directory of the gcc and binutils source directories. You create a separate build directory and use the configure script that came with it to specify the required --prefix for the installation directory and --target to specify the target system.

It would be a good idea to review the other configure options to determine whether you should use any of them for your particular installation; to get a listing of the available options use the --help option of the configure script. In particular, the --newlib-hw-fp option compiles the library routines so they use floating-point arithmetic; by default, the library routines assume floating point is not available and use only integer routines. The floating-point algorithms are generally smaller and faster.

The command make, followed by make install, will create the library.

The GNU Linker Scripting Language

The GNU linker is controlled by a scripting language. If you do not specify a script, the one that was compiled into the linker when it is installed is used by default. You can override this default and provide your own script, as in the following example, which applies the script sprig.link to the linking of the executable load module named sprig:

```
$ ld -T sprig.link start.o loop.o brspr.o -o sprig
```

The -T option specifies the name of the script file. The -c option is a synonym of the -T option.

The primary reason for using a special script is the addressing scheme. Normally, the linker produces an executable file with adjustable addresses that can be set at the time the module is loaded into memory. Each section has two addresses (which quite often are the same value); one is the virtual memory address (VMA) used internally by the module when it is run, and the other is the loadable memory address (LMA), specifying where the section is to be loaded. With an embedded module, all addresses are resolved by the linker into absolute locations so that every addressing reference is completely resolved and immovable. This process of locking down the address is known as *locating* the module. Some systems have a separate utility that processes the relocatable output from the linker into an absolute module, but the GNU linker has the locator built into it.

The linker reads object files produced by the compiler and combines them into a new object file (also called an executable file) as its output. An object file is divided into sections. Each section has a name and a size. The linker combines the input sections of the same name into a single output section. Some sections contain executable code, some contain data with initial values, and others contain uninitialized data. A section with uninitialized data usually has nothing other than a name and a size.

Script Example 1

The following example can be used to generate a linked object file. It takes the sections of the various input object files and combines them together at the specified addresses:

```
SECTIONS
{
    . = 0x0100000;
    .text : {
        *(.text)
    }
    . = 0x8000000;
    .data : {
        *(.data)
    }
    .bss : {
        *(.bss)
    }
}
```

The SECTIONS keyword specifies that this is a map of the memory layout for the linked object module. The statements between the opening and closing braces of the SECTIONS command are taken in order and specify the exact layout of output.

The period is a special variable that contains the current address (also called the location counter) for insertion of data into the output. The first statement in this example sets the current address to the absolute value 0x0100000. If it had not been set, the output address would have defaulted to 0. Once the current address has been set, it will be incremented automatically by each item added to the output.

The statement .text { . . . } places the beginning of the output .text section at the current address. The items between the braces are the ones included as part of the output .text section. In this example, the output .text section contains all the input .text sections. You could list all the input file names here, but the asterisk matches all file names.

Following the .text section, the location counter is set to 0x08000000. It is at this address the .data section is output. Combining all the input .data sections into a single output .data section advances the location counter, which then points to the location just past the end of the .data section, and that's where the output .bss section is placed.

Script Example 2

The following linker script specifies the locations of the sections in a form that is more like the one you are likely to use to create an object file for an embedded system. It addresses the existence of both ROM and RAM:

```
MEMORY
{
    rom (rx)   : ORIGIN = 0x00000000, LENGTH 1024K
    ram (rwx)  : ORIGIN = 0x00100000, LENGTH 512K
}
SECTIONS
{
    .text rom : {
        *(.text)
    }
    .data ram : {
        _StartOfData = . ;
        *(.data)
        _EndOfData = .;
    } >rom
    .bss : {
        *(.bss)
    }
    _HeapLocation = .
    _StackLocation = 0x80000000
}
```

This example begins with the MEMORY keyword, which is used to assign names to blocks of the output address space. This technique can be used to break up the output address space into any number of blocks and, with later instructions, insert specific sections into specific memory blocks. In this example, the MEMORY settings are used to specify the location and size of the RAM and the ROM and to assign a name to each one for use later.

The optional memory attributes `rx` mean that the memory contents can be read and executed. The attributes `rwx` mean the contents are read/write and can be executed. If you omit the attribute settings, all permissions are granted.

The previously defined memory locations allow names instead of numbers to be used to set addresses. The output `.text` section is placed in ROM by defining its name and location as `.text rom`, and the `.data` section is placed in RAM by being specified as `.data ram`. The named items are taken in order, so if an address is not specified, it is assumed to be at the end of the previous item. For example, the `.bss` section is output immediately following the `.data` section.

The symbols, such as `_StartOfData` and `_EndOfData`, included in the script become globally defined variables during the linking process. These names can be used from inside your program to directly access the memory address to which they are set. The `_HeapLocation` symbol is defined as the address in RAM immediately following the `.bss` section, and `_StackLocation` is set to the absolute address `0x80000000`.

Some Other Script Commands

The `OUTPUT_FORMAT` command is important for getting the resulting executable module into a form that can be loaded into your development system. For example, the following command will produce the output object in the Intel hex format:

```
OUTPUT_FORMAT("ihex")
```

Some of the binary file descriptor (BFD) names available for this command are `"binary"`, `"ihex"` (for Intel hex), `"srec"` (for S-records), `"coff-sh"` (for SH-2), and `"coff-m68k"` (for CPU32). Using `OUTPUT_FORMAT` in the script is the same as using `--oformat` on the command line of the linker, and it has the same set of BFD names available.

The `INPUT` command can be used to list a set of libraries and/or object files that you want to include in every link. For example, the following command will cause two libraries and one object file to always be included:

```
INPUT(libc.a libg.a startmod.o)
```

The output file can be named with the `OUTPUT_FILENAME` command as follows:

```
OUTPUT_FILENAME("loadable.out");
```

The
Complete
Reference

## Chapter 18

Output from the Compiler

The fundamental purpose of the compiler is to produce object files, libraries containing object files, and executable programs. But it is also possible to use the compiler to get other types of output. It is not very often that you find yourself in a position of needing this information, but the compiler can be very helpful in some special situations where clues to a problem are scarce.

Options are available that make it possible for you to discover what the compiler thinks your program means syntactically, where the compiler searches for subprocesses and libraries, and get a listing of the intermediate language produced from parsing your program. You can get a complete listing of all the header files included by a program, and you can automatically generate a dependency statement for a makefile based on the source code.

Information about Your Program

The compiler constructs detailed internal tables containing information about the program being compiled, and command-line options are available that make it possible for you to extract some of this information. Not only can you examine the parse tree, which contains the compiler's interpretation of your code, but you can also get a complete listing of all header files included, the amount of time the compile has taken, and how much memory each module of your program requires. For C++ programs you can extract class definition relationships.

The Parse Tree

The compiler parses your program into an internal tree. This tree structure, representing the original source code, can be dumped to a file with the suffix .tu by using the -fdump-translation-unit option, as in the following example:

```
$ gcc -fdump-translation-unit showdump.c -o showdump
```

The output file produced by this command contains a textual representation of the tree in showdump.c.tu. Each node in the tree is numbered (shown as @1, @2, and so on), and the tree structure is represented by each tree node referring to other tree nodes by numbers.

The amount of information displayed with each node can be controlled to some extent. The following form will produce a tree that contains the compiler's internal addressing information that can be used to cross-reference the parse tree with the internal addresses produced by the -d option (described later in this chapter):

```
$ gcc -fdump-translation-unit-address showdump.c -o showdump
```

The following two forms will produce a listing with either more or less information, respectively:

```
$ gcc -fdump-translation-unit-all showdump.c -o showdump
$ gcc -fdump-translation-unit-slim showdump.c -o showdump
```

The tree produced from any of these options is quite easy to read. The following partial tree dump shows that each node is identified by its unique ID number and a somewhat descriptive name. A list of attributes is also included:

```
@1    function_decl    name: @2      type: @3     srcp: showdump.c:5
                        chan: @4      args: @5     extern
@2    identifier_node  strg: main    lngt: 4
@3    function_type    size: @6      algn: 64     retn: @7
                        prms: @8
@4    var_decl         name: @9      type: @7     srcp: showdump.c:3
                        chan: @10     init: @11    size: @12
                        algn: 32      used: 1
@5    parm_decl        name: @13     type: @7     scpe: @1
                        srcp: showdump.c:4          chan: @14
                        argt: @7      size: @12    algn: 32
                        used: 0
```

At this level in the tree, most of the attributes are defined in terms of other tree nodes. For example, a name attribute is the number of a tree node that has strg (string) and lngth (length) attributes. Some nodes, such as the function_type, have algn (alignment) attributes. Variables, such as arguments and declarations, have both type and name attributes, and they also have a used attribute that is a count of the number of times the variable is used in the program. Many of the nodes have srcp (source position) attributes that specify the name and line number of the source file from which each node was produced.

Header Files

The -H option, which can also be written as --trace-includes, generates a nested listing of all the include files. The following example is the output generated on a Linux system for a C program that includes only stdio.h:

```
. /usr/lib/gcc-lib/i586-pc-linux-gnu/3.2/include/stdio.h
.. /usr/include/features.h
```

```
... /usr/include/sys/cdefs.h
... /usr/include/gnu/stubs.h
.. /usr/lib/gcc-lib/i586-pc-linux-gnu/3.2/include/stddef.h
.. /usr/include/bits/types.h
... /usr/lib/gcc-lib/i586-pc-linux-gnu/3.2/include/stddef.h
... /usr/include/bits/pthreadtypes.h
.... /usr/include/bits/sched.h
.. /usr/include/libio.h
... /usr/include/_G_config.h
.... /usr/lib/gcc-lib/i586-pc-linux-gnu/3.2/include/stddef.h
.... /usr/include/wchar.h
..... /usr/lib/gcc-lib/i586-pc-linux-gnu/3.2/include/stddef.h
..... /usr/include/bits/wchar.h
.... /usr/include/gconv.h
..... /usr/include/wchar.h
...... /usr/lib/gcc-lib/i586-pc-linux-gnu/3.2/include/stddef.h
..... /usr/lib/gcc-lib/i586-pc-linux-gnu/3.2/include/stddef.h
... /usr/lib/gcc-lib/i586-pc-linux-gnu/3.2/include/stdarg.h
.. /usr/include/bits/stdio_lim.h
Multiple include guards may be useful for:
/usr/include/bits/pthreadtypes.h
/usr/include/bits/sched.h
/usr/include/bits/stdio_lim.h
/usr/include/gnu/stubs.h
```

Each level of inclusion is indicated by the number of periods preceding the name. Also, at the bottom of the listing are the names of header files that probably should be fixed because including any one more than once could cause problems with multiple definitions.

The Memory Required by the Program

The compiler can be requested to produce a summary of the amount of memory required for the compiled program, along with some details of how that memory has been allocated. The following sample output demonstrates the detailed form of the report:

RTX	Number	Bytes	% Total
address	7	56	0.664
const_int	129	1032	12.239
const_double	21	336	3.985
const_vector	19	152	1.803
pc	1	8	0.095
reg	14	224	2.657

```
mem                        216          3456       40.987
symbol_ref                 391          3128       37.097
cc0                          1             8        0.095
plus                         1            16        0.190
eq                           1            16        0.190
Total                      801          8432
```

```
Size     Allocated        Used     Overhead
8             8192         6216          184
16             12k         4192          180
32           8192          3392           88
64            32k          28k           288
512           28k          24k           196
1024         4096         1024            28
112           52k          42k           416
20           8192         2580           104
Total         152k         112k          1484
```

```
String pool
entries      452
identifiers  452 (100.00%)
slots        16384
bytes        4805   (3339   overhead)
table size   64k
coll/search  0.0168
ins/search   0.7609
avg. entry   10.63 bytes (+/- 5.78)
longest entry 36
```

From this listing you can determine the amount of memory allocated for various parts of your program as well as how much of each allocation is being used. This can be especially useful in analyzing large programs and object modules for embedded systems.

Time Consumed

The -time option can be used when compiling and linking to cause gcc to list the amount of time consumed by each individual process. For example, the following command compiles three C programs into assembly language, invokes the assembler to produce an object file from each one, and uses collect2 to link them together:

```
gcc -time getshow.c strmaker.c showstring.c -o getshow
# cc1 0.15 0.02
```

```
# as 0.01 0.00
# cc1 0.08 0.03
# as 0.01 0.01
# cc1 0.13 0.03
# as 0.01 0.00
# collect2 0.13 0.05
```

The first of the two times listed for each process is the user time (the amount of time spent executing the code of the subprocesses), and the second is the system time (the amount of time the process spent in making system calls). The actual wall-clock time is not listed, but a total time for the entire gcc process, including the wall-clock time, can be added by using the standard time utility to run gcc, as in the following example:

```
$ time gcc -time getshow.c strmaker.c showstring.c -o getshow
```

The C++ Intermediate Tree

The g++ compiler can be instructed to dump the intermediate language produced by the front end translation. The dump can be taken at different points during the compilation process. The following command will show the intermediate language as it was originally generated, before any modifications or optimizations:

```
$ g++ -fdump-tree-original minmax.cpp -o minmax
```

The intermediate language can also be dumped following code optimization:

```
$ g++ -fdump-tree-optimized minmax.cpp -o minmax
```

The process of inlining functions is performed on the intermediate language, and the results of inlining can be dumped with the following:

```
$ g++ -fdump-tree-inlined minmax.cpp -o minmax
```

The format of the output can be specified by tagging a modifier onto the end of each of the dump option names. Appending -address to the end of the option will cause the inclusion of address information that corresponds to the address information produced by the -d option (described later in this chapter). To reduce the amount of information included in the listing, the -slim tag can be specified. To increase the amount of information in the dump, append the -all tag. For example, the following command will produce a verbose dump of the intermediate language following optimization:

```
$ g++ -fdump-tree-optimized-all minmax.cpp -o minmax
```

The C++ Class Hierarchy

The g++ compiler can be instructed to dump the complete class hierarchy and virtual function tables of your program. Included in the dump is the hierarchy of the system classes used by your program, so the output can be quite large. The following command will compile and then dump the complete class hierarchy of a program named `minmax.cpp`:

```
$ g++ -fdump-class-hierarchy minmax.cpp -o minmax
```

The output resulting from this command is the executable program `minmax` and a text file named `minmax.cpp.class` that contains the class hierarchy. The following command has the same result, except the class hierarchy also includes address information that can be cross-referenced with the information dumped by the `-d` option:

```
$ g++ -fdump-class-hierarchy-address -da minmax.cpp -o minmax
```

The `-d` option dumps some internal compiler information, as described later in this chapter.

The amount of information included in the dump can be reduced by using the following option:

```
$ g++ -fdump-class-hierarchy-slim minmax.cpp -o minmax
```

A larger dump file, containing all the information available, can be obtained by using the following option:

```
$ g++ -fdump-class-hierarchy-all minmax.cpp -o minmax
```

Information for the Makefile

A collection of options exists that can be used to instruct the compiler to scan your source files and generate dependencies for insertion into a makefile. For example, the following program includes two header files:

```
/* getshow.c */
#include "strmaker.h"
#include "showstring.h"
int main(int argc,char *argv[])
{
    char *string;
    string = strmaker();
```

```
    showstring(string);
}
```

The following compiler command reads the source file and produces a dependency line for the makefile (in this example, the header file `strmaker.h` includes `motback.h`):

```
$ gcc -M getshow.c
getshow.o: getshow.c strmaker.h motback.h showstring.h
```

The `-M` option sets the `-E` option, which suppresses all output other than the dependency line. If you wish to produce a dependency line and continue with the compilation, enter the following:

```
$ gcc -MD getshow.c -o getshow
```

This command will produce the executable getshow and store the text of the dependencies in a file named `getshow.d`. The `-MF` option can be used to specify the name of the file, as in the following example, which places the dependencies in a file named `depends.text`:

```
$ gcc -MD -MF depends.text getshow.c -o getshow
```

The `-MF` option can also be used along with `-M` to suppress compilation and store the dependencies in a file, as follows:

```
$ gcc -M -MF depends.text getshow.c
```

An alternative way of specifying the name of the output file is to set the environment variable `DEPENDENCIES_OUTPUT`.

The `-M` and `-MM` options will detect and report an error for a missing header file. If you want to suppress this error message, you can specify the `-MP` option along with `-M` and `-MM`, which will also generate a dummy target for each header file.

The `-MT` option can be used with `-M` or `-MM` to specify the name of the target, as in the following example:

```
$ gcc -M -MT spang.o getshow.c
spang.o: getshow.c strmaker.h motback.h showstring.h
```

Information about the Compiler

A few compiler options are available so you can make certain which compiler you are
using and determine just how it has been configured. For example, the version number
of the compiler can be listed with the following command:

```
$ gcc -dumpversion
```

To determine the target machine—the type of computer for which this compiler
creates object files—enter the following:

```
$ gcc -dumpmachine
```

Time to Compile

The `-ftime-report` option can be used to generate a listing of the time consumed for
the various stages of compiling. This is mostly for compiler developers, but it can also
be used to get a feel for the relative complexity of your programs. The output from a
compilation using this option looks like the following:

```
Execution times (seconds)
  garbage collection   :   1.13 (23%) usr    0.00 ( 0%) sys    0.50 (10%) wall
  life analysis        :   0.01 ( 0%) usr    0.00 ( 0%) sys    0.00 ( 0%) wall
  preprocessing        :   0.43 ( 9%) usr    0.08 (24%) sys    1.00 (20%) wall
  lexical analysis     :   0.38 ( 8%) usr    0.10 (29%) sys    0.00 ( 0%) wall
  parser               :   2.72 (56%) usr    0.14 (41%) sys    3.00 (60%) wall
  expand               :   0.02 ( 0%) usr    0.00 ( 0%) sys    0.00 ( 0%) wall
  varconst             :   0.05 ( 1%) usr    0.00 ( 0%) sys    0.50 (10%) wall
  integration          :   0.03 ( 1%) usr    0.01 ( 3%) sys    0.00 ( 0%) wall
  local alloc          :   0.01 ( 0%) usr    0.00 ( 0%) sys    0.00 ( 0%) wall
  global alloc         :   0.01 ( 0%) usr    0.00 ( 0%) sys    0.00 ( 0%) wall
  rest of compilation  :   0.00 ( 0%) usr    0.01 ( 3%) sys    0.00 ( 0%) wall
  TOTAL                :   4.84               0.34               5.00
```

The values are shown in terms of the number of seconds and the percentage each
duration is of the total. The `usr` time is the duration spent in the actual execution of
code inside the compiler. The `sys` time is the duration spent inside system calls (such
as input and output), and the `wall` time is the actual time consumed.

Subprocess Switches

The gcc program is a front end for other programs such as a language compiler, assembler, and linker. At the time gcc was configured and compiled, the names of the subprocesses, and the options passed to them, were configured and installed. To determine the specifications used to construct the command-line arguments of subprocesses, enter the following:

```
$ gcc -dumpspecs | more
```

The specification for the options and arguments passed to a subprocess consists of a single string. A default set of spec definitions for each of the fundamental subprocesses is built into gcc and automatically becomes a part of the compiler front end, but it is possible to override the default spec strings at the time the compiler is configured.

An example of the information listed is the following spec for invoking the C preprocessor:

```
*cpp:
%{posix:-D_POSIX_SOURCE} %{pthread:-D_REENTRANT}
```

With this spec, whenever gcc invokes cpp, the --posix option on the gcc command line will cause the appearance of -D_POSIX_SOURCE on the cpp command line, and the appearance of --pthread on the gcc command line will cause the appearance of -D_REENTRANT on the cpp command line.

The line of spec text defining the conditions for all the possible options passed to a subprocess can become quite involved. An example of a more complicated (but by no means the most complicated) spec set is one used in invoking an assembler:

```
*asm:
%{v:-V} %{Qy:} %{!Qn:-Qy} %{n} %{T}
```

In this example, if -v is specified on the gcc command line, the option -V is specified for the assembler. If -Qy is specified on the gcc command line, it is not passed on to the assembler, but if -Qn is *not* specified, then -Qy is added to the assembler command line. If either -n or -T is specified for gcc, each will be passed on to the assembler. No other options are passed to the assembler.

Verbose Compiler Debugging Information

The -d option can be used to instruct the GCC system to dump internal information at various stages of the compilation process. The information in the dumped files has meaning only to those working on the compiler itself, so even though the information is quite detailed, it will not help you in debugging or analyzing an application.

You can request that a dump be generated from one of several different points during the compilation process. For the complete list, see the −d entry in Appendix D. The output is roughly the same at all the dump points and includes information about unnecessary instructions being deleted, register allocation, register deallocation (when a register has its value clobbered), and the generated instructions in the internal RTL language. For example, the following simple program tests one value against another to decide whether a branch should be taken:

```
/* showdump.c */
int a = 44;
static int b = 22;
int main(int argc,char *argv[])
{
    if(a > b) {
        b = a;
    } else {
        a = b;
    }
}
```

The following command compiles the program and requests a dump be made immediately after the RTL code is generated:

```
$ gcc -dr showdump.c -o showdump
```

The dumped information is stored in a file named `showdump.c.00.rtl` and looks like the following:

```
;; Function main

(note 2 0 5 NOTE_INSN_DELETED -1347440721)

(insn 5 2 6 (nil) (parallel[
            (set (reg/f:SI 7 esp)
                (and:SI (reg/f:SI 7 esp)
                    (const_int -16 [0xfffffff0])))
            (clobber (reg:CC 17 flags))
        ] ) -1 (nil)
    (nil))

(insn 6 5 7 (nil) (set (reg:SI 59)
        (const_int 0 [0x0])) -1 (nil)
    (expr_list:REG_EQUAL (const_int 0 [0x0])
        (nil)))
```

```
(insn 7 6 8 (nil) (parallel[
        (set (reg/f:SI 7 esp)
            (minus:SI (reg/f:SI 7 esp)
                (reg:SI 59)))
        (clobber (reg:CC 17 flags))
    ] ) -1 (nil)
    (nil))

(insn 8 7 3 (nil) (set (reg/f:SI 60)
    (reg/f:SI 55 virtual-stack-dynamic)) -1 (nil)
    (nil))

(note 3 8 4 NOTE_INSN_FUNCTION_BEG -1347440721)

(note 4 3 9 NOTE_INSN_DELETED -1347440721)

(note 9 4 10 NOTE_INSN_DELETED -1347440721)

(note 10 9 12 NOTE_INSN_DELETED -1347440721)

(insn 12 10 13 (nil) (set (reg:SI 61)
    (mem/f:SI (symbol_ref:SI ("a")) [0 a+0 S4 A32])) -1 (nil)
    (nil))

(insn 13 12 14 (nil) (set (reg:CCGC 17 flags)
    (compare:CCGC (reg:SI 61)
        (mem/f:SI (symbol_ref:SI ("b")) [0 b+0 S4 A32]))) -1 (nil)
    (nil))

(jump_insn 14 13 15 (nil) (set (pc)
    (if_then_else (le (reg:CCGC 17 flags)
            (const_int 0 [0x0]))
        (label_ref 22)
        (pc))) -1 (nil)
    (nil))

(note 15 14 16 NOTE_INSN_DELETED -1347440721)

(note 16 15 18 NOTE_INSN_DELETED -1347440721)

(insn 18 16 19 (nil) (set (reg:SI 62)
    (mem/f:SI (symbol_ref:SI ("a")) [0 a+0 S4 A32])) -1 (nil)
    (nil))
```

```
(insn 19 18 20 (nil) (set (mem/f:SI (symbol_ref:SI ("b")) [0 b+0 S4 A32])
        (reg:SI 62)) -1 (nil)
    (nil))

(jump_insn 20 19 21 (nil) (set (pc)
        (label_ref 28)) -1 (nil)
    (nil))

(barrier 21 20 22)

(code_label 22 21 23 2 "" "" [0 uses])

(note 23 22 24 NOTE_INSN_DELETED -1347440721)

(note 24 23 26 NOTE_INSN_DELETED -1347440721)

(insn 26 24 27 (nil) (set (reg:SI 63)
        (mem/f:SI (symbol_ref:SI ("b")) [0 b+0 S4 A32])) -1 (nil)
    (nil))

(insn 27 26 28 (nil) (set (mem/f:SI (symbol_ref:SI ("a")) [0 a+0 S4 A32])
        (reg:SI 63)) -1 (nil)
    (nil))

(code_label 28 27 29 3 "" "" [0 uses])

(note 29 28 33 NOTE_INSN_FUNCTION_END -1347440721)

(insn 33 29 34 (nil) (clobber (reg/i:SI 0 eax)) -1 (nil)
    (nil))

(insn 34 33 31 (nil) (clobber (reg:SI 58)) -1 (nil)
    (nil))

(code_label 31 34 32 1 "" "" [0 uses])

(insn 32 31 35 (nil) (set (reg/i:SI 0 eax)
        (reg:SI 58)) -1 (nil)
    (nil))

(insn 35 32 0 (nil) (use (reg/i:SI 0 eax)) -1 (nil)
    (nil))
```

Information about Files and Directories

A collection of options can be used to request that the compiler look around the disk to find things for you. Because the system configuration determines the directories in which the compiler searches for libraries, you may find yourself in a situation where you need to verify the location of the actual library being used. This can be done using the -print-file-name option. For example, the following command determines the location of the libgcc.a library:

```
$ gcc -print-file-name=libgcc.a
/usr/lib/gcc-lib/i586-pc-linux-gnu/3.2/libgcc.a
```

The -print-file-name option can be used to locate any library, but the libgcc.a library has an option of its own, as shown in the following example:

```
$ gcc -print-libgcc-file-name
/usr/lib/gcc-lib/i586-pc-linux-gnu/3.2/libgcc.a
```

In similar fashion, you can determine the full path name of the internal subprocesses, such as cc1 and cc1obj. For example, enter the following command to locate f771:

```
$ gcc -print-prog-name=f771
/usr/lib/gcc-lib/i586-pc-linux-gnu/3.2/f771
```

You can determine the current GCC installation directory and the complete search path for both programs and libraries by entering the following command:

```
$ gcc -print-search-dirs >path.text
```

The output from this command can be quite large, and the paths are listed as one continuous line, so it is probably best to redirect the output to a file so you can use an editor to help you analyze it. The installation directory is listed first, followed by programs and libraries. Some of the path names are derived by an algorithm that leaves them more verbose than necessary, but if you need to know the search order you can figure it from the output of this command.

The Complete Reference

Chapter 19

Implementing a Language

Inside the GCC compiler, the *front end* analyzes the syntax and semantics of the programming language, and the *back end* generates the code for the target machine. GCC is designed to allow any number of front ends, and every front end is a different programming language. If you write your own front end for GCC, any of the existing back ends (also known as *ports*) can be installed with it, so your language is portable to a number of machines.

The concept is simple but, as the saying goes, the devil is in the details. Assuming that you have a language parser capable of recognizing the elements of the language you wish to implement, the fact is that you must connect this front end to the rest of the GCC. The parser must produce output in a recognized format. The GCC front end is not as isolated from the back end as perhaps it should be, so there is more to consider than just the raw parser output. Also, there is the possible development of a runtime library for the language.

From Front to Back

The purpose of GCC is to read the source code of a programming language and produce an executable program from it. The following series of steps is an overview of the compilation process:

- **Lexical analysis**   The source code is read and tokenized. This process usually involves reading the source in a stream of one character at a time and deciding which of these characters belong together to have meaning for the language. The tokens can be roughly divided into three categories: names, numbers, and punctuation. Every language has its own set of rules about what is valid and what is not valid in each of these categories.

- **Parsing**   The tokens have relationships among themselves, depending largely on their positions relative to one another in the stream coming in from the lexical scan. The parser determines the type of each token (keyword, symbolic name, number, and so on) and uses this information to form the entire source file into a tree. Nodes in the tree represent data declarations, functions, individual statements, and so on. The entire program is represented by the tree.

- **Pruning**   Some amount of optimization is performed by analyzing the entries in the tree. Redundant and unused portions of the tree are removed. Some portions of the tree may be moved to other locations in the tree to prevent statements from being executed more often than necessary.

- **RTL**   The contents of the parse tree are converted to Register Transfer Language (RTL) code. RTL is a special pseudo assembly language that contains opcodes for a hypothetical machine. The parse tree is "unrolled" into a linear sequence of RTL instructions. The instructions in the tree are reorganized as necessary, with branches inserted as necessary, in accordance with if-condition tests defined in the parse tree. Branching for `case`/`switch` type statements and loops is also inserted. Much of the translation done at this stage is target dependent—that is, the RTL code generated is in terms of the target machine and contains such things as the register allocation information.

- **RTL optimizing**   Optimizations are performed on the RTL code. These optimizations include such things as tail recursion elimination, common subexpression elimination, jump optimization, and several others. This is an excellent place to perform optimization because it will apply to every language front end and every target back end.

- **Assembly language**   The RTL is translated into assembly language for the target machine and written to a file.

- **Assembling**   The assembler is invoked to translate the assembly language file into an object file. This file is not in an executable format—it contains executable object code, but not in a loadable form. Besides, it more than likely contains unresolved references to routines and data in other modules.

- **Linking**   The linker combines object files from the assembler (some of which may be stored in libraries filled with object files) into an executable program.

You should note that there is a logical separation of the front end language parser from the back end code generator, with the parse tree being the intermediary. Any parser that is capable of producing the tree structure can be connected to the back end through the RTL code generator and compiled with GCC. Similarly, any machine for which a code generation program has been written to translate RTL language into native assembly language is capable of producing compiled programs from any of the languages handled by the front end.

It is not quite as simple as this description makes it sound, but it works.

Lexical Scan

A compiler reads the source code of a program as a stream of characters and then groups the characters into a stream of *tokens* for processing. Each token is a number, a name, or punctuation. For example, the following line is made up of seven tokens:

```
if (grimle <= 43.1) {
```

The process of breaking the line into its tokens is called a *lexical scan*, or just *lex* for short. The mechanical process of performing a lexical scan is the same for any language, except for changes in the rules that define which characters are valid for symbols and which are the valid punctuation characters. In fact, the process is consistent enough from one programming language to another that a standard utility exists that can be used to write your lexical scanner program for you. The standard UNIX utility named `lex`—or the GNU equivalent named `flex`—can be given the set of rules that your language is to follow, and it will produce a program that will generate the token stream from the input source.

A Simple Lex

As an example of a simple lex definition, the following defines the two keywords howdy and now:

```
%%
howdy printf("(The word is 'howdy')");
now printf("(The time is %ld)",time(0L));
%%
```

The %% characters specify the beginning and end of the list of character matching. This example will detect a match on either of the two words and execute the command following it. The command is actually a C program statement that will be included in the program produced by this script. The following pair of statements will create the C program, named lex.yy.c, and compile it into an executable named howdy:

```
$ flex howdy.lex
$ gcc lex.yy.c -lfl -o howdy
```

The program lex.yy.c produced in this example is over 1500 lines of C code, and it calls routines in the library named libfl.a. One reason the output code is so large is the number of comments—the generated code is commented well enough to make it relatively easy to determine how it works. If you are using the standard UNIX lex utility instead of the GNU flex program, the form of the commands is slightly different:

```
$ lex howdy.lex
$ gcc lex.yy.c -ll -o howdy
```

This program can be run from the command-line. It will run and wait for input, which you can enter from the keyboard. Anything that you enter that is not one of the two recognized keywords is simply echoed to the output, while the two keywords are replaced by the strings in the printf() function calls.

Lex with Regular Expressions

The following lex definitions will recognize the keywords switch and case, any arbitrary symbol, any integers, and both the left and right braces:

```
%%
switch printf("SWITCH ");
case printf("CASE ");
[a-zA-Z][_a-zA-Z0-9]*  printf("WORD(%s) ",yytext);
[0-9]+ printf("INTEGER(%s) ",yytext);
```

```
\{ printf("LEFTBRACE ");
\} printf("RIGHTBRACE ");
%%
```

The first two rules match the keywords `switch` and `case`. The third rule matches any symbol that begins with an upper or lower case letter and continues with zero or more letters, digits, or underscore characters. Note that the output string includes `yytext`, which is a pointer to the token string itself. The fourth rule matches any string of one or more digits. The last two rules match the left and right braces.

This lex example will extract the tokens of the following input text:

```
blatz {
   switch big_time_do
   case HamFram
   case 889
} dend
```

The following sequence of commands will compile the lex script `kwords.lex` into a program named kwords and then use it to tokenize the source file named `kwtry.text`:

```
$ flex kwords.lex
$ gcc lex.yy.c -lfl -o kwords
$ cat kwtry.text | kwords
WORD(blatz)  LEFTBRACE
   SWITCH  WORD(big_time_do)
   CASE  WORD(HamFram)
   CASE   INTEGER(889)
RIGHTBRACE   WORD(dend)
```

Parsing

The example described in this section is intended to demonstrate the process of using a lexical scan to read the tokens and using a parser to organize the tokens logically, as well as calling a collection of C functions with the organized information. In a compiler the C functions are used to generate the output (in GCC the output is code in the RTL intermediate language), but in this example the output is simply lines of text describing the code that would be generated.

The code that actually performs the job of parsing can be produced by the standard UNIX utility named `yacc`, which is an acronym for Yet Another Compiler Compiler. The GNU utility that performs the same task is named `bison`. The two programs are almost identical in purpose and function.

The example is based on a very simple language named clang that accepts commands to draw colored circles and rectangles at specific locations. The following is an example of a clang program:

```
set color blue;
set location (100,200);
draw circle 30;
set color red;
set location (250,200);
draw rectangle (10,10);
```

The set statement is used to specify the color and the location of the next figure to be drawn. The draw statement renders a figure of the specified type and size.

The following is the content of the file named clang.lex:

```
/* clang.lex */
%{
#include "y.tab.h"
extern int yylval;
extern char *yytext;
%}

%%
set             { return(SETTOKEN); }
color           { return(COLORTOKEN); }
location        { return(LOCATIONTOKEN); }
draw            { return(DRAWTOKEN); }
circle          { return(CIRCLETOKEN); }
rectangle       { return(RECTANGLETOKEN); }
\;              { return(SEMICOLON); }
\,              { return(COMMA); }
\(              { return(LEFTPAREN); }
\)              { return(RIGHTPAREN); }
[0-9]+          {  yylval = atoi(yytext);
                   return(NUMBER);
                }
[a-zA-Z][a-zA-Z0-9]*  { yylval = strdup(yytext);
                        return(NAME);
                      }
\n              /* ignore end of line */
[ \t]+          /* ignore white space */
%%
```

The include file `clang.tab.h` is produced by `bison` from the parser file, as described later. Each of the lexical definitions returns a value specifying its type (as defined in the header file). Because the definitions are used to generate C source code, it is much safer to use the backslash character to escape the punctuation characters recognized as tokens.

Each incoming token is stored as a string pointed to by the variable `yytext`. To make the token available to the C routines, it is necessary that the value of the token be stored—as a type that is valid for it—in the variable `yylval`. In this example, the NAME tokens are saved as strings, and the NUMBER tokens are converted into integers with a call to `atoi()`.

The last two token matches produce nothing, but they are necessary if you wish to successfully scan past multiple spaces, tabs, and the end of lines. To create the parser of a line-oriented language, you could have the newline character return a value that could be detected by the parser.

The following is the contents of the file `clang.y`, which contains the syntax definition of the language:

```
%start commands

%token SETTOKEN DRAWTOKEN COLORTOKEN
%token LOCATIONTOKEN CIRCLETOKEN RECTANGLETOKEN
%token SEMICOLON LEFTPAREN RIGHTPAREN COMMA
%token NUMBER NAME


%%

commands:
    /* nothing */
    | commands command
    ;


command: SETTOKEN set SEMICOLON
    | DRAWTOKEN draw SEMICOLON
    ;

set: COLORTOKEN NAME
        { setcolor($2); }
    | LOCATIONTOKEN LEFTPAREN NUMBER COMMA NUMBER RIGHTPAREN
        { setlocation($3,$5); }
    ;

draw: CIRCLETOKEN NUMBER
        { drawcircle($2); }
```

```
|  RECTANGLETOKEN LEFTPAREN NUMBER COMMA NUMBER RIGHTPAREN
      { drawrectangle($3,$5); }
   ;

%%
```

The first line of the file specifies the starting point of the syntax tree definitions. Following that are the token definitions—these are named constants in the generated code that are used as unique identifiers for each token found in the input stream.

Each entry in the parse definition is called a *production*. Each production has a name, and the name is associated with one or more syntax layout definitions to its right. The syntax items on the right are separated by vertical bar (|) characters, and the last one is terminated by a semicolon. The parser matches the incoming stream of tokens against the items on the right side of the production until it finds a match.

The kind of parser generated by bison or yacc reads the tokens from left to right and, to determine a match, will look ahead by no more than one token. This kind of parser is called a LALR(1) parser, or simply an LR(1) parser. This is quite sufficient to handle modern programming languages, but older languages with more ambiguous syntax require special handling. Modern languages are designed with an LR(1) parser in mind.

The starting production is named commands. The commands production can either be empty (which happens at the end of the file) or can contain a list of one or more commands. When you first look at the production, it may appear backwards to you—but the fact that it refers to itself again before it refers to the next production has to do with the nature of the recursive code generated by the parser. It will actually work either way, but things run more efficiently with them in the order shown.

The commands production will match either the set or draw language keyword. The one it matches determines the productions that are used to match the following tokens. The set keyword directs the parser to the production named set, and the draw keyword directs the parser to the draw production. The production names don't have to match the keywords, but it does seem to make them easier to read.

Inside each production is some C code enclosed in braces. This can be any arbitrary C code, but this example simply makes calls to functions that are described further on. The arguments to the functions are determined by the position of the item (or value) in the production. The parameter named $1 is the first one, $2 is the second, and so on. Note that the values passed to the functions in this example are either NAME or NUMBER tokens, which have C code in their lex definitions to assign their values to yylval.

All that is left to do is define the C code that will be used to generate the object code from the source code. This example, instead of producing code, simply prints out a description of the code it would produce. The following C source file contains the functions required to be present in all parsers, along with the functions called from the productions defining the language:

```
/* clmain.c */
#include "clang.tab.h"
#include <stdio.h>

char colorname[30] = "black";
int x = 0;
int y = 0;

main()
{
    yyparse();
}
int yywrap()
{
    return(1);
}
void yyerror(const char *str)
{
    fprintf(stderr,"Clang: %s\n",str);
}

int setcolor(char *name)
{
    strcpy(colorname,name);
    return(0);
}

/* Save the x and y location of the
   next figure to be drawn. */
int setlocation(int xloc,int yloc)
{
    x = xloc;
    y = yloc;
}

/* Draw a circle of the of the specified size and color
   at the current location. */
int drawcircle(int radius)
{
    printf("Draw %s circle at (%d,%d) radius=%d\n",
        colorname,x,y,radius);
}

/* Draw a rectangle of the specified height, width, and color
```

```
   at the current location. */
int drawrectangle(int height,int width)
{
    printf("Draw %s rectangle at (%d,%d) h=%d w=%d\n",
        colorname,x,y,height,width);
}
```

The header file `clang.tab.h` is the one produced from clang.y by `bison`, and it contains some constant definitions that may be useful in the code. The `main()` function is the mainline of the compiler. In this example, it only calls `yyparse()` to perform the action of parsing, but in an actual compiler it would also be responsible for creating the intermediate language, managing the conversion from intermediate language into object code, performing optimizations, determining the names of the input and output files, responding to the command-line options, and any other actions the compiler is to perform.

The `yywrap()` function is called at the end of the current input file and can be used to start the reading of another source file. A return value of 1 indicates that there is no more input.

The `yyerror()` function is called by the parser if an error occurs. The character string passed to the function contains a description of the error. This example simply prints the error message to standard error.

The `setcolor()` function is called by the parser whenever the keyword `set` is used to specify a new color. Depending on the code being generated, as well as the underlying graphics facilities, this function could generate code to make a change to the color or, as in this case, save the color information locally so it can be accessed later as needed.

The `setlocation()` function is similar to the `setcolor()` function, except it defines the location to be used to draw the next figure. In this example, the coordinates are saved locally so they will be available when it comes time to actually draw the figure.

The `drawcircle()` and `drawrectangle()` functions are called to generate code that will do the actual rendering. The previous set color and location information can be used as part of the generated instructions. This example simply prints the information that would be used to generate the code.

The following series of commands can be used to compile and link the source files into a program that can be used to read source code and produce the pseudo instructions for drawing shapes:

```
$ bison -d clang.y
$ flex clang.lex
$ gcc clmain.c lex.yy.c clang.tab.c -o clang
```

The `bison` command reads the input source file `clang.y` and produces the output file `clang.tab.c`. The file `clang.tab.c` contains the C code that parses the input, so it must be compiled and linked into the compiler. Also, because the `-d` option is specified, the file `clang.tab.h` is also produced. This is the header file used in `clmain.c` and `clang.lex` to provide the numeric definitions of all the token types.

The `flex` command is used to produce the file named `lex.yy.c`, which contains the C functions for reading the input stream and organizing it into tokens.

The `gcc` command is used to compile and link the three C source files into an executable named `clang`. As it is written, the compiler accepts source code from standard input, so the source file of the test program, named `figures.clang`, can be processed with the following command:

```
$ cat figures.clang | clang
```

The resulting output looks like the following:

```
Draw blue circle at (100,200) radius=30
Draw red rectangle at (250,200) h=10 w=10
```

Creating the Parse Tree

The output from the parse operation is a parse tree. The actual format of the tree is a linear list of lines of text, with each line being a node in the tree. Each node has an identifier so it can be referred to from any other node, and it contains a character that specifies the node type. The node types, and the characters that designate them, are listed in Table 19-1.

Designator	Type Description
<	Comparison expression
1	Unary arithmetic expression
2	Binary arithmetic expression
b	A lexical block
c	Constant
d	Variable declaration or variable reference
e	An expression that is not a comparison, unary, or binary expression and does not have side effects
r	A reference to a memory location
s	An expression that inherently has side effects
t	A data type
x	A special node that does not fit any other category

Table 19-1. *The Character Designators of the Node Types of the Parse Tree*

The node type indicators are defined in the GCC source file tree.def. Many functions exist to create tree nodes, and they are found in stmt.c. There are many any functions available to create tree nodes—so many, in fact, it seems that any possible statement you can think of has its own RTL code generator. For example, the following function generates code that compares op1 to op2 and branches to label only if the two are equal:

```
static void do_jump_if_equal(op1,op2,label,unsignedp);
```

In this example, both op1 and op2 are expression tree nodes, and label is a memory reference to a location in the executable code. The last parameter specifies whether the comparison is to be signed or unsigned. This function examines the arguments to determine exactly what code should be generated (for example, if op1 and op2 are both constant values and are equal to one another, a simple branch instruction is generated). Once the form of the instruction is determined, a routine is called to actually emit the instruction.

The low-level RTL-generation routines are in the source file emit-rtl.c. Probably the simplest of these is the emit_note() function, which emits an instruction that doesn't do anything other than act as a placeholder. The code that actually creates the instructions and adds them to the RTL output looks like the following:

```
note = rtx_alloc(NOTE);
INSN_UID(note) = cur_insn_uid++;
NOTE_SOURCE_FILE(note) = file;
BLOCK_FOR_INSN(note) = NULL;
add_insn(note);
```

In this code sequence, a new RTL tree node of the appropriate type and size is created with the call to rtx_alloc(). A tree node (defined as the struct rtx_def in the file rtl.h) consists of a collection of identifying flags at its head, followed by a variable length array containing the operands. The macro INSN_UID inserts the unique tree node ID number. The macro NOTE_SOURCE_FILE adds source file information to the node.

The call to add_insn() adds the newly constructed node to the end of the linked list that is the RTL code. The function add_insn_before() can be used to insert a new instruction in front of an existing instruction, and add_insn_after() can be used to insert a new instruction immediately following an existing instruction.

No symbol table information is carried forward into the RTL. It is necessary for a symbol table of some form to exist in the front end to resolve references to names, but it can be ignored at this point because RTL code makes all references directly to tree nodes by their ID numbers. However, the symbol table must exist and be accessible from the back end of the compiler.

Connecting the Back to the Front

The back end of the compiler is not cleanly separated from the front end. A number of global variables and functions must be declared as part of the front end so they can be directly accessed from the back end.

The code for the front end should be isolated in its own subdirectory beneath the main gcc directory. For example, the cp directory contains the code for C++, and the directory ada contains the code for the Ada compiler. In this directory is a file named Make-lang.in that is included by the main makefile in the parent gcc directory and by the makefile for the language. The file Makefile.in is also included, and it is used to create the makefile for the language. The file config-lang.in is used by the configure script.

The driver program gcc must be modified to include the new language, but these modifications occur automatically as part of the build process.

The front end must contain certain global variables and functions that are referenced from the back end. The purpose of these is to provide access to the tree nodes and the symbol table, as well as for general initialization and cleanup. Table 19-2 contains a brief description of the required global variables. Table 19-3 contains a brief description of the functions that must exist in the compiler front end to be addressed from the back end. Many of these functions and variables are also used in the front end, but they must exist as globals with these names.

Name	Description
error_mark_node	The parent node of a tree containing nodes representing error conditions in the input
integer_type_node	A tree node of the fundamental integer type
char_type_node	A tree node of the fundamental character type
void_type_node	A tree node of the fundamental void type
integer_zero_node	A tree node of the integer value 0
integer_one_node	A tree node of the integer value 1
tree_current_function_decl	A tree node representing the current function being translated

Table 19-2.   *Front End Variables Addressed from the GCC Back End*

Name	Description
language_string	The address of a character string naming the language
flag_traditional	Required, but used only by C

Table 19-2.   *Front End Variables Addressed from the GCC Back End* (continued)

Name	Description
lang_init()	Performs all language-specific initializations
lang_finish()	Performs all language-specific finalization and cleanup
lang_decode_option()	Called with the options found on the command line
init_lex()	Performs all initializations required for lexical analysis
init_parse()	Performs all initializations required by the parser
finish_parse()	Performs all parser finalization and cleanup
type_for_mode()	Returns a tree node representing a machine data type
type_for_size()	Returns an integer tree node with the specified number of bits of precision
type_for_unsigned()	Returns an unsigned integer tree node of the specified size
signed_type()	Returns a signed integer tree node of the specified size
signed_or_unsigned_type()	Returns a tree node of the specified type and specified signedness

Table 19-3.   *Front End Functions Called from the GCC Back End*

Name	Description
`init_decl_processing()`	Initializes the tree node variables listed in Table 19-2
`global_bindings_p()`	Returns a value that indicates whether the current scope is global
`kept_level_p()`	Returns a value that indicates whether the current level needs to have a data block created
`getdecls()`	Returns a tree listing all declarations at the current scope level
`pushdecl()`	Inserts a declaration into the symbol table and returns a tree node
`pushlevel()`	Creates a new scope level in the symbol table
`poplevel()`	Abandons the current scope level of the symbol table and restores the previous state
`insert_block()`	Adds a new block to the end of the list of blocks in the current scope level
`set_block()`	Sets the block node for the current scope level
`maybe_build_cleanup()`	May return a tree node that represents an action to be taken to clean up behind previous actions (such as destroying objects)
`truthvalue_conversion()`	Returns an expression that is the same as the specified expression, except it results in `true` or `false`
`mark_addressable()`	Marks the specified expression as one that addresses memory
`copy_lang_decl()`	Duplicates the specified declaration tree node
`incomplete_type_error()`	Prints an error message for using an incomplete type

Table 19-3. *Front End Functions Called from the GCC Back End* (continued)

Name	Description
yyerror()	Prints a parse error message
print_lang_decl()	Outputs a tree node declaration to the specified file
print_lang_type()	Outputs the type information of the tree node to the specified file
print_lang_identifier()	Outputs the identifier information of the tree node to the specified file
set_yydebug()	Sets debugging on or off for syntax analysis

Table 19-3. *Front End Functions Called from the GCC Back End* (continued)

The Complete Reference

Chapter 20

Register Transfer Language

he Register Transfer Language (RTL) is the central point of the compilation process. The purpose of the front end of the compiler is to produce RTL, and the purpose of the back end is to translate the RTL into assembly language. Most of the optimization processing is performed on the program while it is in the RTL form. This chapter is a description of the form of RTL.

The RTL code can be dumped to disk files in a text format. Chapter 18 contains examples of the procedure required for dumping RTL code into its printed form. This chapter contains a description of the RTL code as well as information you will need to be able to read the codes embedded in the dumped format.

RTL Insns

A single statement in the RTL is called an *insn*. The insns are connected internally as a doubly linked list. Some insns are actual instructions while others contain information such as branch tables used for switch statements. Yet others represent data declarations and act as labels for branching targets. Also, each insn has a unique ID by which any insn can refer to any other insn.

The Six Fundamental Expression Codes

There are many different kinds of insns. Each insn has an expression code that designates its type. The RTL code making up the logic flow of a program is composed of only six fundamental types, but each of these can hold references to other types. For example, an expression code of insn, which indicates an executable statement, will include other insns as its operands. For example, the following insn reads the value of the variable named val and stores it in a register. To do this, the RTL code has an expression code of insn and contains an insn with the expression code set, which in turn employs insns with expression codes of reg and mem. The mem insn contains a symbol_ref insn.

```
(insn 12 10 14 (nil) (set (reg:SI 61)
    (mem/f:SI (symbol_ref:SI("val")) [0 a+0 S4 A32])) -1 (nil)
    (nil))
```

The insn expression code is one of the six fundamental expression code types. Every RTL program is composed of a combination of the six expression codes listed in Table 20-1.

The Type and Content of Insns

Each type of insn is unique and is designed to serve a special purpose; therefore, each one contains data that pertains to its purpose. Quite often the contained data is in the form of another insn, but this chain of linked RTL instructions can always be traced to

Expression Code	Description
insn	This expression code is used for instructions that do not jump and do not make function calls. This type of insn loads registers, performs arithmetic, compares values, and so on.
jump_insn	This expression code is used for instructions that will (or may) jump to another location, which means the insn will usually contain one or more label_ref insns. This expression code is also used to return from the current function. A reference to the code_label insn, which is the target of the jump, is included for simple conditional or unconditional jumps. For more complicated jumps, it may be necessary to scan the entire body of insns to find the possible targets.
call_insn	This expression code is used for instructions that will (or may) perform a function call. These instructions must be handled specially because they could unexpectedly modify registers and memory locations. An insn of this type typically contains clobber and mem insns to specify which registers and memory locations are altered. There is either a mem insn that specifies the memory block in which parameters are passed, or there are clobber and use insns that specify the work registers and the registers bearing arguments.
code_label	This expression code is used to mark a label that can be the target of a jump. It contains a code_label_number insn to hold the unique label ID number. The ID number is unique to the entire compilation unit, not just the current function. The code_label insn is generally referred to at the jump location inside a label_ref insn. During and after the optimization, a count is maintained of the number of times this label is used as a jump target. Each code_label is one of the following four kinds: NORMAL This is the only kind of label that cannot be an alternate entry point into a function. STATIC_ENTRY This label is an entry point into the function but is visible only from within the compilation unit. GLOBAL_ENTRY This label is an entry point into the function and is visible (through the linker) to all compilation units. WEAK_ENTRY This label is an entry point into the function and is a global entry, but it can be overridden by another symbol of the same name.

Table 20-1.   *The Six Fundamental RTL Expression Codes*

PERIPHERALS AND
INTERNALS

Expression Code	Description
barrier	This expression code is placed in the sequence of insns to mark a location that cannot be reached through control flow. A barrier insn is inserted following an unconditional jump and following calls to functions that cannot return.
note	This expression code is used to contain certain debugging and declarative information. Each note insn contains one field that contains a number and another field that contains a character string. The number is usually the line number of the source file named by the string. The note insn controls the line number information used for debugging. If the number is not a line number, it is a type designator specifying one of the following types: NOTE_INSN_DELETED The note marks a point at which an insn was deleted. NOTE_INSN_DELETED_LABEL This note replaces a deleted code_label insn, which was removed because it was never the target of a jump. NOTE_INSN_BLOCK_BEG Marks the beginning of a scoping level block of code. NOTE_INSN_BLOCK_END Marks the end of a scoping level block of code. NOTE_INSN_EH_REGION_BEG Marks the beginning of a scoping level for exception handling. NOTE_INSN_EH_REGION_END Marks the end of a scoping level for exception handling. NOTE_INSN_LOOP_BEG Marks the beginning of a while or for loop. NOTE_INSN_LOOP_END Marks the end of a while or for loop. NOTE_INSN_LOOP_CONT Marks the place in a loop to which a continue statement would jump. NOTE_INSN_LOOP_VTOP Marks the place in a loop where the exit test begins. NOTE_INSN_FUNCTION_END Marks the spot near the end of a function just in front of the label jumped to by return statements. NOTE_INSN_SETJMP Marks the code immediately following a call to a setjmp() type of function.

Table 20-1. *The Six Fundamental RTL Expression Codes* (continued)

some fundamental data. The data contained in statements of the RTL language is in the form of one of the five insn types listed in Table 20-2.

The format and content of the RTX varies widely, but three fields are always present: the ID, the address of the previous insn, and the address of the next insn. These three values can be extracted from any insn by using the following three macros:

```
INSN_UID(insn)
PREV_INSN(insn)
NEXT_INSN(insn)
```

The first insn can be retrieved by calling `get_insns()`, and the last one can be retrieved by calling `get_last_insn()`.

Most of the GCC code that deals with insns is written to deal with expressions. An RTL expression insn is referred to as an RTX. These expression insns are the statements that contain the executable code of the program. Inside the GCC code they are stored in a struct that is referenced through a pointer that has the typedef name `rtx`.

Each RTX has its own *expression code* (or RTX code) that specifies which kind of expression it is. The expression codes are defined in the file `rtl.def` as a collection of enumeration constant names. The expression codes are machine independent, which

Insn Type	Description
Expression	An executable statement. An RTL expression is called an RTX.
Integer	An integer data type in the form of a C language `int` data type.
Wide integer	An integer data type in the form defined by `HOST_WIDE_INT`, which is normally defined as a 64-bit value.
String	A sequence of characters stored internally with a terminating null, as in standard C. Strings are mostly used for symbol name references, but they are also used to represent machine description information, as described in Chapter 21. A zero-length string is represented internally as a null pointer.
Vector	An arbitrary number of pointers to expressions. The number of members in a vector is explicitly stated in the insn. Vectors of zero length are represented internally as null pointers.

Table 20-2.   *The Fundamental Insn Data Types of RTL*

means the RTL language is machine independent. The RTX code can be set in an `rtx` struct and then retrieved by using the following two macros defined in `rtl.h`:

```
PUT_CODE(rtx,code);
int code = GET_CODE(rtx);
```

The macro named `DEF_RTL_EXPR` is used to define each RTL in the file `rtl.def`. This macro has four arguments, as shown the following example:

```
DEF_RTL_EXPR(COND_EXEC,"cond_exec","ee",'x')
```

The first argument passed to the macro is the name of the RTL in all uppercase letters. It is used in the C source code as an `enum` as the unique identifier of the RTL. The second argument is the name of the RTL as a lowercase ASCII string. It is this name that is printed in the diagnostic output. The third argument is a list of the data types of the operands, with each type being designated by a single character. A description of the types is found in Table 20-3. The fourth argument is the single-letter class designator of the RTL. The classes are listed in Table 20-4.

Operand Code	Description
*	Unspecified. An attempt to process this type will generate a warning message.
0	An unused field.
b	A pointer to a bitmap header.
B	A definition of a basic block of instructions (one entrance, one exit).
e	A pointer to an RTL expression.
E	A pointer to an array of RTL expressions.
i	An integer.

Table 20-3.   *The Codes Used to Specify RTX Operand Types*

Operand Code	Description
n	An integer that specifies one of the following:
	1 Instruction deleted
	2 The beginning of a block
	3 The end of a block
	4 The beginning of a loop
	5 The end of a loop
	6 The continuation of a loop
	7 An instruction at the top of the loop
	8 A loop-ending conditional
	9 The end of a function
	10 The end of the function prologue
	11 The beginning of the function epilogue
	12 A deleted label
	13 The beginning (entry point) of a function
	14 The beginning of an exception handling region
	15 The ending of an exception handling region
	16 A repeated line number
	17 A basic block
	18 An expected value
	19 A prediction
s	A character string.
S	An optional character string.
u	A pointer to another insn.
t	A tree pointer.
T	Code to be assembled or compiled and executed. It is assembly language source, unless the first character is an asterisk, in which case the language is C.
V	An optional pointer to an array of RTL expressions.

Table 20-3. *The Codes Used to Specify RTX Operand Types* (continued)

Class	Description
<	An RTX code that is a comparison operator, such as less than or equals
1	An RTX code that is a unary arithmetic operator, such as negation or one's compliment
2	An RTX code that is a noncommutative binary operation, such as subtraction or division
3	An RTX code that is a non-bitfield three-input operation, such as if/then/else
a	An RTX code for autoincrement addressing modes
b	An RTX code for a bit-field operation, such as zero extract or sign extract
c	An RTX code for a commutative binary operation, such as addition or multiplication
g	An RTX code for grouping instructions together
i	An RTX code for a machine instruction, such as jump or call
m	An RTX code for something used to match insns
o	An RTX code that represents an object, such as a memory location or a register
x	The code for any RTL that does not fit into any of the other classes

Table 20-4. *The Class Codes of an RTL*

The number of and type of operands vary from one RTL code to the next. Table 20-3 contains a description of the codes used to indicate the data type of the operands. These codes are not strictly adhered to. For example, although the code T is used to indicate the source of executable code, and s is used to indicate a simple string, some of the RTL definitions have C source code included as an s type. Each RTL code is processed separately, so the operands can be almost anything—the letters indicating the types are very general and used only for printing the operand values for debugging.

The following list provides a description of the RTL codes. Each RTL is listed by its name, followed by its class and the character string that specifies the type and number of operands associated with it. Each entry contains a description of its purpose and a list of the meaning and type of the operands it employs. The operands are of the data type and appear in the order shown in the quoted string. In the GCC code, an uppercase form of the name of the RTL code is used to define an enumerated type used as a numeric ID for the RTL—for example, the `eq_attr` RTL has a constant named `EQ_ATTR` as its unique identifier. As noted in the descriptions, some of the RTL codes serve a special purpose—for example, some of them are used to create lists of expressions, while others are used as a convenience and never actually appear in an insn. Rather they are used only as special entries in the machine descriptions.

- **abs '1' "e"**   If the value resulting from the expression is negative, convert it to a positive value.

- **absence_set 'x' "ss"**   This appears only in machine descriptions to specify a list of CPU functional units that cannot be reserved only if certain other functional units are also not reserved. For example, in the VLIW processor, slot0 cannot be reserved following slot1 or slot2. Also see `presence_set`. Operand 0 is a comma separated list of functional units that cannot be reserved unless at least one functional unit from operand 1 is also reserved. Operand 1 is a comma separated list of functional units.

- **addr_diff_vec 'x' "eEee0"**   This contains a vector of address differences between a base operation and a target operation to be used in spacing calculations. The operands 2, 3, and 4 are valid only when `CASE_VECTOR_SHORTEN_MODE` has been defined in the compiler. Operand 0 is the base operation. Operand 1 is the address differences representing the distance of each operand from the base operation. Operand 2 is the label representing the minimum address. Operand 3 is the label representing the maximum address. Operand 4 is a set of flags to determine the rules for flag shortening. The flag "min_align" specifies to use the minimum alignment for any branch. The flag "base_after_vec" specifies that the address of the base is after the `addr_diff_vec`. The flag "min_after_vec" specifies the minimum address target label is after the `addr_diff_vec`. The flag "max_after_vec" specifies the maximum address target label is after the `addr_diff_vec`. The flag "min_after_base" specifies the minimum address target label is after the base. The flag "max_after_base" specifies the maximum address target label is after the base. The flag "offset_aligned" specifies that offsets must be treated as unsigned values. The flag "scale" specifies that it is necessary to make offsets fit into the mode.

- **addr_vec 'x' "E"**   A vector of addresses. Each address is included as a `label_ref` to a `code_label`.

- **address 'm' "e"**   A reference to the address of an argument. Operand 0 is an expression specifying the address.

- **addressof 'o' "eit"**   A reference to an address of a register, which is removed by `purse_addressof()` in the compiler after as many register addresses as possible have been removed by being elided. Operand 0 is the register. Operand 1 is the original pseudo register number for which the insn was generated. Operand 2 is the declaration of the item stored in the register, for use by put_reg_in_stack.

- **and 'c' "ee"** The two operands are evaluated and the result is taken as a bitwise AND of the two values.

- **ashift '2' "ee"** A bitwise logical shift to the left. Operand 0 is the expression producing the value to be shifted. Operand 1 is the expression producing the value of the number of bits to shift.

- **ashiftrt '2' "ee"** A bitwise arithmetic shift to the right (with sign extension). Operand 0 is the expression producing the value to be shifted. Operand 1 is the expression producing the value of the number of bits to shift.

- **asm_input 'x' "s"** A string that is passed through to the assembler as an instruction. This can be used inside other insns as part of a pattern of code, and it can also be used for the insertion of comments in the assembler code.

- **asm_operands 'x' "ssiEEsi"** An assembly language instruction with its operands. Operand 0 is the template defining the instruction. Operand 1 is the constraint for the output. Operand 2 is an identifying value that distinguishes this assembly language statement from the others. Operand 3 is a collection of values to be used as input operands. Operand 4 is a collection of modes and constraints for the input operands. Each member of the array is an asm_input with a constraint string specifying the mode of the input operand. Operand 5 is the name of the containing source file. Operand 6 is the line number of the containing source file.

- **attr 'x' "s"** This is used only in the machine descriptions to define insn attributes. It is a marker that can be inserted to specify the name of an attribute. Operand 0 is the name of the attribute.

- **attr_flag 'x' "s"** This is used only in the machine descriptions to define attributes. If the conditional expression is true, the setting specifies the probability of a branch being taken, and the insn being executed is specified by the flag. The valid flag values are "forward", "backward", "very_likely", "likely", "very_unlikely", and "unlikely". Operand 0 is the value of the flag.

- **automota_option 'x' "s"** This appears only in machine descriptions as an option for generating automata. For operand 0, the option "no-minimization" means the automata cannot be minimized, which only has meaning when the CPU functional unit reservations are to be queried in an automaton state. The option "time" is a request to print additional timing statistics in the generation of automata. The option "v" is a request for the generation of a file with the suffix .dfa, containing verification and debugging information. The option "w" causes the generation of error messages instead of warning messages for noncritical errors. The option `"ndfa"` causes the creation of a nondeterministic finite-state automata.

- **barrier 'x' "iuu"**   A marker that indicates that control flow will not pass through. Operand 0 is the unique ID of this RTX. Operand 1 is a pointer to the previous instruction in the chain. Operand 2 is a pointer to the next instruction in the chain.

- **call 'x' "ee"**   Calls a subroutine. Operand 0 is the address of the subroutine to be called. Operand 1 is the number of arguments being passed to the subroutine.

- **call_insn 'i' "iuuBteieee"**   An insn that can possibly call a subroutine but cannot change the address to which the subroutine is to return. Operand 0 is the unique ID of this RTX. Operand 1 is a pointer to the previous instruction in the chain. Operand 2 is a pointer to the next instruction in the chain. Operand 3 is the basic block of instructions. Operand 4 is a pointer to the tree node. Operand 9 is a `call_insn_function_usage` insn that makes the function call.

- **call_placeholder 'x' "uuuu"**   A placeholder that is to be replaced by a `call_insn` or by code for a sibling call or tail recursion. Operand 0 is the unique ID of this RTX. Operand 1 is a pointer to the previous instruction in the chain. Operand 2 is a pointer to the next instruction in the chain. Operand 3 is a `code_label` insn for the label used in tail recursion. This is null if no tail recursion possibilities were found.

- **clobber'x' "e"**   An indicator that something is being used in a way that's not necessary to explain. For example, a subroutine call will use a register internally and overwrite any value stored there. Also see `use`. Operand 0 is the expression specifying the item being used.

- **cc0 'o' ""**   Represents the condition code register. The logic used with the insn is as if the condition code register contains a value that can be compared to zero but, in fact, is a true/false setting that is the result of a prior comparison.

- **code_label 'x' "iuuB00iss"**   A label followed by instructions. Operand 0 is the unique ID of this RTX. Operand 1 is a pointer to the previous instruction in the chain. Operand 2 is a pointer to the next instruction in the chain. Operand 3 is the basic block of instructions following the label. Operand 4 is the jump count of the label. Operand 5 is a pointer to the chain of label references to this label. Operand 6 is a unique identification number. Operand 7 is the name the user assigned to the label, if any. Operand 8 is an alternate label name used internally.

- **compare '2' "ee"**   The two operands are evaluated and compared for equality to produce a zero value if they match and a nonzero value if they do not match.

- **concat 'o' "ee"**   A concatenation of the two expressions in such a way that it creates a value with the number of bits equal to the sum of the number of bits in the two expressions. This is used for complex numbers and normally appears during RTL generation but not in the final insn chain.

- **cond 'x' "Ee"** A general conditional statement. Operand 0 is a vector of pairs of expressions. The first member of each pair is evaluated in turn, and the second member of each pair is the conditional expression that results in zero for false and a nonzero value for true. Operand 1 is used as the conditional expression if none of the pairs of expressions in operand 0 evaluates to true.

- **cond_exec 'x' "ee"** A conditional expression and a block of code that is executed when the conditional is true. The conditional expression has no side effects. Operand 0 is the conditional expression. Operand 1 is the insn to be executed.

- **const 'o' "e"** An expression that results in a constant value. This forces it to be recognized as a constant value by the compiler instead of as an expression to be generated into the final code.

- **const_double 'o' "ww"** A numeric floating-point constant. The operands are chains of values that make up the entire value of the doubles. The syntax is shown as `"ww"`, but it actually ranges from `"ww"` to `"wwwww"`, depending on the size of the floating-point format on the target hardware.

- **const_int 'o' "w"** A numeric integer constant.

- **const_string 'o' "s"** A string constant. At this time, this is only used for attributes.

- **const_vector 'x' "E"** A vector (array) constant.

- **constant_p_rtx 'x' "e"** A `__builtin_constant_p` expression. This is created during RTL generation only if optimization is turned on, and it is eliminated during the first CSE pass.

- **define_asm_attributes 'x' "V"** Defines attribute computation for assembly language instructions. Operand 0 is a vector containing the list of attributes.

- **define_attr 'x' "sse"** This is used only in the machine descriptions to define insn attributes. Operand 0 is the name of the attribute being defined. Operand 1 is a comma-separated list of possible values for the attribute. Operand 2 is an expression to be used for the default setting of the attribute.

- **define_automaton 'x' "s"** This appears only in machine descriptions to name automata used for pipeline hazards recognition. The name is used in `define_cpu_unit` and `define_query_cpu_unit`. Operand 0 is a comma-separated list of names.

- **define_bypass 'x' "issS"** This appears only in machine descriptions to specify the latency from one set of insns to another. Operand 0 is the latency value. Operand 1 is a comma-separated list of insn names from which the latency timing begins. Operand 2 is a comma-separated list of insn names at which the latency timing ends. Operand 3 is an optional function name that receives the two insns as arguments and returns a bypass value. The return value is zero if the bypass is to be ignored in this particular case.

■ **define_cond_exec 'x' "Ess"**   The definition of a conditional execution meta-operation to generate new instances of define_insn. Operand 0 indicates the expressions to be used for matching. Operand 1 is a C language conditional expression that must result in a nonzero value for a pattern to match. Operand 2 is a block of either C or assembly language code to produce the assembly language output.

■ **define_cpu_unit 'x' "sS"**   This appears only in machine descriptions to define the names of the CPU functional units. Operand 0 is a comma-separated list of the CPU functional unit names. Operand 1 is the name of the automaton, as described in define_automaton.

■ **define_delay 'x' "eE"**   Defines a requirement for delay slots. Operand 0 is a conditional expression that evaluates to true to indicate the insn requires the number of delay slots specified. Operand 1 is a vector (the length of which is three times the length of the number of required slots) containing a set of three conditions for each slot. The first is true to indicate that an insn is to occupy the slot position. The second is true for each insn that can be annulled if the branch is taken. The third is true for each insn that can be annulled if the branch is not taken.

■ **define_expand 'x' "sEss"**   Defines how to generate multiple insns for a standard insn name. Operand 0 is the standard insn name. Operand 1 is the vector of insn patterns to be matched. Operand 2 is a C language expression that must result in a nonzero value for this operation to be available. Operand 3 is some C language code to be executed prior to generating the insns. This could, for example, be code to create an RTX sequence for use in generating code.

■ **define_function_unit 'x' "siieiiV"**   A set of insns that require a function unit. That is, each of these insns produces a result after a delay, and there may be restrictions on the number of insns of this type that can be scheduled to execute simultaneously because of possible restrictions on the number of function units in the CPU. More than one define_function can be declared for the same CPU, but the first operands must be the same for the same function unit. Operand 0 is the name of the function unit. Operand 1 is the number of identical function units in the CPU. Operand 2 is the maximum number of simultaneous function units available in the CPU. The number 0 indicates there is no limit. The number 1 indicates only one insn at a time can use the function unit. Operand 3 is a conditional expression involving the function attribute that results in a nonzero value if the function applies to this insn. Operand 4 is the constant delay value after which the result of the insn using the function will be available. Operand 5 is the constant delay value after which another insn can use the same function unit. Operand 6, if specified, is a list of attribute expressions. If any of these expressions results in a nonzero value, the function unit is currently executing, and an appropriate amount of delay must be inserted. If the result is zero for all expressions, the function unit is available and can be scheduled immediately, subject to the limit specified by operand 2.

- **define_insn 'x' "sEsTV"**   This appears only in machine descriptions and is the definition of one kind of instruction. Operand 0 is the name of the instruction. If the name is a null string, the instruction is part of the machine description solely for the purpose of being recognized in matches and will never appear as an RTX. Operand 1 is the pattern of the expression. Operand 2 is a C expression specifying additional conditions for recognizing this pattern. If this is a null string, there are no further conditions. Operand 3 is assembly language defining the action to be taken if the match is successful. If the exprssion begins with an asterisk, it is C instead of assembly. Operand 4 is an optional vector of attributes for this insn (see `set_attr` and `set_attr_alternative`).

- **define_insn_and_split 'x' "sEsTsESV"**   The definition of an insn and its associated split. This is produced from concatenating a `define_insn` and a `define_split`, where the two share the same patterns. Operand 0 is the name of the instruction. If the name is null, the instruction is stored in the machine descriptions only to be matched and will never be used to create an actual RTX. Operand 1 is the vector of expressions to be matched. Operand 2 is the C source code to be used as an extra expression in matching. This operand can be a null string. Operand 3 is the source code of an action to be executed when a match is found. Operand 4 is the C source code of an expression that must result in a nonzero value. Operand 5 is the vector of expressions to be placed in the `sequence`. Operand 6 is some C language code to be executed prior to generating the insns. This could, for example, be code to create an RTX `sequence` for use in generating code. Operand 7 is a vector of attributes for this insn.

- **define_insn_reservation 'x' "sies"**   This appears only in machine descriptions to describe the reservation of CPU functional units. Operand 0 is a string used as descriptive output for debugging and tracing. Operand 3 is the regular expression used to select the instructions. The regular expression uses the following syntax: The vertical bar (|) is used in the expression as an OR operator, and the plus sign (+) is used as an AND operator. The asterisk (*) is used to repeat an element a specified number of times. The `cpu_function_unit_name` is the name of a CPU function unit. The `reservation_name` is one defined by `define_reservation`. The following is the syntax of the regular expression:

```
regexp  = regexp "," oneof
        | oneof

oneof   = allof "+" repeat
        | repeat

repeat  = element "*" number
        | element
```

```
element = cpu_function_unit_name
        | reservation_name
        | result_name
        | "nothing"
        | "(" regexp ")"
```

- **define_peephole 'x' "sEsTV"**   The definition of a peephole optimization. Operand 0 is the name of the optimization. Operand 1 is the vector of instructions to which this optimization may be applied. Operand 3 is a C language expression that must result in a nonzero value. Operand 4 is an optional list of attributes for this insn (see `set_attr` and `set_attr_alternative`).

- **define_peephole2 'x' "EsES"**   The definition of an RTL peephole optimization operation. Operand 0 is the vector of insns to match. Operand 1 is a C language expression that must result in a nonzero value. Operand 2 is a vector of insns to be placed into the `sequence`. Operand 3 is some C language code to be executed prior to generating the insns. This could, for example, be code to create an RTX `sequence` for use in generating code.

- **define_query_cpu_unit 'x' "sS"**   This appears only in machine descriptions to describe the CPU functional units defined by `define_cpu_unit`. Operand 0 is a comma-separated list of CPU functional unit names. Operand 1 is the name of the automation, as described in `define_automaton`.

- **define_reservation 'x' "ss"**   This appears only in machine descriptions to specify a collection of CPU functional units that are commonly reserved as a group. Operand 0 is the name assigned to the collection of functional units. Operand 1 is the list of CPU functional units that is to be identified by the name.

- **define_split 'x' "EsES"**   A definition of a split operation. Operand 0 is the vector of insns to match. Operand 1 is a C language expression that must result in a nonzero value. Operand 2 is a vector of insns to be placed into the `sequence`. Operand 3 is some C language code to be executed prior to generating the insns. This could, for example, be code to create an RTX `sequence` for use in generating code.

- **div '2' "ee"**   The two expressions are evaluated, and operand 1 is divided into operand 0.

- **eq '<' "ee"**   The generated code evaluates the expressions and performs a signed comparison. The result is true if the first value is equal to the second.

- **eq_attr 'x' "ss"**   This is used only in the machine descriptions to define attributes. It is the name of an attribute of a comparison value to be used to determine whether the attribute applies. Operand 0 is the name of the attribute. Operand 1 is the comparison value.

- **exclusion_set 'x' "ss"** This appears only in machine descriptions to specify CPU functional units that cannot be simultaneously scheduled with other CPU functional units. The functional units listed as the first operand cannot be scheduled with those in the second list. An example of this is where single and double precision floating-point operations cannot be carried on simultaneously. Operand 0 is a comma-separated list of functional units that cannot be scheduled with those in operand 1. Operand 1 is a comma-separated list of functional units.

- **expr_list 'x' "ee"** A linked list of expressions.

- **ffs '1' "e"** Evaluates the expression and counts the number of trailing zero bits in the result from the expression.

- **fix '1' "e"** Converts the value of a floating-point expression to a fixed-point value. Also see `unsigned_fix`.

- **float '1' "e"** Converts the value of a fixed-point expression to a floating-point value. Also see `unsigned_float`.

- **float_extend '1' "e"** Code is generated to evaluate the floating-point expression and, if necessary, to extend it to fit the larger format into which it is being stored.

- **float_truncate '1' "e"** Code is generated to evaluate the floating-point expression and, if necessary, to truncate it to fit the smaller format into which it is being stored.

- **ge '<' "ee"** The generated code evaluates the expressions and performs a signed comparison. The result is true if the first value is greater than or equal to the second.

- **geu '<' "ee"** The generated code evaluates the expressions and performs an unsigned comparison. The result is true if the first value is greater than or equal to the second.

- **gt '<' "ee"** The generated code evaluates the expressions and performs a signed comparison. The result is true if the first value is greater than the second.

- **gtu '<' "ee"** The generated code evaluates the expressions and performs an unsigned comparison. The result is true if the first value is greater than the second.

- **high 'o' "e"** This is the value of the high-order bits in a constant expression on a RISC machine.

- **if_then_else '3' "eee"** A representation of a conditional jump instruction. Operand 0 is the conditional expression. Operand 1 is the expression to be the target of the jump whenever the conditional expression evaluates to true. Operand 2 is the expression to be the target of the jump whenever the conditional expression evaluates to false.

- **include 'x' "s"**   The operand is the name of a file to be included.
- **insn 'i' "iuuBteiee"**   This is an insn that cannot branch. Operand 0 is the unique ID of this RTX. Operand 1 is a pointer to the previous instruction in the chain. Operand 2 is a pointer to the next instruction in the chain. Operand 3 is the basic block of instructions that cannot branch. Operand 4 is a pointer to the tree node.
- **insn_list 'x' "ue"**   A linked list of instructions.
- **ior 'c' "ee"**   The two operands are evaluated and the result is taken as a bitwise inclusive OR of the two values.
- **jump_insn 'i' "iuuBteiee0"**   This is an insn that can possibly branch. Operand 0 is the unique ID of this RTX. Operand 1 is a pointer to the previous instruction in the chain. Operand 2 is a pointer to the next instruction in the chain. Operand 3 is the basic block of instructions. Operand 4 is a pointer to the tree node.
- **label_ref 'o' "u00"**   This is a reference to a label in the assembly language. Operand 0 is a `code_label` insn found elsewhere in the chain. Also see `symbol_ref`. Operand 1 is a `LABEL_NEXTREF` declaration used in `flow.c`. Operand 2 is a `CONTAINING_INSN` declaration used in `flow.c`.
- **le '<' "ee"**   The generated code evaluates the expressions and performs a signed comparison. The result is true if the first value is less than or equal to the second.
- **leu '<' "ee"**   The generated code evaluates the expressions and performs an unsigned comparison. The result is true if the first value is less than or equal to the second.
- **lo_sum 'o' "ee"**   This is the sum of a register and the low-order bits of a constant expression on a RISC machine.
- **lsshiftrt '2' "ee"**   A bitwise logical shift to the right. Operand 0 is the expression producing the value to be shifted. Operand 1 is the expression producing the value of the number of bits to shift.
- **lt '<' "ee"**   The generated code evaluates the expressions and performs a signed comparison. The result is true if the first value is less than the second.
- **ltgt '<' "ee"**   The generated code evaluates the expressions and performs an unordered floating-point comparison. The result is true if the first value is not equal to the second. Also see `uneq`.
- **ltu '<' "ee"**   The generated code evaluates the expressions and performs an unsigned comparison. The result is true if the first value is less than the second.
- **match_insn 'm' "is"**   This appears only in the machine descriptions. Operand 0 is the index into the operand table. Operand 1 is the name of the function to perform the matching.
- **match_dup 'm' "i"**   This appears only in the machine descriptions. A test is made for a match with whatever is stored at the specified location in the operand table. Operand 0 is the index into the operand table.

- **match_op_dup 'm' "iE"** This appears only in the machine descriptions. It matches only something that is stored in the operand table at the specified index. Operand 0 is the index into the operand table. Operand 1 is the vector of expressions to be compared.

- **match_operand 'm' "iss"** This appears only in the machine descriptions. It is a comparison for functional equality of two operands. Operand 0 is the index into the operand table. Operand 1 is the name of the function to be used to perform the comparison. Operand 2 is the first operand name to be compared. Operand 3 is the second operand name to be compared.

- **match_operator 'm' "isE"** This appears only in the machine descriptions. It recursively matches the operands of the expressions in the RTX. Operand 0 is the index into the operand table. Operand 1 is the name of the function to be called to do the matching. Operand 2 is the vector of operands to be matched.

- **match_par_dup 'm' "iE"** This appears only in the machine descriptions. It matches only something that is stored in the operand table at the specified index. Operand 0 is the index into the operand table. Operand 1 is the vector of expressions to be compared.

- **match_parallel 'm' "isE"** This appears only in machine descriptions. It matches the vector of operands—a collection of parallel instructions—by calling the specified function. Operand 0 is the index into the operand table. Operand 1 is the name of the function to be called to do the matching. Operand 2 is the vector of parallel instructions to be matched.

- **match_scratch 'm' "is"** This appears only in the machine descriptions. For the form used as an RTX, see scratch. A comparison is made to test for a scratch register. Operand 0 is the index into the operand table. Operand 1 is the name of the function to be used to perform the comparison.

- **mem 'o' "e0"** A memory location. Operand 0 is the address of the memory location. Operand 1 is the alias set to which this memory belongs.

- **minus '2' "ee"** The two operands are evaluated, and operand 1 is subtracted from operand 0.

- **mod '2' "ee"** The two expressions are evaluated, and operand 1 is divided into operand 0, and the result is taken to be the remainder of an integer division operation.

- **mult '1' "e"** The two operands are evaluated and multiplied to produce a result.

- **ne '<' "ee"** The generated code evaluates the expressions and performs a signed comparison. The result is true if the first value is not equal to the second.

- **neg '1' "e"** The expression is evaluated and the result is negated.

- **nil 'x' "*"** A null pointer.

- **not '1' "e"** The expression is evaluated and a bitwise not operation (one's compliment) is performed to produce the result.

■ **note 'x' "iuuB0ni"**   Specifies where in the code the source code line starts. Operand 0 is the unique ID of this RTX. Operand 1 is a pointer to the previous instruction in the chain. Operand 2 is a pointer to the next instruction in the chain. Operand 3 is the basic block of instructions following the label. Operand 4 is the name of the file if the line number is greater than zero; otherwise, this is data specific to this note. Operand 5 is the line number. If the line number value is zero, this is the value of enum note_insn. Operand 6 is a unique value if the line number is equal to note_insn_deleted_label.

■ **ordered '<' "ee"**   The generated code evaluates the expressions and performs an ordered floating-point comparison. An ordered comparison throws an exception if either value is NaN. The result is true only if the values are equal. Also see unordered.

■ **parallel 'x' "E"**   An array of two or more operations to be executed in parallel.

■ **pc 'o' ""**   The program counter. Jumps are specified as set statements with operand 0 being a pc.

■ **phi 'x' "E"**   The SSA phi operator, which can only appear at the beginning of a basic block. The operand is a vector of $2n$ RTX. Element $2n+1$ is a const_int insn with the ID number of the predecessor block through which control has passed when element $2n$ is used.

■ **plus 'c' "ee"**   The two expressions are evaluated and the resulting values are added together.

■ **post_dec 'a' "e"**   Postdecrementation of the address in memory specified by the expression. The amount of the decrementation is not specified because its type and size can be determined from the expression.

■ **post_inc 'a' "e"**   Postincrementation of the address in memory specified by the expression. The amount of the incrementation is not specified because its type and size can be determined from the expression.

■ **post_modify 'a' "ee"**   Represents generic address side effects (except in the case of increment and decrement, which are handle by other operators). Also see pre_modify. Operand 0 is a reg insn, which is used as the address. Operand 1 is an expression that is assigned to the register. This operand must be of the form plus (reg) (reg) or plus (reg) (const_int), where the first operand of the plus is the same as the first operand of the post_modify.

■ **pre_dec 'a' "e"**   Predecrementation of the address in memory specified by the expression. The amount of the decrementation is not specified because its type and size can be determined from the expression.

■ **pre_inc 'a' "e"**   Preincrementation of the address in memory specified by the expression. The amount of the incrementation is not specified because its type and size can be determined from the expression.

■ **pre_modify 'a' "ee"**   Represents generic address side effects (except in the case of increment and decrement, which are handle by other operators). Operand 0 is a `reg` insn, which is used as the address. Operand 1 is an expression that is assigned to the register. This operand must be of the form `plus(reg)(reg)` or `plus(reg)(const_int)`, where the first operand of the `plus` is the same as the first operand of the `pre_modify`.

- **prefetch 'x' "eee"** A memory prefetch with attributes supported on some target machines. The operands 1 and 2 will be ignored for hardware that does not support them. Operand 0 is the memory address from which the fetch is to be made. Operand 1 is set to 0 for read access and 1 for write access. Operand 2 is a number determining the level of temporal locality, where 0 indicates none, with 1, 2, and 3 specifying increasing levels of temporal locality.

- **presence_set 'x' "ss"** This appears only in machine descriptions to specify a list of CPU functional units that cannot be reserved unless certain other functional units are also reserved. Also see `absence_set`. Operand 0 is a comma-separated list of functional units that cannot be reserved unless at least one functional unit from operand 2 is also reserved. Operand 1 is a comma-separated list of functional units.

- **queued 'x' "eeeee"** A pointer to a member of a queue of instructions to be output later for postincrement or postdecrement so that a queued insn never becomes an actual part of the generated code. A queued expression is put into an instruction so that the value used is the one coming before the increment or decrement. Operand 0 is the variable (or register) to be incremented or decremented. Operand 1 is the insn that performs the incrementing or decrementing. Operand 2 is a `reg` RTX that contains the original value of the variable. Operand 3 is the body to be used as the incrementing or decrementing instruction. Operand 4 is the next `queued` expression in the queue.

- **range_info 'x' "uuEiiiiiibbii"** The header for range information. Operand 0 is a pointer to a `note` insn marking the beginning of the range. Operand 1 is a pointer to a `note` insn marking the end of the range. Operand 2 is a vector containing all the registers that can be substituted within the range. Operand 3 is the number of calls within the range. Operand 4 is the total number of insns in the range. Operand 5 is a unique ID number for this range. Operand 6 is the basic block number of the start of the range. Operand 7 is the basic block number of the end of the range. Operand 8 is the loop depth. Operand 9 is a bitmap specifying which registers are live at the beginning of the range. Operand 10 is a bitmap specifying which registers are live at the end of the range. Operand 11 is a marker number for the start of the range. Operand 12 is a marker number for the end of the range.

- **range_live 'x' "bi"** This is information about the registers that are live at this point. Operand 0 is the bitmap representing the list of live registers. Operand 1 is the original block number of the current block.

- **range_reg 'x' "iiiiiiiitt"** Specifies the registers that can be substituted within the range. Operand 0 is the original pseudo register number. Operand 1 is the value held in the pseudo register for the duration of the range. Operand 2 is the number of references made to the register within the range. Operand 3 is the number of times the register is clobbered in the range. Operand 4 is the number of deaths the register has in the range. Operand 5 contains flags that indicate whether the data needs to be copied from the original register to the new register at the beginning of the range, and whether the data needs to be copied from the new register back to the original register at the end of the range. Operand 6 is the live length. Operand 7 is the number of calls across which this register remains alive. Operand 8 is the symbol node of the variable, if the register is a variable. Operand 9 is the block node in which the variable is declared, if the register is a variable.

- **range_var 'x' "eti"** This is information about the ranges of a local variable. Operand 0 is an `expr_list` containing the ranges in which the variable is copied to a pseudo register. Operand 1 is the block in which the variable is declared. Operand 2 is the number of ranges in which the variable appears.

- **reg 'o' "i0"** This is a hardware or pseudo register. Also see `scratch`. Operand 0 is the register number. If this number is less than `FIRST_PSEUDO_REGISTER`, then it is a hardware register. Operand 1 is the original register number, which will be a different value for a pseudo register that was converted into a hardware register.

- **resx 'x' "i"** This is a placeholder for a possible `_Unwind_Resume` before it has been determined whether a function call or a branch is needed. Operand 0 is the exception region from which control is flowing.

- **return 'x' ""** Returns from a subroutine.

- **rotate '2' "ee"** A bitwise shift to the left without sign extension. Bits shifting off the left end are rotated back to the right end. Operand 0 is the expression producing the value to be shifted. Operand 1 is the expression producing the value of the number of bits to shift.

- **rotatert '2' "ee"** A bitwise shift to the right, with bits shifting off the right end being rotated back to the left end. Operand 0 is the expression producing the value to be shifted. Operand 1 is the expression producing the value of the number of bits to shift.

- **scratch 'o' "0"** A scratch register. This is a register that is used only within a single instruction, and it will be turned into a `reg` insn during register allocation or during reload. This is specified as having an operand only to facilitate it being turned into a `reg`.

- **sequence 'x' "E"** This form of a sequence of insns is the result of generating code based on a `define_expand` that produces a number of insns. The function `emit_insn()` breaks the `sequence` apart into separate insns. Operand 0 is the array of expressions.

- **set 'x' "ee"** An assignment operation for storing a value at a location. All assignment operations must use `set`. Instructions that require multiple assignments must use multiple `set` insns. Operand 0 is the lvalue. This is the location (memory, register, condition code, or whatever) to receive the assigned value. Operand 1 is the rvalue, which is the value, or the location of the value, to be stored in the lvalue.

- **set_attr 'x' "ss"** This can be used as the last operand of `define_insn`, `define_peephole`, and `define_asm_insn` to specify an attribute to assign to insns matching the pattern. Operand 0 is the name of the attribute. Operand 1 is the value of the attribute.

- **set_attr_alternative 'x' "sE"** This can be used as the last operand for `define_insn` and `define_peephole` as a set of alternatives attribute values to be assigned. Which is assigned is determined by a match. Operand 0 is the name of the attribute. Operand 1 is an array of possible attribute values.

- **sign_extend '1' "e"** The result of evaluating the expression is sign-extended. The amount of sign extension is determined by the machine modes and type of expression. Also see `zero_extend`.

- **sign_extract 'b' "eee"** This is the specification of the size and location of a signed bit field. Also see `zero_extract`. Operand 0 is the memory unit containing the first bit of the bit field. Operand 1 is the number of bits in the field. Operand 2 is the offset to the bit field, which is the number of bits in the memory unit before the first bit of the bit field. If `BITS_BIG_ENDIAN` is set, the count is from the most significant bit of the memory unit; otherwise, the count is from the least significant bit.

- **smax 'c' "ee"** A signed comparison in which the result is the maximum of the two expressions.

- **smin 'c' "ee"** A signed comparison in which the result is the minimum of the two expressions.

- **sqrt '1' "e"** Extracts the square root of the value resulting from the evaluation of the expression.

- **ss_minus '2' "ee"** The two expressions are evaluated and the result of operand 1 is subtracted from operand 0 with signed saturation. Also see `us_minus`.

- **ss_plus 'c' "ee"** The two expressions are evaluated and the results are added with signed saturation. Also see `us_plus`.

- **ss_truncate '1' "e"** Evaluates the expression and performs signed saturating truncation. Also see `us_truncate`.

- **strict_low_part 'x' "e"** This is the assignment of a value that only modifies the least significant part of the destination. Operand 0 is the assignment expression that has the `strict_low_part` restriction imposed on it.

- **subreg 'x' "ei"**   One word of a multiword value. Operand 0 is an expression containing the complete value. Operand 1 is the selector of the word of the multiword value.

- **symbol_ref 'o' "s"**   A reference to a named label. Also see `label_ref`. Operand 0 is the label string with the preceding underscore added to it. If the label name begins with an asterisk, the asterisk is removed and the underscore is not added.

- **trap_if 'x' "ee"**   A conditional trap. For an unconditional trap, the conditional expression is set to 1. Operand 0 is the conditional expression. Operand 1 is the code to execute if the conditional expression is a nonzero value.

- **truncate '1' "e"**   The result of the expression is simply truncated to be stored in the receiving location.

- **udiv '2' "ee"**   The two expressions are evaluated and operand 1 is divided into operand 0, performing an unsigned integer division.

- **unordered '<' "ee"**   The generated code evaluates the expressions and performs an unordered floating-point comparison. An unordered comparison does not throw an exception if either value is NaN. The result is true only if the values are equal. Also see `ordered`.

- **umax 'c' "ee"**   In an unsigned comparison operation, the result is the maximum of the two expressions.

- **umin 'c' "ee"**   In an unsigned comparison operation, the result is the minimum of the two expressions.

- **umod '2' "ee"**   The two expressions are evaluated and operand 1 is divided into operand 0, and the result is taken to be the remainder of an unsigned integer division.

- **uneq '<' "ee"**   The generated code evaluates the expressions and performs an unordered floating-point comparison. The result is true if the first value is equal to the second.

- **unge '<' "ee"**   The generated code evaluates the expressions and performs an unordered floating-point comparison. The result is true if the first value is greater than or equal to the second.

- **ungt '<' "ee"**   The generated code evaluates the expressions and performs an unordered floating-point comparison. The result is true if the first value is greater than the second.

- **unle '<' "ee"**   The generated code evaluates the expressions and performs an unordered floating-point comparison. The result is true if the first value is less than or equal to the second.

- **unlt '<' "ee"**   The generated code evaluates the expressions and performs an unordered floating-point comparison. The result is true if the first value is less than the second.

- **UnKnown 'x' "*"** An RTX that, as yet, has an unknown type.

- **unsigned_fix '1' "e"** Converts the value of a floating-point expression to an unsigned fixed-point value. Also see `unsigned_fix`.

- **unsigned_float '1' "e"** Converts the value of an unsigned fixed-point expression to a floating-point value. Also see `unsigned_fix`.

- **unspec 'x' "Ei"** A machine-specific operation. Operand 0 is a vector of operands to be used by the machine-specific operation. Operand 1 is an index into the operands specifying which is to be used.

- **unspec_volatile 'x' "Ei"** A machine-specific operation in which there could possibly be a trap. Operand 0 is a vector of operands to be used by the machine-specific operation. Operand 1 is an index into the operands specifying which is to be used.

- **us_minus '2' "ee"** The two expressions are evaluated and the result of operand 1 is subtracted from operand 0 with unsigned saturation. Also see `ss_minus`.

- **us_plus 'c' "ee"** The two expressions are evaluated and the results are added with unsigned saturation. Also see `ss_plus`.

- **us_truncate '1' "e"** Evaluates the expression and performs unsigned saturating truncation. Also see `ss_truncate`.

- **use 'x' "e"** An indicator that something is used in a way that is not necessary to explain. For example, a subroutine call will use a register as part of its calling sequence. Also see `clobber`. Operand 0 is the expression specifying the item being used.

- **value 'o' "0"** Used by the `cselib` routines to describe a value.

- **vec_concat 'x' "ee"** Defines the concatenation of two vectors. The result is a vector the length of the two vectors combined, with the operand 0 vector preceding the operand 1 vector. Operand 0 is the first vector to be concatenated. Operand 1 is the second vector to be concatenated.

- **vec_duplicate 'x' "e"** Defines an operation that multiplies the size of a vector by replicating all the members of the vector. The resulting vector is an integer multiple of the size of the input vector.

- **vec_merge 'x' "eee"** Defines a merge operation between two vectors. Operand 0 is the first vector to be merged. Operand 1 is the second vector to be merged. Operand 2 is a bitmask that specifies where the parts of the resulting vector are to be extracted. A 0 bit indicates a member is to be taken from operand 0, and a 1 bit indicates a member is to be taken from operand 1.

- **vec_select 'x' "ee"** Defines an operation that selects parts of a vector. Operand 0 is the source vector. Operand 1 is a parallel insn containing constant values that specify which members of the source vector are to be stored in the resulting vector.

- **xor 'c' "ee"**   The two operands are evaluated and the result is taken as a bitwise exclusive OR of the two values.

- **zero_extend '1' "e"**   The result of evaluating the expression is not sign extended but zero filled instead. Also see `sign_extend`.

- **zero_extract 'b' "eee"**   The specification of the size and location of an unsigned bit field. Also see `sign_extract`. Operand 0 is the memory unit containing the first bit of the bit field. Operand 1 is the number of bits in the field. Operand 2 is the offset to the bit field, which is the number of bits in the memory unit before the first bit of the bit field. If `BITS_BIG_ENDIAN` is set, the count is from the most significant bit of the memory unit; otherwise, the count is from the least significant bit.

Modes and Mode Classes

Each RTX expression has a mode that describes the size and type of the data it manipulates and produces. Two identical expressions with different modes can produce entirely different code. An example of this is a floating-point expression compared to an integer expression. The modes are listed in Table 20-5 and are defined as a set of enumerated types in machmode.def.

Mode	Description
BImode	Bit mode. Specifies an operation on a single bit.
QImode	Quarter integer mode. Specifies an operation on a byte being treated as an integer value.
HImode	Half integer mode. Specifies an operation on two bytes being treated as an integer value.
PSImode	Partial single integer mode. Specifies an operation on an integer that occupies four bytes of storage but does not actually use all four bytes.
SImode	Single integer mode. Specifies an operation on a 4-byte integer value.
PDImode	Partial double integer mode. Specifies an operation on an integer that occupies eight bytes of storage but does not actually use all eight bytes.

Table 20-5.   *The Machine Modes That Are Applied to Expressions*

Mode	Description
DImode	Double integer mode. Specifies an operation on an 8-byte integer.
TImode	Tetra integer mode. Specifies an operation on a 16-byte integer.
OImode	Octa integer mode. Specifies an operation on a 32-byte integer.
QFmode	Quarter floating mode. Specifies an operation on a single-byte floating-point number.
HFmode	Half floating mode. Specifies an operation on a 2-byte floating-point number.
TQFmode	Three-quarter floating mode. Specifies an operation on a 3-byte floating-point number.
SFmode	Single floating mode. Specifies an operation on a 4-byte floating-point number. This is commonly the single precision floating-point operation of IEEE, which specifies 8-bit bytes but can be different on machines with 16-bit bytes and on other hardware with its own form of floating-point arithmetic.
DFmode	Double floating mode. Specifies an operation on an 8-byte floating-point number. This is commonly the double precision floating-point operation of IEEE, which specifies 8-bit bytes but can be different on machines with 16-bit bytes and on other hardware with its own form of floating-point arithmetic.
XFmode	Extended floating mode. Specifies an operation on a 12-byte floating-point number. This is commonly the extended precision floating-point operation of IEEE, which specifies 8-bit bytes. Some systems will use less than the full 12 bytes.
TFmode	Tetra floating mode. Specifies an operation on a 16-byte floating-point number. This is used for both the 96-bit extended IEEE floating-point types padded to 128 bits, and for the true 128-bit extended IEEE floating-point types.
CCmode	Condition code. Specifies an operation on the value of a condition code. These are machine-specific sets of hardware bits used to contain the results of comparison operations. This mode is not used on machines that use the cc0 insn.

Table 20-5.   *The Machine Modes That Are Applied to Expressions* (continued)

Mode	Description
BLKmode	Block mode. Specifies an operation on aggregate values to which none of the other modes apply. In RTL this mode is used only for memory references used in vector hardware instructions. This mode is not used on machines that have no such instructions.
VOIDmode	Void mode. This is used in the absence of any specific mode. Constant expressions can have this mode because they can be taken to be of whatever mode is dictated by the context.
QCmode	Quarter complex mode. Specifies a complex number composed of two floating-point values in QFmode.
HCmode	Half complex mode. Specifies a complex number composed of two floating-point values in HFmode.
SCmode	Single complex mode. Specifies a complex number composed of two floating-point values in SFmode.
DCmode	Double complex mode. Specifies a complex number composed of two floating-point values in DFmode.
XCmode	Extended complex mode. Specifies a complex number composed of two floating-point values in XFmode.
TCmode	Tetra complex mode. Specifies a complex number composed of two floating-point values in TFmode.
CQImode	Quarter integer complex mode. Specifies a complex number composed of two integer values in QImode.
CHImode	Half integer complex mode. Specifies a complex number composed of two integer values in HImode.
CSImode	Single integer complex mode. Specifies a complex number composed of two integer values in SImode.
CDImode	Double integer complex mode. Specifies a complex number composed of two integer values in DImode.
CTImode	Tetra integer complex mode. Specifies a complex number composed of two integer values in TImode.
COImode	Octa integer complex mode. Specifies a complex number composed of two integer values in OImode.

Table 20-5. *The Machine Modes That Are Applied to Expressions* (continued)

In RTL debugging dumps, and in the machine descriptions, the name of the mode of an operation is listed with a colon immediately following the expression. For example, a register expression could be written as (reg:SI 7 esp) or, if the register flag is set, as (reg/f:SI 7 esp). The mode name is always written with the word "mode" trimmed from it. If no mode appears in the dump, it is VOIDmode.

Not all machines support all modes. It is only required that a machine support QImode (a single-byte integer), the integer types that match the size defined by BITS_PER_WORD, and the float sizes defined by FLOAT_TYPE_SIZE and DOUBLE_TYPE_SIZE. These constant values are defined in the compiler during configuration, and they match the sizes of the target machine.

Mode Class	Description
MODE_INT	The class of integer modes is made up of BImode, QImode, HImode, SImode, DImode, TImode, and OImode.
MODE_PARTIAL_INT	The class of partial integer modes is made up of PQImode, PHImode, PSImode, and PDImode.
MODE_FLOAT	The class of floating-point modes is made up of QFmode, HFmode, TQFmode, SFmode, DFmode, XFmode, and TFmode.
MODE_COMPLEX_INT	The class of complex numbers composed of integer pairs includes CQImode, CHImode, CSImode, CDImode, CTImode, and COImode.
MODE_COMPLEX_FLOAT	The class of complex numbers composed of floating-point pairs includes QCmode, HCmode, SCmode, DCmode, XCmode, and TCmode.
MODE_CC	The class of condition codes is composed of CCmode and any others that may be defined by the macro EXTRA_CC_MODES.
MODE_RANDOM	The random class is used to represent any mode not in one of the other classes, such as BLKmode and VOIDmode.

Table 20-6. *The Names of the Mode Classes and the Modes They Designate*

Although the mode settings are used explicitly in the RTL code, the compiler itself most often uses references to mode classes. The mode classes are described in Table 20-6 and are defined as enum values in machmode.h.

A global variable named byte_mode contains the mode appropriate for the target machine's value for BITS_PER_UNIT (on a 32-bit machine, it is set to QImode). The global variable named word_mode contains the mode appropriate for the target machine's value for BITS_PER_WORD (on a 32-bit machine, it is set to SImode).

Flags

A number of flags are included in each insn in the RTL code. In the printed form of the RTL, these flags appear as single characters preceded by a backslash, as demonstrated in Chapter 18. The exact meaning of the flag depends on the type of insn in which it is set. Table 20-7 contains a list of the insns that can have flags set as well as the flag that is displayed in the output dump of the RTL.

Insn	Flag	Meaning of the Flag
asm_input	/v	The data at the referenced memory location is volatile. The insn cannot be deleted, reordered, or combined.
asm_operands	/v	The data at the referenced memory location is volatile. The insn cannot be deleted, reordered, or combined.
call_insn	/j	This is a sibling call.
call_insn	/u	The call is to a pure function or a const.
code_label	/s	The label is the target of a nonlocal goto and may not be deleted. If such a label is deleted, it must be replaced with an entry specifying the label was deleted.
const	/i	This RTL was produced by procedure integration.
expr_list	/u	A call is made to a pure function or a const.

Table 20-7.   *The Meaning of Flag Indicators for Different Insns*

Insn	Flag	Meaning of the Flag
insn	/f	This is part of a function prologue that sets the stack pointer. It is a frame pointer, saves a register, or sets up a temporary register to use in place of the frame pointer.
insn	/i	This RTL was produced by procedure integration.
insn	/s	During dead code elimination, this flag indicates dead code. During a reorganization (reorg) in the delay slot of a branch, this flag indicates that the insn is from the target of the branch. During scheduling, this flag indicates that this insn must be scheduled together with the previous insn.
insn	/v	This insn has been deleted.
insn_list	/i	This RTL was produced by procedure integration.
jump_insn	/s	During a reorg in the delay slot of a branch, this flag indicates that the insn is from the target of the branch.
label_ref	/s	A label is being referenced that is outside the innermost loop containing this insn.
label_ref	/v	This is a reference to a nonlocal label.
mem	/f	The reference is to a scalar.
mem	/j	The alias set for this memory reference should be left unchanged when a component of memory is accessed.
mem	/s	The referenced memory is part of an aggregate (structure or array). This flag is not set if the reference is through a C pointer, which could be to a scalar or an aggregate.
mem	/u	The value at the memory location never changes.
mem	/v	The data at the memory location is volatile. The insn cannot be deleted, reordered, or combined.

Table 20-7. *The Meaning of Flag Indicators for Different Insns* (continued)

Insn	Flag	Meaning of the Flag
note	/u	A call is made to a pure function or a const.
reg	/f	The register contains a pointer.
reg	/i	This register contains the value to be returned by the current function. On machines that have a preset register used to return a value, this flag will not be set.
reg	/s	The register content has its entire life contained in the test expression of a loop.
reg	/u	The value in the register never changes.
reg	/v	This flag indicates a user-defined variable; otherwise, it is a temporary variable created by the compiler.
reg_label	/v	This is a reference to a nonlocal label.
set	/f	This is part of a function prologue that sets the stack pointer. It establishes the frame pointer, saves a register, or sets up a temporary register to use in place of the frame pointer.
set	/j	The value is being set to be returned.
subreg	/s	An object is being accessed that has had its mode promoted from a wider mode.
subreg	/u	The reference is to an unsigned value that has had its mode promoted to a wider type.
symbol_ref	/f	The reference addresses this function's string constant pool.
symbol_ref	/i	The referenced symbol is weak.
symbol_ref	/u	The reference is to something inside the constant pool of the current function.
symbol_ref	/v	This flag is used for machine-specific purposes.

Table 20-7. *The Meaning of Flag Indicators for Different Insns* (continued)

Chapter 21

Machine-Specific
Compiler Options

This chapter includes information that can be used when compiling programs for specific platforms. Mostly, the options and settings deal with adjusting the generated code to use (or not use) some specific feature of the hardware, but there are also options for debugging and organizing sections in object files.

The Machine List

The following machine description files are included with the 3.1 release of GCC. These files are found in the config directory of the GCC source distribution:

alpha/alpha.md	m88k/m88k.md
alpha/ev4.md	mcore/mcore.md
alpha/ev5.md	mips/mips.md
alpha/ev6.md	mmix/mmix.md
arc/arc.md	mn10200/mn10200.md
arm/arm.md	mn10300/mn10300.md
avr/avr.md	ns32k/ns32k.md
c4x/c4x.md	pa/pa.md
cris/cris.md	pdp11/pdp11.md
d30v/d30v.md	romp/romp.md
dsp16xx/dsp16xx.md	rs6000/rs6000.md
fr30/fr30.md	s390/s390.md
h8300/h8300.md	sh/sh.md
i370/i370.md	sparc/cypress.md
i386/i386.md	sparc/sparc.md
i386/athlon.md	sparc/hypersparc.md
i386/k6.md	sparc/sparclet.md
i386/pentium.md	sparc/supersparc.md
i386/ppro.md	sparc/ultra1_2.md
i960/i960.md	sparc/ultra3.md
ia64/ia64.md	stormy16/stormy16.md
m32r/m32r.md	v850/v850.md
m68hc11/m68hc11.md	vax/vax.md
m68k/m68k.md	

Each directory corresponds to a single platform. Some of the directories contain more than one .md file because of the include directive, which allows for the full configuration to be organized as a set of files. For example, the alpha.md file in the alpha directory includes the files ev4.md, ev5.md, and ev6.md, and the i386.md file in the i386 directory includes pentium.md, ppro.md, k6.md, and athlon.md.

The GCC Command-Line Options

Some, but not all, of the existing ports have special command-line options that tell the compiler to produce code that will further refine the generated to code to match a specific hardware mode or runtime configuration. The following sections list the –m options available for the ports that have defined them.

Most of the options begin with –m, but there are a few exceptions. Some are used to specify that code be generated for a specific CPU within a family of CPUs, while others can be used to generate code that will take advantage of some specific hardware feature to better merge the characteristics of your program with the hardware. Some of the options are needed to make the generated code fit with a particular hardware configuration.

Alpha Options

The following options are defined for the DEC Alpha implementations.

-malpha-as
Generates code to be assembled by the vendor-supplied assembler. Also see –mgas.

-mcix
Specifies that the compiler is to generate code to use the optional CIX instruction set. The default is to use the instruction sets implied by –mcpu. Code for the CIX instruction set can be disabled by –mno-cix. Also see –mbwx, –mfix, and –mmax.

-mbuild-constants
This option requires the compiler to construct all integer constants using code, even if it takes more instructions (the maximum is six).

Normally GCC examines a 32- or 64-bit integer constant to see whether it can construct the constant from smaller constants in two or three instructions. If it cannot, it will output the constant as a literal and generate code to load it from the data segment at runtime. This option would typically be used to build a shared library dynamic loader. A shared library must relocate itself in memory before it can find the variables and constants in its own data segment.

-mbwx
Specifies that the compiler is to generate code to use the optional BWX instruction set. The default is to use the instruction sets implied by –mcpu. Code for the BWX instruction set can be disabled by –mno-bwx. Also see –mcix, –mfix, and –mmax.

-mcpu=*type*
Sets the instruction set and instruction scheduling parameters for the specified machine type. You can specify either the EV style name or the corresponding chip number. GCC supports scheduling parameters for the EV4, EV5, and EV6 family of processors and will choose the default values for the instruction set from the processor you specify. If

you do not specify a processor type, GCC will default to the processor on which the compiler was built. The valid choices for *type* are listed in Table 21-1.

-mexplicit-relocs
Generates explicit symbol relocation information.

Older Alpha assemblers provided no way to generate symbol relocations except via assembler macros. Use of these macros does not allow optimal instruction scheduling. GNU `binutils` supports a new syntax that allows the compiler to explicitly mark which relocations should apply to which instructions. This option is mostly useful for debugging, because GCC detects the capabilities of the assembler when it is built and sets the default accordingly. The generation of symbol relocation information can be suppressed by -mno-explicit-relocs.

Also see -msmall-data and -mlarge-data.

-mfix
Specifies that the compiler is to generate code to use the optional FIX instruction set. The default is to use the instruction sets implied by -mcpu. Code for the FIX instruction set can be disabled by -mno-fix. Also see -mbwx, -mcix, and -mmax.

-mfloat-ieee
Generates code that uses IEEE single and double precision instead of VAX F and G floating-point arithmetic. Also see -mfloat-vax.

Type	Description
ev4, ev45, 21064	Schedules as an EV4 and has no instruction set extensions
ev5, 21164	Schedules as an EV5 and has no instruction set extensions
ev56, 21164a	Schedules as an EV5 and supports the BWX extension
pca56, 21164pc, 21164PC	Schedules as an EV5 and supports the BWX and MAX extensions
ev6, 21264	Schedules as an EV6 and supports the BWX, FIX, and MAX extensions
ev67, 21264a	Schedules as an EV6 and supports the BWX, CIX, FIX, and MAX extensions

Table 21-1.   *CPU Type Selections for DEC Alpha*

-mfloat-vax
Generates code that uses VAX F and G floating-point arithmetic instead of IEEE single and double precision. Also see -mfloat-ieee.

-mfp-reg
Generates code that uses the floating-point register set. This is the default.

The option -mno-fp-regs does not use the floating-point register set, and it sets the option -msoft-float. If the floating-point register set is not used, floating-point operands are passed in integer registers as if they were integers, and floating-point results are passed in $0 instead of $f0. This is a nonstandard calling sequence, so any function with a floating-point argument or return value called by code compiled with -mno-fp-regs must also be compiled with that -mno-fp-regs.

A typical use of -mno-fp-regs is in building a kernel that does not use, and therefore does not save and restore, any floating-point registers.

-mfp-rounding-mode=*mode*
Selects the IEEE rounding mode. Other Alpha compilers call this option -fprm *mode*. Table 21-2 lists the possible values for *mode*.

-mfp-trap-mode=*mode*
This option controls which floating-point-related traps are enabled. Other Alpha compilers call this option -fptm *mode*. Table 21-3 lists the possible values for *mode*.

Mode	Description
n	Floating-point numbers are rounded toward the nearest machine number or toward the even machine number in case of a tie. This is the default.
m	Rounds toward minus infinity.
c	Chopped rounding mode. Floating-point numbers are rounded toward zero.
d	Dynamic rounding mode. A field in the floating-point control register (fpcr) controls the rounding mode in effect. The C library initializes this register for rounding toward plus infinity. Therefore, unless your program modifies the register, this mode rounds toward plus infinity.

Table 21-2. *Floating-point Rounding Modes*

Mode	Description
n	The only traps enabled are the ones that cannot be disabled in software (for example, the division-by-zero trap). This is the default.
u	Underflow traps are enabled in addition to the traps enabled by n.
su	The instructions are marked to be safe for software completion.
sui	Like su, but inexact traps are enabled as well.

Table 21-3. *Floating-point Trap Mode Settings*

-mgas
Generates code to be assembled by the GNU assembler. Also see -malpha-as.

-mieee
Generates code that is fully IEEE compliant, except that the inexact-flag is not maintained. The Alpha architecture implements floating-point hardware optimized for maximum performance and is mostly compliant with the IEEE floating-point standard. However, for full compliance, software assistance is required.

With this option, the preprocessor macro _IEEE_FP is defined during compilation. The resulting code is less efficient but is able to correctly support denormalized numbers and exceptional IEEE values such as not-a-number (NaN) and plus/minus infinity. Other Alpha compilers call this option -ieee_with_no_inexact.

Also see -mieee-with-inexact.

-mieee-conformant
Generates code as IEEE conformant.

This option must not be used unless you also specify -mtrap-precision=i and either specify -mfp-trap-mode=su or -mfp-trap-mode=sui.

The only effect of this option is to emit the line .eflag 48 in the function prolog of the generated assembly file. Under DEC UNIX, this has the effect that IEEE-conformant math library routines will be linked in.

-mieee-with-inexact
The same as -mieee, except the generated code also maintains the IEEE inexact-flag. This option causes the generated code to implement fully compliant IEEE math.

In addition to the defining of _IEEE_FP, _IEEE_FP_EXACT is also defined as a preprocessor macro. On some Alpha implementations the resulting code may execute significantly slower than the code generated by default. Because very little code depends on the inexact-flag, you should normally not specify this option. Other Alpha compilers call this option -ieee_with_inexact.

-mlarge-data

With this option, the data area is limited to just below 2GB. Programs that require more than 2GB of data must use `malloc()` or `mmap()` to allocate the data in the heap instead of in the program's data segment. This is the default.

When generating code for shared libraries, `-fpic` sets `-msmall-data` and `-fPIC` sets `-mlarge-data`.

-mmax

Specifies that the compiler is to generate code to use the optional MAX instruction set. The default is to use the instruction sets implied by `-mcpu`. Code for the MAX instruction set can be disabled by `-mno-max`. Also see `-mbwx`, `-mcix`, and `-mfix`.

-mmemory-latency=*duration*

Sets the latency the scheduler should assume for typical memory references as seen by the application. This number is highly dependent on the memory access patterns used by the application and the size of the external cache on the machine.

The duration can be specified as a decimal number, which is a number of clock cycles.

The duration can also be specified as `L1`, `L2`, `L3`, or `main`. The compiler contains estimates of the number of clock cycles for typical EV4 and EV5 hardware for the level 1, 2, and 3 caches (also called Dcache, Scache, and Bcache), as well as for the main memory. Note that `L3` is only valid for EV5.

-msmall-data

When `-mexplicit-relocs` is in effect, static data is accessed via `gp-relative` relocations. This option specifies that objects 8 bytes long or smaller are placed in a small data area (the `.sdata` and `.sbss` sections) and are accessed via 16-bit relocations based on the `$gp` register. This limits the size of the small data area to 64KB but allows the variables to be directly accessed via a single instruction.

When generating code for shared libraries, `-fpic` sets `-msmall-data` and `-fPIC` sets `-mlarge-data`.

-msoft-float

Indicates that the compiler is not to use the hardware floating-point instructions for floating-point operations. The functions in libgcc.a will be used to perform floating-point operations.

Unless they are replaced by routines that emulate the floating-point operations or are compiled in such a way as to call such emulation routines, these routines will issue hardware floating-point operations. If you are compiling for an Alpha that does not have floating-point hardware, you must ensure that the library is built. Alpha implementations without floating-point operations still have floating-point registers.

The default is `-mno-soft-float`.

-mtrap-precision=*precision*

Sets the precision used in floating-point traps.

In the Alpha architecture, floating-point traps are imprecise. This means that without software assistance it is impossible to recover from a floating-point trap, and program execution normally needs to be terminated. The compiler generates code that can assist operating system trap handlers in determining the exact location that caused a floating-point trap.

Different levels of precision can be selected from those listed in Table 21-4.

Other Alpha compilers provide the equivalent options called -scope_safe and -resumption_safe.

-mtune=_type_
Sets only the instruction-scheduling parameters for the specified machine type. The instruction set is not changed. The valid choices for type are listed in Table 21-1.

Alpha/VMS Options

The following option is defined for the DEC Alpha/VMS implementation.

-mvms-return-codes
Returns a VMS condition from main(). The default is to return a POSIX condition code.

ARC Options

The following options are defined for ARC implementations:

-mcpu=_cpu_
Generates code for the specified ARC cpu.

Which CPU variants are supported depends on the configuration. All variants support -mcpu=base, which is the default.

Precision	Description
p	Program precision. This option means a trap handler can only identify which program caused a floating-point exception. This is the default.
f	Function precision. The trap handler can determine the function that caused a floating-point exception.
i	Instruction precision. The trap handler can determine the exact instruction that caused a floating-point exception.

Table 21-4.   *Floating-point Trap Precision Settings*

-mdata=*section*

Places data in the specified code section. This selection can be overridden in the code
by specifying the `section` attribute.

 Also see `-mtext` and `-mrodata`.

-mmangle-cpu

Prepends the name of the CPU onto all public symbol names.

 In multiple-processor systems, there are many ARC variants with different
instruction and register set characteristics. This flag prevents code compiled for one
CPU to be linked with code compiled for another. No facility exists for handling
variants that are almost identical.

-mrodata=*section*

Places read-only data in the specified code section. This selection can be overridden in
the code by specifying the `section` attribute.

 Also see `-mtext` and `-mdata`.

-mtext=*section*

Places functions in the specified code section. This selection can be overridden in the
code by specifying the `section` attribute.

 Also see `-mdata` and `-mrodata`.

-EL

Generates code for little endian mode. This is the default.

-EB

Generates code for big endian mode.

ARM Options

The following options are defined for Advanced RISC Machines (ARM) architectures.

-mabort-on-noreturn

Generates a call to the function `abort()` at the end of a `noreturn` function. The call
is placed so that it will be executed if the function tries to return.

-malignment-traps

Generates code that will not trap even if the MMU has alignment traps enabled. The
generated code is a series of byte accesses instead of a direct half-word access. This
option is ignored when compiling for ARM architecture 4 or later because these
processors are capable of directly accessing half-word locations in memory.

 The specification of `-mno-alignment-traps` generates code that assumes that
the MMU will not trap unaligned accesses. This option produces better code when the
target instruction set does not have half-word memory operations. Note that you cannot

use this option to access unaligned word objects, because the processor will only fetch one 32-bit aligned object from memory.

The default setting for most targets is `-mno-alignment-traps`. This produces better code when no half-word memory instructions are available.

On ARM architectures prior to ARMv4, there were no instructions to access half-word objects stored in memory. However, when reading from memory, a feature of the ARM architecture allows a word load to be used even if the address is unaligned, and the processor core will rotate the data as it is being loaded. The `-malignment-traps` option tells the compiler that such misaligned accesses will cause an MMU trap and that it should instead generate the access as a series of byte accesses. The compiler can still use word accesses to load half-word data if it knows that the address is aligned to a word boundary.

-mapcs
The same as `-mapcs-frame`.

-mapcs-26
Generates code for a processor running with a 26-bit program counter and conforming to the function calling standards for the APCS 26-bit option.

The `-mapcs-26` option replaces the `-m2` and `-m3` options that existed in previous versions of the compiler.

-mapcs-32
Generates code for a processor running with a 32-bit program counter and conforming to the function calling standards for the APCS 32-bit option.

The `-mapcs-32` option replaces the `-m6` option that existed in previous versions of the compiler.

-mapcs-frame
Generates a stack frame that is compliant with the ARM Procedure Call Standard for all functions, even if this is not strictly necessary for correct execution of the code. The default is `-mno-apcs-frame`.

Specifying the option `-fomit-frame-pointer` in conjunction with this option will cause the stack frames not to be generated for leaf functions.

-march=*name*
This option specifies the name of the target ARM architecture. GCC uses this name to determine what kind of instructions it can emit when generating assembly code. This option can be used in conjunction with or instead of the -mcpu option. The recognized selections for *name* are `armv2`, `armv2a`, `armv3`, `>armv3m`, `armv4`, `armv4t`, `armv5`, `armv5t`, and `armv5te`.

-mbig-endian
Generates code for a processor running in big-endian mode; the default is to
compile code for a little-endian processor. Also see `-mwords-little-endian`
and `-mlittle-endian`.

-mcallee-super-interworking
Gives all externally visible functions in the file being compiled an ARM instruction set
header that switches to Thumb mode before executing the rest of the functions. This
configuration allows these functions to be called from noninterworking code.

-mcaller-super-interworking
Allows calls via function pointers (including virtual functions) to execute correctly
regardless of whether the target code has been compiled for interworking. There is
a small overhead in the cost of executing a function pointer if this option is enabled.

-mbsd
This option can only be used on the RISC iX to emulate the native BSD-mode compiler.
This is the default if `-ansi` is not specified. Also see `-mxopen`.

-mcpu=_name_
This option is used to specify the name of the target ARM processor. GCC uses this
name to determine what kind of instructions it can emit when generating assembly
code. The recognized names are `arm2`, `arm250`, `arm3`, `arm6`, `arm60`, `arm600`, `arm610`,
`arm620`, `arm7`, `arm7m`, `arm7d`, `arm7dm`, `arm7di`, `arm7dmi`, `arm70`, `arm700`, `arm700i`,
`arm710`, `arm710c`, `arm7100`, `arm7500`, `arm7500fe`, `arm7tdmi`, `arm8`, `strongarm`,
`strongarm110`, `strongarm1100`, `arm8`, `arm810`, `arm9`, `arm9e`, `arm920`, `arm920t`,
`arm940t`, `arm9tdmi`, `arm10tdmi`, `arm1020t`, and `xscale`.
    Also see `-mtune`.

-mfp=_number_
Same as `-mfpe-`_number_.

-mfpe=_number_
This option specifies the version of the floating-point emulation available on the target.
Permissible values for _number_ are 2 and 3.

-mhard-float
Generates code containing floating-point operations. This is the default.
See `-msoft-float`.

-mlittle-endian
Generates code for a processor running in little-endian mode. This is the default for
all standard configurations. Also see `-mbig-endian`.

-mlong-calls

This option causes code to be generated that performs function calls by first loading the address of the function into a register and then making the call based on the address stored in the register.

The default behavior is -mno-long-calls, which has the default result of placing the function calls within the scope of a #pragma long_calls_off directive.

These option settings have no effect on how the compiler generates code to handle function calls via function pointers.

This option is needed if the target function lies outside of the 64MB addressing range of the offset based version of the subroutine call instruction. Even with this option set, certain functions will not be turned into long calls. Examples include static functions, functions bearing the short-call attribute, functions that are inside the scope of a #pragma no_long_calls directive, and functions whose definitions have already been compiled within the current compilation unit. On the other hand, functions that have weak definitions, functions with the long-call attribute, functions in a section with the long-call attribute, and functions that are within the scope of a #pragma long_calls directive will always be turned into long calls.

-mnop-fun-dllimport

Disables support for the dllimport attribute.

-mpic-register=reg

Specifies the register to be used for PIC addressing. The default is R10, unless stack-checking is enabled, when R9 is used. Also see -msingle-pic-base.

-mpoke-function-name

Writes the name of each function into the text section, directly preceding the code of the function prolog. The generated code is similar to the following:

```
        .ascii "arm_poke_function_name", 0
        .align
t1
        .word 0xff000000 + (t1 - t0)
arm_poke_function_name
    mov     ip, sp
    stmfd   sp!, {fp, ip, lr, pc}
    sub     fp, ip, #4
```

During a stack backtrace, code can inspect the value of the program counter stored at fp+0. If the trace function then looks at location pc-12 and finds the top eight bits are set, then you know that a function name is embedded immediately preceding this location. The length of the name is ((pc[-3]) & 0xff000000).

-msched-prolog

This is the default. Specifying `-mno-sched-prolog` prevents the reordering of instructions in the function prolog or the merging of those instruction with the instructions in the body of the function.

The code generated when `-mno-sched-prolog` is specified causes all functions to begin with a more easily recognized set of instructions. This fact can be used to locate the start of functions inside executable code.

-mshort-load-bytes

Deprecated form of `-malignment-traps`.

-mshort-load-words

Deprecated form of `-malignment-traps`.

-msingle-pic-base

Treats the register used for PIC addressing as read-only, rather than loading it in the prolog for each function. The runtime system is responsible for initializing this register with an appropriate value before execution of the program begins. Also see `-mpic-register`.

-msoft-float

Generates code containing library calls for floating-point operations. The default is `-mhard-float`.

You should be aware that the required libraries are not available for all ARM targets. Normally the libraries of the C compiler for the target machine are used, but this cannot be done directly in cross-compilation. If you use this option, you will also need to provide your own libraries.

This option changes the calling conventions used in the code, so it is useful only if you compile the entire program with this option. You will need to compile libgcc.a (the library that comes with GCC) using `-msoft-float` for this to work.

-mstructure-size-boundary=*number*

The size of all structures and unions will be rounded up to a multiple of the number of bits set by this option. Permissible values for *number* are 8 and 32. Specifying the larger number can produce faster and more efficient code, but it can also increase the size of the program.

The default value varies for different toolchains. For the COFF-targeted toolchain, the default value is 8.

The two values are potentially incompatible. Code compiled with one value cannot necessarily be expected to work with code or libraries compiled with the other value if they exchange information using structures or unions.

PERIPHERALS AND INTERNALS

-msymrename

This is the default. This option can only be used on the RISC iX as `-mno-symrename` to suppress running the assembler postprocessor, `symrename`, after code has been assembled. Normally it is necessary to modify some of the standard symbols in preparation for linking with the RISC iX C library. Specifying `-mno-symrename` suppresses this pass.

The postprocessor is never run when the compiler is built for cross-compilation.

-mthumb

Generates code for the 16-bit Thumb instruction set. The default is to use the 32-bit ARM instruction set.

-mthumb-interwork

Generates code that supports calling between the ARM and Thumb instruction sets. Without this option, the two instruction sets cannot be reliably used within a single program.

This option causes the generation of slightly larger code, so the default is `-mno-thumb-interwork`.

-mtpcs-frame

Generates a stack frame that is compliant with the Thumb Procedure Call Standard for all non-leaf functions. (A leaf function is one that does not call any other functions.) The default is `-mno-tpcs-frame`. Also see `-mtpcs-leaf-frame`.

-mtpcs-leaf-frame

Generates a stack frame that is compliant with the Thumb Procedure Call Standard for all leaf functions. (A leaf function is one that does not call any other functions.) The default is `-mno-apcs-leaf-frame`. Also see `-mtpcs-frame`.

-mtune=*name*

This option is very similar to the `-mcpu` option, except that instead of specifying the actual target processor type and restricting which instructions can be used, it specifies that GCC should tune the performance of the code as if the target were of the type specified, but continue to choose the actual instructions generated based on the CPU specified by the `-mcpu` option.

The possible values for *name* are the ones listed for `-mcpu`. For some ARM implementations, better performance can be obtained by using this option.

-mwords-little-endian

Generates code for a little-endian word order but a big-endian byte order.

This option should only be used if you require compatibility with code for big-endian ARM processors generated by versions of the compiler prior to 2.8.

This option only applies when generating code for big-endian processors—that is, a desired byte order of the form `32107654`.

-mxopen
This option can only be used on the RISC iX to emulate the native X/Open-mode compiler. Also see –mbsd.

AVR Options

The following options are defined for AVR implementations.

-mcall-prologues
Reduces code size by generating function prologs and epilogs as calls to the appropriate subroutines.

-minit-stack=*address*
Specifies the initial stack address, which may be a symbol or numeric value. The value of __stack is the default.

-mmcu=*setting*
The value of *setting* specifies either the ATMEL AVR instruction set or the MCU type. Table 21-5 lists the valid names for *setting*. The first column contains the AVR instruction set names, and the second column contains the corresponding MCU types. Any name from either the first or second column can be used as the setting.

-mno-interrupts
Reduces code size by generating code that is not compatible with hardware interrupts.

-mno-tablejump
Reduces code size by not generating tablejump instructions, which can sometimes increase code size.

-msize
Outputs instruction size information into the assembly language file.

-mtiny-stack
Generates code that changes only the low eight bits of the stack pointer.

CRIS Options

The following options are defined for the CRIS ports.

-m8-bit
Arranges for the stack frame, writable data, and constants all to be 8-bit aligned.
    Also see –mdata-align, –mconst-align, –mstack-align, –m32-bit, and –m16-bit.

AVR	MCU	Description
avr1	at90s1200, attiny10, attiny11, attiny12, attiny15, attiny28	This is the minimal AVR core instruction set, which is not supported by the C compiler. This setting is only for assembler programs.
avr2	at90s2313, at90s2323, attiny22, at90s2333, at90s2343, at90s4414, at90s4433, at90s4434, at90s8515, at90c8534, at90s8535	This avr2 instruction set is the default. This is the classic AVR core, with up to 8KB of program memory space.
avr3	atmega103, atmega603, at43usb320, at76c711	This is for the classic AVR core, with up to 128KB of program memory space.
avr4	atmega8, atmega83, atmega85	This is for the enhanced AVR core, with up to 8KB of program memory space.
avr5	atmega16, atmega161, atmega163, atmega32, atmega323, atmega64, atmega128, at43usb355, at94k	This is for the enhanced AVR core, with up to 128KB of program memory space.

Table 21-5.   *The AVR and MCU Settings*

-m16-bit
Arranges for the stack frame, writable data, and constants all to be 16-bit aligned.
   Also see -mdata-align, -mconst-align, -mstack-align, -m32-bit, and -m8-bit.

-m32-bit
Arranges for the stack frame, writable data, and constants all to be 32-bit aligned. This is the default.
   Also see -mdata-align, -mconst-align, -mstack-align, -m16-bit, and -m8-bit.

-maout
Legacy `no-op` option only recognized with the `cris-axis-aout` target.

-march=*architecture*
Same as `-mcpu`.

-mcc-init
Suppresses the use of condition-code results from previous instructions and always generates compare and test instructions before the use of condition codes.

-mconst-align
Arranges for constants to be aligned for the maximum single data access size for the chosen CPU model. The default is `-mno-const-align`, which sets a 32-bit alignment. ABI details, such as structure layout, are not affected.
   Also see `-mdata-align`, `-m32-bit`, `-m16-bit`, and `-m8-bit`.

-mcpu=*architecture*
Generates code for the specified architecture. The valid choices for *architecture* are v3 for ETRAX4, v8 for ETRAX100, and v10 for ETRAX100LX. The default is v0, except for cris-axis-linux-gnu, where the default is v10.

-mdata-align
Arranges for individual data items to be aligned for the maximum single data access size for the chosen CPU model. The default is `-mno-data-align`, which sets a 32-bit alignment. ABI details, such as structure layout, are not affected.
   Also see `-mstack-align`, `-mconst-align`, `-m32-bit`, `-m16-bit`, and `-m8-bit`.

-melf
Legacy `no-op` option only recognized with the `cris-axis-elf` and `cris-axis-linux-gnu` targets.

-melinux
Selects a GNU/Linux-like multilib, include files, and an instruction set for `-mcpu=v8`. This option is valid only for the `cris-axis-aout` target.

-melinux-stacksize=*number*
Arranges for indications in the program informing the kernel loader that the stack of the program should be set to *number* bytes. This option is only available for the `cris-axis-aout` target.

-metrax100
Same as `-mcpu=v8`.

-metrax4
Same as -mcpu=v3.

-mgotplt
In conjunction with -fpic and -fPIC, instruction sequences are generated that load addresses for functions from the PLT part of the GOT rather than calls to the PLT. This is the default, which can be suppressed by -mno-gotplt.

-mlinux
Legacy no-op option, only recognized with the cris-axis-linux-gnu target.

-mmax-stack-frame=*number*
Issues a warning when the stack frame of a function exceeds *number* bytes.

-mno-side-effects
Suppresses the generation of instructions with side effects in addressing modes other than postincrement.

-mpdebug
Enables CRIS-specific verbose debug-related information in the assembly code. This option also has the effect of turning off the #NO_APP formatted-code indicator to the assembler at the beginning of the assembly file.

-mprologue-epilogue
It is the default to generate prolog and epilog code that sets up the stack frame.
Specifying -mno-prologue-epilogue suppresses the generation of the normal function prolog and epilog that set up the stack frame. No return instructions or return sequences are generated in the code. Use this option only together with a visual inspection of the compiled code because no warnings or errors are generated when call-saved registers must be saved or when storage for local variable needs to be allocated.

-mstack-align
Arranges for the stack frame to be aligned for the maximum single data access size for the chosen CPU model. The default is -mno-stack-align, which sets a 32-bit alignment. ABI details, such as structure layout, are not affected.
Also see -mdata-align, -mconst-align, -m32-bit, -m16-bit, and -m8-bit.

-mtune=*architecture*
Tunes to the specified architecture everything applicable about the generated code, except for the ABI and the set of available instructions. The choices for *architecture* are the same as for -mcpu.

-sim
Links with input and output functions from a simulator library. Code, initialized data, and zero-initialized data are allocated consecutively. This option is valid only for the cris-axis-aout and cris-axis-elf targets. Also see -sim2.

-sim2
Similar to -sim but passes linker options to locate initialized data at 0x40000000 and zero-initialized data at 0x80000000.

D30V Options

The following options are defined for D30V implementations.

-masm-optimize
Enables passing -O to the assembler when optimizing. The assembler uses the -O option to automatically "parallelize" adjacent short instructions, where possible. This is the default, which can be overridden by specifying -mno-asm-optimize.

-mbranch-cost=*number*
Increases the internal costs of branches to *number*. Higher costs mean that the compiler will issue more instructions to avoid doing a branch. The default is 2.
    Also see -mcond-exec.

-mcond-exec=*number*
Specifies the maximum number of conditionally executed instructions that replace a branch. The default is 4.
    Also see -mbranch-cost.

-mextmem
Links the .text, .data, .bss, .strings, .rodata, .rodata1, and .data1 sections into external memory, which starts at location 0x80000000.

-mextmemory
Same as -mextmem.

-monchip
Links the .text section into on-chip text memory, which starts at location 0x00000000. It also links the .data, .bss, .strings, .rodata, .rodata1, and .data1 sections into on-chip data memory, which starts at location 0x20000000.

H8/300 Options

The following options are defined for the H8/300 implementations.

-malign-300
On the H8/300H and H8/S, the same alignment rules are used as for the H8/300.
    The default for the H8/300H and H8/S is to align long and float data items on 4-byte boundaries. This option causes them to be aligned on 2-byte boundaries.
    This option has no effect on the H8/300.

-mh
Generates code for the H8/300H.

-mint32
Generates `int` data as 32-bit values.

-mrelax
Shortens some address references at link time, if possible. This option sets the linker option `-relax`.

-ms
Generates code for the H8/S.

-ms2600
Generates code for the H8/S2600. This switch must be used in combination with `-ms`.

HPPA Options

The following options are defined for the HPPA family of computers.

-march=*architecture*
Generates code for the specified architecture. The known names for *architecture* are `1.0` (for PA 1.0), `1.1` (for PA 1.1), and `2.0` (for PA 2.0).

Code compiled for lower numbered architectures will run on higher numbered architectures, but not the other way around. Refer to /usr/lib/sched.models on an HPUX system to determine the proper architecture option for your machine.

-mbig-switch
Generates code suitable for big switch tables. Use this option only if the assembler/ linker complain about out-of-range branches within a switch table.

-mdisable-fpregs
Prevents floating-point registers from being used in any manner.

This is necessary for compiling kernels that perform lazy context switching of floating-point registers. If you use this option and attempt to perform floating-point operations, the compiler will abort.

-mdisable-indexing
Prevents the compiler from using indexing address modes. This avoids some rather obscure problems when compiling MIG generated code under MACH.

-mfast-indirect-calls
Generates code that assumes calls never cross space boundaries.

This allows the compiler to generate code that performs faster indirect calls. This option will not work in the presence of shared libraries or nested functions.

-mgas
Enables the use of assembler directives only the gas assembler understands.

-mjump-in-delay
Fills delay slots of function calls with unconditional jump instructions by modifying the return pointer for the function call to be the target of the conditional jump.

-mlinker-opt
Enables the optimization pass in the HPUX linker. This option makes symbolic debugging impossible. Also, it triggers a bug in the HPUX 8 and HPUX 9 linkers in which they give bogus error messages when linking some programs.

-mlong-load-store
Generates three-instruction load and store sequences, as sometimes required by the HPUX 10 linker. This is equivalent to the +k option used with HP compilers.

-mno-space-regs
Generates code that assumes the target has no space registers.
This allows GCC to generate faster indirect calls and use unscaled index address modes. Such code is suitable for level 0 PA systems and kernels.

-mpa-risc-1-0
The same as -march=1.0.

-mpa-risc-1-1
The same as -march=1.1.

-mpa-risc-2-0
The same as -march=2.0.

-mportable-runtime
Uses the portable calling conventions proposed by HP for ELF systems.

-mschedule=*type*
Schedules code according to the constraints for the specified machine type. The valid selections for *type* are 700, 7100, 7100LC, 7200, 7300, and 8000. Refer to /usr/lib/sched.models on an HPUX system to determine the proper scheduling option for it. The default scheduling is 8000.

-msoft-float
Generates output containing library calls for floating-point operations.
The libraries are not available for all HPPA targets. Under normal circumstances, the facilities of the machine's usual C compiler are used, but this cannot be done directly in cross-compilation. You must provide suitable library functions for cross-compilation. The embedded target hppa1.1-*-pro does provide software floating-point support.

This option changes the calling convention in the object file, so it is only useful if you compile all modules, including all libraries, of a program with this option. This includes libgcc.a, the library that comes with GCC.

IA-64 Options

The following options are defined for the Intel IA-64 architecture.

-mauto-pic
Generates code that is self-relocatable. This option also sets −mconstant-gp. This is useful when compiling firmware code.

-mb-step
Generates code that works around Itanium B step errata.

-mbig-endian
Generates code for a big endian target. This is the default for HPUX.
  Also see −mlittle-endian.

-mconstant-gp
Generates code that uses a single constant global pointer value. This is useful when compiling kernel code.
  Also see −mauto-pic.

-mdwarf2-asm
Generates assembler code for the DWARF2 line number debugging info. This may be useful when the GNU assembler is not being used. The option can be reversed by specifying −mno-dwarf2-asm.

-mfixed-range=*range*
Generates code that treats the given register range as fixed registers. A register range is specified as two registers separated by a dash. Multiple register ranges can be specified separated by a comma.
  A fixed register is one that the register allocator cannot use. This is useful when compiling kernel code.

-mgnu-as
Generates code for the GNU assembler. This is the default, which can be reversed by specifying −mno-gnu-as.

-mgnu-ld
Generates code for the GNU linker. This is the default, which can be reversed by specifying −mno-gnu-ld.

-minline-divide-max-throughput

Generates code for inline divides using the maximum throughput algorithm. Also see `-minline-divide-min-latency`.

-minline-divide-min-latency

Generates code for inline divides using the minimum latency algorithm. Also see `-minline-divide-max-througput`.

-mlittle-endian

Generates code for a little endian target. This is the default for AIX5 and Linux.
 Also see `-mbig-endian`.

-mno-pic

Generates code that does not use a global pointer register for addressing. The result is code that is not position independent and violates the IA-64 ABI.

-mregister-names

Generates `in`, `loc`, and `out` register names for the stacked registers. This may make assembler output more readable. This option can be reversed with `-mno-register-names`.

-msdata

Enables optimizations that use the small data section. This is the default, which can be reversed with `-mno-sdata`, and may be useful for working around optimizer bugs.

-mvolatile-asm-stop

Generates a stop bit immediately before and after volatile assembler statements. This option can be reversed with `-mno-volatile-asm-stop`.

Intel 386 and AMD x86-64 Options

The following options are defined for the i386 and x86-64 family of computers.

-m128bit-long-double

Specifies the size of the `long double` type to be 128 bits (16 bytes). The i386 application binary interface specifies the size to be 12 bytes, while newer architectures (Pentium and later) prefer `long double` aligned on an 8- or 16-byte boundary. This is impossible to achieve with 12-byte `long doubles` being accessed as an array.
 If you specify this option, the structures and arrays containing `long double` data will change size. Also, the function calling convention for functions using `long double` will be modified.
 Also see `-m96bit-long-double`.

-m32
On AMD x86-64 processors in a 64-bit environment, this option sets int, long, and pointer data to 32 bits and generates code that runs on any i386 system.

-m386
The same as -mcpu=i386. This form of the option is deprecated.

-m3dnow
Enables the use of built-in functions that allow direct access to the 3Dnow extensions. The usage can be disallowed with -mno-3dnow.

-m486
The same as -mcpu=i486. This form of the option is deprecated.

-m64
On AMD x86-64 processors in a 64-bit environment, this option sets int to 32 bits, sets long and pointer data to 64 bits, and generates code specifically for AMD's x86-64 architecture.

-m96bit-long-double
Specifies that the size of long double data items be 96 bits (12 bytes), as required by the i386 application binary interface. This is the default.
  Also see -m128bit-long-double.

-maccumulate-outgoing-args
Specifies that the maximum amount of space required for outgoing arguments will be computed in the function prolog. This is faster on most modern CPUs because of reduced dependencies, improved scheduling, and reduced stack usage when the preferred stack boundary is not equal to 2. The drawback is an increase in code size. Setting this option also sets -mno-push-args.

-malign-double
Specifies that the compiler align double, long double, and long long variables on a two-word boundary. Specifying -mno-align-double aligns them on a one-word boundary.
  Aligning double variables on a two-word boundary will produce code that runs somewhat faster on a Pentium at the expense of the program being larger.
  The -malign-double option causes structures containing the preceding types to be aligned differently than the published application binary interface specifications for the 386.

-march=*architecture*
Generates instructions for the machine architecture. The choices for *architecture* are the same as for *type* in the -mcpu option. Specifying -march implies -mcpu for the same type.

-masm=*dialect*

Outputs assembly language instructions using the specified dialect. Valid selections for *dialect* are `intel` and `att`. The default is `att`.

-mcpu=*type*

Tunes the generated code to everything applicable to the specified type, except for the ABI and the set of available instructions. The valid choices for *type* are `i386`, `i486`, `i586`, `i686`, `pentium`, `pentium-mmx`, `pentiumpro`, `pentium2`, `pentium3`, `pentium4`, `k6`, `k6-2`, `k6-3`, `athlon`, `athlon-tbird`, `athlon-4`, `athlon-xp`, and `athlon-mp`.

The type `i586` is equivalent to `pentium`. The type `i686` is equivalent to `pentiumpro`. The `k6` and `athlon` types are the AMD chips.

Although selecting a specific CPU will cause things to be scheduled appropriately for that particular chip, the compiler will not generate any code that does not run on the i386 without the `-march` option being specified.

-mfpmath=*unit*

Generates floating-point instructions for the selected hardware unit.

Specifying *unit* as `387` uses the standard 387 floating-point coprocessor, present in the majority of chips and emulated otherwise. Code compiled with this option will run almost everywhere. The temporary results are computed with 80-bit precision.

Also see `-ffloat-store` in Appendix D. This is the default choice for the i386 architecture.

Specifying *unit* as `sse` uses scalar floating-point instructions, present in the SSE instruction set. This instruction set is supported by Pentium3 and newer chips as well as in the AMD line by the Athlon-4, Athlon-xp, and Athlon-mp chips. The earlier version of the SSE instruction set supports only single-precision operations, thus the double- and extended-precision operations are still performed using 387. The newer version, present only in Pentium4 and the AMD x86-64 chips, supports double-precision operations.

When specifying *unit* as `i387`, you must also specify a `-march`, `-msse`, or `-msse2` option to enable SSE extensions and make this option effective. For the x86-64 compiler, these extensions are enabled by default. The resulting code should be considerably faster (in most cases) and avoid the numerical instability problems of `387` code. However, this option may break some existing code that expects temporaries to be 80-bit values.

Specifying *unit* as `sse,387` attempts to utilize both instruction sets at once. This effectively doubles the number of available registers on chips with separate execution units for 387 and SSE. This option is experimental, because gcc register allocation does not model separate functional units well.

-mieee-fp

Specifies that the compiler uses IEEE floating-point comparisons. These comparisons correctly handle the case in which the result of a comparison is unordered. The use of IEEE floating-point comparisons can be suppressed by specifying `-mno-ieee-fp`.

-minline-all-stringops
All string operations are inlined. The default is that string operations are inlined only when the destination is known to be aligned at least to a 4-byte boundary. This option enables more inlining, which increases code size, but may improve performance of the code that depends on fast memcpy(), strlen(), and memset() for short lengths.

-mmmx
Enables the use of built-in functions that allow direct access to the MMX extensions. This usage can be disallowed with -mno-mmx.

-mno-align-stringops
Does not align the destination of inlined string operations. This option reduces code size and improves performance in cases where the destination is already aligned and the compiler doesn't know it.

-mno-fancy-math-387
Some 387 emulators do not support the sin, cos, and sqrt instructions for the 387. This option avoids generating those instructions. It has no effect unless you also specify the -funsafe-math-optimizations option.

  This option is the default on FreeBSD, OpenBSD, and NetBSD. It is ignored when -march indicates that the target CPU will always have an FPU and the instruction will not need emulation.

-mno-fp-ret-in-387
Specifies not to use the FPU registers for return values of functions.

  The usual calling convention has functions return values of types float and double in an FPU register, even if there is no FPU. The idea is that the operating system should emulate an FPU. Specifying this option will cause the values to be returned in ordinary CPU registers instead.

-mno-red-zone
On AMD x86-64 processors in a 64-bit environment, this option suppresses the use of a so-called *red zone* for x86-64 code. The red zone is mandated by the x86-64 ABI and is a 128-byte area beyond the location of the stack pointer that will not be modified by signal or interrupt handlers and therefore can be used for temporary data without adjusting the stack pointer. This option disables the red zone.

-momit-leaf-frame-pointer
Does not retain the frame pointer in a register for leaf functions. This avoids the instructions to save, set up, and restore frame pointers and makes an extra register available inside the leaf functions.

  The option -fomit-frame-pointer can be used to remove the frame pointer for all functions, but this does make debugging more difficult.

-mpentium

The same as -mcpu=pentium. This form of the option is deprecated.

-mpentiumpro

The same as -mcpu=pentiumpro. This form of the option is deprecated.

-mpreferred-stack-boundary=*number*

Attempts to keep the stack boundary aligned to a 2 raised to *number* byte boundary. The default for *number* is 4 (16 bytes or 128 bits).

Optimizing for code size by specifying -Os sets the minimum to the correct alignment (four bytes for x86 and eight bytes for x86-64). On Pentium and Pentium Pro, double and long double values should be aligned to an 8-byte boundary to prevent the code from running slower. On the Pentium III, the Streaming SIMD Extension (SSE) data type __m128 suffers similar speed penalties if it is not aligned on a 16-byte boundary.

To ensure proper alignment of values on the stack, the stack boundary must be aligned to the boundary required by any value stored on the stack. Also, every function must be generated so that it keeps the stack aligned. This means calling a function compiled with a higher preferred stack boundary from a function compiled with a lower preferred stack boundary will most likely misalign the stack. It is recommended that libraries that use callbacks always use the default setting.

This extra alignment does consume stack space and generally increases code size. For code that is sensitive to stack space usage, such as embedded systems and operating system kernels, you may want to reduce the preferred alignment to -mpreferred-stack-boundary=2.

Also see -malign-double.

-mpush-args

Uses push operations to store outgoing parameters. This method is shorter and usually equally as fast as the method using sub/mov operations, and it's enabled by default. The default can be overridden with -mno-push-args and, in some cases, disabling it may improve performance because of improved scheduling and reduced dependencies.

-mregparm=*number*

Specifies the number of registers used to pass integer arguments. By default, no registers are used to pass arguments. The largest value for *number* is 3. You can control this behavior for a specific function by using the function attribute regparm.

When using this option with *number* being a nonzero value, you must build all modules, including libraries, with the same value.

-mrtd

Uses a different function calling convention, in which functions that take a fixed number of arguments return with the ret num instruction, which pops their arguments while returning. This saves one instruction in the caller because there is no need to pop the arguments after the return.

You can specify that an individual function is called with this calling convention with the function attribute `stdcall`. You can also override the `-mrtd` option by using the function attribute `cdecl`.

The use of this calling convention is incompatible with the one normally used on UNIX, so you cannot use it if you need to call libraries compiled with the UNIX compiler. Also, you must provide function prototypes for all functions that take variable numbers of arguments; otherwise, incorrect code will be generated for calls to those functions.

Incorrect code will result if you call a function with too many arguments. Normally, extra arguments are harmlessly ignored.

-msoft-float
Generates code containing library calls for floating-point operations. The libraries are not part of GCC. The libraries of the target computer's C compiler can be used, but this can't be done directly in cross-compilation. It will be necessary for you to provide your own libraries for a cross compiler.

On machines where a function returns floating-point results in the 80387 register stack, some floating-point opcodes may be emitted even when `-msoft-float` is specified.

-msse
Enables the use of built-in functions that allow direct access to the SSE extensions. The usage can be disallowed with `-mno-sse`.

-msse2
Enables the use of built-in functions that allow direct access to the SSE2 extensions. The usage can be disallowed with `-mno-sse2`.

-mthreads
Supports thread-safe exception handling for Mingw32. Code that relies on thread-safe exception handling must compile and link all code with the `-mthreads` option. Setting this option defines `-D_MT`. When linking, it includes a special thread helper library with `-lmingwthrd` that cleans up per-thread exception handling data.

-msvr3-shlib
Specifies that the compiler place uninitialized local variables into the `bss` data segment. To specify that they be placed in the `data` data segment, use `-mno-svr3-shlib`. These options are meaningful only on System V Release 3.

Intel 960 Options

The following options are defined for the Intel 960 implementations.

-m*type*
Assumes the defaults for the specified machine type. This includes settings for instruction scheduling, floating-point support, and addressing modes. The possible choices for *type* are `ka`, `kb`, `mc`, `ca`, `cf`, `sa`, and `sb`. The default is `kb`.

-masm-compat
Enables compatibility with the iC960 assembler.

-mcode-align
Aligns code to 8-byte boundaries for faster fetching. This is currently turned on, by default, for C-series implementations only. For the others, the default is `-mno-code-align`.

-mcomplex-addr
The compiler is to assume that the use of a complex addressing mode is desired on this implementation of the i960. Complex addressing modes may not be worthwhile on the K-series, but they definitely are on the C-series. The default is `-mcomplex-addr` for all processors except `cb` and `cc`, where the default is `-mno-complex-addr`.

-mic-compat
Enables compatibility with iC960.

-mic2.0-compat
Enables compatibility with iC960 version 2.0.

-mic3.0-compat
Enables compatibility with iC960 version 3.0.

-mintel-asm
Same as `-masm-compat`.

-mleaf-procedures
This option specifies that the compiler should attempt to alter leaf procedures to be callable with the `bal` instruction as well as `call`. This option can be suppressed by specifying `-mno-leaf-procedures`.

The result of specifying `-mleaf-procedures` is more efficient code for explicit calls when the `bal` instruction can be substituted by the assembler or linker, but less efficient code in other cases, such as calls via function pointers.

-mlong-double-64
Implements data type `long double` as a 64-bit floating-point number. Without this option, `long double` is implemented as an 80-bit floating-point number.

The only reason for this option is the lack of 128-bit `long double` support in `fp-bit.c`. This option is only useful for people using soft-float targets.

-mnumerics
This option specifies that the processor does support floating-point instructions. Also see `-msoft-float`.

-mold-align
Enables structure-alignment compatibility with Intel's gcc release version 1.3 (which is based on gcc 1.37). Setting this option also sets `-mstrict-align`.

-msoft-float
This option specifies that the processor does not support floating-point instructions. Also see -mnumerics.

-mstrict-align
Does not permit unaligned accesses. To permit unaligned access, specify -mno-strict-align.

-mtail-call
Instructs the compiler to take additional attempts (beyond those of the machine-independent portions of the compiler) to optimize tail-recursive calls into branches. You may not want to do this because the detection of cases where this is not valid is not totally complete. The default is -mno-tail-call.

M32R/D Options

The following options are defined for the Mitsubishi M32R/D architectures.

-m32r
Generates code for the M32R. This is the default.

-m32rx
Generates code for the M32R/X.

-mcode-model=*name*
Specifying *name* as small instructs the compiler to assume all objects live in the lower 16MB of memory so that their addresses can be loaded with the ld24 instruction. The compiler also assumes all subroutines are reachable with the bl instruction. This is the default.

Specifying *name* as medium instructs the compiler to assume objects may be anywhere in the 32-bit address space (the compiler will generate seth/add3 instructions to load their addresses). The compiler also assumes all subroutines are reachable with the bl instruction.

Specifying *name* as large instructs the compiler to assume objects may be anywhere in the 32-bit address space (the compiler will generate seth/add3 instructions to load their addresses). The compiler also assumes subroutines may not be reachable with the bl instruction (the compiler generates the much slower seth/add3/jl instruction sequence).

-msdata=*setting*
This options specifies which items are stored in the small data area. The small data area consists of the sections .sdata and .sbss. Objects may be explicitly put into the small data area with the section attribute specifying one of these two sections. Also see the -G option.

Specifying *setting* as none disables the use of the small data area. Variables will be put into one of .data, .bss, or .rodata (unless the section attribute has been specified). This is the default.

Specifying *setting* as sdata places small global and static data in the small data area but does not generate special code to reference them.

Specifying *setting* as use places small global and static data in the small data area and generates special instructions to reference them.

-G *number*

Puts global and static objects less than or equal to *number* bytes into the small data or bss sections instead of the normal data or bss sections. The default value of *number* is 8.

The −msdata option must be set to either sdata or use for this option to have any effect.

All modules should be compiled with the same −msdata and −G settings. Compiling with different values for *number* may or may not work. If it does not work, the linker will detect the error preventing incorrect code from being generated.

M680x0 Options

The following options are defined for the 680x0 series. The default values for these options vary, depending on which CPU in the 680x0 series was selected when the compiler was configured.

-m5200

Code is generated for a 520X "coldfire" family CPU. This is the default when the compiler is configured for 520X-based systems. Use this option for microcontrollers with a 5200 core, including the MCF5202, MCF5203, MCF5204, and MCF5202.

This option also sets −mnobitfield.

-m68000

Code will be generated for the 6800. This option is for microcontrollers with a 68000 or EC000 core, including the 68008, 68302, 68306, 68307, 68322, 68328, and 68356. This is the default when the compiler is configured to generate code for the 68000 series.

This option also sets −mnobitfield.

-m68020

Code will be generated for a 68020. This is the default when the compiler is configured for 68020-based systems.

This option also sets −mbitfield.

-m68020-40

Code is generated for a 68040, without using any of the new instructions. This results in code that can run relatively efficiently on either a 68020/68881, 68030, or 68040. The generated code does use the 68881 instructions that are emulated on the 68040.

-m68020-60

Code is generated for a 68060, without using any of the new instructions. This results in code that can run relatively efficiently on a 68020/68881, 68030, or 68040. The generated code does use the 68881 instructions that are emulated on the 68060.

-m68030

Code will be generated for a 68030. This is the default when the compiler is configured for 68030-based systems.

-m68040

Code will be generated for a 68040. This is the default when the compiler is configured for 68040-based systems. This option inhibits the use of 68881/68882 instructions that have to be emulated by software on the 68040. Use this option if your 68040 does not have code to emulate those instructions.

-m68060

Code is generated for a 68060. This is the default when the compiler is configured for 68060-based systems. This option inhibits the use of 68020 and 68881/68882 instructions that have to be emulated by software on the 68060. Use this option if your 68060 does not have code to emulate those instructions.

-m68881

Code will be generated containing 68881 instructions for floating point. This is the default for most 68020 systems, unless --nfp was specified when the compiler was configured.

-malign-int

This option specifies the alignment of int, long, long long, float, double, and long double variables on a 32-bit boundary. The default is -no-align-int, which places the alignment on a 16-bit boundary. Aligning variables on 32-bit boundaries produces larger code that runs somewhat faster on processors with 32-bit busses.

Using the -malign-int option, GCC aligns structures containing the preceding types differently than most published application binary interface specifications for the m680x0.

-mbitfield

Enables the use of the bit-field instructions. The -m68020 option implies this option. This is the default if the compiler is configured for a 68020.

-mc68000

Same as -m6800.

-mc68020

Same as -m68020.

-mcpu32

Code is generated for a CPU32. This is the default when the compiler is configured for CPU32-based systems. Use this option for microcontrollers with a CPU32 or CPU32+ core, including the 68330, 68331, 68332, 68333, 68334, 68336, 68340, 68341, 68349, and 68360.

This option also sets `-mnobitfield`.

-mfpa

Code is generated containing Sun FPA instructions for floating point.

-mno-strict-align

The compiler will assume that unaligned memory references will be handled by the system. To force the compiler to align the referenced data, specify `-mstrict-align`.

-mnobitfield

Disables the use of the bit-field instructions. The options `-m68000`, `-mcpu32`, and `-m5200` imply this option.

-mpcrel

Uses the PC-relative (program counter-relative) addressing mode of the 68000 directly, instead of using a global offset table.

This option also sets `-fpic` to allow, at most, a 16-bit offset for PC-relative addressing. The `-fPIC` option is not currently supported with this option.

-mrtd

Uses a different function calling convention, in which functions take a fixed number of arguments and return with the `rtd` instruction by popping the arguments while returning. This saves one instruction in the caller because there is no need to pop the arguments. The `rtd` instruction is supported by the 68010, 68020, 68030, 68040, 68060, and CPU32 processors, but not by the 68000 and 5200.

This calling convention is incompatible with the one normally used on UNIX, so you cannot use it if you need to call libraries compiled with the UNIX compiler. Also, you must provide your own function prototypes for all functions, such as `printf()`, that take variable numbers of arguments. Without appropriate prototypes, incorrect code will be generated for calls to those functions.

Incorrect code will result if a function is called with too many arguments. Using the default calling sequence, extra arguments are harmlessly ignored.

-mshort

Causes the type `int` to be a 16-bit number, the same as `short int`.

-msoft-float

Code is generated to make library calls for floating-point operations.

To use this option you will need to acquire suitable libraries for cross-compilation, and the libraries are not available for all m680x0 targets. Often the facilities of the C compiler on the target machine are used, but this can't be done directly in cross-compilation. The embedded targets m68k-*-aout and m68k-*-coff do provide software floating-point support.

M68HClx Options

These options are defined for the 68HC11 and 68HC12 microcontrollers. The default values for these options depend on which style of microcontroller was selected when the compiler was configured.

-m6811
Code will be generated for a 68HC11. This is the default when the compiler is configured for 68HC11-based systems.

-m6812
Code will be generated for a 68HC12. This is the default when the compiler is configured for 68HC12-based systems.

-m68hc11
Same as -m6811.

-m68hc12
Same as -m6812.

-mauto-incdec
Enables the use of 68HC12 for both pre and post auto-increment and auto-decrement addressing modes.

-mshort
Considers an int data type to be a 16-bit number, the same as short int.

-msoft-reg-count=*count*
Specifies *count* as the number of pseudo-soft registers, which are used in code generation. The maximum number is 32. Using more pseudo-soft registers may or may not result in better code, depending on the program. The default is 4 for 68HC11 and 2 for 68HC12.

M88K Options

The following options are defined for Motorola 88K architectures.

-m88000
Generates code that works well on both the m88100 and the m88110.

-m88100
Generates code that works best for the m88100 but also runs on the m88110.

-m88110
Generates code that works best for the m88110 and may not run on the m88100.

-mbig-pic
A deprecated option. Use `-fPIC` instead.

-mhandle-large-shift
Includes code to detect bit-shifts of more than 31 bits. Such shifts are trapped or code is generated to handle them properly. By default, GCC makes no special provision for large bit shifts.

-midentify-revision
Includes an `ident` directive in the assembler output, recording the source file name, compiler name and version, timestamp, and the set of compilation flags used.

-mno-check-zero-division
Generates code that does not detect integer division by zero. The default is `-mcheck-zero-division`, which detects integer division by zero.

Some models of the MC88100 processor fail to trap upon integer division by zero under certain conditions. By default, when compiling code that might be run on such a processor, GCC generates code that explicitly checks for zero-valued divisors and traps with exception number 503 when one is detected. Use of `-mno-check-zero-division` suppresses such checking for code generated to run on an MC88100 processor.

GCC assumes that the MC88110 processor correctly detects all instances of integer division by zero. When -m88110 is specified, no explicit checks for zero-valued divisors are generated, and both `-mcheck-zero-division` and `-mno-check-zero-division` are ignored.

-mno-underscores
Specifies that the assembly language generated by the compiler does not have an underscore character added at the beginning of each symbol. The default is to add an underscore at the beginning of each name.

-mocs-debug-info
Includes debugging information about registers used in each stack frame, as specified in the 88open Object Compatibility Standard (OCS). This extra information makes it possible to debug code that has had the frame pointer eliminated.

The default for DG/UX, SVr4, and Delta 88 SVr3.2 is to include this information, which can be suppressed by specifying `-mno-ocs-debug-info`. Other 88K configurations omit this information by default.

-mocs-frame-position

When generating COFF debugging information for automatic variables and parameters stored on the stack, this option specifies the use of the offset from the canonical frame address, which is the stack pointer (register 31) upon entry to the function.

Specifying `-mno-ocs-frame-position` instructs the compiler, when generating COFF debugging information for automatic variables and parameters stored on the stack, to use the offset from the frame pointer register (register 30). When this option is in effect, the frame pointer is not eliminated when debugging information is selected by the `-g` switch.

The DG/UX, SVr4, Delta88 SVr3.2, and BCS configurations use the offset by default, which can be suppressed by `-mno-ocs-frame-position`. Other 88K configurations have the default of `-mno-ocs-frame-position`.

-moptimize-arg-area

This option saves space by reorganizing the stack frame. This option generates code that does not agree with the 88open specifications, but it uses less memory.

Specifying `-mno-optimize-arg-area` suppresses the reorganization of the stack frame to save space. This is the default, which conforms to the specification but uses more memory.

-mshort-data-*number*

Generates smaller data references by making them relative to r0, which allows loading a value using a single instruction rather than the usual two. The value of *number* should be greater than zero but has no effect for values greater than 65535.

This option controls which data references are affected by specifying *number* as the maximum offset. For example, if you specify `-mshort-data-512`, the data references affected are those involving displacements of less than 512 bytes.

-mserialize-volatile

Generates code to guarantee sequential consistency of volatile memory references. This is the default, which can be overridden by `-mno-serialze-volatile`.

The order of memory references made by the MC88110 processor does not always match the order of the instructions requesting those references. In particular, a load instruction may execute before a preceding store instruction. Such reordering violates sequential consistency of volatile memory references when there are multiple processors. When consistency must be guaranteed, GCC generates special instructions as needed to force execution in the proper order.

The MC88100 processor does not reorder memory references, so it always provides sequential consistency. However, by default, GCC generates the special instructions to guarantee consistency even when you use `-m88100` to make it possible for that code to be run on an MC88110 processor. If you intend to run your code only on the MC88100 processor, you may want to specify `-mno-serialize-volatile`. The extra code generated to guarantee consistency may affect the performance of your application, which you can avoid if you know that you can safely forgo this guarantee.

-msvr3
Turns off the compiler extensions related to System V release 4 (SVr4). See –msvr4.

-msvr4
Turns on the compiler extensions related to System V release 4 (SVr4). This option determines which variant of the assembler syntax to generate, makes the C preprocessor recognize #pragma weak, and makes GCC issue additional declaration directives used in SVr4.

　　This is the default for the m88k-motorola-sysv4 and m88k-dg-dgux m88k configurations. For these configurations, the default can be reversed by using –msvr3. For other M88K configurations, the default is –msvr3.

-mtrap-large-shift
Same as –mhandle-large-shift.

-muse-div-instruction
Generates code to use the div instruction for signed integer division on the MC88100 processor. By default, the div instruction is not used.

　　On the MC88100 processor, the signed integer division instruction div traps to the operating system on a negative operand. The operating system transparently completes the operation, but at a large cost in execution time. By default, when compiling code that might be run on an MC88100 processor, GCC emulates signed integer division using the unsigned integer division instruction divu, thereby avoiding the large penalty of a trap to the operating system. Such emulation has its own, smaller execution cost in both time and space. To the extent that your code's important signed integer division operations are performed on two nonnegative operands, it may be desirable to use the div instruction directly.

　　On the MC88110 processor, the div instruction (also known as the divs instruction) processes negative operands without trapping to the operating system. When –m88110 is specified, –muse-div-instruction is ignored, and the div instruction is used for signed integer division.

　　The result of dividing INT_MIN by -1 is undefined. In particular, the behavior of such a division with and without –muse-div-instruction may differ.

-mversion-03.00
This option is obsolete and is ignored.

-mwarn-passed-structs
Issues a warning when a function passes a struct as an argument or return value. Structure-passing conventions have changed during the evolution of the C language and are often the source of portability problems. By default, GCC issues no such warning.

MCore Options

The following options are defined for the Motorola MCore processors.

-m210
Generates code for the 210 processor.

-m340
Generates code for the 340 processor.

-m4byte-functions
Forces all functions to be aligned on a 4-byte boundary. This option can be reversed with -mno-4byte-functions.

-mbig-endian
Generates code for a big endian target. Also see -mlittle-endian.

-mcallgraph-data
Emits callgraph information. This option can be reversed with -mno-callgraph-data.

-mdiv
Uses the hardware divide instruction. This is the default, which can be reversed by -mno-div.

-mhardlit
Constants are inlined into the code stream if it can be done in two instructions or less. This option can be suppressed by -mno-hardlit.

-mlittle-endian
Generates code for a little endian target. Also see -mbig-endian.

-mrelax-immediate
Allows arbitrarily sized immediate values in bit operations. This option can be suppressed by -mno-relax-immediate.

-mslow-bytes
Prefers word access when reading byte quantities. This option can be reversed with -mno-slow-bytes.

-mwide-bitfields
Bit fields are stored as int data types. This option can be reversed with -mno-wide-bitfields.

MIPS Options

The following options are defined for the MIPS family of computers.

-m4650
Turns on `-msingle-float`, `-mmad`, and `-mcpu=r4650`.

-mabi=*name*
Generates code for the named ABI. The recognized ABI names are `32`, `o64`, `n32`, `64`, `eabi`, and `meabi`.

The name `eabi` selects the embedded ABI defined by Cygnus. The name `meabi` selects the embedded ABI defined by MIPS. Both these ABIs have 32-bit and 64-bit variants. By default, the compiler will generate 64-bit code when you select a 64-bit architecture, but you can specify `-mgp32` to get 32-bit code instead.

-mabicalls
Generates the pseudo operations `.abicalls`, `.cpload`, and `.cprestore` that some System V.4 ports use for position-independent code. This action can be suppressed by `-mno-abicalls`.

-march=*architecture*
Generates code that will run on the specified architecture, which can either be the name of a generic MIPS ISA or the name of a specific processor.

The generic ISA names are `mips1`, `mips2`, `mips3`, `mips4`, `mips32`, and `mips64`.

The specific processor names are `r2000`, `r3000`, `r3900`, `r4000`, `vr4100`, `vr4300`, `r4400`, `r4600`, `r4650`, `vr5000`, `r6000`, `r8000`, `4kc`, `4kp`, `5kc`, `20kc`, and `orion`. In the processor names, a terminating `000` can be abbreviated as `k`—that is, `r2000` can be written as `r2k`. Also, prefix letters are optional, so `vr5000` can be written as `r5000`, `r5k`, or `vr5k`.

The special architecture name `from-abi` selects the most compatible architecture for the selected ABI, which is `mips1` for 32-bit ABIs and `mips3` for 64-bit ABIs.

The macro `_MIPS_ARCH` is defined to contain the name of target architecture as a string. Also, the macro `_MIPS_ARCH_*architecture*` is defined using the capitalized name of the string in `_MIPS_ARCH`. For example, `-march=r2000` defines `_MIPS_ARCH` as `"r2000"` and also defines the macro `_MIPS_ARCH_R2000`. The `_MIPS_ARCH` definition uses the full prefixed form of the name, as listed earlier, so it will never abbreviate `000` as `k`. Specifying `from-abi` results in the macro definition of either `"mips1"` or `"mips3"`. The default architecture name is used when no `-march` option is specified.

-mdouble-float
Permits the compiler to use double precision operations. This is the default.

Also see `-msingle-float`.

-membedded-data

Allocates variables to the read-only data section first, if possible, and next to the small data section, if possible. Otherwise, they are allocated in data. This results in slightly slower code than the default, but it reduces the amount of RAM required while executing and therefore may be preferred for some embedded systems. This action can be suppressed by -mno-embedded-data.

-membedded-pic

Generates PIC code suitable for some embedded systems. All calls are made using PC-relative addresses, and all data is addressed using the $gp register. No more than 65,536 bytes of global data may be accessed. This option requires GNU as and GNU ld, which do most of the work. This currently works only on targets that use ECOFF; it does not work with ELF.

-mentry

Uses the entry and exit pseudo ops. This option can only be used with -mips16.

-mfix7000

Passes an option to gas, which will cause noops to be inserted if the read of the destination register of an mfhi or mflo instruction occurs within the following two instructions.

-mflush-func=*function*

Specifies the name of the function to call to flush the I and D caches. Specifying -mno-flush-func instructs the compiler not to call any such function.

If called, the function must take the same arguments as the common _flush_func() —that is, the address of the memory range for which the cache is being flushed, the size of the memory range, and the number 3 (to flush both caches). The default depends on the target GCC was configured for, but commonly is either _flush_func() or __cpu_flush().

-mfp32

Assumes that floating-point registers are 32 bits wide.

-mfp64

Assumes that floating-point registers are 64 bits wide.

-mfused-madd

Generates code that uses the floating-point multiply and accumulate hardware instructions, when they are available. These instructions are generated by default if they are available. However, this may be undesirable if the extra precision causes problems, or on certain chips in the mode where denormals are rounded to zero and where denormals generated by multiply and accumulate instructions cause exceptions anyway.

The use of hardware floating-point operations can be disabled by specifying `-mno-fused-madd`.

-mgas
Generates code for the GNU assembler. This is the default on the OSF/1 reference platform, using the OSF/rose object format. Also, this is the default if the configure option `--with-gnu-as` is specified.

Also see `-mmips-as`.

-mgp32
Assumes that general purpose registers are 32 bits wide.

-mgp64
Assumes that general purpose registers are 64 bits wide.

-mgpopt
Instructs the compiler to write all the data declarations before the instructions in the text section, which allows the MIPS assembler to generate one-word memory references instead of using two words for short global or static data items. This is the default when optimization is turned on, but it can be suppressed by specifying `-mno-gpopt`.

-mhalf-pic
Puts pointers to external references into the data section and loads them from there, rather than putting the references in the text section. This action can be suppressed by `-mno-half-pic`.

-mhard-float
Generates output containing hardware floating-point instructions. This is the default.

Also see `-msoft-float`.

-mint64
Forces `int` and `long` types to be 64 bits wide.

The default size of `int`, `long`, and pointer data depends on the ABI. All the supported ABIs use an `int` of 32 bits. The n64 ABI and the 64-bit Cygnus EABI use a `long` of 64 bits. All others use a `long` of 32 bits. A pointer is the same size as a `long`, or the same size as integer registers, whichever is smaller.

Also see `-mlong64` and `-mlong32`.

-mips1
The same as `-march=mips1`.

-mips2
The same as `-march=mips2`.

-mips3
The same as -march=mips3.

-mips4
The same as -march=mips4.

-mips16
Enables 16-bit instructions. This can be suppressed by specifying -mno-mips16.

-mips32
The same as -march=mips32.

-mips64
The same as -march=mips64.

-mlong-calls
Generates code to make all function calls with the JALR instruction, which requires loading up a function's address into a register before the call. This option is necessary for calls outside the current 512MB segment to functions that are not addressed through pointers. This option can be suppressed by -mno-long-calls.

-mlong32
Forces long, int, and pointer types to be 32 bits wide.
    The default size of int, long, and pointer data depends on the ABI. All the supported ABIs use an int of 32 bits. The n64 ABI and the 64-bit Cygnus EABI use a long of 64 bits. All others use a long of 32 bits. A pointer is the same size as a long, or the same size as integer registers, whichever is smaller.
    Also see -mint64 and -mlong64.

-mlong64
Forces long types to be 64 bits wide.
    The default size of int, long, and pointer data depends on the ABI. All the supported ABIs use an int of 32 bits. The n64 ABI and the 64-bit Cygnus EABI use a long of 64 bits. All others use a long of 32 bits. A pointer is the same size as a long, or the same size as integer registers, whichever is smaller.
    Also see -mint64 and -mlong32.

-mmad
Permits the use of the mad, madu, and mul instructions, as on the r4650 chip. This can be reversed by specifying -mno-mad.

-mmemcpy
Generates code to make all block moves call the appropriate string function, memcpy() or bcopy(), instead of possibly generating inline code. The function calls can be suppressed by specifying -mno-memcpy.

-mmips-as

Generates code for the MIPS assembler and invokes `mips-tfile` to add normal debug information. This is the default for all platforms, except for the OSF/1 reference platform, using the OSF/rose object format. If either the -gstabs or the -gstabs+ option is specified, the `mips-tfile` program will encapsulate the STABS within MIPS ECOFF.

Also see -mgas.

-mmips-tfile

The object file output by the MIPS assembler is postprocessed with the `mips-tfile` program to add debug support. This action can be suppressed by specifying -mno-mips-tfile. The -mno-mips-tfile option should only be specified when there are bugs in the `mips-tfile` program that prevent compilation.

If `mips-tfile` is not run, no local variables will be available to the debugger. Also, `stage2` and `stage3` objects will have the temporary file names passed to the assembler embedded in the object file, which means the objects will not compare the same.

-mrnames

Instructs the compiler to output code using the MIPS software names for the registers instead of the hardware names (that is, `a0` instead of `$4`). The only known assembler that supports this option is the Algorithmics assembler. This option can be suppressed by -mno-rnames.

-msingle-float

Assumes that the floating-point coprocessor only supports single precision operations, as on the `r4650` chip. Also see -mdouble-float.

-msoft-float

Generates output containing library calls for floating-point operations.

The required libraries are not part of GCC. Normally the facilities of the target machine's usual C compiler are used, but this can't be done directly in cross-compilation. You must provide your own suitable library functions for cross-compilation.

Also see -mhard-float.

-msplit-addresses

Generates code to load the high and low parts of address constants separately. This allows the compiler to optimize away redundant loads of the high order bits of addresses. This optimization requires GNU as and GNU ld. This optimization is enabled by default for some embedded targets where GNU as and GNU ld are standard. This option can be disabled by specifying -mno-split-addresses.

-mstats
For each noninline function processed, this option causes the compiler to output one line to the standard error file containing statistics about the program (the number of registers saved, stack size, and so on). This action can be suppressed by `-mno-stats`.

-mtune=*architecture*
Optimizes for the specified architecture. Among other things, this option controls the way instructions are scheduled as well as the perceived cost of arithmetic operations. The list of `architecture` names is the same as for `-march`.

When this option is not specified, the compiler optimizes for the processor specified by `-march`. By using both `-march` and `-mtune`, it is possible to generate code that will run on a family of processors but optimize the code for one particular member of that family.

This option causes the definition of the macros `_MIPS_TUNE` and `_MIPS_TUNE_` *architecture*, which are created using the same rules as the two macros defined by `-march`.

-muninit-const-in-rodata
When used together with `-membedded-data`, this option will always store uninitialized const variables in the read-only data section.

-EL
Compiles code for the processor in little endian mode. Also see `-EB`.

-EB
Compiles code for the processor in big endian mode. Also see `-EL`.

-G *number*
Puts global and static items less than or equal to `number` bytes in size into the small data or bss section instead of the normal data or bss section. This allows the assembler to emit one-word memory reference instructions based on the global pointer (`gp` or `$28`), instead of the normal two words used. By default, `number` is 8 when the MIPS assembler is used and 0 when the GNU assembler is used.

This option setting is also passed to the assembler and linker, so all modules should be compiled with the same `number` value.

-nocpp
Tells the MIPS assembler to not run its preprocessor over user assembler files (files with a .s suffix) when assembling them.

-no-crt0
Does not include the default `crt0`.

MMIX Options
The following options are defined for the MMIX.

-mabi=*setting*

Specifying *setting* as mmisware generates code that passes function parameters and return values that, inside the called function, are seen as registers $0 and up.

Specifying *settings* as gnu generates the GNU ABI, which uses global registers $231 and up.

-mbase-addresses

Generates code that uses base addresses.

Using a base address automatically generates a request (handled by the assembler and the linker) for a constant to be set up in a global register. The register is used for one or more base address requests, within the range 0 to 255, from the value held in the register. This generally leads to short and fast code, but the number of data items that can be addressed is limited, which means that a program that uses lots of static data may require -mno-base-addresses to suppress this option.

-mbranch-predict

Uses the probable-branch instructions when static branch prediction indicates a probable branch. This action can be suppressed by -mno-branch-predict.

-melf

Generates an executable in the ELF format, rather than the default mmo format used by the MMIX simulator.

-mepsilon

Generates floating-point comparison instructions that compare with respect to the rE epsilon register. This option can be reversed by -mno-epsilon.

-mknuthdiv

Makes the result of a division yielding a remainder have the same sign as the divisor. The default is -mno-knuthdiv, in which the sign of the remainder follows the sign of the dividend. Both methods are considered arithmetically valid, the latter being almost exclusively used.

-mlibfuncs

Specifies that intrinsic library functions are being compiled, passing all values in registers, no matter the size. This option can be reversed by -mno-libfuncs.

-msingle-exit

Forces generated code to have a single exit point in each function. This option can be suppressed by -mno-single-exit.

-mtoplevel-symbols

Prepends a colon onto the front of all global symbols so that the assembly code can be used with the PREFIX assembly directive. This action can be suppressed by specifying -mno-toplevel-symbols.

-mzero-extend
When reading data from memory in sizes shorter than 64 bits, zero-extending load instructions are used by default, rather than sign-extending ones. This option can be reversed by -mno-zero-extend.

MN10200 Options

The following option is defined for Matsushita MN10200 architecture.

-mrelax
Specifies that the linker should perform a relaxation optimization pass to shorten branches, calls, and absolute memory addresses. This option only has an effect when used on the command line for the final link step. Also, this option makes symbolic debugging impossible.

MN10300 Options

The following options are defined for the Matsushita MN10300 architecture.

-mam33
Generates code that uses features specific to the AM33 processor. The default is -mno-am33, which does not generate code for the special features.

-mmult-bug
Generates code to avoid bugs in the multiply instructions for the MN10300 processors. This is the default. This option can be turned off with -mno-mult-bug.

-mno-crt0
The default is to link the C runtime initialization routines, but this option causes them not to be linked to the program.

-mrelax
Specifies that the linker should perform a relaxation optimization pass to shorten branches, calls, and absolute memory addresses. This option only has an effect when used on the command line for the final link step. This option makes symbolic debugging impossible.

NS32K Options

The following options are defined for the 32000 series. The default values for these options depend on which style of 32000 was selected when the compiler was configured.

-m32032
Generates code for a 32032. This is the default when the compiler is configured for 32032. and 32016 based systems.

-m32081

Generates code containing 32081 instructions for floating point. This is the default for all systems.

Also see -m32381.

-m32332

Generates code for a 32332. This is the default when the compiler is configured for 32332-based systems.

-m32381

Generates code containing 32381 instructions for floating point. This also sets -m32081. The 32381 is compatible only with the 32332 and 32532 CPUs. This is the default for the pc532-netbsd configuration.

-m32532

Generates code for a 32532. This is the default when the compiler is configured for 32532-based systems.

-mbitfield

Generates code to use the bit-field instructions. This is the default for all platforms except the PC532.

Also see -mnobitfield.

-mhimem

Causes code to be generated that can be loaded above 512MB.

Many NS32000 series addressing modes use displacements of up to 512MB. If an address is above 512MB, displacements from zero cannot be used. This option may be useful for operating systems or ROM code.

Also see -mnosb.

-mieee-compare

Specifies that the compiler uses IEEE floating-point comparisons. These comparisons handle correctly the case where the result of a comparison is unordered. However, the required kernel support may not be available. This can be disabled with -mno-ieee-compare.

-mmulti-add

Tries to generate the multiply-add floating-point instructions polyF and dotF. This option is only available if the -m32381 option is in effect.

Using these instructions requires changes to the register allocation, which generally has a negative impact on performance. This option should only be used when compiling code that is likely to make heavy use of multiply-add instructions.

Also see -mnomulti-add.

-mnobitfield

Specifies to not use the bit-field instructions. On some machines it is faster to use shifting and masking operations. This is the default for the PC532.

Also see -mbitfield.

-mnohimem

Assumes code will be loaded in the first 512MB of virtual address space. This is the default for all platforms.

-mnomulti-add

Specifies to not try and generate the multiply-add floating-point instructions polyF and dotF. This is the default.

Also see -mmulti-add.

-mnoregparam

Specifies to not pass any arguments in registers. This is the default for all targets.

Also see -mrtd and -mregparam.

-mnosb

The sb register is not available for use or has not been initialized to zero by the runtime system. This is the default for all targets except pc532-netbsd. This option is set whenever -mhimem or -fpic is specified.

-mregparam

Uses a different function-calling convention, where the first two arguments are passed in registers. This calling convention is incompatible with the one normally used on UNIX, so you cannot use it if you need to call libraries compiled with the UNIX compiler.

Also see -mrtd and -mnoregparam.

-mrtd

Uses a different function-calling convention, in which functions taking a fixed number of arguments pop their arguments on return by using the ret instruction.

This calling convention is incompatible with the one normally used on UNIX, so you cannot use it if you need to call libraries compiled with the UNIX compiler. Also, you must provide function prototypes for all functions that take variable numbers of arguments; otherwise, incorrect code will be generated for calls to those functions.

Incorrect code will result if you call a function with too many arguments. Normally, extra arguments are harmlessly ignored.

This option takes its name from the 680x0 rtd instruction.

Also see -mregparam and -mnoregparam..

-msb

Allows the compiler to use the sb register as an index register, which is always loaded with zero. This is the default for the pc532-netbsd target.

Also see -mnosb.

-msoft-float

Generates output containing library calls for floating point. However, the libraries containing the called functions may not be available.

PDP-11 Options

The following options are defined for the PDP-11.

-mabshi

Uses the abshi2 pattern. This is the default, which can be reversed with -mno-abshi.

-mbranch-cheap

Specifies to not pretend that branches are expensive. This is the default.

Also see -mbranch-expensive.

-mbranch-expensive

Pretends that branches are expensive. This is for experimenting with code generation only.

Also see -mbranch-cheap.

-m10

Generates code for a PDP-11/10.

-m40

Generates code for a PDP-11/40.

-m45

Generates code for a PDP-11/45. This is the default.

-mac0

Returns floating-point results in ac0 (fr0 in UNIX assembler syntax). The default is -mno-ac0, which returns floating-point results in memory.

-mbcopy

Specifies to not use inline movstrhi patterns for copying memory.

Also see -mbcopy-builtin.

-mbcopy-builtin

Uses inline movstrhi patterns for copying memory. This is the default.

Also see -mbcopy.

-mdec-asm

Uses DEC assembler syntax. This is the default when configured for any PDP-11 target other than pdp11-*-bsd.

-mfloat32
Defines float data as 32 bits. This option can also be specified as `-mno-float64`.

-mfloat64
Defines float data as 64 bits. This is the default. This option can also be specified as `-mno-float32`.

-mfpu
Uses hardware FPP floating point. This is the default. (FIS floating point on the PDP-11/40 is not supported.)

-mint16
Defines int data as 16 bits. This is the default. This option can also be specified as `-mno-int32`.

-mint32
Defines int data as 32 bits. This option can also be specified as `-mno-int16`.

-msoft-float
Suppress the use of hardware floating point.

-msplit
Generates code for a system with split I&D. The default is `-mno-split`, which generates code for a system without a split I&D.

-munix-asm
Uses UNIX assembler syntax. This is the default when the compiler is configured for `pdp11-*-bsd`.

RS/6000 and PowerPC Options

The following options are defined for the IBM RS/6000 and PowerPC.

GCC supports two related instruction set architectures for the RS/6000 and PowerPC. The *Power* instruction set is those instructions supported by the RIOS chipset used in the original RS/6000 systems. The *PowerPC* instruction set is the architecture of the Motorola MPC5xx, MPC6xx, MPC8xx microprocessors, and the IBM 4xx microprocessors.

Neither architecture is a subset of the other. However, there is a large common subset of instructions supported by both. An MQ register is included in processors supporting the power architecture.

-mabi=altivec
Extends the current ABI to include the AltiVec ABI extensions. This does not change the default ABI; instead, it adds the AltiVec ABI extensions to the current ABI. To suppress this extension, specify `-mabi=no-altivec`.

-mabi=spe

Extends the current ABI to include the SPE ABI extensions. This does not change the default ABI but rather only adds the SPE ABI extensions. To disable the inclusion of these extensions, specify `-mabi=no-spe`.

-misel

Enables the generation of ISEL instructions. This option can also be written as `-misel=yes`. To disable the generation of ISEL instructions, use `-misel=no`.

-mads

On embedded PowerPC systems, this option assumes that the startup module is called crt0.o and the standard C libraries are libads.a and libc.a.

-maix-struct-return

Returns all structures in memory (as specified by the AIX ABI).

-maix32

This is the default. This option disables the 64-bit ABI and implies `-mno-powerpc64`.
   Also see `-maix64`.

-maix64

Enables the 64-bit AIX ABI and calling convention, which includes 64-bit pointers, 64-bit long types, and the infrastructure needed to support them. This option also implies `-mpowerpc64` and `-mpowerpc`.
   Also see `-maix32`.

-maltivec

This option enables the use of built-in functions that allow access to the AltiVec instruction set. You may also need to set `-mabi=altivec` to adjust the current ABI with AltiVec ABI enhancements. To disable the use of the built-in functions, specify `-mno-altivec`.

-mbig

On System V.4 and embedded PowerPC systems, this option compiles code for the processor in big endian mode.
   Also see `-mlittle`.

-mbig-endian

Same as `-mbig`.

-mbit-align

On System V.4 and embedded PowerPC systems, this option forces structures and unions that contain bit-fields to be aligned to the base type of the bit-field. This is the default. To not force this alignment, specify `-mno-bit-align`.
   For example, by default a structure containing nothing but eight unsigned bit-fields of length 1 would be aligned to a 4-byte boundary and have a size of four bytes. By

specifying -mno-bit-align, the structure would be aligned to a 1-byte boundary and be one byte in size.

-mcall-aix
On System V.4 and embedded PowerPC systems, this option compiles code using calling conventions that are similar to those used on AIX. This is the default if you configured GCC using powerpc-*-eabiaix.

-mcall-gnu
On System V.4 and embedded PowerPC systems, this option compiles code for the Hurd-based GNU system.

-mcall-linux
On System V.4 and embedded PowerPC systems, this option compiles code for the Linux operating system.

-mcall-netbsd
On System V.4 and embedded PowerPC systems, this option compiles code for the NetBSD operating system.

-mcall-solaris
On System V.4 and embedded PowerPC systems, this option compiles code for the Solaris operating system.

-mcall-sysv
On System V.4 and embedded PowerPC systems, this option compiles code using calling conventions that adhere to the March 1995 draft of the System V Application Binary Interface, PowerPC processor supplement. This is the default unless you configured GCC using powerpc-*-eabiaix.

-mcall-sysv-eabi
Specifies both -mcall-sysv and -meabi.

-mcall-sysv-noeabi
Specifies both the -mcall-sysv and -mno-eabi options.

-mcpu=*type*
Specifies the architecture type, register usage, choice of mnemonics, and instruction-scheduling parameters to those of the specified *type* of machine. The recognized machine type names are rios, rios1, rsc, rios2, rs64a, 601, 602, 603, 603e, 604, 604e, 620, 630, 740, 7400, 7450, 750, power, power2, powerpc, 403, 505, 801, 821, 823, 860, and common.

The option -mcpu=common generates code for a generic processor that will run on any Power or PowerPC processor. GCC will use only the instructions in the common subset of both architectures and will not use the MQ register. GCC assumes a generic processor model for scheduling purposes.

The options –mcpu=power, –mcpu=power2, –mcpu=powerpc, and –mcpu= powerpc64 specify generic Power, Power2, pure 32-bit PowerPC (that is, not MPC601), and 64-bit PowerPC machine types, with a generic processor model assumed for scheduling purposes.

The remainder of the options produce code for a specific processor. Code generated under one of those options will run best on that processor, and it may not run at all on another.

Table 21-6 lists other options that are set by the –mcpu option. Selecting the value in the first column of the table implies the options named in the second column.

-meabi

On System V.4 and embedded PowerPC systems, this option adheres to the Embedded Applications Binary Interface (eabi), which is a set of modifications to the System V.4 specifications. The stack is aligned to an 8-byte boundary, the function __eabi() is called from main() to set up the eabi environment, and the –msdata option can use both r2 and r13 to point to two separate small data areas.

Specifying –mno-eabi aligns the stack to a 16-byte boundary, does not call an initialization function from main(), and causes the –msdata option to only use r13 to point to a single small data area.

The –meabi option is on by default if you configured GCC using one of the powerpc*-*-eabi* options.

-memb

On embedded PowerPC systems, this option sets the PPC_EMB bit in the ELF flags header to indicate that eabi extended relocations are used.

-mcpu Options	Implied Options
common	-mno-power, -mno-powerc
power, power2, rios1, rios2, rsc	-mpower, -mno-powerpc, -mno-new-mnemonics
powerpc, rs64a, 602, 603, 603e, 604, 620, 630, 740, 7400, 7450, 750, 505	-mno-power, -mpowerpc, -mnew-mnemonics
601	-mpower, -mpowerpc, -mnew-mnemonics

Table 21-6. *Setting an -mcpu Option Implies the Setting of Other Options*

-mfull-toc
This is the default. The compiler will allocate at least one TOC (table of contents) entry for each unique, nonautomatic variable reference in your program. Also, floating-point constants will be included in the TOC. The TOC is limited to a maximum of 16,384 entries.

To reduce the amount of information stored in the TOC, see `-mno-fp-in-toc`, `-mno-sum-in-toc`, and `-mminimal-toc`.

-mfused-madd
Generates code that uses the floating-point multiply and accumulate instructions. This option is selected by default if hardware floating is used. To suppress this option, specify `-mno-fused-madd`.

-mhard-float
Generates code that does not use the floating-point register set.

Also see `-msoft-float`.

-minimal-toc
This option can be used in the case of a linker error message stating that the available TOC (table of contents) space has been exceeded. This option reduces the amount of TOC space used, making only one TOC entry for each file. The code produced is slightly larger and slower, but it makes an extreme reduction in the size of the TOC.

Also see `-mfull-toc`.

-mlittle
On System V.4 and embedded PowerPC systems, this option compiles code for the processor in little endian mode.

Also see `-mbig`.

-mlittle-endian
Same as `-mlittle`.

-mlongcall
Specifies that all function calls be made via pointers so that functions that reside further than 64MB (67,108,864 bytes) from the current location can be called. This setting can be overridden by specifying the `shortcall` function attribute or `#pragma longcall(0)`. The long calls can be disabled by specifying `-mno-longcall`.

Some linkers are capable of detecting out-of-range calls and generating glue code on the fly. On these systems, long calls are unnecessary and the code is slower than necessary. As of this writing, the AIX linker can do this, as can the GNU linker for the PowerPC/64. This feature is planned to be added to the GNU linker for 32-bit PowerPC systems as well.

-mmultiple
Generates code that uses the "load multiple word" instructions and the "store multiple word" instructions. These instructions are generated by default on Power systems and are not generated on PowerPC systems.

To disable the generation of these instructions, specify `-mno-multiple`.

Do not use this option on little endian PowerPC systems, because those instructions do not work when the processor is in little endian mode. The exceptions are PPC740 and PPC750, which permit the instructions usage in little endian mode.

-mmvme
On embedded PowerPC systems, this option assumes that the startup module is called crt0.o and the standard C libraries are libmvme.a and libc.a.

-mnew-mnemonics
Selects the assembly language mnemonics defined for the PowerPC architecture. This option will be ignored if the mnemonics are not defined for the selected architecture.

Also see `-mold-mnemonics`.

-mno-fp-in-toc
This option can be used in the case of a linker error message stating that the available TOC (table of contents) space has been exceeded. This option reduces the amount of TOC space used by preventing the inclusion of floating-point constants.

Also see `-mfull-toc`.

-mno-sum-in-toc
This option can be used in the case of a linker error message stating that the available TOC (table of contents) space has been exceeded. This option reduces the amount of TOC space used by generating code to calculate the sum of an address and a constant at runtime instead of putting that sum into the TOC.

Also see `-mfull-toc`.

-mold-mnemonics
Selects the assembly language mnemonics defined for the Power architecture. This option will be ignored if the mnemonics are not defined for the selected architecture.

Also see `-mnew-menonics`.

-mpe
Generates code that supports the IBM RS/6000 SP Parallel Environment (PE) by linking special startup code with an application that has been written to use message passing.

The system must either have PE installed in the standard location (/usr/lpp/ppe.poe/) or the specs file must be overridden by using the `-specs` option to specify the directory location. The Parallel Environment does not support threads, so the -mpe option and the -pthread option are incompatible.

-mpower

Generates instructions that are found only in the Power architecture to use the MQ register. If the GCC installation specified this configuration, it can be suppressed by -mno-power.

By specifying both -mno-power and -mno-powerpc, GCC will use only the instructions in the common subset of both architectures, plus some special AIX common-mode calls, and will not use the MQ register. Specifying both -mpower and -mpowerpc permits GCC to use any instruction from either architecture and to allow the use of the MQ register. Specify this for the Motorola MPC601.

-mpower2

Generates instructions that are present in the Power2 architecture but are not present in the original Power architecture. Setting this option also sets the -mpower option. If the GCC installation specified this configuration, it can be suppressed by -mno-power2.

-mpowerpc

Generates instructions that are found only in the 32-bit subset of the PowerPC architecture. If the GCC installation specified this configuration, it can be suppressed by -mno-powerpc.

Also see -mpower.

-mpowerpc-gpopt

Generates code to use the optional PowerPC architecture instructions in the General Purpose group, including floating-point square root. Setting this option also sets -mpowerpc. If the GCC installation specified this configuration, it can be suppressed by -mno-powerpc-gopt.

-mpowerpc-gfxopt

Generates code to use the optional PowerPC architecture instructions in the Graphics group, including floating-point select. Setting this option also sets -mpowerpc. If the GCC installation specified this configuration, it can be suppressed by -mno-powerpc-gfxopt.

-mpowerpc64

Generates the additional 64-bit instructions that are found in the full PowerPC64 architecture and to treat GPRs as 64-bit double-word quantities. The default is -mno-powerpc64.

-mprototype

On System V.4 and embedded PowerPC systems, this option assumes that all calls to variable argument functions are properly prototyped.

Without this option, or by specifying -mno-prototype, the compiler must insert an instruction before every nonprototyped call to set or clear bit 6 of the condition code register (CR) to indicate whether floating-point values were passed in the floating-point registers. With -mprototype, only calls to prototyped variable argument functions will set or clear the bit.

-mregnames
On System V.4 and embedded PowerPC systems, this option emits register names into the assembly language using symbolic forms. This option can be suppressed by -mno-regnames.

-mrelocatable
On embedded PowerPC systems, this option generates code that allows the program to be relocated to a different address at runtime. If you specify this option for any module, all objects linked together must be compiled with -mrelocatable or -mrelocatable-lib. The default is -mno-relocatable.

-mrelocatable-lib
On embedded PowerPC systems, this option generates code that allows the program to be relocated to a different address at runtime. Modules compiled with this option can be linked with modules compiled without the -mrelocatable and -mrelocatable-lib options, and they can be linked with modules compiled with the -mrelocatable option.

-msdata=*setting*
Specifying -msdata=eabi on System V.4 and embedded PowerPC systems puts small initialized const global and static data in the .sdata2 section, which is pointed to by register r2. Also, small initialized non-const global and static data is put in the .sdata section, which is pointed to by register r13. Also, small uninitialized global and static data is put in the .sbss section, which is adjacent to the .sdata section. The -msdata=eabi option sets the -memb option but is incompatible with the -mrelocatable option.

Specifying -msdata=sysv on System V.4 and embedded PowerPC systems puts small global and static data in the .sdata section, which is pointed to by register r13. It also puts small uninitialized global and static data in the .sbss section, which is adjacent to the .sdata section. The -msdata=sysv option is incompatible with the -mrelocatable option.

Specifying -msdata=none (which can also be written as -mno-sdata) on embedded PowerPC systems puts all initialized global and static data in the .data section and all uninitialized data in the .bss section.

Specifying -msdata=default (which can be written simply as -msdata) on System V.4 and embedded PowerPC systems, in combination with -meabi, will compile code the same as -msdata=eabi. If -meabi is not specified, the code is compiled the same as -msdata=sysv.

-msdata-data
On System V.4 and embedded PowerPC systems, this option puts small global and static data in the `.sdata` section. It also puts small uninitialized global and static data in the `.sbss` section. It does not use register `r13` to address small data, however.

This is the default behavior unless other -msdata options are used.

-msim
On embedded PowerPC systems, this option assumes that the startup module is called sim-crt0.o and that the standard C libraries are libsim.a and libc.a. This is the default for `powerpc-*-eabisim` configurations.

-msoft-float
Generates code that uses software floating-point emulation.

Also see `-mhard-float`.

-mstrict-align
On System V.4 and embedded PowerPC systems, this option generates code that assumes unaligned memory references will be handled by the system. This is the default. To not make this assumption, specify `-mno-strict-align`.

-mstring
Generates code that uses the "load string" instructions and the "store string word" instructions to save multiple registers and perform small block moves. These instructions are generated by default on Power systems and are not generated on PowerPC systems.

To disable the generation of these instructions, specify `-mno-string`.

Do not use this option on little endian PowerPC systems, because those instructions do not work when the processor is in little endian mode. The exceptions are PPC740 and PPC750, which permit the instructions usage in little endian mode.

-msvr4-struct-return
Returns structures smaller than 8 bytes in registers (as specified by the SVR4 ABI).

-mtoc
On System V.4 and embedded PowerPC systems, this option assumes that register 2 contains a pointer to a global area pointing to the addresses used in the program. Specifying `-mno-mtoc` will suppress the assumption.

-mtune=*type*
Specifies the instruction scheduling parameters for specified machine *type* but does not set the architecture type, register usage, or choice of mnemonics, as is done by -mcpu. The same set of values recognized by -mcpu is recognized by -mtune. If both options are specified, the code generated will use the architecture, registers, and mnemonics set by -mcpu but the scheduling parameters set by -mtune.

-mupdate
Generates code that uses the load or store instructions that update the base register to the address of the calculated memory location. This is the default.

To suppress the generation of this code, specify `-mno-update`, which opens a small window of time between updating the stack pointer and updating the address of the previous frame in which code that walks the stack frame across interrupts or signals may get corrupted data.

-mvxworks
On System V.4 and embedded PowerPC systems, this option specifies that you are compiling for a VxWorks system.

-mwindiss
Specifies that the compilation is for the WindISS simulation environment.

-mxl-call
Uses the convention of certain AIX compilers of passing floating-point arguments on the stack. To disable this option, specify `-mno-xl-call`.

On AIX, floating-point arguments are passed to prototyped functions beyond the register save area (RSA) on the stack in addition to argument FPRs. The AIX calling convention was extended but not initially documented to handle an obscure K&R C case of calling a function that takes the address of its arguments with fewer arguments than declared. AIX XL compiler floating-point arguments that do not fit in the RSA are accessed from the stack when a subroutine is compiled without optimization. Because always storing floating-point arguments on the stack is inefficient and rarely needed, this option is not enabled by default and is only necessary when calling subroutines compiled by AIX XL compilers without optimization.

-myellowknife
On embedded PowerPC systems, this option assumes that the startup module is called crt0.o and the standard C libraries are libyk.a and libc.a.

-G *number*
On embedded PowerPC systems, this option puts global and static items less than or equal to *number* bytes into the small data or bss section instead of the normal data or bss section. The default value of *number* is 8.

This option is also passed to the linker, so all modules should be compiled with the same value for *number*.

-pthread
Adds support for multithreading with the pthreads library. This option sets flags for both the preprocessor and the linker.

RT Options

The following options are defined for the IBM RT PC.

-mcall-lib-mul

Generates a call to `lmul$$` for integer multiples.
> Also see `-min-line-mul`.

-mfp-arg-in-fpregs

Uses a calling sequence incompatible with the IBM calling convention in which floating-point arguments are passed in floating-point registers. The stdarg.h header will not work with floating-point operands if this option is specified.
> Also see `-mfp-arg-in-gregs`.

-mfp-arg-in-gregs

Uses the normal calling convention for floating-point arguments. This is the default.
> Also see `-mfp-arg-in-fpregs`.

-mfull-fp-blocks

Generates full-size floating-point data blocks, including the minimum amount of scratch space recommended by IBM. This is the default.
> Also see `-mminimum-fp-blocks`.

-mhc-struct-return

Structures of more than one word are returned in memory rather than in a register. This provides compatibility with the MetaWare HighC (`hc`) compiler. Use the option `-fpcc-struct-return` for compatibility with the Portable C Compiler (`pcc`).

-min-line-mul

Uses an inline code sequence for integer multiplies. This is the default.
> Also see `-mcall-lib-mul`.

-mminimum-fp-blocks

Specifies not to include extra scratch space in floating-point data blocks. This results in smaller code but slower execution, because scratch space must be allocated dynamically.
> Also see `-mfull-fp-blocks`.

-mnohc-struct-return

Returns some structures that are larger than one word in registers, as convenient. This is the default. For compatibility with the IBM-supplied compilers, use the option `-fpcc-struct-return` or the option `-mhc-struct-return`.

S/390 and zSeries Options

The following options are defined for the S/390 and zSeries architecture.

-m31

Generates code compliant with the Linux for S/390 ABI. For the s390 targets, the default is –m31, while the s390x targets default to –m64.

-m64

Generates code compliant with the Linux for zSeries ABI. This allows GCC, in particular, to generate 64-bit instructions. For the s390 targets, the default is –m31, whereas the s390x targets default to –m64.

-mbackchain

Generates code that maintains an explicit backchain within the stack frame that points to the caller's frame, which is needed to allow debugging. This is the default, which can be reversed by –mbackchain.

-mhard-float

Uses the hardware floating-point instructions and registers for floating-point operations. The compiler generates IEEE floating-point instructions. This is the default.

Also see –msoft-float.

-mdebug

Prints additional debug information when compiling. The default is –mno-debug, which indicates to not print debug information.

-mmvcle

Generates code using the mvcle instruction to perform block moves. The default is –mno-mvcle, which uses an mvc loop.

-msmall-exec

Generates code using the bras instruction to do subroutine calls. This only works reliably if the total executable size does not exceed 64KB. The default is –mno-small-exec, which uses the basr instruction instead. It does not have the size limitation.

-msoft-float

Specifies to not use the hardware floating-point instructions and registers for floating-point operations. Functions in libgcc.a are to be used to perform floating-point operations.

Also see –mhard-float.

SH Options

The following options are defined for the SH implementations.

-m1

Generates code for the SH1.

-m2
Generates code for the SH2.

-m3
Generates code for the SH3.

-m3e
Generates code for the SH3e.

-m4-nofpu
Generates code for the SH4 without a floating-point unit.

-m4-single-only
Generates code for the SH4 with a floating-point unit that only supports single-precision arithmetic.

-m4-single
Generates code for the SH4, assuming the floating-point unit is in single-precision mode by default.

-m4
Generates code for the SH4.

-mb
Generates code for the processor in big endian mode.
    Also see -ml.

-mbigtable
Generates 32-bit offsets in switch tables. The default is to use 16-bit offsets.

-mdalign
Aligns doubles at 64-bit boundaries. This changes the calling conventions, and therefore some functions from the standard C library will not work unless you recompile it first with the -mdalign option set.

-mfmovd
Enables the use of the instruction fmovd.

-mhitachi
Complies with the calling conventions defined by Hitachi.
    Also see -mnomacsave.

-mieee
Increases IEEE compliance for floating-point code.

-misize
Dumps the instruction size and location in the assembly code.

-ml
Generates code for the processor in little endian mode.
    Also see –mb.

-mnomacsave
Marks the MAC register as clobbered by a call, even if –mhitachi is specified.

-mpadstruct
This option is deprecated. It pads structures to multiples of four bytes, which is incompatible with the SH ABI.

-mprefergot
Generates function calls using the Global Offset Table instead of the Procedure Linkage Table when generating position-independent code.

-mrelax
Shortens some address references at link time. This option sets the linker –relax option.

-mspace
Optimizes for size instead of speed. This option is set by –Os.

-musermode
Generates a library function call to invalidate instruction cache entries, after fixing up a trampoline. This is the default when the target is sh–*–linux*.
    This library function call doesn't assume it can write to the entire memory address space.

SPARC Options

The following are the options defined for the Sun Microsystems SPARC processor.

-m32
On the SPARC V9 processor in a 64-bit environment, this option sets int, long, and pointer values to 32 bits.

-m64
On the SPARC V9 processor in a 64-bit environment, this option sets int to 32 bits while setting long and pointer values to 64 bits.

-mapp-regs>
Generates code using the global registers 2 through 4, which the SPARC SVR4 ABI reserves for applications. This is the default.
    To be fully SVR4 ABI compliant (at the cost of some performance loss), specify –mno-app-regs. Libraries and system software should be compiled with –mno-app-regs.

-mcmodel=*setting*
On the SPARC V9 processor in a 64-bit environment, this option generates code for the specified code model. The settings for the code models are listed in Table 21-7.

-mbroken-saverestore
On the SPARCLET processor, this option will generate code that does not use nontrivial forms of the `save` and `restore` instructions.

The reason for this option is that early versions of the SPARCLET processor do not correctly handle `save` and `restore` instructions when used with arguments, but they are correctly handled when used without arguments. A `save` instruction used without arguments increments the current window pointer but does not allocate a new stack frame because it is assumed that the window overflow trap handler will properly handle this case, as do interrupt handlers.

-mcpu=*type*
The instruction set, register set, and instruction scheduling parameters are set for the specific machine named as the *type*. Supported values for *type* are v7, cypress, v8, supersparc, sparclite, hypersparc, sparclite86x, f930, f934, sparclet, tsc701, v9, and ultrasparc.

Setting	Code Model
medlow	The Medium/Low code model means the program must be linked in the low 32 bits of the address space. Pointers are 64 bits. Programs can be statically or dynamically linked.
medmid	The Medium/Middle code model means the program must be linked in the low 44 bits of the address space, the text segment must be less than 2G bytes in size, and the data segment must be within 2G of the text segment. Pointers are 64 bits.
medany	The Medium/Anywhere code model means the program may be linked anywhere in the address space, the text segment must be less than 2G bytes in size, and the data segment must be within 2G of the text segment. Pointers are 64 bits.
embmedany	The Medium/Anywhere code model for embedded systems assumes a 32-bit text and a 32-bit data segment, both starting anywhere (determined at link time). Register %g4 points to the base of the data segment. Pointers are 64 bits. Programs are statically linked. PIC is not supported.

Table 21-7. *The SPARC V9 Model Settings*

Default instruction scheduling parameters are used for values that select an architecture and not an implementation. Table 21-8 lists the architectures and the implementations that support them.

-mcypress

This is the default. The compiler optimizes code for the Cypress CY7C602 chip, as used in the SparcStation/SparcServer 3xx series. This is also appropriate for the older SparcStation 1, 2, IPX, and so on.

This option is deprecated and will be removed from a future version of the compiler. Use –mcpu=cypress instead.

-mfaster-structs

This option enforces the assumption that structures have an 8-byte alignment. This enables the use of pairs of ldd and std instructions for copies in structure assignment. This code is in place of twice as many ld and st pairs.

However, the use of this changed alignment directly violates the SPARC ABI, so it is intended only for use on targets where it is understood that the resulting code will not be in line with the ABI rules.

The default is –mno-faster-structs.

-mflat

This option specifies that the compiler should not generate save and restore instructions but instead should use a "flat" or "single register window" calling convention. The default is –mno-flat.

This model uses %i7 as the frame pointer and is compatible with the normal register window model. Code from the two models may be intermixed. The local registers and the input registers (0–5) will still be saved on the stack as necessary.

By specifying –mno-flat, the compiler emits save and restore instructions (except for leaf functions), which is the normal mode of operation.

Architecture	Implementations
v7	cypress
v8	supersparc, hypersparc
sparclite	f930, f934, sparclite86x
sparclet	tsc701
v9	ultrasparc

Table 21-8. *The Implementations That Support Various Architectures*

-mfpu
This is the default, which is to generate code containing hardware floating-point instructions.

To generate code containing library calls for floating-point operations, specify `-mno-fpu`. The libraries for this are not available for all SPARC platforms. The libraries used by the native compiler of the target machine can be used, but these cannot be used in cross-compilation. The embedded targets `sparc-*-aout` and `sparclite-*-*` do provide software floating-point support.

The option `-mfpu` can also be written `-mhard-float`.

Also see `-msoft-float`.

-mhard-float
Same as `-mfpu`.

-mhard-quad-float
The code output with this option set contains quad-word (`long double`) floating-point instructions.

-mlittle-endian
On the SPARCLET processor and on the SPARC V9 possessor in a 64-bit environment, this option will generate code for a processor running in little-endian mode.

-mlive-g0
On the SPARCLET processor, this option will treat register `%g0` as a normal register. GCC will continue to clobber it, as necessary, but will not assume it always reads as 0.

-msoft-float
Same as `-mno-fpu`, except changes are made to the calling convention in the generated code. This means this option can only be used if you compile the entire program with this option. Also, you must compile libgcc.a, the library that comes with GCC, with the `-msoft-float` option so that all the code will be consistent.

-msoft-quad-float
This is the default. The code output with this option set contains library calls for quad-word (`long double`) floating-point instructions. The functions called are those specified in the SPARC ABI.

There is no `-mhard-quad-float` option because there are no SPARC implementations that have hardware support for quad-word floating-point operations. They all invoke a trap handler for one of these instructions, and then the trap handler emulates the effect of the instruction. Because of the trap handler overhead, this is much slower than calling the ABI library routines. This is the reason for the `-msoft-quad-float` option being the default.

-msparclite

This option selects a variation in the SPARC architecture. Unless the compiler is specifically configured for the Fujitsu SPARClite, GCC generates code for the v7 variant of the SPARC architecture. The integer multiply, integer divide, and scan (ffs) instructions exist in SPARClite but not in SPARC V7.

This option is deprecated and will be removed from a future version of the compiler. Use –mcpu=sparclite instead.

-mstack-bias

On the SPARC V9 processor in a 64-bit environment, this option makes the assumption that the stack pointer (and frame pointer, if present) are offset by -2047, which must be added back when making stack frame references. The default is –no-stack-bias, which assumes no such offset is present.

-msupersparc

The compiler optimizes code for the SuperSparc CPU, as used in the SparcStation 10, 1000, and 2000 series. This option also enables use of the full SPARC V8 instruction set.

This option is deprecated and will be removed from a future version of the compiler. Use –mcpu=supersparc instead.

-mtune=*type*

Sets the instruction scheduling parameters for the specified machine *type* but does not specify the instruction set or register set, which would be specified if the –mcpu option were used.

The same values that can be used for –mcpu can also be used for –mtune. The only useful values are the ones that specify a particular CPU implementation (that is, the names listed in the second column of Table 21-8).

-munaligned-doubles

This option imposes the assumption that doubles have 8-byte alignment only if they are contained in another type, or if they have an absolute address. All other doubles are assumed to have 4-byte alignment. Specifying this option avoids some rare compatibility problems with code generated by other compilers. This is not the default because it results in a performance loss, especially for floating-point code.

The default is –mno-unaligned-doubles, which assumes all doubles have 8-byte alignment.

-mv8

This option selects a variation on the SPARC architecture. This option produces SPARC V8 code. The only difference from V7 code is that the compiler emits the integer multiply and integer divide instructions that exist in SPARC V8 but not in SPARC V7.

This option is deprecated and will be removed from a future version of the compiler. Use –mcpu=v8 instead.

System V Options

The following are some additional options available on System V Release 4.

-G
Creates a shared object. It is recommended that `-symbolic` or `-shared` be used instead of this option.

-Qn
Refrains from adding any `.ident` directives to the output file. This is the default.

-Qy
Identifies the versions of each tool used by the compiler by using an `.ident` assembler directive in the output.

-Ym,*directory*
Looks in the *directory* to find the M4 preprocessor. The assembler uses this option.

-YP,*directories*
Searches the specified *directories*, and no others, for libraries specified by the `-lname` option.

TMS320C3x/C4x Options

The following options are defined for TMS320C3x/C4x implementations.

-mbig
Generates code for the big memory model. The big memory model is the default and requires reloading of the DP register for every direct memory access.
    Also see `-msmall`.

-mbig-memory
Same as `-mbig`.

-mbk
Allows allocation of general integer operands into the block count register BK. To disallow the allocation, specify `-mno-bk`.

-mcpu=type
Sets the instruction set, register set, and instruction scheduling parameters for the specified machine type. The valid choices for *type* are `c30`, `c31`, `c32`, `c40`, and `c44`. The default is `c40`, which generates code for the TMS320C40.

-mdb
Enables generation of code using decrement and branch DBcond(D) instructions. This is enabled by default for the C4x. It can be disabled by specifying `-mno-db`.

This is disabled for the C3x for safety because the maximum iteration count on the C3x is 2^23 + 1. Note that GCC will try to reverse a loop so that it can utilize the decrement and branch instructions, but it will give up if there is more than one memory reference in the loop. Therefore, a loop where the loop counter is decremented can generate slightly more efficient code, in cases where the RPTB instruction cannot be utilized.

-mdp-isr-reload

Forces the DP register to be saved on entry to an interrupt service routine (ISR), reloaded to point to the data section, and restored on exit from the ISR. This should not be required unless the small memory model has been violated by a modification being made to the DP register.

-mfast-fix

Disables the generation of the additional code required to correct the results of the FIX instruction. The default is -mno-fast-fix.

The C3x/C4x FIX instruction to convert a floating-point value to an integer value chooses the nearest integer less than or equal to the floating-point value rather than to the nearest integer. Therefore, if the floating-point number is negative, the result will be incorrectly truncated and additional code is necessary to detect and correct this case.

-mloop-unsigned

Allows an unsigned iteration count. The default is -mno-loop-unsigned.

The maximum iteration count when using RPTS and RPTB (and DB on the C40) is 2^31 + 1, because these instructions test whether the iteration count is negative to terminate the loop. If the iteration count is unsigned, there is a possibility that the 2^31 + 1 maximum iteration count may be exceeded.

Also see -mrptb and -mrpts.

-mmemparm

Generates code that uses registers for passing arguments to functions. By default, arguments are passed in registers where possible, rather than by pushing arguments onto the stack.

Also see -mregparm.

-mmpyi

Uses the 24-bit MPYI instruction for integer multiplies on the C3x instead of the default of making a library call to guarantee 32-bit results. This option can be suppressed by -mno-mpyi.

If one of the operands is a constant, the multiplication will be performed using shifts and adds. If this option is not specified for the C3x, squaring operations are performed inline instead of a library call.

-mparallel-insns

Allows the generation of parallel instructions. This is enabled by default by -O2 but can be disabled by -mno-parallel-insns.

Also see -mparallel-mpy.

-mparallel-mpy
Allows the generation of MPY||ADD and MPY||SUB parallel instructions, provided
-mparallel-insns is also specified. These instructions have tight register constraints that
can "pessimize" the code generation of large functions. This option can be disabled by
-mno-parallel-mpy.

-mparanoid
Same as -mdp-isr-reload.

-mregparm
Generates code that uses the stack for passing arguments to functions. By default,
arguments are passed in registers where possible, rather than by pushing arguments
onto the stack.
    Also see -mmemparm.

-mrptb
Enables the generation of repeat block sequences using the RPTB instruction for zero
overhead looping. This is enabled by default by -O2 but can be disabled with -mno-rptb.
    The RPTB construct is only used for innermost loops that do not call functions or
jump across the loop boundaries. There is no advantage to having nested RPTB loops
due to the overhead required to save and restore the RC, RS, and RE registers.
    Also see -mrpts and -mloop-unsigned.

-mrpts=*number*
Enables the use of the single instruction repeat instruction RPTS. The default is
-mno-rpts.
    If a repeat block contains a single instruction, and the loop count can be guaranteed
to be less than the value specified by *number*, GCC will generate an RPTS instruction
instead of an RPTB. If no number is specified, an RPTS will be generated even if the
loop count cannot be determined at compile time.
    The repeated instruction following RPTS does not have to be reloaded from memory
for each iteration, thus freeing up the CPU busses for operands. However, because
interrupts are blocked by this instruction, it is disabled by default.
    Also see -mrptb and -mloop-unsigned.

-msmall
Generates code for the small memory model. The small memory model assumes that
all data fits into one 64K word page. At runtime, the content ofthe DP register must be
set to point to the 64K page containing the .bss and .data program sections.
    Also see -mbig.

-msmall-memory
Same as -msmall.

-mti

Tries to generate an assembler syntax that satisfies the TI assembler (asm30). This also enforces compatibility with the API employed by the TI C3x C compiler. For example, a long double is passed as a structure rather than in floating-point registers.

V850 Options

The following options are defined for V850 implementations.

-mbig-switch

Generates code suitable for big switch tables. This option should be used only if the assembler/linker complains about out-of-range branches within a switch table.

-mep

Optimizes basic blocks that use the same index pointer four or more times to copy a pointer into the ep register and that use the shorter sld and sst instructions. This is the default if optimization is turned on, but it can be disabled by –mno-ep.

-mlong-calls

Treats all calls as being far away. If calls are assumed to be far away, the compiler will always load the function's address up into a register and call indirectly through the pointer.

This option can be suppressed by –mno-long-calls.

-mprolog-function

Uses external functions to save and restore registers at the prolog and epilog of a function. The external functions are slower but use less code space if more than one function needs to save the same set of registers. This is the default if optimization is turned on, but it can be disabled by –mno-prolog-function.

-msda=*number*

Puts static or global variables whose size is *number* bytes or less into the small data area that register gp points to. The small data area can hold up to 64KB.

Also see –mtda and –mzda.

-mspace

Tries to make the code as small as possible by turning on the –mep and –mprolog-function options.

-mtda=*number*

Puts static or global variables whose size is *number* bytes or less into the tiny data area that registers ep addresses. The tiny data area can hold up to 256 bytes in total (128 bytes for byte references).

Also see –msda and –mzda.

-mv850
Specifies that the target processor is the V850.

-mzda=*number*
Puts static or global variables whose size is *number* bytes or less into the first 32KB of memory.
    Also see -msda and -mtda.

VAX Options

The following are the options defined for the DEC VAX processor.

-mg
Outputs code for the VAX g-format floating-point numbers instead of d-format.

-mgnu
Performs output jump instructions on the assumption that the GNU assembler is being used.

-munix
Specifies to not output certain jump instructions (such as aobleq) that the UNIX assembler for the VAX cannot handle across long ranges.

Xstormy16 Options

The following option is defined for Xstormy16.

-msim
Chooses startup files and linker scripts suitable for the simulator.

The
Complete
Reference

Part IV

Appendixes

The Complete Reference

Appendix A

GNU General Public License

493

The GCC compiler is licensed under the GNU General Public License (which is also called the GNU GPL, or just the GPL).

The type of license granted by the GPL is known as a *copyleft*. Briefly, this means that anyone has the right to copy and use the software but that if it is incorporated into a product, that product must also be licensed by the GPL. That is, you cannot take GPL software and convert it to proprietary software. However, there is no restriction whatsoever on you using GCC as a tool to create software that is licensed in any way you wish. The binary bits and pieces that become a part of the produced program do not require the program to be licensed under the GPL.

An alternative to the GPL is the Lesser General Public License (LGPL). This license was formerly called the Library GPL, but the name was changed because it was somewhat misleading—it is suitable for some, but not all, libraries. The LGPL allows library routines to be used in proprietary programs as long as the libraries are shared and not statically linked. An example of this is the GNU version of the standard C library.

The following is the text of the GPL. It describes the details of the license in very clear language. At the end of the document is a description of the process to be followed for you to place your software under the GPL.

GNU General Public License[11]

Everyone is permitted to copy and distribute verbatim copies of this license document, but changing it is not allowed.

Preamble

The licenses for most software are designed to take away your freedom to share and change it. By contrast, the GNU General Public License is intended to guarantee your freedom to share and change free software—to make sure the software is free for all its users. This General Public License applies to most of the Free Software Foundation's software and to any other program whose authors commit to using it. (Some other Free Software Foundation software is covered by the GNU Library General Public License instead.) You can apply it to your programs, too.

When we speak of free software, we are referring to freedom, not price. Our General Public Licenses are designed to make sure that you have the freedom to distribute copies of free software (and charge for this service if you wish), that you receive source code or can get it if you want it, that you can change the software or use pieces of it in new free programs; and that you know you can do these things.

---

[1] Version 2, June 1991

Copyright (C) 1989, 1991 Free Software Foundation, Inc.

59 Temple Place, Suite 330, Boston, MA 02111-1307 USA

To protect your rights, we need to make restrictions that forbid anyone to deny you these rights or to ask you to surrender the rights. These restrictions translate to certain responsibilities for you if you distribute copies of the software, or if you modify it.

For example, if you distribute copies of such a program, whether gratis or for a fee, you must give the recipients all the rights that you have. You must make sure that they, too, receive or can get the source code. And you must show them these terms so they know their rights.

We protect your rights with two steps: (1) copyright the software, and (2) offer you this license which gives you legal permission to copy, distribute and/or modify the software.

Also, for each author's protection and ours, we want to make certain that everyone understands that there is no warranty for this free software. If the software is modified by someone else and passed on, we want its recipients to know that what they have is not the original, so that any problems introduced by others will not reflect on the original authors' reputations.

Finally, any free program is threatened constantly by software patents. We wish to avoid the danger that redistributors of a free program will individually obtain patent licenses, in effect making the program proprietary. To prevent this, we have made it clear that any patent must be licensed for everyone's free use or not licensed at all.

The precise terms and conditions for copying, distribution and modification follow.

GNU GENERAL PUBLIC LICENSE

TERMS AND CONDITIONS FOR COPYING, DISTRIBUTION AND MODIFICATION

0. This License applies to any program or other work which contains a notice placed by the copyright holder saying it may be distributed under the terms of this General Public License. The "Program", below, refers to any such program or work, and a "work based on the Program" means either the Program or any derivative work under copyright law: that is to say, a work containing the Program or a portion of it, either verbatim or with modifications and/or translated into another language. (Hereinafter, translation is included without limitation in the term "modification".) Each licensee is addressed as "you".

   Activities other than copying, distribution and modification are not covered by this License; they are outside its scope. The act of running the Program is not restricted, and the output from the Program is covered only if its contents constitute a work based on the Program (independent of having been made by running the Program). Whether that is true depends on what the Program does.

1. You may copy and distribute verbatim copies of the Program's source code as you receive it, in any medium, provided that you conspicuously and appropriately publish on each copy an appropriate copyright notice and disclaimer of warranty; keep intact all the notices that refer to this License

and to the absence of any warranty; and give any other recipients of the Program a copy of this License along with the Program.

You may charge a fee for the physical act of transferring a copy, and you may at your option offer warranty protection in exchange for a fee.

2. You may modify your copy or copies of the Program or any portion of it, thus forming a work based on the Program, and copy and distribute such modifications or work under the terms of Section 1 above, provided that you also meet all of these conditions:

   a) You must cause the modified files to carry prominent notices stating that you changed the files and the date of any change.

   b) You must cause any work that you distribute or publish, that in whole or in part contains or is derived from the Program or any part thereof, to be licensed as a whole at no charge to all third parties under the terms of this License.

   c) If the modified program normally reads commands interactively when run, you must cause it, when started running for such interactive use in the most ordinary way, to print or display an announcement including an appropriate copyright notice and a notice that there is no warranty (or else, saying that you provide a warranty) and that users may redistribute the program under these conditions, and telling the user how to view a copy of this License. (Exception: if the Program itself is interactive but does not normally print such an announcement, your work based on the Program is not required to print an announcement.)

   These requirements apply to the modified work as a whole. If identifiable sections of that work are not derived from the Program, and can be reasonably considered independent and separate works in themselves, then this License, and its terms, do not apply to those sections when you distribute them as separate works. But when you distribute the same sections as part of a whole which is a work based on the Program, the distribution of the whole must be on the terms of this License, whose permissions for other licensees extend to the entire whole, and thus to each and every part regardless of who wrote it.

   Thus, it is not the intent of this section to claim rights or contest your rights to work written entirely by you; rather, the intent is to exercise the right to control the distribution of derivative or collective works based on the Program.

   In addition, mere aggregation of another work not based on the Program with the Program (or with a work based on the Program) on a volume of a storage or distribution medium does not bring the other work under the scope of this License.

3. You may copy and distribute the Program (or a work based on it, under Section 2) in object code or executable form under the terms of Sections 1 and 2 above provided that you also do one of the following:

a) Accompany it with the complete corresponding machine-readable source code, which must be distributed under the terms of Sections 1 and 2 above on a medium customarily used for software interchange; or,

b) Accompany it with a written offer, valid for at least three years, to give any third party, for a charge no more than your cost of physically performing source distribution, a complete machine-readable copy of the corresponding source code, to be distributed under the terms of Sections 1 and 2 above on a medium customarily used for software interchange; or,

c) Accompany it with the information you received as to the offer to distribute corresponding source code. (This alternative is allowed only for noncommercial distribution and only if you received the program in object code or executable form with such an offer, in accord with Subsection b above.)

The source code for a work means the preferred form of the work for making modifications to it. For an executable work, complete source code means all the source code for all modules it contains, plus any associated interface definition files, plus the scripts used to control compilation and installation of the executable. However, as a special exception, the source code distributed need not include anything that is normally distributed (in either source or binary form) with the major components (compiler, kernel, and so on) of the operating system on which the executable runs, unless that component itself accompanies the executable.

If distribution of executable or object code is made by offering access to copy from a designated place, then offering equivalent access to copy the source code from the same place counts as distribution of the source code, even though third parties are not compelled to copy the source along with the object code.

4. You may not copy, modify, sublicense, or distribute the Program except as expressly provided under this License. Any attempt otherwise to copy, modify, sublicense or distribute the Program is void, and will automatically terminate your rights under this License. However, parties who have received copies, or rights, from you under this License will not have their licenses terminated so long as such parties remain in full compliance.

5. You are not required to accept this License, since you have not signed it. However, nothing else grants you permission to modify or distribute the Program or its derivative works. These actions are prohibited by law if you do not accept this License. Therefore, by modifying or distributing the Program (or any work based on the Program), you indicate your acceptance of this License to do so, and all its terms and conditions for copying, distributing or modifying the Program or works based on it.

6. Each time you redistribute the Program (or any work based on the Program), the recipient automatically receives a license from the original licensor to copy, distribute or modify the Program subject to these terms and conditions. You may not impose any further restrictions on the recipients' exercise of the rights

granted herein. You are not responsible for enforcing compliance by third parties to this License.

7. If, as a consequence of a court judgment or allegation of patent infringement or for any other reason (not limited to patent issues), conditions are imposed on you (whether by court order, agreement or otherwise) that contradict the conditions of this License, they do not excuse you from the conditions of this License. If you cannot distribute so as to satisfy simultaneously your obligations under this License and any other pertinent obligations, then as a consequence you may not distribute the Program at all. For example, if a patent license would not permit royalty-free redistribution of the Program by all those who receive copies directly or indirectly through you, then the only way you could satisfy both it and this License would be to refrain entirely from distribution of the Program.

If any portion of this section is held invalid or unenforceable under any particular circumstance, the balance of the section is intended to apply and the section as a whole is intended to apply in other circumstances.

It is not the purpose of this section to induce you to infringe any patents or other property right claims or to contest validity of any such claims; this section has the sole purpose of protecting the integrity of the free software distribution system, which is implemented by public license practices. Many people have made generous contributions to the wide range of software distributed through that system in reliance on consistent application of that system; it is up to the author/ donor to decide if he or she is willing to distribute software through any other system and a licensee cannot impose that choice.

This section is intended to make thoroughly clear what is believed to be a consequence of the rest of this License.

8. If the distribution and/or use of the Program is restricted in certain countries either by patents or by copyrighted interfaces, the original copyright holder who places the Program under this License may add an explicit geographical distribution limitation excluding those countries, so that distribution is permitted only in or among countries not thus excluded. In such case, this License incorporates the limitation as if written in the body of this License.

9. The Free Software Foundation may publish revised and/or new versions of the General Public License from time to time. Such new versions will be similar in spirit to the present version, but may differ in detail to address new problems or concerns.

Each version is given a distinguishing version number. If the Program specifies a version number of this License which applies to it and "any later version," you have the option of following the terms and conditions either of that version or of any later version published by the Free Software Foundation. If the Program does not specify a version number of this License, you may choose any version ever published by the Free Software Foundation.

10. If you wish to incorporate parts of the Program into other free programs whose distribution conditions are different, write to the author to ask for permission. For software which is copyrighted by the Free Software Foundation, write to the Free Software Foundation; we sometimes make exceptions for this. Our decision will be guided by the two goals of preserving the free status of all derivatives of our free software and of promoting the sharing and reuse of software generally.

NO WARRANTY

11. BECAUSE THE PROGRAM IS LICENSED FREE OF CHARGE, THERE IS NO WARRANTY FOR THE PROGRAM, TO THE EXTENT PERMITTED BY APPLICABLE LAW. EXCEPT WHEN OTHERWISE STATED IN WRITING THE COPYRIGHT HOLDERS AND/OR OTHER PARTIES PROVIDE THE PROGRAM "AS IS" WITHOUT WARRANTY OF ANY KIND, EITHER EXPRESSED OR IMPLIED, INCLUDING, BUT NOT LIMITED TO, THE IMPLIED WARRANTIES OF MERCHANTABILITY AND FITNESS FOR A PARTICULAR PURPOSE. THE ENTIRE RISK AS TO THE QUALITY AND PERFORMANCE OF THE PROGRAM IS WITH YOU. SHOULD THE PROGRAM PROVE DEFECTIVE, YOU ASSUME THE COST OF ALL NECESSARY SERVICING, REPAIR OR CORRECTION.

12. IN NO EVENT UNLESS REQUIRED BY APPLICABLE LAW OR AGREED TO IN WRITING WILL ANY COPYRIGHT HOLDER, OR ANY OTHER PARTY WHO MAY MODIFY AND/OR REDISTRIBUTE THE PROGRAM AS PERMITTED ABOVE, BE LIABLE TO YOU FOR DAMAGES, INCLUDING ANY GENERAL, SPECIAL, INCIDENTAL OR CONSEQUENTIAL DAMAGES ARISING OUT OF THE USE OR INABILITY TO USE THE PROGRAM (INCLUDING BUT NOT LIMITED TO LOSS OF DATA OR DATA BEING RENDERED INACCURATE OR LOSSES SUSTAINED BY YOU OR THIRD PARTIES OR A FAILURE OF THE PROGRAM TO OPERATE WITH ANY OTHER PROGRAMS), EVEN IF SUCH HOLDER OR OTHER PARTY HAS BEEN ADVISED OF THE POSSIBILITY OF SUCH DAMAGES.

END OF TERMS AND CONDITIONS

How to Apply These Terms to Your New Programs

If you develop a new program, and you want it to be of the greatest possible use to the public, the best way to achieve this is to make it free software which everyone can redistribute and change under these terms.

To do so, attach the following notices to the program. It is safest to attach them to the start of each source file to most effectively convey the exclusion of warranty; and each file should have at least the "copyright" line and a pointer to where the full notice is found.

```
<one line to give the program's name and a brief idea of what it does.>
Copyright (C) <year>  <name of author>
```

This program is free software; you can redistribute it and/or modify it under the terms of the GNU General Public License as published by the Free Software Foundation; either version 2 of the License, or (at your option) any later version.

This program is distributed in the hope that it will be useful, but WITHOUT ANY WARRANTY; without even the implied warranty of MERCHANTABILITY or FITNESS FOR A PARTICULAR PURPOSE. See the GNU General Public License for more details.

You should have received a copy of the GNU General Public License along with this program; if not, write to the Free Software Foundation, Inc., 59 Temple Place, Suite 330, Boston, MA 02111-1307 USA

Also add information on how to contact you by electronic and paper mail. If the program is interactive, make it output a short notice like this when it starts in an interactive mode:

```
Gnomovision version 69, Copyright (C) year name of author
Gnomovision comes with ABSOLUTELY NO WARRANTY; for details type 'show w'.
This is free software, and you are welcome to redistribute it under certain
conditions; type 'show c' for details.
```

The hypothetical commands 'show w' and 'show c' should show the appropriate parts of the General Public License. Of course, the commands you use may be called something other than 'show w' and 'show c'; they could even be mouse-clicks or menu items—whatever suits your program.

You should also get your employer (if you work as a programmer) or your school, if any, to sign a "copyright disclaimer" for the program, if necessary. Here is a sample; alter the names:

```
Yoyodyne, Inc., hereby disclaims all copyright interest in the program
'Gnomovision' (which makes passes at compilers) written by James Hacker.
  <signature of Ty Coon>, 1 April 1989
  Ty Coon, President of Vice
```

This General Public License does not permit incorporating your program into proprietary programs. If your program is a subroutine library, you may consider it more useful to permit linking proprietary applications with the library. If this is what you want to do, use the GNU Library General Public License instead of this License.

Appendix B

Environment Variables

A number of environment variables can be set to affect the way GCC compiles programs. The controls imposed by these variables can also be imposed by using the appropriate command-line options.

Several of the environment variables are set to a list of directory names. These names are listed in the same format as is used on the PATH environment variable. The special character named PATH_SEPARATOR (defined during the installation of the compiler) is used between the directory names. On UNIX systems the separator is a colon, and on Window systems it is a semicolon.

C_INCLUDE_PATH

This environment variable applies when compiling C programs. The list of one or more directory names specified by this environment variable is searched for header files, just as if they had been specified on the command line with the -isystem option. Any directories specified by -isystem are searched first.

   Also see CPATH, CPLUS_INCLUDE_PATH, and OBJC_INCLUDE_PATH.

COMPILER_PATH

This environment variable can be set to a list of one or more directories to be searched when the compiler is looking for its subprograms, if the subprograms are not located by the GCC_EXEC_PREFIX specification.

   Also see LIBRARY_PATH, GCC_EXEC_PREFIX, and the -B command-line option.

CPATH

This environment variable applies when compiling C, C++, and Objective-C programs. The list of one or more directory names specified by this environment variable is searched for header files, just as if they had been specified on the command line with the -I option. Any directories specified by -I are searched first.

   Also see C_INCLUDE_PATH, CPLUS_INCLUDE_PATH, and OBJC_INCLUDE_PATH.

CPLUS_INCLUDE_PATH

This environment variable applies when compiling C++ programs. The list of one or more directory names specified by this environment variable is searched for header files, just as it had been specified on the command line with the -isystem option. Any directories specified by -isystem are searched first.

   Also see CPATH, C_INCLUDE_PATH, and OBJC_INCLUDE_PATH.

DEPENDENCIES_OUTPUT

Setting this environment variable to a file name will cause the preprocessor to write a dependency-based makefile rule to the file. System header file names are not included.

   If the environment variable is set to a single name, it is taken to be the name of the file, and the name on the dependency rule is taken from the name of the source file. If there are two names in the definition, the second name is the name of the target used on the dependency rule.

The result of setting this environment variable is the same as using a combination of the command-line options -MM, -MF, and -MT. Also see SUNPRO_DEPENDENCIES.

GCC_EXEC_PREFIX

If this environment variable is defined, it will be used as a prefix string on the names of all the subprograms executed by the compiler. For example, if you were to set the variable to testver instead of looking for as, the assembler, it would first try to find it under the name testveras. If it is not found under this name, the compiler continues by looking for it by its normal name. You can use slash characters in the prefix name to specify a path name.

The default setting for GCC_EXEC_PREFIX is *prefix*/lib/gcc-lib/, where *prefix* is the name specified by the configure script when the compiler was installed. This prefix is also used to locate standard linker files to be included as part of the executable program.

If you use the -B command-line option, it will override this setting. Also see COMPILER_PATH.

LANG

This environment variable is used to specify the character set used by the compiler for the creation of wide character literals, string literals, and comments.

Defining LANG as C-JIS instructs the preprocessor to interpret multibyte characters as Japanese Industrial Standard (JIS) characters. C-SJIS can be used to specify SHIFT-JIS characters and C-EUCJP indicates Japanese EUC.

If LANG is not defined or is defined to be something that is not recognized, the function mblen() is used to determine the character width, and mbtowc() is used to convert multibyte sequences into wide characters.

LC_ALL

If set, the value of this environment variable overrides any setting for both LC_MESSAGES and LC_CTYPE.

LC_CTYPE

This environment variable specifies the character classification of multibyte characters defined in quoted strings. It is primarily used to determine character boundaries in a string, which is required for character encodings that use quote or escape characters that could be misinterpreted as the end of the string or a special character. It can be set to a value such as en_AU for Australian English or es_MX for Mexican Spanish. If this variable is not set, the value defaults to the LANG variable or, if LANG is not set, the C English behavior is used. Also see LC_ALL.

LC_MESSAGES

This environment variable specifies the language to be used to issue diagnostic messages from the compiler. It can be set to a value such as en_AU for Australian English or es_MX for Mexican Spanish. If this variable is not set, the value defaults to the LANG variable or, if LANG is not set, the C English behavior is used. Also see LC_ALL.

LD_LIBRARY_PATH

This environment variable does not affect the compiler, but it does have an effect when a program is run. The variable specifies a list of directories that the program will search to locate shared libraries. This variable must be set for the execution of a program only if the shared libraries are to be found in some location other than where they were when the program was compiled.

LD_RUN_PATH

This environment variable does not affect the compiler, but it does have an effect when a program is run. It is used at runtime to specify the name of a file from which the running program is to get its symbol names and addresses. The addresses are not relocated, making it possible to refer symbolically to absolute address locations in other files. This is identical to the -R option on the ld utility.

LIBRARY_PATH

This environment variable can be set to a list of one or more directory names to be searched when the linker is looking for special linker files and for libraries specified by name with the -l (letter *l*) command-line option.

Directories specified by the -L command-line option take precedence over this environment variable and will be searched first. Also see COMPILER_PATH.

OBJC_INCLUDE_PATH

This environment variable applies when compiling Objective-C programs. The list of one or more directory names specified by this environment variable is searched for header files, just as if they had been specified on the command line with the -isystem option. Any directories specified by -isystem are searched first.

Also see CPATH, CPLUS_INCLUDE_PATH, and C_INCLUDE_PATH.

SUNPRO_OUTPUT

Setting this environment variable to a file name will cause the preprocessor to write a dependency-based makefile rule to the file. System header file names are included.

If the environment variable is set to a single name, it is taken to be the name of the file, and the name on the dependency rule is taken from the name of the source file. If there are two names in the definition, the second name is the name of the target used on the dependency rule.

The result of setting this environment variable is the same as using a combination of the command-line options -M, -MF, and -MT. Also see DEPENDENCIES_OUTPUT.

TMPDIR

This variable contains the path name of a directory that will be used by the compiler to contain the temporary work files. These are the files that are normally deleted at the end the compile process. An example of this would the file that is output from the preprocessor and used as input to the compiler.

Appendix C

Command-Line Cross Reference

This appendix is a cross reference for the command-line options. The command-line options are listed alphabetically by keyword and by category. The keywords are words extracted from the option names, and the categories are derived from the general purpose of the options. You will be able to find options listed under the name of the language to which they apply, whether the options apply to the compiler's internal operations, and so on. For example, if you want to know which command-line options affect the preprocessor or the linker, you will find them listed here.

Cross Reference

Ada -gnat, -I, --include-directory, --no-standard-includes, -nostdinc

alias -fargument-alias, -fargument-noalias, -fargument-noalias-global, -fstrict-aliasing

align -falign-functions, -falign-jumps, -falign-labels, -falign-loops, -Wcast-align

argument -fargument-alias, -fargument-noalias, -fargument-noalias-global, -fugly-args, -Wformat-extra-args

asm --assemble, -fasm, -fdata-sections, -ffunction-sections, -finhibit-size-directive, --for-assembler, -fverbose-asm, -Wa

assert -A, -A-, --assert

atexit -fuse-cxa-atexit

bitfields -fsigned-bitfields, -funsigned-bitfields

boehm -fuse-boehm-gc

bounds -fbounds-check, -ffortran-bounds-check

C --ansi, -ansi, -aux-info, -c, -C, -fallow-single-precision, -fasm, -fbuiltin, -fcommon, -fcond-mismatch, -fdollars-in-identifiers, -fdump-translation-unit, -ffreestanding, -fhosted, -finline, -fshort-wchar, -fsigned-bitfields, -fsigned-char, -funsigned-bitfields, -funsigned-char, -fwritable-strings, -pedantic, -pedantic-errors, -std, -traditional-cpp, -Waggregate-return, -Wbad-function-cast, -Wcast-align, -Wcast-qual, -Wchar-subscripts, -Wcomment, -Wconversion, -Wdeprecated-declarations, -Werror-implicit-function-declaration,

-Wformat, -Wformat-extra-args, -Wformat-nonliteral,
-Wformat-security, -Wformat-y2k, -Wimplicit,
-Wimplicit-function-declaration, -Wimplicit-int, -Wimport,
-Winline, -Wlarger-than-size, -Wlong-long, -Wmain, -Wmissing-braces,
-Wmissing-declarations, -Wmissing-format-attribute,
-Wmissing-noreturn, -Wmissing-prototypes, -Wmultichar,
-Wnested-externs, -Wpacked, -Wpadded, -Wparentheses,
-Wpointer-arith, -Wredundant-decls, -Wreturn-type,
-Wsequence-points, -Wshadow, -Wsign-compare, -Wstrict-prototypes,
-Wswitch, -Wsystem-headers, -Wtraditional, -Wtrigraphs, -Wundef,
-Wuninitialized, -Wwrite-strings

C++ --ansi, -ansi, -faccess-control, -falt-external-templates,
-fasm, -fcheck-new, -fconserve-space, -fconst-strings,
-fdefault-inline, -fdollars-in-identifiers,
-fdump-class-hierarchy, -fdump-translation-unit,
-fdump-tree-switch, -felide-constructors, -fenforce-eh-specs,
-fexternal-templates, -ffor-scope, -fgnu-keywords,
-fimplement-inlines, -fimplicit-inline-templates,
-fimplicit-templates, -finline, -fmemoize-lookups,
-fms-extensions, -fnonansi-builtins, -foperator-names,
-foptional-diags, -fpermissive, -frepo, -frtti, -fshort-wchar,
-fstats, -ftemplate-depth-number, -fuse-cxa-atexit, -fvtable-gc,
-fweak, -fwritable-strings, -nostdinc++, -pedantic,
-pedantic-errors, -Waggregate-return, -Wcast-align, -Wcast-qual,
-Wchar-subscripts, -Wcomment, -Wconversion, -Wctor-dtor-privacy,
-Wdeprecated, -Wdeprecated-declarations, -Weffc++,
-Wextern-inline, -Wformat, -Wformat-extra-args, -Wformat-nonliteral,
-Wformat-security, -Wformat-y2k, -Wimport, -Winline,
-Wlarger-than-size, -Wlong-long, -Wmain, -Wmissing-braces,
-Wmissing-format-attribute, -Wmissing-noreturn, -Wmultichar,
-Wnon-template-friend, -Wnon-virtual-dtor, -Wold-style-cast,
-Woverloaded-virtual, -Wpacked, -Wpadded, -Wparentheses,
-Wpmf-conversions, -Wpointer-arith, -Wredundant-decls, -Wreorder,
-Wreturn-type, -Wshadow, -Wsign-compare, -Wsign-promo, -Wswitch,
-Wsynth, -Wsystem-headers, -Wundef, -Wuninitialized, -Wwrite-strings

call -fcall-saved-register, -fcall-used-register, -fcaller-saves,
-fnon-call-exceptions, -foptimize-sibling-calls

case -fcase-initcap, -fcase-lower, -fcase-preserve,
-fcase-strict-lower, -fcase-strict-upper, -fcase-upper,
-fignore-case, -fintrin-case-spec, -fmatch-case-spec,
-fsource-case-spec, -fsymbol-case-spec

cast   -Wbad-function-cast, -Wcast-align, -Wcast-qual, -Wold-style-cast

char   -fsigned-char, -funsigned-char, -Wchar-subscripts

check   -fbounds-check, -fcheck-new, -fcheck-references, -fdelete-null-pointer-checks, -fforce-classes-archive-check, -ffortran-bounds-check, -fruntime-checking, -fstack-check, -fstore-check

Chill   -fchill-grant-only, -fgrant-only, -fignore-case, -flocal-loop-counter, -fold-string, -fruntime-checking, -I, --include-directory, -lang-chill

class   --bootclasspath, -fconstant-string-class, -fdump-class-hierarchy, -fforce-classes-archive-check, -foptimize-static-class-initialization, -foutput-class-dir, --main, --output-class-directory

comment   -C, -Wcomment

compile   -c, --compile, -E, -fassume-compiled, -fcommon, -fcompile-resource, -fgnu-linker, -fgrant-only, -fhosted, -fmerge-all-constants, -fmerge-constants, -fsyntax, -ftest-coverage, -ftime-report, --help, -pass-exit-codes, -pipe, --preprocess, -Q, -s, -S, -save-temps, -syntax-only, -time, -v

complex   -femulate-complex, -fugly-complex

constant   -fconst-strings, -fconstant-string-class, -fkeep-static-consts, -fmerge-all-constants, -fmerge-constants, -fsingle-precision-constant

conversion   -Wconversion, -Wpmf-conversions

cse   -fcse-follow-jumps, -fcse-skip-blocks, -ffunction-cse, -frerun-cse-after-loop

debug   -a, -d, --debug, -fdump-class-hierarchy, -fdump-translation-unit, -fdump-tree-switch, -fdump-unnumbered, -finstrument-functions, -fmem-report, -foptional-diags, -fpermissive, -fsilent, -fstats, -ftemplate-depth-number, -ftrapping-math, -ftrapv, -fverbose-asm, -g, -gcoff, -gdwarf, -gdwarf-2, -ggdb, -gstabs, -gvms, -gxcoff, -H, -v

declaration -gen-decls, -Wdeprecated-declarations,
-Werror-implicit-function-declaration,
-Wimplicit-function-declaration, -Wmissing-declarations,
-Wredundant-decls

dependencies --dependencies, -M, -MD, -MF, -MG, -MM, -MMD, -MP, -MQ,
-MT, -pass-exit-codes, --print-missing-file-dependencies,
--user-dependencies, -Wout-of-date, --write-dependencies,
--write-user-dependencies

deprecated -Wdeprecated, -Wdeprecated-declarations

directory -B, --bootclasspath directory, -foutput-class-dir,
-I, -I-, -idirafter, -include, --include-barrier,
--include-directory, --include-directory-after,
--include-prefix, --include-with-prefix,
--include-with-prefix-after, -iprefix, -isystem,
-iwithprefix, -iwithprefixbefore, -L, --library-directory,
--output-class-directory, --prefix, -print-multi-directory,
-print-prog-name, -print-search-dirs

dollar -fdollar-ok, -fdollars-in-identifiers

dump -d, --dump, -dumpbase, -dumpmachine, -dumpspecs, -dumpversion,
-fdump-class-hierarchy, -fdump-translation-unit,
-fdump-tree-switch, -fdump-unnumbered

error -fmessage-length, -pedantic-errors, -Werror,
-Werror-implicit-function-declaration

exception -fasynchronous-unwind-tables, -fcheck-new,
-fenforce-eh-specs, -fexceptions, -fnon-call-exceptions,
-fnonansi-builtins

extern -falt-external-templates, -fexternal-templates,
-Wextern-inline, -Wnested-externs

file -aux-info, -B, --bootclasspath, -include, --include-barrier,
--include-directory-after, --include-prefix,
--include-with-prefix, --include-with-prefix-after,
--language, -llibrary, -MF, --output, -print-file-name,
-print-libgcc-file-name, --print-missing-file-dependencies,
-print-prog-name, -remap, -save-temps, -x

float -ffloat-store, -fpretend-float, -Wfloat-equal

form   -ffixed-form, -ffree-form

format   -Wformat, -Wformat-extra-args, -Wformat-nonliteral,
-Wformat-security, -Wformat-y2k, -Wmissing-format-attribute

Fortran   -fautomatic, -fbackslash, -fbadu77-intrinsics-spec,
-fbounds-check, -fcase-initcap, -fcase-lower, -fcase-preserve,
-fcase-strict-lower, -fcase-strict-upper, -fcase-upper,
-fdollar-ok, -femulate-complex, -ff2c, -ff2c-intrinsics-spec,
-ff66, -ff77, -ff90, -ff90-intrinsics-spec, -ffixed-form,
-ffixed-line-length-len, -ffortran-bounds-check, -ffree-form,
-fglobals, -fgnu-intrinsics-spec, -finit-local-zero, -finline,
-fintrin-case-spec, -fmatch-case-spec, -fmil-intrinsics-spec,
-fonetrip, -fpedantic, -fsecond-underscore, -fsilent,
-fsource-case-spec, -fsymbol-case-spec, -fsyntax, -ftypeless-boz,
-fugly-args, -fugly-assign, -fugly-assumed, -fugly-comma,
-fugly-complex, -fugly-init, -fugly-logint, -funderscoring,
-funix-intrinsics, -fversion, -fvxt, -fvxt-intrinsics, -fzeros,
-maligned-data, -pedantic, -pedantic-errors, -Wglobals, -Wimplicit,
-Wsurprising, -Wuninitialized

function   -falign-functions, -ffunction-cse,
-ffunction-sections, -finline-functions,
-finstrument-functions, -fkeep-inline-functions,
-Wbad-function-cast, -Werror-implicit-function-declaration,
-Wimplicit-function-declaration, -Wunused-function

garbage   -fuse-boehm-gc, -fvtable-gc

gcse   -fgcse, -fgcse-lm, -fgcse-sm

global   -fargument-noalias-global, -fglobals, -fvolatile-global,
-Wglobals

gnu   -fgnu-intrinsics-spec, -fgnu-keywords, -fgnu-linker,
-fgnu-runtime

implicit   -fimplicit-inline-templates, -fimplicit-templates,
-Werror-implicit-function-declaration, -Wimplicit,
-Wimplicit-function-declaration, -Wimplicit-int

include   -include, --include-barrier, --include-directory,
--include-directory-after, --include-prefix,
--include-with-prefix, --include-with-prefix-after,

--include-with-prefix-before, --no-standard-includes, --trace-includes

inline -fasm, -fdefault-inline, -fimplement-inlines, -fimplicit-inline-templates, -finline, -finline-functions, -finline-limit, -fkeep-inline-functions, -Wextern-inline, -Winline

intrinsics -fbadu77-intrinsics-spec, -ff2c-intrinsics-spec, -ff90-intrinsics-spec, -fgnu-intrinsics-spec, -fmil-intrinsics-spec, -funix-intrinsics, -fvxt-intrinsics iprefix

Java --bootclasspath, -C, -D, --define-macro, --encoding, -fassume-compiled, -fbounds-check, -fcheck-references, -fcompile-resource, -fencoding, -fforce-classes-archive-check, -fhash-synchronization, -fjni, -foptimize-static-class-initialization, -foutput-class-dir, -fstore-check, -fuse-boehm-gc, -fuse-divide-subroutine, -I, --include-directory, --main, --output-class-directory, -Wextraneous-semicolon, -Wlarger-than-size, -Wout-of-date, -Wredundant-modifiers, -Wshadow

label -falign-labels, -Wunused-label

length -ffixed-line-length-len, -fmessage-length

lib -B, -L, -l, --library-directory, --no-standard-libraries, -print-libgcc-file-name, -print-multi-lib, -shared, -shared-libgcc, -static, -static-libgcc, -symbolic

link -c, --compile, -fcommon, -fgnu-linker, -fhosted, -fmerge-all-constants, -fmerge-constants, --for-linker, --force-link, -fvtable-gc, -L, --library-directory, -llibrary, -no-standard-libraries, -nodefaultlibs, -nostartfiles, -nostdlib, -s, -shared, -shared-libgcc, -static, -static-libgcc, -symbolic, -u, -Wl, -Xlinker

machine -b, --target, --target-help

macro --ansi, -D, --define-macro, -ffast-math, -ffixed-register, -imacros, -U, -undef, --undefine-macro

math -fallow-single-precision, -femulate-complex, -ffast-math, -ffloat-store, -fmath-errno, -fpretend-float, -fschedule-insns, -fschedule-insns2, -fshort-double, -fsingle-precision-constant, -ftrapping-math, -ftrapv, -ftypeless-boz, -fugly-complex,

-funsafe-math-optimizations, -funsigned-bitfields,
-funsigned-char, -fuse-divide-subroutine, -Wdiv-by-zero,
-Wfloat-equal, -Wsign-compare, -Wsign-promo, -Wsurprising

missing --print-missing-file-dependencies, -Wmissing-braces,
-Wmissing-declarations, -Wmissing-format-attribute,
-Wmissing-noreturn, -Wmissing-prototypes

Objective-C --ansi, -ansi, -fasm, -fbuiltin, -fconstant-string-class,
-fgnu-runtime, -finline, -gen-decls, -Waggregate-return,
-Wcast-align, -Wcast-qual, -Wchar-subscripts, -Wcomment,
-Wconversion, -Wdeprecated-declarations, -Wformat,
-Wformat-extra-args, -Wformat-nonliteral, -Wformat-security,
-Wformat-y2k, -Wimport, -Winline, -Wlarger-than-size, -Wlong-long,
-Wmissing-braces, -Wmissing-format-attribute, -Wmissing-noreturn,
-Wmultichar, -Wpacked, -Wpadded, -Wparentheses, -Wpointer-arith,
-Wprotocol, -Wredundant-decls, -Wselector, -Wshadow, -Wsign-compare,
-Wswitch, -Wsystem-headers, -Wundef, -Wuninitialized

optimization -fasynchronous-unwind-tables, -fbranch-probabilities,
-fcall-saved-register, -fcall-used-register, -fcaller-saves,
-fcommon, -fconserve-space, -fcprop-registers, -fcse-follow-jumps,
-fcse-skip-blocks, -fdata-sections, -fdefer-pop, -fdelayed-branch,
-fdelete-null-pointer-checks, -fdiagnostics-show-location,
-felide-constructors, -fexpensive-optimizations, -ffloat-store,
-ffunction-cse, -ffunction-sections, -fgcse, -fgcse-lm,
-fglobals, -fguess-branch-probability, -finit-local-zero,
-fkeep-static-consts, -fmemoize-lookups, -fmove-all-movables,
-fomit-frame-pointer, -foptimize-register-move,
-foptimize-sibling-calls, -foptimize-static-class-initialization,
-fpack-struct, -fpeephole, -fpeephole2, -fppc-struct-return,
-fprefetch-loop-arrays, -freduce-all-givs, -freg-struct-return,
-fregmove, -frename-registers, -frerun-cse-after-loop,
-frerun-loop-opt, -fruntime-checking, -fschedule-insns,
-fschedule-insns2, -fshort-double, -fshort-enums, -fssa, -fssa-ccp,
-fssa-dce, -fstack-check, -fstore-check, -fstrength-reduce,
-fstrict-aliasing, -fthread-jumps, -funroll-all-loops,
-funroll-loops, -funwind-tables, -fvtable-gc, -fzeros, -O, --optimize
optimize, --optimize, --param, -Wdisabled-optimization

preprocessor -A, -A-, --assert, -C, -D, --define-macro,
--dependencies directory, -E, -fident, -fpreprocessed, -H,
-I, -I-, -idirafter, -imacros, -include, --include-barrier,

```
--include-directory, --include-directory-after,
--include-prefix, --include-with-prefix,
--include-with-prefix-after, --include-with-prefix-before,
-iprefix, -isystem, -iwithprefix, -iwithprefixbefore, -M,
-MD, -MF, -MG, -MM, -MMD, -MP, -MQ, -MT, --no-line-commands,
--no-standard-includes, -nostdinc, -nostdinc++, -P,
--preprocess, --print-missing-file-dependencies, -remap,
--trace-includes, -trigraphs, -U, -undef, --undefine-macro,
--user-dependencies, -Wp, --write-dependencies,
--write-user-dependencies, -Wsystem-headers, -Wundef,
-Wunknown-pragmas
```

profile -a, -fdata-sections, -fprofile-arcs, -ftest-coverage, -p, -pg, --profile, --profile-blocks

prototypes -Wmissing-prototypes, -Wstrict-prototypes

register -fcall-saved-register, -fcall-used-register, -fcprop-registers, -ffixed-register, -fforce-addr, -fforce-mem, -foptimize-register-move, -freg-struct-return, -fregmove, -frename-registers, -fstack-limit-register, -remap

return -fppc-struct-return, -freg-struct-return, -Waggregate-return, -Wreturn-type

sign -fsigned-bitfields, -fsigned-char, -Wsign-compare, -Wsign-promo

ssa -fssa, -fssa-ccp, -fssa-dce

stack -fstack-check, -fstack-limit-register, -fstack-limit-symbol

standard --ansi, -ansi, -ff2c, -ff2c-intrinsics, -ff66, -ff77, -ff90, -ff90-intrinsics, -ffixed-form, -ffixed-line-length-len, -ffor-scope, -ffree-form, -fgnu-keywords, -fmil-intrinsics, -fms-extensions, -fnext-runtime, -fnonansi-builtins, -foperator-names, -fpedantic, -fpermissive, -fsigned-bitfields, -fsigned-char, -ftrapping-math, -ftrapv, -fugly-args, -fugly-assign, -fugly-assumed, -fugly-comma, -fugly-complex, -fugly-init, -fugly-logint, -fvxt, -fvxt-intrinsics, -fwritable-strings, --no-standard-includes, --no-standard-libraries, -pedantic, -std, -traditional-cpp, -Wtraditional

static   -fkeep-static-consts,
-foptimize-static-class-initialization,
-fvolatile-static, -static, -static-libgcc

strings   -fconst-strings, -fconstant-string-class,
-fold-string, -fwritable-strings, -Wwrite-strings

syntax   -fsyntax, -syntax-only

template   -falt-external-templates, -fexternal-templates,
-fimplicit-inline-templates, -fimplicit-templates,
-ftemplate-depth-number, -Wnon-template-friend

underscore   -fleading-underscore, -fsecond-underscore,
-funderscoring

version   -dumpversion, -fversion, --use-version, -v, -V

warn   --all-warnings, --extra-warnings, -fmessage-length,
--no-warnings, -w, -W, -Waggregate-return, -Wall,
--warn-, -Wbad-function-cast, -Wcast-align, -Wcast-qual,
-Wchar-subscripts, -Wcomment, -Wconversion, -Wctor-dtor-privacy,
-Wdeprecated, -Wdeprecated-declarations,
-Wdisabled-optimization, -Wdiv-by-zero, -Weffc++, -Werror,
-Werror-implicit-function-declaration, -Wextern-inline,
-Wextraneous-semicolon, -Wfloat-equal, -Wformat,
-Wformat-extra-args, -Wformat-nonliteral,
-Wformat-security, -Wformat-y2k, -Wglobals, -Wimplicit,
-Wimplicit-function-declaration, -Wimplicit-int, -Wimport,
-Winline, -Wlarger-than-size, -Wlong-long, -Wmain,
-Wmissing-braces, -Wmissing-declarations,
-Wmissing-format-attribute, -Wmissing-noreturn,
-Wmissing-prototypes, -Wmultichar, -Wnested-externs,
-Wnon-template-friend, -Wnon-virtual-dtor, -Wold-style-cast,
-Wout-of-date, -Woverloaded-virtual, -Wpacked, -Wpadded,
-Wparentheses, -Wpmf-conversions, -Wpointer-arith, -Wprotocol,
-Wredundant-decls, -Wredundant-modifiers, -Wreorder,
-Wreturn-type, -Wselector, -Wsequence-points, -Wshadow,
-Wsign-compare, -Wsign-promo, -Wstrict-prototypes, -Wsurprising,
-Wswitch, -Wsynth, -Wsystem-headers, -Wtraditional, -Wtrigraphs,
-Wundef, -Wuninitialized, -Wunknown-pragmas, -Wunreachable-code,
-Wunused, -Wunused-function, -Wunused-label, -Wunused-parameter,
-Wunused-value, -Wunused-variable, -Wwrite-strings

The Complete Reference

Appendix D

Command Line Options

T his appendix contains an alphabetic listing of the command line options. Some of the options apply to every language, and some of them apply to a subset of one or more languages. There are also options that apply only to the preprocessor, the assembler, or the linker. Each option is marked with the language, or languages, to which it applies. If an option applies to all languages, it has no such mark.

It is possible to compile any of the languages by using the gcc command, but it is possible that some language-specific options would not be available. Each language has its own front end driver process so, if an option exists only for one specific language, it will probably be necessary to use the driver as a front end for gcc for the option to be recognized.

Option Prefix

All of the options begin with a hyphen. A number of them have two hyphens. There are also some special meanings to options that begin with -f and -W.

The -- Prefix

The traditional method for indicating an option on the command line is to have a letter preceded by a single hyphen. The newer form is to have an option preceded with a pair of hyphens. Many of the options listed in this index have both the older (single hyphen) and new (double hyphen) formats that do exactly the same thing. For example, the traditional option setting to have debugging information included in the generated code is:

L D-1
```
-g
```

This same option can be specified in a longer file, like this:

L D-2
```
--debug
```

The -f Prefix

The letter *f* stands for *flag*. Most of these options are either on or off. For example, the following option sets a flag that will cause peephole optimization to occur:

L D-3
```
-fpeephole
```

Because a flag is either on or off, each flag option has an inverse that is invoked by using the same name with a *no-* prefix. For example:

L D-4
```
-fno-peephole
```

Almost all of these options toggle a true or false flag setting, so one or other of the options is the default setting. But there are some exceptions. For example, either of the two following options can be used to specify the scope of variables declared in a `for` loop:

```
-ffor-scope
-fno-for-scope
```

Neither of the scope settings is the default. The default is to follow the standard, but both of these settings are variations from the standard.

Any `-f` option can also be entered as a double hyphen option. For example, the following pair of options are exactly the same:

```
-frtti
--rtti
```

The -W Prefix

The -W prefix is used to specify whether certain warning messages are to be generated by the compiler. In a manner similar to the -f flag settings, the warnings can be turned both on and off by using *no-* on the front of the name. For example, the following setting will cause the compiler to issue a warning if there are too many arguments on a function call:

```
-Wformat-extra-args
```

To suppress the warning messages, you can use the following:

```
-Wno-format-extra-args
```

The Order on the Command Line

The order of the options can be important. If you have two options on the command line that conflict with one another, normally the second option on the line will override the first by simply changing the setting that the first one made. The command line is read from left to right, and each option sets either a value or a flag (or a collection of values and flags), so anything that is set at one point on the command line can be changed later.

This ordering requirement can actually be used as a convenience. For example, the `-O3` optimizing flag turns on the `-finline-functions` option. If, however, you want to keep `-O3` but turn off the inlining of functions, you can do so by entering the flags in the following order:

```
-O3 -fno-inline-functions
```

The File Types

The compiler determines the contents of a file by examining the suffix of the file name looking for a match to the ones in Table D-1. Any file with an unknown suffix is assumed to be input for the linker on the target machine and is passed to it during the link phase. The −x option can be used to instruct the compiler to ignore the suffix and assume the file is of a certain type.

Suffix	File Contains
.a	A static library (also called an archive file) containing one or more .o files to be used by the linker.
.c	C source code that is to be preprocessed.
.adb	Ada *body* file, which is source code containing a library unit body.
.ads	Ada *spec* file, which is source code containing a library unit declaration or a library unit, renaming a declaration.
.C .c++ .cc .cp .cpp .cxx	C++ source code that is to be preprocessed.
.class	A file containing the bytecodes produced by compiling a Java program.
.f .for .FOR	Fortran source code that is not to be preprocessed.
.F .fpp .FPP	Forttran source code that is to be preprocessed.
.h	C, C++, or Objective-C header file.
.i	C source code that is not to be preprocessed.
.ii	C++ source code that is not to be preprocessed.
.java	Java source code.
.m	Objective C source code that is to be preprocessed.
.mi	Objective C source code that is not to be preprocessed.
.mo	Binary file containing translations for internationalization.
.o	An object file in a format appropriate to be supplied to the linker.

Table D-1.   *File Name Suffixes Recognized by GCC*

Suffix	File Contains
.po	Text file containing translations for internationalization.
.r	Fortran source code to be preprocessed by a RATFOR preprocessor.
.S	Assembly language source code that is to be preprocessed.
.s	Assembly language source code that is not to be preprocessed.
.so	A dynamic library (also called a shared library) containing one or more .o files to be used by a program at execution time.
<other>	Files with an unrecognized suffix, or with no suffix, are assumed to be input for the linker and are passed to it unmodified.

Table D-1.   *File Name Suffixes Recognized by GCC* (continued)

Alphabetic List of Options

-###
Displays the current version number of the compiler and then displays all of the commands that would be used to run each phase of the compile and link process, but none of the commands are executed. When used alone, this option will display the current version number of the compiler. When used in combination with the --help option, a complete list of the command line options is displayed.

Also see -v.

-a
Generate extra code for profiling at the top of each basic block of executable code. The profiling will record each time a basic block of code is executed. The recorded information includes the basic block starting address and the name of the function containing the basic block. If the -g option is also specified, the recorded information for each block will include the file name and the starting line number of each block. The information is written to a file named bb.out (unless another name was specified in the machine description).

Also see -ax, -fprofile-arcs, and -ftest-coverage. This option can be written --profile-blocks.

-A *question(answer)*   Pre
Specifies a question and answer for an assertion in the following form:

L D-10   `#if #question(answer)`

This option can be written `--assert`. Also see `-A-`.

-A-   Pre
Disables standard assertions that normally describe the target machine. Also see `-A`.

--all-warnings
Same as `-Wall`.

--ansi   C C++   ObjC
Same as `-ansi`.

--ansi   C C++   ObjC
This option instructs the compiler to successfully compile programs that are standards
compliant, but does not constrain the code in any way that does not conflict with the
standard. That is, non-conflicting GNU extensions remain enabled. For C, this option
will correctly compile ISO C89 compliant programs. For C++, GNU extensions that
conflict with ISO C++ are disabled.
    This option also set the options `-fno_asm`, `-fno_nonansi_builtin`, `-trigraphs`,
and `-fno_dollars_in_identifiers`. For C++ it also sets the options `-fno_gnu_`
`keywords` and `-fno-nonansi-builtins`.
    This option defines the macro `__STRICT_ANSI__` which prevents some header files
from declaring functions or macros that may conflict names in the program being
compiled.
    This option disables the GNU C extension keywords `asm`, `typeof`, and `inline`, but
the alternate forms `__asm__`, `__typeof__`, and `__inline__` remain available.
    To constrain code strictly to the standard, use `-pedantic` in addition to `-ansi`.
Also see `-std`.
    This option can be written `--ansi`.

--assemble
Same as `-S`.

--assert *question(answer)*   Pre
Same as `-A`.

-aux-info *filename*   C
Outputs prototype declarations for all the functions declared or defined in a single
compilation unit (a C source file and all the header files it includes) to the named file.

-b *machine*

This option specifies the target machine for which the program is to be compiled. If this option is not specified, the default is to compile code for the machine on which the compiler is being run. The machine is determined by naming the directory containing the compiler which is normally /user/local/lib/gcc-lib/*machine*/*version*.

    Also see -B and -V. This option can be written --target.

-B*prefix*

The *prefix* path specifies the location of the libraries, include files, executable programs, and data files of the compiler. To run a subprogram such as cpp, as, or ld, the prefix is tried as the path to locate each program. You may specify a directory separator character at the end of the prefix, or not, as you prefer.

    The same standard search procedure is used in all cases. The following steps are executed in order until the item being sought is located:

1. If a prefix is specified by the -B option, it is used to construct a path name.

2. A path is constructed by using the prefix /usr/lib/gcc/.

3. A path is constructed by using the prefix /usr/local/lib/gcc-lib/.

4. Each directory path defined in the PATH variable is used in the order they appear in the variable.

    The -B option also is used to locate libraries for the linker because the compiler translates this option into a -L option to pass to the linker.

    The -B option also is used to locate header files because the specified prefix has the directory name appended to it and is translated into a -isystem option passed to the preprocessor.

    The environment variable GCC_EXEC_PREFIX can be set to the name of the prefix directory and will have the same effect as if it were specified as a -B option.

    Special case for bootstrapping the compiler: If the prefix is in the form *dirpath*/stage0 through *dirpath*/stage9, it will be replaced by *dirpath*/include.

    This option can be written --prefix.

—bootclasspath=*pathname*

The *pathname* species the location of the standard Java packages and classes (such as java.lang.String). The path name can be that of a directory, a jar file, or a zip file.

    Also see --classpath and -I.

-c

Do not invoke the linker. This option will allow compiling and assembling of source files into object files, but the linker will not be run to create an executable. The object files produced will be stored in a file of the same name as the source file with a .o suffix. Any input files that do not have a recognizable suffix according to Table D-1 or do not have their types indicated by -x are ignored.

    This option can be written --compile.

APPENDIXES

-C   Java

Causes the compiler to produce bytecode class files instead of the default executable object code. Also see -foutput-class-dir.

-C   Pre

This option, used in conjunction with the -E option, causes all comments to be discarded.

This option can be written --comments.

--compile

Same as -c.

-d*letters*

One or more letters can be listed to specify when a debugging dump (or dumps) should occur and what the dump is to contain. This option is for use in debugging the compiler by making it possible to examine detailed information at various stages of compilation. Each output file is identified with a suffix of the pass number followed by some identifying letters. For example, the file dumped following pass 21, which is global register allocation, while compiling doline.c would be named doline.21.greg.

Also see -dumpbase, -fdump-unnumbered, -fdump-translation-unit, -fdump-class-hierarchy, and -fdump-tree-switch. This option can also be written --dump.

Table D-2 lists all of the available letters for the -d option, which can be inserted in any combination and in any order. This feature has been implemented strictly for purposes of debugging the compiler, so you will find that not all the letters are implemented in every release. Note that the letters D, I, M, and N have a special meaning to the preprocessor only when used in conjunction with the -E option.

Letter	Produces
A	Annotates the assembly language output with miscellaneous debugging information.
a	Sets the flags so that all the named files are dumped except the *name.pass*.vcg files, which can only be specified by the v option letter.
b	Dump to *name*.14.bp after computing branch probabilities.
B	Dump to *name*.29.bbro after block reordering.
c	Dump to *name*.16.combine after instruction combination.

Table D-2.   *The Letters That Can Be Used in Combination with the -d Option*

Letter	Produces
C	Dump to *name*.17.ce after first if-conversion.
d	Dump to *name*.31.dbr after delayed branch scheduling.
D	When used along with the -E option, in addition to the normal output after preprocessing, include all macro definitions in the output.
e	Dump to *name*.04.ssa and *name*.07.ussa after static single assignments optimizations.
E	Dump to *name*.26.ce2 after the second if-conversion.
f	Dump to *name*.13.cfg after data flow analysis and *name*.15.life after life analysis.
F	Dump to *name*.09.addressof after purging ADDRESSOF codes.
g	Dump to *name*.21.greg after global register allocation.
G	Dump to *name*.10.gcse after GCSE.
h	Dump to *name*.02.eh after finalization of exception handling.
i	Dump to *name*.01.sibling after sibling call optimizations.
I	When used in conjunction with the -E option, the preprocessor outputs the #include directives in addition to the other preprocessor output.
j	Dump to *name*.03.jump after the first jump optimizations.
k	Dump to *name*.28.stack after register-to-stack conversion and to *name*.32.stack after the conversion from registers to stack.
l	Dump to *name*.20.lreg after local register allocation.
L	Dump to *name*.11.loop after loop optimization.
M	Dump to *name*.30.mach after the machine dependent reorganization pass. When used along with the -E option, the preprocessor will output a list of the macro definitions in effect at the end of all preprocessing.
m	At the end of the compile, print the memory usage information to standard error.
n	Dump to *name*.25.rnreg after register renumbering.

Table D-2. *The Letters That Can Be Used in Combination with the -d Option (continued)*

Letter	Produces
N	Dump to *name*.18.regmove after the register move pass. When used along with the -E option, in addition to the normal output after preprocessing, include a list of all macros in the simplified form of #define *name*.
o	Dump to *name*.22.postreload after post-reload optimizations.
p	Annotate the assembly language with the length of each instruction and a comment indicating which pattern and alternative was used for optimization.
P	Annotate the assembly language with the RTL code that produced each instruction. This also sets the -dp option for more annotation.
r	Dump to *name*.00.rtl after generating the RTL. Also see the letter x.
R	Dump to *name*.27.sched2 after the second scheduling pass.
s	Dump to *name*.08.cse after CSE and the jump optimization that sometimes follows the first CSE pass.
S	Dump to *name*.19.sched after the first scheduling pass.
t	Dump to *name*.12.cse2 after the second CSE pass and the jump optimization that sometimes follows the second CSE pass.
u	Dump to *name*.06.null after SSA optimizations.
v	Dump to *name*.*pass*.vcg a representation of the control flow graph for each of the other files dumped (except *name*.00.rtl). The file is formatted in such a way that it can be read and displayed by vcg.
w	Dump to *name*.23.flow2 after the second flow pass.
W	Dump to *name*.05.ssaccp after the SSA conditional code propogation.
X	Dump to *name*.06.ssadce after the SSA dead code elimination pass.
x	Generate the RTL for a function but do not compile it. This letter is often used with the letter r.
y	The parser will dump debugging information to standard error.
z	Dump to *name*.24.peephole2 after the peephole optimization pass.

Table D-2.   *The Letters That Can Be Used in Combination with the -d Option (continued)*

-D*property[=string]*

This option can be specified on the same command line that specifies
--main and will define a property that can be retrieved by calling the
java.lang.System.getProperty() method. If the *string* is not
specified, the property is defined with the empty string.

This option can be written --define-macro.

-D*macro[=string]*

If the *string* is specified, a macro by that name is defined just as if it had been included
as part of the code. For example, -Dbrunt=logger generates the following definition:

```
#define brunt=logger
```

If the *string* is not specified, the macro is defined as the string "1". For example,
-Dminke generates the following definition:

```
#define minke 1
```

All -D options are processed before any -U options, and all -U options are processed
before any -include or -imacros options.

This option can be written --define-macro.

--debug*[level]*

Same as -g.

--define-macro *macro[=string]*

Same as -D.

--dependencies

The same as -M.

--dump *letters*

Same as -d.

-dumpbase *base*

The base is the base name to be used for naming the dump files produced by the
-d option.

This option can be written --dumpbase.

-dumpmachine

Print the name of the target machine of this compiler and take no further action.

-dumpspecs
Print the specifications used to build the compiler and take no further action. This is a long listing including all the option (and default) settings that were used for compiling, assembling, and linking the GCC compiler itself.

-dumpversion
Print the version number of the compiler and take no further action.

-E   `Pre`
Stop after preprocessing the source code and output the result. The output is written to standard out unless the -o option is used to send it to a file. Input files that do not require preprocessing are ignored, which is determined either by the file name suffixes in Table D-1 or by not having their types indicated by the -x option.

　　This option defines the environment variables __GNUC__, __GNUC_MINOR__, and __GNUC_PATCHLEVEL__.

　　The -dD, -dI, -dM, and -dN options take on special meanings only when used in conjunction with -E. Also see the -C and -P options. This option can be written --preprocess.

--encoding=*name*   `Java`
Same as -fencoding.

--extra-warnings
Same as -W.

-faccess-control   `C++`
This is the default. If you specify -fno-access-control the compiler will not check for access permision requirements. The only purpose of this flag is for working around an access permission bug in the compiler.

-falign-functions[=*number*]
Aligns the starting address of functions on a boundary that is a power of 2 equal to or greater than *number*, but only if it is necessary to skip no more than *number* bytes to do it. For example, if *number* is 20, the resulting alignment is on a 32 byte boundary as long as no more than 20 bytes must be skipped to place it there.

　　Setting number to a power of 2 causes all functions to be aligned to the boundary. If the number is not specified the machine default is used. For some machines the number is rounded up to a power of 2 thus aligning all functions. Specifying *number* as 1 is equivalent to -fno-align-functions and no alignment will take place.

-falign-jumps[=*number*]
Aligns branch targets that cannot be reached any other way to a boundary that is a power of 2 equal to or greater than *number*, but only if it is not necessary to skip no more than *number* bytes to do it. For example, if *number* is 20 the resulting alignment is on a 32-byte boundary as long as no more than 20 bytes must be skipped to place it there. Unlike the similar option -falign-labels, this option does not require the insertion of dummy instructions before the branch target.

If *number* is not specified the machine default is used, which is normally 1. Specifying the number as 1 is equivalent to -fno-align-jumps and no alignment takes place.

-falign-labels[=*number*]
Aligns the targets of all branches to a boundary that is a power of 2 equal to or greater than *number*, but only if it is not necessary to skip no more than *number* bytes to do it. For example, if *number* is 20, the resulting alignment is on a 32-byte boundary as long as no more than 20 bytes must be skipped to place it there. This option can make code slower and larger because of the insertion of dummy instructions before the branch target. For a similar, but cheaper, version of this option see -falign-jumps.

If -falign-loops or -falign-jumps is used, with a greater value than *number*, the greater value is used here. If *number* is not specified, the machine default is used, which is normally 1. Specifying number as 1 is equivalent to -fno-align-labels and no alignment takes place.

-falign-loops[=*number*]
Aligns the top of loops to a boundary that is a power of 2 equal to or greater than *number*, but only if it is not necessary to skip more than *number* bytes to do it. For example, if *number* is 20, the resulting alignment is on a 32-byte boundary as long as no more than 20 bytes must be skipped to place it there. This option could make code larger because of the insertion of dummy instructions to bring about alignment, but, depending on the machine, the loop could execute faster because of branching to an aligned location from the bottom of each iteration.

If *number* is not specified, the machine default is used, which is normally 1. Specifying number as 1 is equivalent to -fno-align-loops, and no alignment takes place.

-fallow-single-precision
This is the default. Do not perform single precision floating point math operations as double precision. If you use the -traditional option, all floating point operations are performed as double precision, but you can use this option to allow single precision operations to take place.

-falt-external-templates
This option is deprecated. Template instances may or may not be emitted depending on the location of the original template instantiation. The instantiation obeys #pragma interface and #pragma implementation. Also see -fexternal-templates.

-fargument-alias
Specifies that arguments passed to functions may be aliases of one another. That is, two or more parameters may represent the same memory location. It is also possible that an argument can be an alias of a global value. This option is intended for internal compiler use only.

This is the default for C, C++, and ObjC.

Also see -fargument-noalias and -fargument-noalias-global.

-fargument-noalias
Specifies that arguments passed to functions will never be aliases of one another. That is, two or more parameters will not represent the same memory location. However, it is possible that an argument can be an alias of a global value. This option is intended for internal compiler use only.

Also see `-fargument-alias` and `-fargument-noalias-global`.

-fargument-noalias-global
Specifies that arguments passed to functions will never be aliases of one another. That is, two or more parameters will not represent the same memory location. It is also not possible that an argument is an alias of a global value. This option is intended for internal compiler use only.

This is the default for Fortran.

Also see `-fargument-alias` and `-fargument-noalias`.

-fasm   `C   C++   ObjC`
This is the default, which enables the keywords `asm`, `inline`, and `typeof`.

For C, specifying `-fno-asm` disables the keywords `asm`, `inline`, and `typeof`. This option has no effect on the keywords `__asm__`, `__inline__`, and `__typeof__`.

For C++, specifying `-fno-asm` disables the keyword `typeof`, but has no effect on `asm` and `inline` because they are part of the language.

Other flags that effect these keywords are `-ansi`, `-gnu-keywords`, and `-std`.

-fassume-compiled=classname   `Java`
The compiler can generate different code depending on whether it can assume that certain classes have already been compiled into native code. The options `-fassume-compiled` and `-fno-assume-compiled` can be used repeatedly to construct lists of classes that can be assumed, or not assumed, to have been compiled.

-fasynchronous-unwind-tables
Generate unwind table in DWARF2 format if supported on the target machine. The resulting table is in a format that can be used by asynchronous events such as a debugger or garbage collector.

Also see `-fexceptions`, `-fnon-call-exceptions`, and `-funwind-tables`.

-fautomatic   `Fortran`
This is the default. Specifying `-fno-automatic` has the same result as if the `SAVE` statement had been specified for every local variable and array. It has no effect on common blocks. This can be disabled by specifying `-fno-automatic`.

Also see `-finit-local-zero`.

-fbackslash   `Fortran`
This is the default. Specifying `-fno-backslash` will prevent the backslash character from being used as an escape character in Hollerith strings (as they are in C) to define

special characters. The default is to interpret \n as a newline character and \007 as the octal representation of the BEL (beep) character).

-fbadu77-intrinsics-*spec* `Fortran`

The *spec* specifies the status of the UNIX intrinsics that have inappropriate forms. The *spec* can be any one of the following:

- `enable` The intrinsics are recognized and enabled. This is the default.
- `hide` The intrinsics are recognized and enabled only if the first mention of the name of each one is in an INTRINSIC statement.
- `disable` The intrinsics are recognized, but references to them must be made through an INTRINSIC statement.
- `delete` The intrinsics are not recognized.

-fbounds-check `Java Fortran`

For Java, this is the default. Specifying `-fno-bounds-check` disables the bounds checking on all array accesses. This option will improve performance of array indexing, but could result in unpredictable behavior if the bounds of an array are exceeded.

For Fortran, this option causes the generation of code that will make checks at runtime to verify array subscripts and CHARACTER substring accesses are within the declared minimum and maximum values.

Also see `-ffortran-bounds-check`.

-fbranch-probabilities

After using `-fprofile-arcs` to compile a program and then running it to create the file containing execution counts for each block of code, the program can be compiled again with this option, and the information from the file is used to optimize the code for the branches that are taken most often. Without this information, GCC will guess which path is taken most often to perform optimization. The information is stored in a file with the name as the source and a `.da` suffix.

Also see `-fguess-branch-probability`.

-fbuiltin `C ObjC`

This is the default, which is to recognize built in functions by their name. The option `-fno-builtin` specifies that no built in function is to be recognized unless it is referenced by using the prefix `__builtin_`. For example, to get the built in version, instead of calling the function named `strcpy()` you should call `__builtin_strcpy()`.

Instead of using -fno-builtin to suppress all built in functions, you can append the name of the function to the option name to select specific built in functions that will not be used. For example, to allow all built in functions except `bzero()` and `sqrt()`, you can use the following options:

```
-fno-builtin-bzero -fno-builtin-sqrt
```

For C++ -fno-builtin is always in effect, so the only way to make a direct call to one of the C built in functions is to use the __builtin_ prefix, but the GNU C++ standard library uses many built in functions.

Also see -fbuiltin-*function*, -ffreestanding, and -fnonansi-builtins.

-fcall-saved-*register*

Treat the named *register* as a register that can be allocated to contain a value, and that value will be retained even through a function call. Functions compiled with this option set must save and restore the contents of the register.

This option must not be specified for registers that have fixed roles (such as a frame pointer or stack pointer).

The register names are platform dependent and are named in the REGISTER_NAMES macro of the machine description.

Also see -fcall-used-*register* and -ffixed-*register*.

-fcall-used-*register*

Treat the named *register* as a register that is available for allocation, but will have its contents destroyed by a function call. It may be allocated for temporary storage, but must be reloaded after a function call.

This option must not be specified for registers that have fixed roles (such as a frame pointer or stack pointer).

The register names are platform dependent and are named in the REGISTER_NAMES macro of the machine description.

Also see -ffixed-*register* and -fcall-saved-*register*.

-fcaller-saves

Extra instructions are included to save registers before a function call and then restore them afterward. The registers can then be used in the function call and inside the function itself. Only registers that contain useful values are saved, and then only if it seems better to save and restore than it does to reload the value later, when it is needed again. This option is enabled by default on some machines and is always enabled by -O2, -O3, and -Os, but can be overridden by -fno-caller-saves.

-fcase-initcap   `Fortran`

Requires most source code to be written with initial upper case letters. Sets the options -fintrin-case-initcap, -fmatch-case-initcap, -fsource-case-preserve, and -fsymbol-case-initcap.

-fcase-lower   `Fortran`

Maps source code to lower case. Sets the options -fintrin-case-any, -fmatch-case-any, -fsource-case-lower, and -fsymbol-case-any.

-fcase-preserve   Fortran
Preserves all case in user defined symbols while allowing any case for matching
keywords and intrinsics. Sets the options `-fintrin-case-any`, `-fmatch-case-any`,
`-fsource-case-preserve`, and `-fsymbol-case-any`.

-fcase-strict-lower   Fortran
Requires most source code to be in lower case. Sets the options `-fintrin-case-lower`,
`-fmatch-case-lower`, `-fsource-case-preserve`, and `-fsymbol-case-lower`.

-fcase-strict-upper   Fortran
Requires most source code to be in upper case. Sets the options `-fintrin-case-upper`,
`-fmatch-case-upper`, `-fsource-case-preserve`, and `-fsymbol-case-upper`.

-fcase-upper   Fortran
Maps source code to upper case. Sets the options `-fintrin-case-any`,
`-fmatch-case-any`, `-fsource-case-upper`, and `-fsymbol-case-any`.

-fcheck-new   C++
Inserts code to check that the pointer returned from operator `new`, used in C++ to
allocate memory, does not return a NULL pointer. This is not normally necessary
because the version of `new` in the C++ library throws an exception if it is out of memory.
If an overloaded version of `new` could return NULL but does not throw an exception,
this option could be used to test the returned pointer.

-fcheck-references   Java
Insert inline code to check for null pointer references when accessing an object through
a reference. This is usually unnecessary because most processors detect such null pointer
references.

-fcommon   C
This is the default. Specifying `-fno-common` will cause the compiler to make an explicit
allocation of space in the data section for each global variable. The default is to allocate
them in a common block that is resolved by the linker, so declaring the same global
variable more than once causes the linker to resolve the two into one.

You can specify `-fno-common` to verify that the program will compile and link on
another system that does not use GCC.

For Fortran, the `-fno-common` option must not be used.

Also see "Attributes" in Chapter 4.

-fcompile-resource=*resourcename*   Java
The *resourcename* is the name of a file containing property defintions and other resources
that is compiled into object code and can be accessed at run time by the core protocol
handler as `core:/`*resourcename*.

-fcond-mismatch

Allow type mismatches in conditional expressions.

-fconserve-space

Place global variables that are not initialized at compile time into the common segment (as is done in C). This reduces the size of the executable file because no space is allocated for them until the program loads. This flag no longer serves a purpose for most platforms because support has been added to store variables in BSS without making them common.

Warning: If use of this option causes your program to crash when it is terminating, it could be because an object is being destroyed twice because object definitions were merged and assigned the same address.

-fconst-strings

This is the default. If you specify -fno-const-strings, string literal declarations are defined as char * instead of the default const char *. To be able to actually write to the strings, you would also need to use the -fwriteable-strings option.

-fconstant-string-class=*classname*

Use the specified *classname* as the name of the class instantiated for each literal string of the form @"...". The default *classname* is NXConstantString.

-fcprop-registers

After all the register allocation has been completed, this option analyzes the pattern of data copied into the registers to try to find places where it is not necessary to copy a value into a register, but propogate a previous copy forward so it can be used again. This option is set by -O but can be overridden with -fno-cprop-registers.

-fcse-follow-jumps

When the target of a jump cannot be reached any other way except by the jump being taken, the common subexpression elimination scan follows the path of the jump. That is, any values that exist before the jump is taken will always exist at the point of the destination of the jump and can be used there. This flag is set by -O2, -O3, and -Os, but can be overridden by -fno-cse-follow-jumps. Also see -fcse-skip-blocks and --param.

-fcse-skip-blocks

If the body of an if statement is simple enough that it does not contain code that would disrupt the previously calculated values, the common subexpression analysis flow skips over the if statement and is applied to the statements that follow it. This flag is set by -O2, -O3, and -Os, but can be overridden by -fno-cse-skip-blocks. Also see -fcse-skip-blocks and --param.

-fdata-sections

Each data item is placed into its own named section in the assembly language output. The section name is derived from the name of the data item. This only has an advantage on machines with a linker that can use sectioning to optimize allocation of space. For the same optimization with the executable code, see -ffunction-sections.

Setting this option for a machine that does not support sectioning in its assembler code will result in a warning message, and the option will be ignored. Even on machines that support such sectioning there will be no advantage unless that linker uses the organization for optimization. In fact, it could have a detrimental effect by making the object code larger and slower to load.

If the `-p` option is set for profiling, this option will have no effect. Also, because of the rearrangement of the code, you may have problems with the `-g` option and debugging.

-fdefault-inline

This is the default. Member functions that have their bodies defined at the point of declaration inside the class will be defined inline whether or not the `inline` keyword is used to declare them. To prevent automatic inlining specify `-fno-default-inline`. Also see `--param`.

-fdefer-pop

The arguments that were pushed onto the stack to make a function call are not popped off immediately after the return of the function, but are allowed to accumulate along with the arguments of several function calls, and the stack is later cleared of them all. This option is set by default, so to force the stack to be cleared after each function call, specify `-fno-defer-pop`.

-fdelete-null-pointer-checks

The code that checks for an attempt to dereference a null pointer is removed if dataflow analysis indicates that the pointer cannot be null. In some environments it is possible to process the result of an attempt to dereference a null pointer, so this option should not be used in programs that rely on these checks. This flag is set by `-O2`, `-O3`, and `-Os`, but can be overridden by `-fno-delete-null-pointer-checks`.

-fdelayed-branch

This flag only has effect on machines with delayed branch slots. This has to do with loading and executing instructions at the same time the decision is being made whether to take a branch. After the decision is made the result of the instruction may be discarded depending on the location of the instruction and the decision made. This flag is set by every level of optimization if the target machine supports it, but it can be overridden by `-fno-delayed-branch`. Also see `--param`.

-fdiagnostics-show-location=*where*

It is possible for a diagnostic (error or warning) message to be long and split so it is displayed on more than one line. The default setting of *where* is `once`, which causes the source file location causing the diagnostic message to be included only once. Specifying *where* as `every-line` will cause the inclusion of the source code location on every line of the diagnostic message.

This option may not be implemented in all cases, and it only applies when the setting (or default value) of `-fmessage-length` is some value other than zero.

APPENDIXES

-fdollar-ok
Allows dollar ($) characters in symbol names.

-fdollars-in-identifiers
Accepts the character $ as a valid character in an identifier. The option -fno-dollars-in-identifiers will explicitly prohibit their use. The default varies depending on the platform and language. Traditional C allowed them, but the modern standards prohibit them, so if you want to specify their use it would be best to do so explicitly.

-fdump-class-hierarchy[-*format*]
For each class, dump the hierarchy and virtual function table to a file with the same name as the class and the suffix .class. The optional *format* can be specified as one of the following:

- **address** The address of each node is printed and can be used to cross-reference tree node addresses with other dumps, such as those produced by -d.
- **slim** Reduce the size of the output by inhibiting the dumping of the bodies of functions or the members of scope.
- **all** Increase the size of the output by turning on all options.

-fdump-translation-unit[-*format*]
Dump the compiler's internal tree structure representing the source code to a file with the same name as the source file with the suffix .tu. The optional *format* can be specified as one of the following:

- **address** The address of each node is printed and can be used to cross-reference tree node addresses with other dumps, such as those produced by -d.
- **slim** Reduce the size of the output by inhibiting the dumping of the bodies of functions or the members of scope.
- **all** Increase the size of the output by turning on all options.

-fdump-tree-*switch*[-*format*]
Dumps various stages of the intermediate language tree to files. The file names are created from the source file name with the suffix named as the *switch* specified as part of the option. The *switch* must be specified as one of the following:

- **original** Dump the tree to *name*.original prior to any tree-base optimization.
- **optimized** Dump the tree to *name*.optimized following all tree-base optimization.
- **inlined** Dump the tree to *name*.inlined following function inlining.

The optional *format* can be specified as one of the following:

- **address** The address of each node is printed and can be used to cross-reference tree node addresses with other dumps, such as those produced by -d.
- **slim** Reduce the size of the output by inhibiting the dumping of the bodies of functions or the members of scope.
- **all** Increase the size of the output by turning on all options.

-fdump-unnumbered
When debugging the compiler with the -d option, this option will suppress instruction numbers and line numbers in the output files, which makes it easier to use diff to compare dumps.

-felide-constructors
C++

This is the default. The generated code that calls a function returning an object by value may be simplified by having the function construct the object directly in the specified return location instead of using a copy constructor to duplicate the one constructed inside the function. This could cause a problem if there are side effects in a constructor, and the default can be overridden with -fno-elide-constructors.

-femulate-complex
Fortran

Implement complex arithmetic by emulation instead of using the gcc back end that provides direct support for complex arithmetic.

This option was implemented as a work-around of bugs in the gcc complex arithmetic, which are now believed to be fixed.

-fencoding=*name*
Java

The name is the encoding name for a particular character set to be used to read source files. The default is supplied the current locale setting of the computer or, if no locale name is specified, the default is UTF-8.

-fenforce-eh-specs
C++

This is the default. GCC generates code to enforce runtime exception violations according to the C++ standard, but specifying -fno-enforce-eh-specs will suppress the generation of the code. The size of the code is reduced without the code to check the violations.

-fexceptions
Enables exception handling. This option generates the extra code necessary to process the throwing and catching of exceptions. If you do not specify this option, it will be specified automatically for languages such as Ada, Java, and C++ that normally throw exceptions.

There is no performance penalty with the generated code, but there is a size penalty so you may want to specify `-fno-exceptions` if you are compiling C++ code that does not use exceptions.

Also see `-fnon-call-exceptions`, `-funwind-tables`, and `-fasynchornous-unwind-tables`.

-fexpensive-optimizations

This flag enables a few optimizations that are effective but cost in terms of compile time. For example, common subexpression elimination is run again following global common subexpression elimination. Some of the other optimizations are carried out in more depth when this flag is set. This flag is set by `-O2`, `-O3`, and `-Os`, but can be overridden by `-fno-expensive-optimizations`.

-fexternal-templates   C++

This option is deprecated. Template instances may or may not be emitted depending on the location of the template definition. The instantiation obeys `#pragma interface` and `#pragma implementation`. Also see `-falt-external-templates`.

-ff2c   Fortran

This is the default, which is to generate code compatible with f2c.

Specifying `-fno-f2c` will suppress generating code compatible with f2c and use the GNU calling convention instead. This has no effect on code that interfaces with the `libf2c` library other than disallowing library intrinsics from libf2c to be passed as arguments.

The `-fno-f2c` option must be used consistently for all code that is to be linked into a single program.

-ff2c-intrinsics-*spec*   Fortran

The *spec* specifies the status of the f2c specific intrinsics that have inappropriate forms. The *spec* can be any one of the following:

- `enable` The f2c-specific intrinsics are recognized and enabled. This is the default.

- `hide` The f2c-specific intrinsics are recognized and enabled only if the first mention of the name of each one is in an INTRINSIC statement.

- `disable` The f2c-specific intrinsics are recognized, but references to them must be made through an INTRINSIC statement.

- `delete` The f2c-specific intrinsics are not recognized.

-ff66   Fortran

The source code being compiled is in the Fortran 66 dialect

Also see `-ff77` and `-ff90`.

-ff77

The source code being compiled is in the Fortran 77 dialect.

This also specifies that the dialect is the one expected by the f2c utility that converts Fortran source to C source.

Also see `-ff66` and `-ff90`.

-ff90

The compiler will recognize certain constructs of the Fortran 90 dialect.

More Fortran 90 constructs can be enabled by using the `-fvxt` and `-ff90-instrinsics-enable` options.

Also see `-ff66` and `-ff77`.

-ff90-intrinsics-*spec*

The *spec* specifies the status of the Fortran 90 intrinsics that have inappropriate forms. The *spec* can be any one of the following:

- `enable`   The Fortran 90 intrinsics are recognized and enabled. This is the default.

- `hide`   The Fortran 90 intrinsics are recognized and enabled only if the first mention of the name of each one is in an INTRINSIC statement.

- `disable`   The Fortran 90 intrinsics are recognized, but references to them must be made through an INTRINSIC statement.

- `delete`   The Forran 90 intrinsics are not recognized.

Also see `-ff90` and `-fvxt`.

-ffast-math

Certain mathematical calculations are made faster by violating some of the ISO and IEEE rules. For example, with this option set it is assumed that no negative values are passed to `sqrt()` and that all floating point values are valid.

Setting this option causes the preprocessor macro `__FAST_MATH__` to be defined and also sets `-fno-math-errno`, `-funsafe-math-optimizations`, and `-fno-trapping-math`. Setting `-fno-fast-math` will also set `-fmath-errno`.

-ffixed-*register*

Treat the named *register* as a fixed register that cannot be allocated for use by the compiler. It may still be used as a stack pointer, frame pointer, or some other fixed purpose.

The register names are platform dependent and are named in the REGISTER_NAMES macro of the machine description.

Also see `-fcall-used-*register*` and `-fcall-saved-*register*`.

-ffixed-form

This is the default. Specifies that the Fortran source code is in the traditional fixed form instead of the free-form format like that of Fortran 90.

Same as `-fno-free-form`.

-ffixed-line-length-*len*
Fortran

The *len* number specifies the column number after which all characters are ignored in the fixed form of source input.

Specifying either –ffixed-line-length-0 or –ffixed-line-length-none allows the input source line to be any length.

The value of *len* is traditionally 72 (leaving 8 spaces on an 80 column card for sequencing).

-ffloat-store

Do not allocate registers to hold floating point values. On some machines this option may cause the registers to extend the precision beyond that defined for the language, and thus will carry more precision than the floating point data stored in memory.

The default is –fno-float-store, which allows the use of registers.

This flag is only useful if your program must restrict its precision to exactly that defined by the IEEE standard.

-ffor-scope
C++

The default is to follow the standard. This setting determines the scope of variables declared in the initialization section of the for statement.

Specifying –ffor-scope limits the scope of the variables to the body of the loop.

Specifying –fno-for-scope limits the scope of the variables from the point at which it is declared to the closing of the scope containing the for statement itself. The following example is valid with this option:

L D-14

```
#include <stdio.h>
int main(int argc,char *argv[])
{
    for(int i=0; i<10; i++) {
        printf("Loop one %d\n",i);
    }
    printf("Out of loop %d\n",i);
    return(0);
}
```

-fforce-addr

Address must be copied into registers to have arithmetic performed on them. This improves the generated code because addresses needed will often have been previously loaded into a register and do not need to be loaded again. The default is –fno-force-addr. Also see –fforce-mem.

-fforce-classes-archive-check
Java

This option will force a check for the presence of an attribute in the class file java.lang.Object to make certain it was compiled by the GNU compiler.

The attribute has zero size and is named `gnu.gcj.gcj-compiled`. This attribute is checked except when the output from the compiler is to be bytecodes.

-fforce-mem
Values must be copied into registers to have arithmetic performed on them. This improves the generated code because values needed will often have been previously loaded into a register and do not need to be loaded again. This flag is set by -O2, -O3, and -Os; otherwise the default is `-fno-force-mem`. Also see `-fforce-addr`.

-ffortran-bounds-check
Causes the generation of checks that will be made at runtime to verify that array subscripts and CHARACTER substring accesses are within the declared minimum and maximum values.

The same as `-fbounds-check`.

-ffree-form
Specifies that the Fortran source code is in a free-form format like that of Fortran 90.

Same as `-fno-fixed-form`.

-ffreestanding
The compiled program is to run in a freestanding environment, which may not have the standard library, and execution may not begin with `main()`. This option sets `-fno-builtin`. This option is the same as `-fno-hosted`.

-ffunction-cse
This is the default. Function calls are made with the function address stored in a register. Using `-fno-function-cse` will cause each instruction making a call to implicitly include the address of the function. The default produces more efficient code. Also see `--param`.

-ffunction-sections
Each function is placed into its own named section in the assembly language output. The section name is derived from the function name. This only has an advantage on machines with a linker that can use sectioning to optimize allocation of space. For the same optimization with data, see `-fdata-sections`.

Setting this option for a machine that does not support sectioning in its assembler code will result in a warning message, and the option will be ignored. Even on machines that support such sectioning there will be no advantage unless that linker uses the organization for optimization. In fact, it could have a detrimental effect by making the object code larger and slower to load.

If the -p option is set for profiling, this option will have no effect. Also, because of the rearrangement of the code, you may have problems with the -g option and debugging.

Also see "Attributes" in Chapter 4.

-fgcse
Performs global common subexpression elimination optimization. This option could
be detrimental if there are computed gotos in the program. This flag is set by -O2, -O3,
and -Os; which can be overridden with -fno-gcse. Also see --param.

-fgcse-lm
Performs global common subexpression elmination optimization by detecting load and
store operations inside a loop, in which the load operation is in a form that can be moved
in front of the loop and thus only occur once. This is the default, but will have no effect
except when -Os is set. It can be overridden with -no-fgcse-lm.

-fgcse-sm
Performs global common subexpression elmination optimization by detecting load and
store operations inside a loop, in which the store operation is in a form that can be moved
after the loop and thus only occur once. This is the default, but will have no effect except
when -Os is set. It can be overridden with -no-fgcse-sm.

-fglobals   Fortran
This is the default. Specifying -fno-globals disables the diagnosis of such global
conflicts as the same procedure name being called with different argument types. This
option also disables inlining to prevent crashes from incorrect code generation.

-fgnu-intrinsics-*spec*   Fortran
The *spec* specifies the status of the GNU intrinsics that have inappropriate forms.
The *spec* can be any one of the following:

- enable   The GNU intrinsics are recognized and enabled. This is the default.
- hide   The GNU intrinsics are recognized and enabled only if the first mention
  of the name of each one is in an INTRINSIC statement.
- disable   The GNU intrinsics are recognized, but references to them must be
  made through an INTRINSIC statement.
- delete   The GNU intrinsics are not recognized.

-fgnu-keywords
This is the default. The option -fno-gnu-keywords disables the typeof keyword.
Also see --ansi.

-fgnu-linker
This is the default. If you specify -fno-gnu-linker it means that the GNU linker is
not to be used, so code to perform certain global initialization (such as constructors and
destructors) is not generated. Without the GNU linker it is necessary that the collect2
utility be used to make certain the linker that is used will include constructors and
destructors.
     On systems that require it, gcc is configured to automatically invoke collect2.

-fgnu-runtime

This is the default for most systems. This option instructs the compiler to generate code using the standard GNU Objective C runtime.

-fguess-branch-probability

This is the default. GCC will guess whether a branch is to be taken more often than it is not, and will optimize the code accordingly.

A randomized model is used to make some of the guesses, so compiling the same source could possibly generate different code. To disable this option and force the same code to be generated with every compilation, specify `-fno-guess-branch-probability`. For other options to prevent the randomness and have the same code generated every time, see `-fbranch-probabilities` and `-fprofile_arcs`.

-fhash-synchronization

This option will cause the location of `synchronize`, `wait`, and `notify` to be stored in a hash table instead of inside each object.

-fhosted

The compiled program is to run in a hosted environment, which has the entire standard library available, and `main()` has a return type of `int`. This option sets `-fbuiltin`. This option is the same as `-fno-freestanding`.

-fident

This is the default. If `-fno-ident` is specified, the preprocessor will ignore the `#ident` directive.

-fimplement-inlines

This is the default. Functions that are generated as inline code also have function bodies generated for them where they are defined. The option `-fno-implement-inlines` will suppress the generation of the function bodies for inline functions controlled by `#pragma implementation`. If no function body is generated, every call to it must be generated as inline code.

-fimplicit-templates

This is the default. Reference to a template, or the function of a template, that does not already exist will cause an instantiation of the template. The option `-fno-implicit-templates` will suppress the implicit instantiation of templates *except* those that are compiled inline. Also see `-fimplicit-inline-templates`.

-fimplicit-inline-templates

This is the default. Reference to a template, or the function of a template, that does not already exist will cause an instantiation of the template. The option `-fno-implicit-templates` will suppress the implicit instantiation of templates *including* those that are compiled inline. Also see `-fimplicit-templates`.

-finhibit-size-directive

Do not output a `.size` assembler directive, nor any other directive that could cause problems if the function is split and the two halves are separated in memory.

This option is a special case used to compile `crtstuff.c` (part of GCC) and is not expected to have any other purpose.

-finit-local-zero `Fortran`

All variables declared local to the compilation unit are initialized to zero. This has no effect on common blocks and variables passed as arguments.

It may be advisable to also specify `-fno-automatic` to prevent the runtime penalty of initializing automatic variables.

-finit-priority

This option is for internal use by the compiler and is used to specify runtime initialization order.

-finline `C    C++    ObjC    Fortran`

This is the default, which allows the `inline` keyword to specify that a function be expanded inline at the place the function is called. Using the `-fno-inline` option will cause the compiler to ignore the `inline` keyword. Note: no inline expansion is done unless some level of optimization has been set with the `-O` option. Also see `--param` and the "Attributes" section of Chapter 4.

-finline-functions

The compiler is allowed to select certain simple functions to be expanded in line at the point of the function call. If the function is declared in such a way that all calls to it are known (for example, a static function in a C source file cannot be addressed from outside the file) the body of the function is omitted because it is never actually called. This option is automatically turned on by `-O3` unless the `-fno-inline-functions` flag is specified. Also see `-fkeep-inline-functions`. Also see `--param` and the "Attributes" section of Chapter 4.

-finline-limit=*size*

The compiler will not expand functions inline that require more than the specified number of pseudo instructions. The default value for *size* is 600. Also see `--param`.

-finstrument-functions

Insert code that will call a function at the entry and exit point of each function. The prototypes of the function calls are as follow:

```
void __cyg_profile_func_enter(void *this_fn,void *call_site);
void __cyg_profile_func_exit(void *this_fn,void *call_site);
```

The `this_fn` argument is the address of the function being called, which can be identified by symbol table information. The `call_site` argument identifies the caller. (On some platforms the `call_site` information is not available.)

If a function is expanded inline, the function calls are inserted before and after the inline code. For purposes of identification there must be a non-inline version of the function available, even if all the calls to it generate inline code.

To prevent a function from having the code inserted, it can be declared with the attribute `no_instrument_function`. This may be necessary for interrupt handlers and functions from which the profiling routines cannot be called.

Also see the "Attributes" section of Chapter 4.

-fintrin-case-*spec*

Fortran

The *spec* determines the case of intrinsic names. It may be any of the following:

- `initcap` The first letter of the name is capitalized and the others are all lower case.
- `upper` The name is all upper case.
- `lower` The name is all lower case. This is the default.
- `any` The name can be in any mixture of upper and lower case letters.

Also see `-fmatch-case-`, `-fsource-case-`, `-fsymbol-case-`, and `-fcase-`.

-fjni

Java

This option compiles native methods into JNI instead of the default CNI. Stubs are also generated to invoke the underlying JNI methods.

-fkeep-inline-functions

The compiler will generate a body for a function even if all of the references to it are expanded inline and there are actually no calls to it. The default is `-fno-keep-inline-functions`, which does not create bodies for functions that are not called. Also see `-finline-functions` and `--param`.

-fkeep-static-consts

This is the default unless some level of optimization is set. Constant values that are private to the compilation unit are allocated storage even if they are not referenced. To prevent allocating space for unused constants, use `-fno-keep-static-consts`.

-fleading-underscore

This option forces each symbol written to the object file to be modified to begin with an underscore character. The option `-fno-leading-underscore` will suppress the addition of an underscore character.

This option is available for use when attempting to link with legacy assembly code.

-fmatch-case-*spec*

The *spec* determines the case of Fortran keywords. It may be any of the following:

- `initcap`   The first letter of the name is capitalized and the others are all lower case.
- `upper`   The name is all upper case.
- `lower`   The name is all lower case. This is the default.
- `any`   The name can be in any mixture of upper and lower case letters.

Also see `-fintrin-case-`, `-fsource-case-`, `-fsymbol-case-`, and `-fcase-`.

-fmath-errno

This is the default. An error code resulting from such math functions as `sqrt()` will be stored in the global variable named `errno`. Setting `-fno-math-errno` will cause no `errno` value to be stored, which can interfere with standard IEEE exception handling. See also `-ffast-math`.

-fmem-report

When the compiler finishes, it prints a detailed listing of the amount of storage that has been allocated for each data type and other permanent memory allocation information.

-fmemoize-lookups

C++

The result of the latest internal symbol table lookups are cached to speed subsequent lookups.

-fmerge-all-constants

This option sets `-fmerge-constants` and adds the merging duplicate character strings and arrays. Standard C and C++ require that each variable have a distinct location, so this option may create non-conforming object code.

-fmerge-constants

An attempt is made for all constant values, except strings, to be merged into a single copy across compilation units. This is the default when any level of optimization is turned on. The default is `-fno-merge-constants`, which will allow for the merging of constant values only within a compilation unit.

-fmessage-length=*size*

Error messages are formatted so they are no longer than *size* characters. If size is 0, no line formatting is done and each error message will appear on a single line. The default size is 72 for C++ and 0 for all other languages. This option may not be implemented in all cases.

-fmil-intrinsics-*spec*
`Fortran`

The *spec* specifies the status of the MIL-STD-1753 intrinsics that have inappropriate forms. The *spec* can be any one of the following:

- `enable`   The MIL-STD-1753 intrinsics are recognized and enabled. This is the default.
- `hide`   The MIL-STD-1753 intrinsics are recognized and enabled only if the first mention of the name of each one is in an INTRINSIC statement.
- `disable`   The MIL-STD-1753 intrinsics are recognized, but references to them must be made through an INTRINSIC statement.
- `delete`   The MIL-STD-1753 intrinsics are not recognized.

-fmove-all-movables

All invariant expressions are moved outside the loop. Whether this produces better or worse code depends on the structure of the loops in the source code. The default is `-fno-move-all-movables` except for Fortran. Also see `-freduce-all-givs`.

-fms-extensions
`C++`

Disables warning messages when using constructs defined in MFC, such as implicit int definition in data declarations and acquiring a pointer to a member function using non-standard syntax. The default is `-fno-ms-extensions`, which enables the warnings.

-fnext-runtime

Generates output compatible with NeXT runtime. The is the default for NeXT based systems such as Darwin and Mac OS X.

-fno-*

Any option beginning with *-fno-* has two forms and is listed alphabetically under the name that does not have the *no-* preceding it. For example, you will find a description of `-fno-for-scope` listed under `-ffor-scope`. Most, but not all, options preceded by *-f* have a companion *-fno* form.

-fnon-call-exceptions

Generate code that makes it possible for trapping instructions (such as invalid floating point operations or invalid memory addressing) to throw exceptions. This option is not universally available because it requires platform-specific runtime support.

This is limited to hardware trap signals only and does not include general signals such as SIGALRM or SIGTERM.

Also see `-fexceptions`, `-funwind-tables`, and `-fasynchronous-unwind-tables`.

-fnonansi-builtins
`C++`

This is the default. Specifying `-fno-nonansi-builtins` will disable the automatic generation of built-in functions that are not specifically required by ANSI/ISO C. Also see `-ansi`, `-fbuiltin.`, and `-fnonansi-builtins`.

-fomit-frame-pointer

Don't store the frame pointer in a register for functions that don't need one, thus omitting the code to store and retrieve the address as well as making another register available for general use. This flag is automatically set for all levels of -O optimization, but only if the debugger can be run without a frame pointer. If the debugger cannot be run with this setting you will have to set it explicitly. Some platforms have no frame pointer and this flag will have no effect. The default is -fno-omit-frame-pointer.

-fonetrip   Fortran

A DO loop is to be executed at least once (the test is made at the bottom of the loop instead of the top).

Prior to Fortran 77 some compilers performed the test at the bottom of the loop and some at the top. Beginning with Fortran 77 the test is made at the top of the loop, which means that if the test is false from the beginning, the loop will never execute.

-foperator-names

This is the default. Specifying -fno-operator-names will prevent the keywords and, bitand, bitor, compl, not, or, and xor from being recognized by the compiler as alternate operators for &&, &, |, ~, !, ||, and ^ respectively. This will prevent breaking old code by making the names available to be used for other purposes.

-foptimize-register-move

Register allocation is optimized by changing the assignment of registers used in operations that move data from one memory location to another. This is especially effective on machines that have instructions that can move data directly from one memory location to another. This flag is set by -O2, -O3, and -Os, but can be overridden by -fno-optimize-register-move.

-foptimize-sibling-calls

Optimizes recursive tail calls and sibling calls. This flag is automatically set by -O2, -O3, and -Os. The default is -fno-optimize-sibling-calls.

The following is an example of a recursive tail call:

L D-16

```
int rewhim(int x,int y) {
    . . .
    return(rewhim(x+1,y));
}
```

Optimization can be performed by, instead of making a new function call, inserting a command that jumps to the top of the function. A similar situation is shown in the following example of a sibling call:

```
int whim(int x,int y) {
    . . .
    return(wham(x+1,y));
}
```

In a sibling call, the call to the function whim() must be made, but the stack frame of whim() can be deleted by the call, causing wham() to return its value directly to the caller of whim().

-foptimize-static-class-initialization `Java`
This is the default. When optimization is set to -O2, -O3, or -Os and the output is object code instead of bytecodes, static classes are initialized on their first use. This optimization can be turned off by specifying -fno-optimize-static-class-initialization.

-foptional-diags `C++`
This is the default. Specifying -fno-optional-diags will suppress diagnostic messages that, according to the C++ standard, a compiler is not required to issue.

--for-assembler *optionlist* `Asm`
Same as -Wa.

--for-linker *option* `Linker`
Same as -Xlinker.

--force-link *name* `Linker`
Same as -u.

-foutput-class-dir=*directory* `Java`
When used with the -C option, the class files output from the compiler are stored in *directory* (or the appropriate subdirectory of *directory*) instead of using the current directory as the base.

This option can be written --output-class-directory.

-fpack-struct
Pack the members of structures together in such a way that no alignment space is inserted between the members of the structure.

This could cause the executable code accessing structure members to be less efficient, and it could also cause the code to be incompatible with the system libraries.

For Fortran, the -fpack-struct option must not be used.

Also see "Attributes" in Chapter 4.

-fpedantic `Fortran`
Same as -pedantic for Fortran.

-fpeephole
This is the default, but it can be turned off with -fno-peephole. Enables peephole optimization at the time the assembly language is output. It looks for matches on sets of instructions and replaces them with an optimized set. This flag has no effect unless optimization is also specified. This option is platform dependent and may have no effect.

-fpeephole2
Enables RTL peephole optimization after registers have been allocated but before scheduling. The optimization is a machine specific translation of one specific set of instructions into another. This option is platform dependent and may have no effect. There is no effect unless optimization is also specified. This flag is set by -O2, -O3, and -Os, but can be overridden by -fno-peephole2.

-fpermissive

Diagnostic messages specifying that code does not conform to the standard are issued as warnings instead of errors. If nether -fpermissive nor -pedantic is specified, the -fpedantic-errors option is assumed.

-fpic
Generate position independent code (PIC) that can be used in a shared library. All internal addressing is done through a global offset table (GOT). To determine an address, the memory location of the code itself is added to an entry in the table. This option requires operating system support, so it is not available on all systems.

   This option produces object modules that can be stored in and loaded from shared libraries.

   If the -fpic option produces an error message from the linker that position independent code does not work, recompile using -fPIC instead.

   Some systems have a size limit for the offset table. The limit is 16k on the Motorola m88k, 32k on the m68k and RS/6000, and 8k on the Sparc. Position independent code requires support, so it only exists on certain machines.

   See also -fPIC and -shared.

-fPIC
This option is the same as the -fpic option, with the added benefit that it can be used to overcome the table size limitations of position independent code that can possibly be encountered on the m68k, m88k, and Sparc.

   See also -fpic and -shared.

-fppc-struct-return
Generate code to return all structures by storing them in memory even if they are small enough to fit in a register. The precise convention for returning structures in memory or in registers depends on the platform.

   While producing less efficient code, this option may be needed when linking to object files created using another compiler.

In Fortran, this option should only be used if it was used to compile the version of `libg2c` that this program will be linked with.

Also see `-freg-struct-return`.

-fprefetch-loop-arrays

If it is supported by the platform, instructions are generated to prefetch arrays to improve loop performance.

-fpreprocessed

No preprocessing will take place even if files on the command line have suffixes that would indicate that the files should be preprocessed. The suffixes are listed in Table D-1.

Even with this option specified, the `-C` option can still be used to have the preprocessor remove comments.

-fpretend-float

When cross compiling object for another system, this flag will format floating point operations as if they were going to be performed on the local machine. The result is likely to be in a form that will not run on the target machine, but the sequence of instructions is likely to be the same as it will be when producing code for the target machine.

-fprofile-arcs

After using this option to compile a program and then running it to create the file containing execution counts for each block of code, the program can be compiled again with the `-fbranch-probabilities` option, and the information from the file is used to optimize the code for the branches that are taken most often. Without this information, GCC will guess which path is taken most often to perform optimization. The information is stored in a file with the name as the source and a `.da` suffix.

A second use of this option is to use it in conjunction with the `-ftest-coverage` option to support `gcov`. This option combination creates a flow graph for each function in the program, then determines a spanning tree for the graph. Code is then inserted into each function not in the spanning tree that will generate a count of the number of times it is executed. For each block with a single entry and exit, the code is added directly to the block. Blocks with multiple entries or exits cause the creation of a new block that tracks each entry and exit.

A program compiled with these options and run with gcov will run a bit slower than a program compiled with `-a` and `-ax`, but the counts produced by the `-a` option don't provide enough information to estimate all branch possibilities.

Also see `-a`, `-ax`, `-fbranch-probabilities`, and `-fguess-branch-probability`.

-freduce-all-givs

Forces all general induction variables (loop counters) to be strength reduced. Whether this produces better or worse code depends on the structure of the loops in the source code. The default is `-fno-reduce-all-givs` except for Fortran.

Also see `-fmove-all-movables`.

-freg-struct-return
Generate code to return short structures by storing them in registers. If they are not small enough to fit in a register, they are returned in memory. The precise convention for returning structures in memory or in registers depends on the platform.

In Fortran, this option should only be used if it was used to compile the version of libg2c that this program will be linked with.

Also see -fpcc-struct-return.

-fregmove
Same as -foptimize-register-move.

-frename-registers
This is an optimization technique that attempts to eliminate false dependencies in scheduled code by making use of registers left over after register allocation and scheduling has been completed. This optimization is mostly advantageous for machines with a large number of registers. The code generated by this option can be very difficult to debug. This flag is set by -O3 but can be overridden by -fno-rename-registers.

-frepo
Enables automatic template instantiation. Setting this option also sets -fno-implicit-templates, which suppresses automatic instantiation of non-inline templates.

-frerun-cse-after-loop
This option will cause the common subexpression optimization to be applied again following loop optimizations. This is done because it is possible that loop optimization creates the presence of new subexpressions. This flag is set by -O2, -O3, and -Os, but can be overridden by -fno-rerun-cse-after-loop. Also see --param.

-frerun-loop-opt
Run the loop optimization twice. The second time does not unroll loops, but it does analyze the loops again with the instructions from the first optimization pass removed. This flag is set by -O2, -O3, and -Os, but can be overridden by -fno-rerun-loop-opt.

-frtti

This is the default. Code is generated for run time identification of every class containing virtual methods. If you use neither dynamic_cast nor typeid, you can save some space in each class by using -fno-rtti to supress the code generation. This flag has no effect on exception handling which generates rtti code as necessary.

-fschedule-insns
On machines that have relatively slow floating point or memory access operations when compared to other operations, and on machines that support the execution of more than one instruction at a time, an attempt is made to change the order of the instructions to

eliminate stalling. Other instructions are executed during the time the slower instruction is being executed. This flag is set by -O2, -O3, and -Os, but can be overridden by -fno-scedule-insns.

-fschedule-insns2

This is the same as -fschedule_insns except that it is performed after allocation of both the global registers and the local registers for each function. This can be effective on machines with a small number of registers and relatively slow instructions to load registers. This flag is set by -O2, -O3, and -Os, but can be overridden by -fno-scedule-insns2.

-fshared-data

This option requests that the data be shared rather than private. This only has meanings on operating systems where shared data is accessible among separate processes running the same program, and each process has its own copy of private data.

-fshort-double

Use the same size for the double data type that is used for float.
   For Fortran, this option may cause problems.

-fshort-enums

Reduce the size of an enum to the smallest integer type required to store the range of values.

-fshort-wchar

Changes the data type of wchar_t to be unsigned short int instead of the default for the current target.

-fsigned-char

With this option the char data type defaults to signed (a value from 0 to 255). If no flag is used to specify whether char data types should be signed or unsigned, the default will vary depending on the platform. Specifying -fno-signed-char is the same as -funsigned-char.

-fsigned-bitfields

This is the default. Bit fields are treated as signed int data types, but specifying -fno-signed-bitfields will cause them to be treated as unsigned int types. Specifying -traditional forces all bit fields to be unsigned. Specifying -fno-signed-bitfields is the same as -funsigned-bitfields.

-fsilent

This is the default. Specifying -fno-silent lists to stderr the name of each program unit as it is being compiled.

-fsingle-precision-constant
Constant declarations of floating point numbers are stored as single precision floating point numbers instead of doubles.

-fsource-case-*spec*

The *spec* determines whether the source text is to be translated to all upper case, lower case, or left unchanged. Holerith constants are not affected. The *spec* may be any of the following:

- upper   The source is translated to all upper case.
- lower   The source is translated to all lower case. This is the default.
- preserve   The source text is left unchanged.

Also see -fintrin-case-, -fmatch-case-, -fsymbol-case-, and -fcase-.

-fssa
Experimental feature. The entire body of a function is converted to a SSA (Static Single Assignment) flow graph, optimizations are performed, and then the code is converted out of an SSA graph to the original format.

-fssa-ccp
Experimental feature. Enables SSA conditional code propagation in which variables that are actually used as constants are converted to constants and also eliminates branches which can never be taken. This option requires -fssa and any level of -O.

-fssa-dce
Experimental feature. Enables SSA dead code elimination which removes any code that cannot be executed. This option requires -fssa and any level of -O.

-fstack-check
Generate code that will perform the test necessary to prevent the program from overflowing the stack. The generated code does not actually do the checking, but the code is generated to make certain the operating system detects it when the stack is extended.

This may be necessary when running a program in a multi-threaded environment, but stack overflow is automatically checked in a single-threaded program.

-fstack-limit-register=*register*
Specify the name of the register that contains the address limiting the size of the stack. This option can only be used to reduce the stack; it cannot be used to expand it beyond the size specified by the operating system.

Also see -fstack-limit-symbol.

-fstack-limit-symbol=*symbol*
Specify the name of the variable that contains the address limiting the size of the stack. This option can only be used to reduce the stack; it cannot be used to expand it beyond the size specified by the operating system.

The values used for the address depend on the platform. For example, if the stack begins with the address 0x80000000 and grows by decreasing the address, a stack limit of 128k can be imposed with the following option settings:

```
-fstack-limit-symbol=__stack_limit -Wl,__stack_limit=0x7FFE0000
```

It is also possible to declare the stack limit variable inside the program, but it would still be necessary to specify the -fstack-limit-symbol option on the command line.
Also see -fstack-limit-register.

-fstats

Displays statistical information about front-end processing. This information pertains to compiler internals and has no effect on its output.

-fstore-check

This is the default. Specifying -fno-store-check removes the run time checks made to ensure the correct object type is being stored in an array.

-fstrength-reduce

Performs loop strength reduction and elimination variables being used inside loops. This is the process of replacing time-consuming operations, such as multiply and divide, with simpler and faster operations, such as add and subtract. This option is always set by -funroll_loops and -funroll-all-loops. It is also set by -O2, -O3, and -Os but can be overridden by -fno-strength-reduce.

As a simple example, the following loop uses a temporary variable to contain a calculated index:

```
for(int i=0; i<10; i++) {
    index = i * 2;
    frammis(valarr[index]);
}
```

The internal variable index can be eliminated, and the multiplication can be changed to a simple shift resulting in the following:

```
for(int i=0; i<10; i++) {
    frammis(valarr[i << 1]);
}
```

Shifting the loop counter one position to the left effectively doubles it, and the value is then used directly as the index on the array without being stored in a temporary variable.

-fstrict-aliasing

The strictest aliasing rules are applied depending on the language being compiled. With strict aliasing in C, for example, an `int` cannot be the alias of a `double` or a pointer, but it can be the alias of an `unsigned int`. Even with strict aliasing there is not a problem with union members as long as the references are through the union and not through a pointer to the address of a union member. The following code could cause a problem:

L D-21

```
int *iptr;
union {
    int ivalue;
    double dvalue;
} migs;
  .  .  .
    migs.ivalue = 45;
    iptr = &migs.ivalue;
    frammis(*iptr);
    migs.dvalue = 88.6;
    frammis(*iptr);
```

In this example is possible that strict aliasing would not recognize that the value pointed to by `iptr` had changed between the two function calls. However, referring to the union members directly would not cause a problem.

-fsymbol-case-*spec* `Fortran`

The *spec* determines the case of user defined symbols. It may be any of the following:

- `initcap` The first letter of the name is capitalized and the others are all lower case.
- `upper` The name is all upper case.
- `lower` The name is all lower case.
- `any` The name can be in any mixture of upper and lower case letters. This is the default.

Also see `-fmatch-case-`, `-fsource-case-`, `-fintrin-case-`, and `-fcase-`.

-fsyntax `Fortran`

Check the source code for syntax and proceed no further.

-ftemplate-depth-*number*

Sets the maximum template instantiation depth to *number* to detect recursive or circular template definitions. Programs adhering to the standard must not use a depth greater than 17. The default depth is 500.

-ftest-coverage

The compiler will produce files that contain information used by gcov. The output files bear the same name as the source file, but with different suffixes to indicate their contents.

A file with the suffix .bb contains the mappings from basic blocks of executable code to line numbers in the source file. This information is used by gcov to relate execution counts to line numbers.

A file with the suffix .bbg contains a list of all arcs in the program's flow graph. This information is used by gcov to reconstruct the flow graph and compute the execution counts from the data in a file with the suffix .da produced by setting the -fprofile-arcs option.

Also see -a, -ax, -ftest-coverage, and -fprofile-arcs.

-fthread-jumps

If the value of the conditional expression of a jump goes to a location where the values are such that another jump will also be taken, the original jump is redirected to the final destination. This option is set for all optimization levels, but can be overridden with -fno-thread-jumps.

-ftime-report

When the compilation is complete, the compiler will print statistics about the time spent in compilation. Times are printed for user, system, and the wall clock for each pass and summed at the end.

-ftrapping-math

This is the default. Setting the option -fno-trapping-math causes the code to assume that floating point operations will not cause exceptions that could be trapped and to issue signals. The -fno-trapping-math option may cause code to be generated that violates standards rules for floating point operations.

-ftrapv

Generate code to trap overflow conditions on signed addition, subtraction, and multiplication. This option can be used during software testing to create a core file whenever an integer overflow condition occurs, which normally goes undetected. The default is -fno-trapv.

-ftypeless-boz

Fortran

Specifies that prefix-radix non-decimal constants such as Z'ABCD' are typeless instead of defaulting to INTEGER(KIND=1).

-fugly-args

Fortran

This is the default. Specifying -fno-ugly-args will disallow the passing of typeless Hollerith constants as arguments in a function call. For example, the two following function calls are valid by default:

```
CALL FRED(4HABCX)
CALL SAM('123'O)
```

-fugly-assign `Fortran`

Use the same storage to contain assigned labels and numeric data. For example, the two following statements would use the same storage location:

L D-23

```
I = 3
ASSIGN 10 TO I
```

This option will be necessary if the program attempts to access the assigned value as data because the compiler default is to create separate storage locations for the two different types of information.

-fugly-assumed `Fortran`

An array with a specified size of 1 is assumed to have been declared as a size of *. For example, DIMENSION X(1) will be treated as if it had been written DIMENSION X(*).

-fugly-comma `Fortran`

A trailing comma implies that a null argument is to be added to the list of those passed to the subroutine. For example, with this option set, CALL BLOG() will pass a single null argument and CALL RIM(,) will pass two null arguments.

Without this option the trailing comma is ignored and causes no null argument to be passed, even in the presence of other arguments in the list.

-fugly-complex `Fortran`

Allows any kind of complex expression to be used with the intrinsics REAL(expr) and AIMAG(expr). The default is to limit the complex expression to COMPLEX(KIND=1).

With the -ff90 option set, these intrinsics return the unconverted real and imaginary parts of their arguments.

-fugly-init `Fortran`

This is the default. Specifying -fno-ugly-init disallows the use of Hollerith formatted data in PARAMETER and DATA statements. It also disallows the use of character constants to initialze numeric data types, and vice versa.

-fugly-logint `Fortran`

Automatic conversion between INTEGER and LOGICAL data types is enabled in most circumstances, enough so the two can be used interchangeably.

-funderscoring `Fortran`

This is the default. Two underscores are appended to names with an underscore. One underscore is appended to external names with no underscore. Two underscores are also appended to internal names with underscores to avoid naming collisions with external names.

Specifying -fno-underscoring will prohibit the transformation of names by appending underscore characters to them. Specifying -fno-second-underscoring instead will prevent only the appending of the second underscore character.

The use of these underscore control options is not recommended unless you are making adjustments to try to make the output compatible with code produced by another compiler. Among other problems, omitting the underscoring can cause a name conflict with a system library.

-fuse-boehm-gc   Java
Enables use of the Boehm garbage collection bitmap marking code.

-fsecond-underscore   Fortran
This is the default. See -funderscoring.

-funix-intrinsics-*spec*   Fortran
The *spec* specifies the status of the UNIX intrinsics. The *spec* can be any one of the following:

- enable   The UNIX intrinsics are recognized and enabled. This is the default.

- hide   The UNIX intrinsics are recognized and enabled only if the first mention of the name of each one is in an INTRINSIC statement.

- disable   The UNIX intrinsics are recognized, but references to them must be made through an INTRINSIC statement.

- delete   The UNIX intrinsics are not recognized.

-funroll-all-loops
This option sets -funroll-loops and removes the limit on the size of the loop to be unrolled, and will unroll the loop even if the number of iterations cannot be determined. This flag will normally produce slower and bigger code than would otherwise be produced.

To unroll a loop where the number of iterations cannot be determined exactly, the loop is unrolled a number of times with a test for an exit at the end of each of the blocks of code. This creates a larger loop that contains multiple copies of itself, so it will not iterate as often as it would have otherwise.

-funroll-loops
If it can be determined at compile time that the number of iterations is small enough, and if the number of instructions inside the loop is small enough, the loop is unrolled by removing the loop and duplicating the instructions so they will be executed the correct number of times. A loop is determined to be small enough if the number of insns in the loop multiplied by the number of iterations is less than a constant (currently set to 100). This option always sets both -fstrength-reduce and -frerun-cse-after-loop.

-funsafe-math-optimizations
Removes checking for floating point operations and assumes that values are valid. It allows math operations to violate IEEE and ANSI standards. This option may also cause the linker to include code that optimizes the operation of the hardware FPU (Floating Point Unit) in non-standard ways.

-funsigned-bitfields
Specifying this option will cause bit fields to be treated as unsigned int data types. By default, bit fields are treated as signed int data types. Specifying -traditional also forces all bit fields to be unsigned. Specifying -fno-unsigned-bitfields is the same as -fsigned-bitfields.

-funsigned-char
With this option the char data type defaults to unsigned (a value from -127 to +128). If no flag is used to specify whether char data types should be signed or unsigned, the default will vary depending on the platform. Specifying -fno-unsigned-char is the same as -fsigned-char.

-funwind-tables
This option is similar to -fexceptions, except only the necessary static data is generated and has no other effect on the generated code. This flag is intended for internal use and should not be specified on the command line.

Also see -fexceptions, -fnon-call-exceptions, and -fasynchornous-unwind-tables.

-fuse-cxa-atexit
Causes global destructors to be run in the reverse order that the constructors completed instead of the reverse order that the constructors started. The order will differ only if one global constructor is invoked from inside another. This option will work only if the cxa_exit() function is part of the C runtime library. Without this option the atexit() function is used.

-fuse-divide-subroutine
A library routine is called to perform integer division, which makes it possible to have exceptions thrown for integer division by zero.

-fverbose-asm
Inserts more verbose comments than normal into the generated assembly language to make it more readable.

This option is primarily for debugging the compiler itself by making the assembly code easier to read. The default, -fno-verbose-asm, is more useful when comparing assembly listings.

-fversion
Fortran

Runs internal tests to verify GNU Fortran is installed correctly, and then displays the version number. This option is set by both `-v` and `--verbose`.

-fvolatile

Treat all memory referenced through pointers as volatile.

Also see `-fvolatile-global` and `-fvolatile-static`.

-fvolatile-global

Treat all external and global memory references to contain volatile data. This switch does not cause static data items (data accessible only within the compilation unit) to be considered volatile.

Also see `-fvolatile` and `-fvolatile-static`.

-fvolatile-static

Treat all memory references to static data items (data accessible anywhere within the compilation unit) to be volatile.

Also see `-fvolatile-global` and `-fvolatile`.

-fvtable-gc
C++

Causes the creation of relocation information, making it possible for a linker to eliminate vtable entries for unused virtual functions. This option requires the use of both the GNU assembler and linker.

This information can also be used in the removal of unused functions. See `-ffunction-sections` and `-Wl`.

-fvxt
Fortran

Certain source code constructs can vary in meaning between GNU Fortran and VXT Fortran. Specifying this option will cause those constructs to be interpreted as VXT Fortran.

Also see `-ff90`, `-ffvxt-intrinsics-`, and `-ff90-intrinsics-`.

-fvxt-intrinsics-*spec*
Fortran

The *spec* specifies the status of the VXT intrinsics. The *spec* can be any one of the following:

- `enable`   The VXT intrinsics are recognized and enabled. This is the default.
- `hide`   The VXT intrinsics are recognized and enabled only if the first mention of the name of each one is in an INTRINSIC statement.
- `disable`   The VXT intrinsics are recognized, but references to them must be made through an INTRINSIC statement.
- `delete`   The VXT intrinsics are not recognized.

Also see `-fvxt`.

APPENDIXES

-fweak   C++
This is the default. Specifying -fno-weak will prevent the use of weak symbol support even if it is supported by the linker. The -fno-weak option should not be used, as it produces inferior code that has no benefit beyond testing the compiler.

-fwritable-strings   C   C++
The compiler allows data to be written into string constants. This flag is set by the -traditional option.

To have the ability to actually write into C++ string constants, you will also need to specify -fno-const-strings.

-fzeros   Fortran
Treat an initial value of zero the same as any other value. Without this option it is possible to have multiple DATA statements set the initial value of a variable to zero, and the fact will be undiagnosed by the compiler.

-g[*level*]
The output includes debugging information in a form that can be used by gdb. The format and content depends on the object format produced by the compiler (stabs, COFF, XCOFF, or DWARF).

The *level* setting is optional. The *level* number specifies the amount of debugging information to be included. The default is level 2. Level 1 produces the global information required for backtraces, but does not include local variables nor line numbers. Level 2 includes all of the level 1 information plus local variables and line numbers. Level 3 includes the level 2 information along with extra information such as macro definitions.

On a system that uses the stabs format, this option will produce debugging information in a form that can be used only by gdb.

It is possible to use this option in combination with -O to produce optimized code. With optimization the debugging procedure may not be as easy to follow as it would have been otherwise because optimization makes changes to the generated code, and there is no longer a one-to-one correspondence between the source and the object it produced. Some object code will be relocated, and some source may appear to have not produced any executable code at all.

Also see -ggdb, -gstabs, -gcoff, -gxcoff, and -gdwarf. This option can be written --debug.

-gcoff[*level*]
Produce debugging information in COFF format if it is supported. This format is used most often by SDB on System V prior to SVR4. The *level* setting is optional. See -g for a description of *level* settings 1, 2, and 3.

-gdwarf[*level*]
If supported, produce debugging information in DWARF version 1 format. The *level* setting is optional. Only if *level* is set to + will gdb extensions be included, which may disable the use of other debuggers. See -g for a description of *level* settings 1, 2, and 3.

This is the format used by SDB on most SVR4 systems.

-gdwarf-2[*level*]
If supported, produce debugging information in DWARF version 2 format. The *level* setting is optional. See –g for a description of *level* settings 1, 2, and 3.
This is the format used by DBX on IRIX 6.

-gen-decls   `ObjC`
Interface declarations for a class in the input source files are written to a file named w.decl.

-ggdb[*level*]
Produce detailed debugging information specifically formatted for gdb, including any available gdb extensions. The *level* setting is optional. See –g for a description of *level* settings 1, 2, and 3.

-gnat*option*   `Ada`
Specifies an option to be provided to GNAT, the Ada front end. All of the options are single letters that are appended to the option word gnat. For example, to specify the options e and l, you could specify them this way on the command line:

```
$ gcc -gnate -gnatl
```

The two options can be combined into one. The following is the same as the previous:

```
$ gcc -gnatel
```

Some of the options require values to be supplied with them. For example, the k option is used to specify the maximum number of error message output from the compiler, and the following command specifies the value as 15:

```
$ gcc -gnatk15
```

An option that requires a value can be combined with the other options if it is placed last in the list. The following examples shows a combined specification of e, l, and k:

```
$ gcc -gnatelk15
```

The following options, specified as numbers without preceding letters, enforce the restrictions defined for Ada 83 or Ada 95:

```
$ gcc -gnat83
$ gcc -gnat95
```

The default is –gnat95. Table D-3 contains a list of the available option letters used with the –gnat prefix.

Letter	Description
a	Enables assertions. This option enables the specifying of both Pragma Assert and Pragma Debug. Without this option these two pragmas are ignored.
b	Generate brief messasges to standard error even if the verbose option is also set.
c	Only check syntax and semantics. The .ali file is generated, but no executable code is generated.
e	Error messages are displayed as they occur instead of being saved and displayed all at once at the end.
E	Full dynamic elaboration checks are performed.
f	Every possible error is reported. Multiple errors may be detected on each line. All undefined references are reported, instead of only the first occurrence.
g	Enable Ada style checking (column alignment, indention, capitalization patterns, and so on).
i*char*	The value of *char* specifies the identifier character set. The standard ASCII characters (values 1 through 127) are always the same, but the remainder of the 8-bit values (128 through 255) can have different meanings. The character sets are identied as follows: 1 Latin-1 2 Latin-2 3 Latin-3 4 Latin-4 p IBM PC f full upper case n no upper case w wide character

Table D-3. *The Letters and Values Using with the* -gnat *Option*

Letter	Description
j*char*	The value of *char* specifies the method used to encode wide characters. The available methods are as follows: n none h Hex encoding u Upper-half coding s Shift JIS e EUC coding
k*number*	The vakue of *number* specifies an upper limit (1 to 999) to the number of characters in an identifier.
l	Output a full source listing including error messages.
m*number*	The value of *number* is the maximum number of error messages that will be reported.
n	Activate inlining across unit boundaries for subprograms for which the inline pragma is specified. This option is overridden if -fno-inline is specified.
N	This is the same as specifying -gnatn and adding pragma inline to each source file. This option is overridden by -fno-inline.
o	Enable runtime checking that that is not normally enabled, such as integer overflow and access before elaboration. This option causes the program to be larger and run more slowly. (This option has no effect on floating point operations).
p	Suppress all runtime checking. This has the same effect as pragma Suppress(all_checks). By removing the runtime safety checks, the program is smallter and runs more efficiently.
q	Don't halt the compiler on a syntax error. The code generation continues with whatever information the parser was able to gather.
r	Requires the column layout format to match that of the reference manual.
s	Only check the syntax.

Table D-3.   *The Letters and Values Using with the -gnat Option* (continued)

Letter	Description
t	Produce the .adt tree file used for dead code elimination.
u	List all of the units involved in this compilation.
v	Verbose mode. Full error output, along with the source lines causing the errors, to standard ouptut.
w*mode*	The mode determines how warnings are handled. If *mode* is s, warning messages are suppressed. If *mode* is e, warning messages are treated as error messages. If mode is l (ell), elaboration order warnings are generated.
z*type*	Specifies the generation of stubs. If *type* is r, reciever stubs are generatred. If type is s, sender stubs are generated.

Table D-3.   *The Letters and Values Using with the* -gnat *Option* (continued)

-gstabs[*level*]
If supported, produce debug information in stabs format if. The *level* setting is optional. Only if *level* is set to + will the gdb extensions be included. See -g for a description of *level* settings 1, 2, and 3.

This option can be used with DBX on most BSD systems, but doesn't work with DBX or SDB on MIPS, Alpha, or SVR4. Also, on SVR4, the GNU assembler is required.

-gvms[*level*]
If supported, produce debugging information in VMS debug format. The *level* setting is optional. See -g for a description of *level* settings 1, 2, and 3.

This is the format used by DEBUG on VMS.

-gxcoff[*level*]
If supported, produce debug information in XCOFF format. The *level* setting is optional. Only if *level* is set to + will the gdb extensions be included, which may disable the use of other debuggers and may cause problems with assemblers other than the GNU assember. See -g for a description of *level* settings 1, 2, and 3.

This is the format used by DBX on RS/6000.

-H
Print a nested listing of all the header files used, along with a list of the ones that are missing a multiple include guard.

This option can be written --trace-includes.

--help

Displays a list of the command line options understood by gcc. If the -v option is also specified, the list will include options accepted by various processes invoked by gcc. If the -W option is also specified, the undocumented command line options will also be listed. Also see --target-help.

--include-directory　　　　　　　　　　　　　　　　　　　Pre　Ada　Java

Same as -I.

-I *name*　　　　　　　　　　　　　　　　　　　　　　　　Pre　Ada　Java

For the preprocessor, the *name* is a directory to the primary list of directories to be searched for include files. This option can be used repeatedly to add several directories.

The directories specified with this option are searched first, so it is possible to override any system header files that would normally be included.

Specifying the current directory with a dot reference as in -I. specifies the directory to be the current working directory of the compiler.

For Ada, the *name* is the directory to be searched for source files.

For Java, the *name* is path of a location to be searched before any of the others (such as the ones named by the --classpath option or the CLASSPATH environment variable). The location is a directory, a jar file, or a zip file. It is recomended that -I be used in preference to --classpath.

Also see -I-, -isystem, -B, -nostdinc and -withprefixbefore and the environment variable CPATH. To set up a secondary list of directories searched for header files, see -idirafter. This option can be written --include-directory.

-I-　　　　　　　　　　　　　　　　　　　　　　　　　　Pre

The special form -I- may be specified once to declare that all -I directives that came before it on the command line will work for #include " . . ." but will not work for #include < . . .>. Any -I options following the -I- option will work for #include < . . . >.

The -I- option will also omit the default searching of same directory as the source file. This option can be written --include-barrier.

-idirafter *directory*　　　　　　　　　　　　　　　　　　Pre

Add the *directory* name to the second list of directories searched for header files. To find a header file, GCC looks through the directories in the first list (the one that has names added to it by the -I option). If the header file is not found in the first list, the second list is searched.

This option can be written --include-directory-after.

-imacros *filename*　　　　　　　　　　　　　　　　　　　Pre

The preprocessor will read and process the named file prior to reading the program source code. All information stored in *filename* is discarded except the macros it defined, which may be used in the source file.

Any -D or -U options that are also on the command line will be processed before any -imacros option. The -include and -imacros options are processed in the order they appear on the command line.

This option can be written --imacros.

-include *filename* `Pre`
The preprocessor will read and process the named file prior to reading the program source code just as if it had been included as the first statement in the source file.

Any -D or -U options that are also on the command line will be processed before any -include option. The -include and -imacros options are processed in the order they appear on the command line.

This option can be written --include.

--include-barrier `Pre`
Same as -I-.

--include-directory-after *directory* `Pre`
The same as -idirafter.

--include-prefix *prefix* `Pre`
The same as -iprefix.

--include-with-prefix *directory* `Pre`
Same as -iwithprefix.

--include-with-prefix-after *directory* `Pre`
Same as -iwithprefix.

--include-with-prefix-before *directory* `Pre`
Same as -withprefixbefore.

-iprefix *prefix* `Pre`
Specifies the *prefix* is to be used to construct the path to the directories named on the -iwithprefix and -withprefixbefore options.

This option can be written --include-prefix.

-isystem *directory* `Pre`
Adds the named *directory* at the beginning of the second include path, and the directory is marked as a system directory so it gets the same special treatment that is used for the standard system directories.

Also see -I and -B.

-iwithprefix *directory* `Pre`
Add the *directory* name to the second list of directories searched for header files. The name is constructed by appending the prefix specified by -iprefix with the named *directory*. If no prefix has been specified on the command line prior to this option, the directory containing the installed passes of the compiler itself is used as the default.

To find a header file, GCC looks through the directories in the first list (the one that has names added to it by the `-I` option). If the header file is not found in the first list, the second list is searched.

This option can be written `--include-with-prefix` or `--include-with-prefix-after`.

-iwithprefixbefore *directory*   `Pre`

Add a name to the list of directories in the main include path. The name is constructed by appending the prefix specified by `-iprefix` with the named *directory*. If no prefix has been specified on the command line prior to this option, the directory containing the installed passes of the compiler itself is used as the default.

This option can be written `--include-with-prefix-before`.

--library-directory *directory*   `Linker`

Same as `-L`.

-L*directory*   `Linker`

Add the named directory as one to be searched for libraries specified with the `-l` (ell) option.

Also see `-B` and the environent variable `LIBRARY_PATH`. This option can be written `--library-directory`.

-l*library*   `Linker`

Specifies the name of a library to be used by the linker in resolving references. The actual library name is constructed by appending the prefix `lib` and the suffix `.a` onto the specified name. For example, specifying `-lconsole` results in the library name `libconsole.a`.

A search for the named library will be made in the standard set of libraries and in any directory named using the `-L` option.

The option `-lobjc` is a special case required for linking Objective-C programs.

To resolve references, libraries are searched in the order they are found on the command line, which means the order in which they appear is important. For example, in the following command line any references made from `glower.o` to objects in `libjpeg.a` will be resolved, but references from `flower.o` will not be resolved:

```
gcc glower.o -ljpeg flower.o -o showall
```

This ordering can also be important when a member from one library requires a member from another library to resolve a reference. It is also possible to have a circular reference between two libraries requiring that they appear on the line more than once:

```
gcc sprig.o -ldflat -lturbo -ldflat -o sprig
```

The same library can be specified on the command line as either `libjpeg.a` or `-ljpeg`, but only the `-l` option instructs the linker to look in the standard directories and in any directories specified with the `-L` option.

For POSIX compliance, it is valid to leave a space between the option flag and the library name.

Also see `-L`.

--language *language*
Same as `-x`.

-M
The preprocessor outputs a rule suitable for inclusion in a makefile. The rule is composed of the object file name, a colon, the name of the source file and the name of the included files. The include files are listed on separate lines by their full path names. If the `-include` or `-imacros` options are on the command line, those files are also in the list.

The `-M` option implies `-E`.

The resulting rule contains the name of the object file and the list of dependencies; it does not include a rule to compile the source.

Unless either the `-MT` or `-MQ` option is used to specify the name, the object file name in the produced rule is the same as the input source with the suffix replaced.

The source file can be any of those listed in Table D-1 that require preprocessing. For example, if the source is Java, the path to the system Jar file is listed.

The other preprocessor options involved with producing makefile rules are `-MD`, `-MMD`, `-MF`, `-MG`, `-MM`, `-MP`, `-MQ`, and `-MT`.

This option can be written `--dependencies`.

--main=*classname*
Specifies the name of the class containing the `main()` method that is to be the starting point of program execution.

It is valid for every class to have its own `main()` method, so when several are compiled and linked together it is necessary to specify which one is to be used as the program's entry point.

-maligned-data
This option only applies to Fortran on Intel x86.

Fortran programs that make heavy use of REAL(KIND=2)(DOUBLE PRECISION) benefit greatly from having double precision floating point data aligned on 64-bit boundaries.

-MD
This is the same as `-M` except that `-E` is not implied. The compilation continues as normal and the makefile rule is output to a file that has the same base name as the source with a `.d` suffix. It is also possible to specify `-MF`, `-o`, or `-E` along with this option to specify the name of the rule output file.

This option can be written `--write-dependencies`.

-MMD

The same as -MD except no system header files are listed.

This option can be written --write-user-dependencies.

-MF *filename*

When used with -M,-MM, -MD, or -MMD, this option specifies the name of the output file.

An alternative way of specifying the name of the output file is to set the environment variable DEPENDENCIES_OUTPUT.

-MG

This option can be used in conjunction with -M or -MM to specify that missing header files are assumed to be generated files that reside in the same directory as the source file. The dependency list is generated just as if the header file existed and included no other headers.

This option can be written --print-missing-file-dependencies.

-MM

The same as -M except no system header files are listed.

This option can be written --user-dependencies.

-MP

Used in conjunction with -M or -MM to produce a dummy target for each include file. The only purpose of this is to prevent make from generating error messages when you remove a header file without updating the makefile.

-MQ *filename*

This option is the same as -MT except the target name is quoted appropriately for the makefile. For example, the command gcc -M -MT '$(OBJMRK)mrk.o' brink.c will produce the following:

```
$$(OBJMRK)mrk.o: brink.c
```

-MT *filename*

Used in conjunction with -M or -MM to specify the name of the target file of the produced makefile rule. By default, the target file is the same name as the input source file with a .o suffix appended to it. The -MT option can be used to specify a different name, a complete path name, or a name based on an environment variable. For example, the command gcc -M -MT '$(OBJMRK)mrk.o' brink.c will produce the following:

```
$(OBJMRK)mrk.o: brink.c
```

Also see -MQ.

--no-line-commands   Pre

Same as -P.

--no-standard-includes   Pre Ada

Same as -nostdinc.

--no-standard-libraries   Linker

Same as -nostdlib.

--no-warnings

Do not issue warning messages. Same as -w.

-nodefaultlibs   Linker

The standard system library routines should not be included as part of the linked executable program. The only libraries that will be used are the ones specifically listed on the command line.

It is possible that the compiler will generate calls to the system functions memcpy(), memcmp(), and memset() (for standard C and for System V) and bcopy(), and bzero() (for BSD). These references are normally resolved in libc.a, so you will need to resolve these references by providing the routines yourself.

The library libgcc.a contains a set of special routines that are specific to the target platform or can be considered part of the compiler, so you should normally specify -lgcc even when omitting the standard libraries.

Also see -nostartfiles and -nostdlibs.

-nostartfiles   Linker

The standard startup object files should not be included as part of the linked executable program. Also see -nostdlib and -nodefaultlibs.

-nostdinc   Pre Ada

Prevents the compiler from searching for heading files in the standard system directories. The only directories searched are the current directory and those specified by the -I option.

For Ada, this option specifies that that system library is not to be used for source files.

This option can be written --no-standard-includes.

-nostdinc++   Pre C++

Prevents the compiler from searching for header files in the standard C++ directories, but continues to search in the other standard directories. This option is specifically for use in compiling the C++ libraries.

-nostdlib   Linker

Only the items you specify on the command line will be passed to the linker. None of the standard startup files or libraries will be passed to the linker. This option implies both -nostartfiles and -nodefaultlibs.

This option can be written --no-standard-libraries.

-Olevel
Specifies the level of optimization to be applied to the code generated by the compiler. There is always a trade-off between optimizing for the size of the code or for speed of execution. The default is -O0 for no optimization.

If no optimization level is specified, the compiler runs to produce code that matches the structure of the input source. Optimization not only requires more processing, it requires much more memory. Compiling without optimization has the double advantage of shortening the compile time (optimization can take much longer), and the code produced can be tracked easily in a debugger. Both of these actions are ideal for the software development process. You can use the debugger on code that has been optimized, but some of the output code may be rearranged making it much more difficult to follow.

This option can be written --optimize.

Level	Description
-O	The compiler attempts to reduce both code size and execution time, but not to make modifications that would cause difficulties with debugging. Turns on the options -fno_optimize_size, -fdefer_pop, -fthread_jumps, -jguess_branch_prob, -cprop-registers, and -fdelayed_branch. The -fomit_frame_pointer flag is set only if the debugger is able to work without it on this platform.
-O0	The default. Disables all optimization. Turns off all size optimization and sets -fno-merge-constants.
-O1	The same as -O.
-O2	This level turns on all optimizations that do not involve size and speed trade-offs. In addition to the options turned on for -O, this level turns on -foptimize-sibling-calls, -fcse-follow-jumps, -fcse-skip-blocks, -fgcse, -fexpensive-optimizations, -fstrength-reduce, -frerun-cse-after-loop, -frerun-loop-opt, -fcaller-saves, -fforce-mem, -fpeephole2, -fschedule-insns, -fschedule-insn-after-reload, -fregmove, -fstruct-aliasing, -fdelete-null-pointer-checks, and -freorder-blocks. This level does no loop unrolling, inlining, nor register renaming.

Table D-4. *The Six Levels of Optimization*

Level	Description
-O3	In addition to the options turned on for -O2, this level turns on -finline-functions and -frename-registers.
-Os	Optimizes for size. All of the -O2 options flags are set. The -falign-loops, -falign-jumps, -falign-labels, and -falign-functions are all set to 1, which prevents any space being inserted for alignment.

Table D-4. *The Six Levels of Optimization* (continued)

The optimization levels are listed in Table D-4.

-o *filename*
Write the output to the named file. This applies no matter what kind of output is being generated; it could be preprocessed source, assembly language, an object file, or a linked executable. Because only one output file can be specified, the -o option should not be used if several files are being produced.

If the compiler produces a linked executable and the -o option is not specified to name it, the default name is a.out.

This option can be written --output.

--optimize *level*
Same as -O.

--output *filename*
Same as -o.

--output-class-directory=*directory*   `Java`
Same as -foutput-class-dir.

-p
Include extra code that will output information suitable for analysis by the profiling program prof. This option must be used both to compile the source files and to link the object files.

Also see -pg. This option can be written --profile.

-P   `Pre`
The preprocessor is not to generate #line directives when used with the -E option.

This option can be written --no-line-commands.

--param *name=value*

There are some internal limits used by GCC to determine the amount of optimization to be done, so adjustments to these values are adjustments to the optimization. The following table lists names and values of the available parameter settings.

This option can be written --param.

Name	Value
max-delay-slot-insn-search	The maximum number of instructions to consider when looking for one to fill a delay slot. A larger value can improve the generated code, but slows compile time. The default is 100.
max-delay-slot-live-search	The maximum number of blocks to search when attempting to find a block with valid live register information. A larger value can improve the generated code, but slows compile time. The default is 333.
max-gcse-memory	Maximum amount of memory that can be allocated to perform GCSE (Global Command Subexpression Elimination). If there is not enough memory to perform the operation, the optimization is not performed. The default is 50 megabytes (52428800).
max-gcse-passes	Maximum number of iterations of GCSE (Global Command Subexpression Elimination). The default is 1.
max-inline-insns	Maximum number of instructions in a method that can be a candidate for being expanded inline. The default is 600.
max-pending-list-length	Maximum number of branch elements that can be stored by the slot scheduler in a pending dependency list before the tracking mechanism resets the list and starts over. A large function can generation thousands of dependencies. The default is 32.

Table D-5. *The Names Accepted By the* --params *Option*

APPENDIXES

-pass-exit-codes

An exit code from any phase of the compilation process that indicates an error will be ignored, and the compiler will continue. The return value from GCC is the largest error code value resulting from any one pass. Normally the compiler halts and returns the exit code value whenever it is non-zero.

-pedantic

Issues warnings required by strict compliance to the ISO standards for C and C++. Without this option the GNU extensions are enabled, but ISO compliant programs should compile successfully (although some may require the -ansi option).

For C, the standard applied is the one specified by the -std option. If -std is used to specify gnu89, then -pedantic applies the rules for C89. The -pedantic option issues only the diagnostic messages required by the ISO standard, so it is possible for code that does not comply with the standard to compile without a warning. There are no plans for GCC to implement an option that would force strict standards compliance.

For C, the -pedantic option does not apply to any expression following __extension__.

For C++, if nether the -fpermissive nor the -pedantic option is specified, the -fpedantic-errors option is assumed.

For Fortran, warnings are issued for uses of extensions to Fortran 77. Warnings are issued for C-like constructs in character constants (such as \n). Warnings are issued for certain GNU language extensions and some traditional Fortran features, but valid Fortran 77 should compile properly with or without this option. It should be noted, however, that this option does not force the program to strictly adhere to the standard.

This option can be written --pedantic.

-pedantic-errors

This option is the same as -pedantic, except the diagnostics are issued as errors instead of warnings.

For C++, if neither the -fpermissive nor the -pedantic option is specified, the -fpedantic-errors option is assumed.

This option can be written --pedantic-errors.

-pg

Include extra code that will output information suitable for analysis by the profiling program gprof. This option must be used both to compile the source files and to link the object files. Also see -p.

-pipe

Use pipes instead of intermediate files to communicate the output from one phase of the compiler to the input of another. This could fail if the local assembler is incapable of reading input from a pipe.

This option can be written --pipe.

--prefix *prefix*
Same as -B.

--preprocess
Same as -E.

`Pre`

-print-file-name=*library*
Print the full path name of the named library. No other action is taken by the compiler other than listing the path name. Also see -print-libgcc-file-name and -print-prog-name.
    This option can be written --print-file-name.

-print-libgcc-file-name
Print the full path name of the library named libgcc.a. This option is the same as -print-file-name=libgcc.a.
    This option can be written --print-libgcc-file-name.

--print-missing-file-dependencies
Same as -MG.

`Pre`

-print-multi-directory
Print the directory name corresponding to the library selected by any multilib selection option specified on the command line. The directory name is determined by the GCC_EXEC_PREFIX environment variable.
    This option can be written --print-multi-directory.

-print-multi-lib
Print the directory names of the multilib selections along with the command line options used to make the selections.
    The output produced by this option uses a semicolon (;) as a separator and uses an at sign (@) in place of the hyphen - to specify command line option names. This is done to simplify shell processing of the text.
    This option can be written --print-multi-lib.

-print-prog-name=*program*
Print the full path name of the named program (such as cc1 or cpp0). No other action is taken by the compiler other than listing the path name. Also see -print-file-name.
    This option can be written --print-prog-name.

-print-search-dirs
Print a list of the complete path names of all the directories that GCC will search for programs to be run as subprocesses and for libraries to be used for linking. No other action is taken by the compiler.
    If a program is not being found, you can either place it in one of the directories searched or add its directory to the environment variable GCC_EXEC_PREFIX.
    This option can be written --print-search-dirs.

APPENDIXES

--profile
Same as -p.

--profile-blocks
Same as -a.

-Q
The compiler will print the name of each function as it is being compiled, and will print diagnostic statistics at the end of each pass including the amount of time taken to compile and link the program.

-remap   Pre
This option instructs the preprocessor to check for the existence of a file named header.gcc in each directory containing include files. If the file exists, it is used to determine the actual name of the file being sought. Each line of the file contains the name of the header file being sought followed by the actual file name. For example, the following lines in a header.gcc file would cause header files with long names to be found under shorter names:

L D-33
```
NotSupportedException.h notsup.h
RollbackException.h rollbak.h
TransactionRequiredException.h transreq.h
```

-s   Linker
The symbol table and all relocation information is removed from the executable. The result is the same as that achieved by running the strip utility.

-S
Do not invoke the assembler nor the linker. This option will allow compiling of source files into assembly language files, but the assembler will not be run to create an executable. The output produced is stored in files of the same name as the source file with a .s suffix. Any input files that do not have a recognizable suffix, as listed in Table D-1, or do not have their types indicated by -x are ignored.
    This option can be written --assemble.

-save-temps
Do not follow the normal procedure of deleting the temporary intermediate files produced by the compiler. They are left in the current directory with the suffixes indicating their content. The content of the files can be identified by the file suffixes listed in Table D-1.
    This option can be written --save-temps.

-shared

The linker will produce a shared object which can be dynamically linked to a program at run time to form a complete executable. Also, if the gcc command is being used to create a shared library as its output, this option will prevent that absence of a main() method from being considered an error by the linker.

For this to work properly the -fpic, -fPIC, and target platform options should be used consistently to compile shared object modules that are to be placed in the same library. In particular this option may require the generation of special code for constructors to work properly. The errors produced from incorrect flag settings can be very subtle, and there is no penalty for specifying them unnecessarily.

Also see -shared-libgcc, -static-libgcc, and -static. This option can be written --shared.

-shared-libgcc

This option specifies that the shared version of libgcc be used. On systems that do not support shared libraries, or if no shared version of the library was constructed, this option has no effect.

If the linker is invoked through g++, gcj, or g77 this flag is automatically specified because of the requirement for throwing exceptions. The shared version of libgcc should be used when an application is going to throw an exception from code in one shared library that is to be caught by code in another shared library. Under these circumstances the shared version of libgcc should be used by both the thrower and the catcher.

Also see -shared, -static-libgcc, and -static.

-specs=*filename*

The gcc driver program reads a spec file to determine which flags should be passed to which subprocesses (as described in Chapter 19). This option can be used to override the default specifications by naming a spec file to be processed after the default files to alter the set of rules used to invoke subprocesses.

This option can be written --specs.

-static

The linker will ignore any dynamically linkable libraries and resolve all references by including static object files directly into the resulting object file. On systems without dynamic linking capabilities, this option has no effect.

Also see -shared. This option can be written --static.

-static-libgcc

This option specifies that the static version of libgcc be used. This option may cause problems with exceptions in C++ and Java.

Also see -shared, -shared-libgcc, and -static.

-std=_name_

Specifies the C language standard. The names recognized are listed in Table D-6.

This option disables the GNU C extension keywords `asm`, `typeof`, and `inline`, but the the alternate forms `__asm__`, `__typeof__`, and `__inline__` remain available.

Also see `-ansi`. This option can be written `--std`.

-symbolic

Bind references to global symbols when building shared objects. This is an alternative to linking an executable as either -shared or -static. Only a few systems support this option, such as certain SVR4 systems and DG/UX.

This option can be written `--symbolic`.

-syntax-only

Check the syntax of the input source code, report any warnings or errors, and stop.

Name	Description
iso9899:1990	The ISO C 89 standard. This option also sets the flags `-fno-traditional`, `-fno-writeable-strings`, `-fno-asm`, `-fno-nonansi-builtin`, and `-fno-noniso-default-format-attributes`.
iso9899:199409	The ISO C 89 standard as amended. This option also sets the flags `-fno-traditional`, `-fno-writeable-strings`, `-fno-asm`, `-fno-nonansi-builtin`, and `-fno-noniso-default-format-attributes`.
iso9899:1999	The ISO C 99 standard. This option also sets the flags `-fno-traditional`, `-fno-writeable-strings`, `-fno-asm`, `-fno-nonansi-builtin`, and `-fno-noniso-default-format-attributes`.
c89	Same as iso9899:1990.
c99	Same as iso9899:1999.
gnu89	The ISO C 89 standard with GNU extensions and some ISO C 99 features. This option also sets the flags `-fno-traditional`, `-fno-writeable-strings`, `-fasm`, `-fnonansi-builtin`, and `-fnoniso-default-format-attributes`.

Table D-6.   _The Options for Specifying the Language Standard_

--target *machine*
Same as –b.

--target-help
Displays a list of the target-specific command-line options. Also see ––help.

--trace-includes `Pre`
Same as –H.

-traditional `C`
This option is deprecated. It attempts to support characteristics of the original K&R C language. A traditional program will not compile if it includes the ISO C header files. This option also sets –traditional-cpp and –fwritable-strings.
Also see –fallow-single-precision. This option can be written ––traditional.

-traditional-cpp `C`
The C preprocessor supports characteristics of the original preprocessor.
This option can be written ––traditional-cpp.

-trigraphs `Pre`
Support ISO C trigraphs. This option is implied by –ansi and by –std.
With this option set, each of the three-character sequences (each beginning with ??) that make up the nine trigraphs will be translated into a single character, according to the following table:

??=	#	??(	[	??<	{
??/	\	??)	]	??>	}
??'	^	??!	|	??-	~

This option can be written ––trigraphs.

-time
Output the time consumed by each subprocess to compile a program. The times listed on each line are the user time (the time spent in the code of the subprocess) and the system time (the time spent in system calls). The following example shows the output from compiling a C++ program into an executable object file:

```
gcc -time fortest.cpp -o fortest.o
# cc1plus 0.14 0.05
# as 0.00 0.01
# collect2 0.10 0.03
```

This option can be written ––time.

-u *name*   `Linker`
The specified name is inserted into the linker's symbol table as one that must be resolved.
The linker will then resolve the symbol by loading the object module that contains
a definition of the symbol.
    This option can be written `--force-link`.

-U*macro*   `Pre`
If it has been previously defined, the *macro* definition is removed.
    All `-D` options are processed before any `-U` options, and all `-U` options are processed
before any `-include` or `-imacros` options.
    This option can be written `--undefine-macro`.

-undef   `Pre`
The preprocessor will not predefine any nonstandard macros. This option suppresses
the architecture definitions such as `__unix__`, `__OpenBSD__`, `__mips__`, `__linux__`,
`__vax__`, and so on.

--undefine-macro *macro*   `Pre`
Same as `-U`.

--use-version version *version*
Same as `-V`.

--user-dependencies   `Pre`
Same as `-MM`.

-v
Displays the current version number of the compiler and displays all of the commands
used to run each phase of the compile and link process. When used alone, this option
will display the current version number of the compiler. When used in combination
with the `--help` option, a complete list of the command line options is displayed.
    Also see `-###`. This option can be written `--verbose`. This flag also sets `-fversion`
for Fortran.

-V *version*
Specify the version of `gcc` that is to be run. This option only has meaning if you
have more than one version of the compiler installed. The default is to run the latest
version installed.
    This works by modifying the prefix used to select the compiler and its components,
which are normally kept in `/usr/local/lib/gcc-lib/`*machine*`/`*version*.
    Also see `-b` and `-B`. This option can be written `--use-version`.

--verbose
Same as `-v`.

-w

Do not issue warning messages. Same as `--no-warnings`.

-W

This option enables the issuing of a family of warning messages dealing primarily with code that could possibly cause a problem, but it could also be what was intended by the programmer. This option enables all of the following:

- **Comparison** A warning is issued if an unsigned value is tested for being less than zero. For example, because unsigned values can never be negative, the following test will always be false:

```
unsigned int x;
    . . .
if(x < 0) . . .
```

- **Comparison** A warning is issued for the comparison of a signed value with an unsigned value. An incorrect result can be produced when the unsigned value is converted to a signed value for the comparison. This warning can be suppressed by `-Wno-sign-compare`.

- **Comparison** Algebraic notation and the C sytnax for comparison are not the same. A warning will be issued for the following statement:

```
if(a < b < c) . . .
```

  In algebraic notation this expression is true only if b lies in the open interval between a and c. In C, this expression is the same as the following, which is very different:

```
int result;
result = a < b;
if(result < b) . . .
```

- **Const return** Issue a warning for the return value of a function being declared as `const`. The `const` declaration has no meaning here because the return value from a function is an rvalue.

- **Aggregate initializers** A warning is issued if initial values are specified for an aggregate data type, but values are not supplied for all members of the aggregate. In the following example an error message would be issued for both the array and the struct:

```
struct {
    int a;
    int b;
    int c;
} trmp = { 1, 2 };
int arr[10] = { 1, 2, 3, 4, 5 };
```

- **No side effect**   A warning is issued for a statement that has no effect. For example, the result of the following addition is not used:

```
int a = 1;
int b = 2;
a + b;
```

- **Overflow**   In Fortran, warnings are issued when floating point constant declarations overflow.

- **Return value**   Issue a warning if a function is written so that it may or may not return a value, as in the following example which does not return value if x is negative:

```
ambigret(int x)
{
    if(x >= 0)
        return(x);
}
```

- **Static syntax**   Issue a warning if the keyword static does not come first on a declaration line. This ordering is no longer a requirement in standard C.

- **Unused arguments**   If either -Wall or -Wunused is specified along with -W, a warning is issued for any unused arguments in the body of a function.

This option can be written --extra-warnings.

-Wa,*optionlist*   `Asm`
The *optionlist* is a list of one or more comma separated lists of options to be passed to the assembler. The options are split at the commas and each one is provided to the assembler as a command line option.

Also see -Wp and -Wl. This option can be written as --for-assembler.

-Waggregate-return   `C   C++   ObjC`
Issue a warning if a function returns a structure, union, or an array.

-Wall
For C and ObjC, setting this option is the same as setting -Wreturn-type, -Wunused, -Wimplicit, -Wswitch, -Wformat, -Wparentheses, -Wmissing-braces, -Wsign-compare, and -Wmultichar. The -Wunknown-pragmas option is set to detect only those not found in system headers. The -Wuninitialized option is set if -O is also specified.

For C++, the additional options set are -Wctor-dtor-privacy, -Wnon-virtual-dtor, -Wreorder, and -Wnon-template-friend.

For Fortran, the only option settings that have any effect are -Wunused and -Wuninitialized.

For Java, this is the same as setting `-Wredundant-modifiers`, `-Wextraneous-semicolon`, and `-Wunused`.

This option can be written `--all-warnings`.

--warn-

Same as `-W`.

-Wbad-function-cast

Issue a warning whenever a function is cast to a non-matching type. For example, the following will cause a warning to be issued on the function call:

```
int glim()
{
    return(88);
}
 . . .
char *cp;
cp = (char *)glim();
```

-Wcast-align

Issue a warning there is a possible problem with the alignment resulting from casting a pointer to a different type. For example, on some machines it is possible to address an `int` only on 2- or 4-byte boundaries, so casting a `char` pointer to an `int` pointer could result in an invalid address value.

-Wcast-qual

Issue a warning whenever a function call removes a qualifier. For example, the following removes the `const` qualifier:

```
const char *conchp;
char *chp;
 . . .
chp = (char *)conchp;
```

-Wchar-subscripts

Issue a warning if a `char` data type is used as the subscript of an array. Because `char` often defaults to being signed, this can be the cause of an error.

-Wcomment

Issue a warning when a `/*` is found inside a `/* . . . */` comment. Also issue a warning when a `//` comment line ends with a backslash (which continues the comment to the following line).

-Wconversion
Issue a warning if a prototype causes a type conversion other than the one that would occur if the conversion were made without the prototype. This includes converting between real and integer data types, signed and unsigned values, as well as changing the width of the value. Warnings are issued only for implicit conversions (coercion), but not for specific casts. For example, the first of the following assignment statements will issue a warning but the second will not:

L D-44

```
unsigned int recp;
recp = -1;
recp = (unsigned int)-1;
```

-Wctor-dtor-privacy
Issue a warning if a class appears to be unusable because it has only private constructors or destructors, no friends, and no public or static members. This option is set by -Wall.

-Wdeprecated
This is the default. Warnings are issued about the use of deprecated features of C++ unless the option -Wno-deprecated is specified.

-Wdeprecated-declarations
This is the default. Warnings are issued about the use of items marked with the deprecated attribute unless -Wno-deprecated=declarations is specified.

-Wdisabled-optimization
Issue a warning if a requested optimization is disabled. This circumstance occurs not because of a problem with your code, but because of a limitation within the compiler itself. GCC will refuse to perform optimizations that are too complex and/or will take too long to perform.

-Wdiv-by-zero
This is the default. Issues a warning when the compiler can detect integer division by zero unless the option -Wno-div-by-zero is specified. There is no warning for floating point division by zero.

-Weffc++
Issues warnings for violations of some of the style guidelines from the book *Effective C++* by Scott Myers. The standard library headers do not follow these guidelines, so you will also get warnings issued from them.

-Werror
Convert all warnings into error messages.

-Werror-implicit-function-declaration
Issue an error whenever a function is used before being declared. Also see -Wimplicit-function-declaration.

-Wextern-inline `C++`
Issue a warning if a function is declared as both `extern` and `inline`.

-Wextraneous-semicolon `Java`
Issue a warning for a semicolon that has no statement to terminate. Empty statements have been deprecated.

-Wfloat-equal
If two floating point numbers are compared for equality, a warning is issued because this is often an error in the logic of the program.

It is the nature of floating point arithmetic that calculated real numbers are rarely equal to one another. This means that comparison for exact equality on two real numbers can fail even if the numbers are close enough together for the logic of your program to treat them as if they were identical. The following is a technique for comparing floating point numbers if your program considers equality being within 0.00001 of one another:

```
double delta = 0.00001;
  . . .
if((val1 > val2-delta) && (val1 < val2+delta) {
    /* val1 and val2 are considered equal */
}
```

-Wformat `C   C++   ObjC`
Check the calls to functions such as `printf()` and `scanf()` and issue a warning if the arguments' types on the command do not match with the ones specified in the formatting string. For example, the following statement attempts to format a `double` value as an `int` and produces a warning message:

```
double dvalue = 44.44;
  . . .
printf("The value %d is bad.\n",dvalue);
```

The formats are tested against the features supported in GNU `libc` version 2.2, which includes the ones in C89, C99, POSIX, and some BSD GNU extensions. If the `-pedantic` option is also specified, warnings will be issued for formats that are not part of the standard.

The functions with format strings tested by this option are `printf()`, `fprintf()`, `sprintf()`, `scanf()`, `fscanf()`, `strftime()`, `vprintf()`, `vfprintf()`, and `vsprintf()`. For C99 the list includes `snprintf()`, `vsnprintf()`, `vscanf()`, `vfscanf()`, and `vsscanf()`. For X/Open the list includes `strfmon()`, `printf_unlocked()`, and `fprintf_unlocked()`.

Also see `-Wformat-extra-args`, `-Wformat-nonliteral`, and `-Wformat-security`. See the section "Attributes" in Chapter 4. This option is set by `-Wall`.

-Wformat=2   `C    C++    ObjC`
The same as setting `-Wformat`, `-Wformat-nonliteral`, and `-Wformat-security`.

-Wformat-extra-args   `C    C++    ObjC`
This is the default. If `-Wformat` is specified, specifying `-Wno-format-extra-args`
will suppress warning messages about extra (unused) arguments passed to the function
calls such as `printf()` and `scanf()`.

-Wformat-nonliteral   `C    C++    ObjC`
Issues a warning if `-Wformat` is specified and the formatting string on a call to functions
such as `printf()` and `scanf()` is not a literal constant, which cannot be checked.

-Wformat-security   `C    C++    ObjC`
Issues a warning if `-Wformat` is specified and a call to a function such as `printf()` and
`scanf()` presents a possible security problem. Function calls using a variable instead
of a literal constant string for the formatting is not trusted because it could contain a `%n`.

-Wformat-y2k   `C    C++    ObjC`
This is the default. Specifying `-Wno-format-y2k` will suppress warnings about
`strftime()` formats that produce two-digit years.

-Wglobals   `Fortran`
This is the default. Specifying `-Wno-globals` suppresses warnings about the global name
of a subroutine, function, data block, or common block being the same as the name of
an intrinsic. Warnings are also inhibited about inconsistent invocations of global functions
and subroutines (such as a different number or different types of arguments).

-Wimplicit   `Fortran`
Issue a warning whenever a variable, array, or function is implicitly declared. The effect
is similar to the effect of the declaration `IMPLICIT NONE`.

-Wimplicit-int   `C`
Issue a warning when a declaration does not specify a type. This option is set by
`-Wimplicit` and `-Wall`.

-Wimplicit-function-declaration   `C`
Issue a warning whenever a function is used before being declared. Also see
`-Werror-implicit-function-declaration`. This option is set by `-Wimplicit`
and `-Wall`.

-Wimplicit   `C`
Same as `-Wimplicit-int` and `-Wimplicit-function-definition`. This option
is set by `-Wall`.

-Wimport   `C    C++    ObjC`
This is the default. Specifying `-Wno-import` will suppress warning messages from the
preprocessor about the use of `#import`.

-Winline

Issue a warning if a function that was declared as `inline` could not be expanded as inline code.

-Wl,*optionlist*

The *optionlist* is a list of one or more comma separated lists of options to be passed to the linker. The options are split at the commas, and each one is provided to the linker as a command-line option.

Also see `-Xlinker`, `-Wa` and `-Wp`.

-Wlarger-than-*size*

Issue a warning whenever an object larger than *size* bytes is declared, if the return value from a function is larger than *size* bytes.

-Wlong-long

This is the default, but will only work if the `-pedantic` option is also specified. This option will issue a warning if the `long long` data type is used. The default can be overridden by specifying `-Wno-long-long`.

-Wmain

Issue a warning if the definition of `main()` looks suspicious. It should be a function that has external linkage and returns an `int`. It should have zero, two, or three arguments of the appropriate types.

-Wmissing-braces

Issues a warning if the initial values of an array are not completely bracketed. In the following example, both arrays a and b are initialized correctly, but braces are used for array b to be more specific about the placement of the values:

```
int a[2][2] = { 0, 1, 2, 3 };
int b[2][2] = { { 1, 2 }, { 3, 4} };
```

This option is set by `-Wall`.

-Wmissing-declarations

Issue a warning if a global function is defined without a previous declaration with or without specifying the argument types. Also see `-Wstrict-prototypes` and `-Wmissing-prototypes`.

-Wmissing-format-attribute

Issue warnings which might be candidates for the `format` attribute. It should be noted that the warnings are issued for *possible* `noreturn` candidates. This option has no effect unless the option `-Wformat` or `-Wall` has also been specified.

-Wmissing-noreturn

Issues a warning about a function which may be suitable for the `noreturn` attribute. It should be noted that the warnings are issued for *possible* `noreturn` candidates, and that care should be taken not to specify the `noreturn` attribute on a function that actually returns because it will introduce subtle bugs into your program.

-Wmissing-prototypes

Issue a warning if a global function is defined without a previous prototype declaration specifying the argument types. Also see `-Wstrict-prototypes` and `-Wmissing-declarations`.

-Wmultichar

This is the default. Issues warnings if a character constant is declared containing more than one character such as 'ab' or 'Plop'. The code resulting from this kind of declaration depends on the platform and should never be used in portable code, but the warning can be suppressed by `-Wno-multichar`.

-Wnested-externs

Issue a warning for an `extern` declaration inside a function.

-Wnon-template-friend

This is the default. A warning is issued when a non-templatized friend function is declared as the member of a template.

Prior to the C++ standards definition, GNU C++ implemented the name of a friend to be declared as an unqualified id. By default this is no longer the behavior but, for existing code, you can turn off the warning message by specifying `-Wno-non-template-friend`. This option is set by `-Wall`.

-Wnon-virtual-dtor

Issue a warning if a non-virtual destructor should probably be virtual. Non-virtual destructors will not be executed if an object is destroyed while being referenced as one of its super classes. This option is set by `-Wall`.

-Wold-style-cast

Issues a warning when a traditional style (C language style) cast is used instead of one of the new forms from the C++ standard with one of the casting operators `static_cast`, `const_cast`, or `reinterpret_cast`. For example:

L D-48

```
class A { ... };
class B: public A { ... };
  . . .
A* a = new A();
B* b = a;                   //implicit conversion
A* a2 = static_cast<A*>(b); //reversing an implicit conversion
```

-Wout-of-date

This is the default. Specifying `-Wno-out-of-date` will suppress the warning issued by the compiler when a source file is newer than its class file.

-Woverloaded-virtual

Issues a warning when a function declaration hides a virtual function declared in a base class. In the following example the function fn() in class A is hidden:

```
class A {
    virtual void fn();
};
class B: public A {
    void fn(int);
};
```

-Wp,*optionlist*

The *optionlist* is a list of one or more comma separated list of options to be passed to the preprocessor. The options are split at the commas, and each one is provided to the preprocessor as a command-line option.

Also see -Wa and -Wl.

-Wpacked

Issue a warning when the packed attribute is specified, but has no effect. For example, the following struct would consume four bytes even without the packed attribute:

```
struct fourbyte {
    short x;
    char a;
    char b;
}__attribute__((packed));
```

See "Attributes" in Chapter 4. Also see -fpack-struct and -Wpadded.

-Wpadded

Issue a warning if the compiler inserts padding between the members of a structure to either align an item within the structure or to align the entire structure. In some cases it is possible to rearrage the members of the structure to align the members and reduce the size of the structure by removing the padding. For example, the following struct will cause a byte to be inserted before the short data type to align in on a 2-byte boundary:

```
struct pad {
    char a;
    short b;
    char c;
};
```

-Wparentheses

Issue warnings for constructions that, while syntactically correct, could possibly be confusing to the programmer because of operator precedence or the structure of the code.

The following expression will cause a warning to be issued because it is difficult to remember whether logical operators associate left to right or right to left:

L D-52
```
if(a && b || c) . . .
```

The following will issue a warning because, in the absence of braces, the relationships among the if and else statements could be misleading:

L D-53
```
if(a)
    if(b)
        m = p;
else
    a = 0;
```

It is apparent from the indention that the programmer intended for the else statement is to be associated with the first if statement, but it is not.

This option is set by -Wall.

-Wpmf-conversions C++

This is the default. Specifying -Wno-pmf-conversions will cause a warning to be issued when there is a conversion from a pointer to the address of a member function.

-Wpointer-arith

Issue a warning for anything that depends on the size of a function type or the size of a void. For the sake of pointer arithmetic, the GCC default size for these items is 1.

-Wprotocol ObjC

This is the default. Specifying -Wno-protocol suppresses warnings issued when methods required by a protocol are not implemented in the class adopting the protocol.

-Wredundant-decls C C++ ObjC

Issue a warning for any item declared more than once in the same scope. This warning is issued even when the declarations are identical.

-Wredundant-modifiers Java

Issue a warning if an unnecessary modifier is used in a declaration. For example, a warning is issued if a method in an interface is declared public.

-Wreorder

Issue a warning if the compiler rearranges member initializers to match the order in which they are declared. For example, the following initializers must be rearranged:

```
class Reo {
    int i;
    int j;
    Reo(): j(5), i(10) { }
};
```

This option is set by -Wall.

-Wreturn-type

Issue a warning when any declared function is declared without a return type and allowed to default to int. Also issue a warning if there is a return statement without a value in a function that is not declared as void. This option is set by -Wall.

--write-dependencies

Same as -MD.

--write-user-dependencies

Same as -MMD.

-Wselector

Issue a warning if a selector defines multiple methods of different types.

-Wsequence-points

Issues a warning if a variable is referenced more than once in an expression, and one of the references modifies its value. The definition of the C language allows expressions between sequence points to be evaluated in any order (as long as operator precedences are maintained), so modification of a variable in one location makes its value undetermined if it is used in another.

A sequence point is specified in the code by the presence of one of the following operators:

```
; , && || ? :
```

The following are some examples of expressions that have ambiguous results because of a sequence point violation:

```
s = a[s++];
s = s--;
a[s++] = b[s];
a[s] = b[s += c];
```

-Wshadow

Issue a warning whenever a local variable shadows a parameter, global variable, or another local variable. Also issue a warning if a built-in function is shadowed.

-Wsign-compare

Issue a warning when a comparison between a signed and unsigned value could produce an incorrect result by converting the signed value to unsigned before making the comparison. This option is set by -Wall but can be overridden by specifying -Wno-sign-compare.

-Wsign-promo

Issue a warning when overloading from an unsigned (or enumerated type) data type to a signed data type of the same size. The standard specifies this type of conversion, but it could cause loss of data.

-Wstrict-prototypes

Issue a warning if a function is declared or defined without specifying the type and number of arguments. Also see -Wmissing-prototypes and -Wmissing-declarations.

-Wsurprising

This option will issue warnings about constructs that could be interpreted in more than one way, and cause a surprising result for the programmer. These are language constructs that are treated differently by different compilers. The warnings include:

■ Expressions with two operators in a row. An example of this is x ** y * z. In the absence of parentheses it is possible for a compiler to interpret the expression as x** (y * z) or as ((x**y) * z. The -fpedantic option also issues warnings for these situations.

■ Expression with an ambiguous unary minus. For example, -2 ** x because the expression could be interpreted as -(2 ** x) or as (-2)**x. Expressions such as -x*y can cause surprising results if a value is close to the maximum range of the x or y data type and the interpretation is - (x*y) instead of (-x) *y.

■ A DO loop that uses a real number instead of an integral value as its loop counter can cause surprising restults. This is not normally a problem, but the result can vary from one compiler to the next.

-Wswitch

Issue a warning if an enumerated type is used as the index for a switch statement and there is no default and a case statement is not present for all the possible values. This option is set by -Wall.

-Wsynth

Issue a warning when operator synthesis is different from cfront. In the following example GCC will synthesize the operator A& operator = (const A&); where cfront employs the user-defined default operator =.

```
class A {
    operator int();
```

```
    A& operator = (int);
};

main() {
    A a1;
    A a2;
    a1 = a2;
}
```

-Wsystem-headers

C C++ ObjC

Issue warning messages for code in the system header files as well in the program being compiled. Normally warnings caused by system headers are suppressed.

To generate warnings about unknown pragmas in system headers it will be necessary to specify -Wunknown-pragmas because using -Wall only checks the pragmas in the program and ignores the ones in the system headers.

-Wtraditional

Issue warnings for standard C constructs that may have a different meaning, or did not exist, in traditional C. Some of these are ambiguous or problematic constructs that should be avoided.

- **Conversion**   Issue a warning for any conversion between a fixed and floating point number caused by a prototype definition. Also see -Wconversion. For example, a warning would be issued for the following function call:

```
void takedouble(double dval);
 . . .
int eighty = 80;
takedouble(eighty);
```

- **External**   Issue a warning if a function is declared as external within a block of code, and the function is used outside of the scope of the block.

- **Initial values**   Issue a warning for the declaration of an initial value for an automatic aggregate data type (such as an array or struct declared inside a function).

- **Initial values**   Issue a warning for specifying an initial value of a union, unless the value of the initializing constant is zero.

- **Label**   Issue a warning for a label having the same name as a variable.

- **Literal constants**   Warnings are issued for integer constants declared with the U suffix, and real number constants with the suffixes F or L.

- **Literal constants**   A warning is issued if a base ten standard C literal constant has a different width or signed/unsigned characeristics than it would have in traditional C. This warning is only for base ten constants because hexadecimal and octal constants are assumed to be bit patterns.

- **Literal constants** A warning is issued for the standard C method of string constant concatenation.

- **Preprocessor** A warning is issued for a macro named appearing as part of a string literal. The string literals of traditional C can contain macro definitions but standard C does not allow them.

- **Preprocessor** Issues warnings for any preprocessor directives starting in column one that are unknown to traditional C. You can specify newer preprocessor directives, such as #pragma and #elif, by indenting them so they do not begin in the first column. (The traditional preprocessor requires that all directives begin in the first column.)

- **Preprocessor** Issue a warning for a macro defined in the form of a function but has no arguments.

- **Static** A warning is issued if a non-static function is declared following a static function. (This is not accepted by some traditional compilers).

- **Switch** A warning is issued if a switch statement's operand is of type long.

- **Unary plus** Issue a warning for the presence of a unary plus.

-Wtrigraphs

Issue a warning for a trigraph that may change the meaning of the program. Because trigraphs are translated everywhere except inside comments, it occasionally happens that a trigraph appears inside a quoted string. For example, one version of the Linux kernel contained the string "imm: parity error (???)\n" which standard C translated to "imm: parity error (?]\n".

-Wundef

The proprocessor will issue a warning whenever an undefined identifier is found in an expression evaluated by an #if directive.

-Wuninitialized

Issue a warning if an automatic variable is used before it is initialized. Also issue a warning if a setjmp() call may destroy the value of an automatic variable. This option can only be used in conjunction with -O because it is the optimizing data flow information that is required for these situations to be detected.

Because this option requires data flow analysis, it is not possible for it to be completely accurate. For example, in the following code it is not possible to guarantee that value will or will not be initialized for the printf() statement:

```
int value;
if(a < b)
    value = 5;
else if(a > c)
```

```
    value = 10;
printf("%d\n",value);
```

Because of the nature of the data flow analysis, this option does not apply to structures, unions, arrays, any variable declared as `volatile`, any variable that has its address taken, or a variable used to compute a value that is never used.

The data flow analysis is aware of the `setjmp()` statement, but it has no way of knowing from where `longjmp()` may be called, so a warning could be issued when there is no problem.

The same sort of data flow analysis is required for Fortran source, as demonstrated by the following example where it may not be possible to determine whether TVAL is always initialized:

```
IF (IVAL .EQ. 1) TVAL = 5
IF (IVAL .EQ. 2) TVAL = 10
CALL SMON(TVAL)
```

Some of the false warnings issued by this option can be suppressed by declaring functions that do not return as `noreturn`.

This option is set by `-Wall` if the `-O` option is also specified.

-Wunknown-pragmas
Issue a warning if an unknown `#pragma` directive is encountered. This option will issue warnings for any unknown `#pragma` directives in the system header files unless it has been set by `-Wall`.

-Wunreachable-code
Issue a warning if code is detected that cannot be reached during the execution of the program. This can happen if the code follows a branch that will always be taken or follows a function call that does not return.

Care should be taken in removing code causing this warning to be issued. It is possible to get a warning from a function that generated inline code or from the expansion of a macro, but there are other instances of the code that do not generate unreachable code. Also, unreachable code could be the result of a compile-time option causing code to be intentionally skipped.

-Wunused
This option sets the options `-Wunused-function`, `-Wunused-label`, `-Wunused-parameter`, `-Wunused-value`, and `-Wunused-variable`.

For Fortran, a warning is issued whenever a variable is declared but not used.

This option is set by `-Wall`.

-Wunused-function
Issue a warning for the definition of a static function that is not used or for a static function that is declared but not defined. This option is also set by -Wunused and -Wall.

-Wunused-label
Issue a warning for an unused label defined without the unused attribute. This option is also set by -Wunused and -Wall.

-Wunused-parameter
Issue a warning for an unused parameter declared without the unused attribute. This option is also set by -Wunused and -Wall.

-Wunused-value
Issue a warning for an unused local variable or non-constant static variable declared without the unused attribute. This option is also set by -Wunused and -Wall.

-Wunused-variable
Issue a warning for an unused local variable or non-constant static variable declared without the unused attribute. This option is also set by -Wunused and -Wall.

-Wwrite-strings   `C    C++`
Issue a warning if a C program stores the address of a literal string constant into a pointer that is not declared as const. Issue a warning if a C++ converts string constants to type char *.

This option is useful only if care has been taken in writing the code to declare data types and prototypes as const, otherwise the warnings can become a nuisance.

-x*language*
Specifies the content of files named on the command line. Without this option the content of the files is assumed from the suffixes on the file names. This option applies to all names following it on the command line. The following example specifies that the files named morg.jmp and frampl are both C source code files:

L D-61

```
gcc -xc morg.jmp frampl
```

The option can be used more than once to change the expected language, and the special name none can be used to turn the option off again. For example, the following command line specifies that the files named murk and stim.wad both contain C++ source code, the file named hummer.c is actually Java source code, while slamm.c defaults to being C source code:

62

```
gcc -xc++ murk stim.wad -xjava hummer.c -xnone slamm.c
```

The –x option can be written --language. See Table D-7.

-Xlinker *option*   Linker

Pass an option through to the linker. This is primarily used to specify system-specific linker options.

For example, if you are using the System V linker and want to specify the –all option for it, you can do that by specifying -Xlinker -all. It is necessary to use -Xlinker repeatedly to specify more than one item on the linker's command line. For example, to specify -woff 5,17 you would need to specify it as -Xlinker -woff -Xlinker 5,17. It will not work as -Xlinker "-woff 5,17".

Also see -Wl. This option can be written --for-linker.

Language Name	Description
ada	Ada source code.
assembler	Assembler langauge that is not to be preprocesssed.
assembler-with-cpp	Assembler language that is to be preprocessed.
c	C source code that is to be preprocessed.
c++	C++ source code that is to be preprocessed.
c++-cpp-output	C++ source code that is not to be preprocessed.
c-header	C header file
cpp-output	C source code that is not to be preprocessed.
f77	Fortran source code that is not to be preprocessed.
f77-cpp-input	Fortran source code that is to be preprocessed.
java	Java source code.
objc-cpp-output	Objective C source code that is not to be preprocessed.
objective-c	Objective C source code that is to be preprocessed.
ratfor	Fortran source code to be preprocessed by a RATFOR preprocessor.

Table D-7.   *The Language Specifiers of the –x Option*

APPENDIXES

Appendix E

Glossary

absolute address

An absolute address is a unique numeric value that specifies a specific byte of memory. Also see *relative address*.

address

See *absolute address* and *relative address*.

aggregate

A data type that contains more than one of the fundamental data types. For example, an array is an aggregate, as is a C struct.

aliasing

The same memory location being addressed directly or indirectly by two or more different names, and possibly different data types, is known as *aliasing*. This is a special consideration for optimization because it is common to retain values in registers.

ANSI (American National Standards Institute)

An organization that administers and coordinates U.S. voluntary standardization.

archive

See *library*.

assembler

A platform-specific program that reads assembly language source (mnemonic representations of the hardware opcodes) and translates it into a binary object file that can be fed to the linker.

backtrace

The GNU debugger can print a list of function names and addresses that were called to get the program to the current point of execution. This information, which includes function addresses and argument values, is called a *backtrace*.

BFD (Binary File Descriptor)

A library that includes routines that work with the various binary file formats to perform low-level operations.

BSD (Berkeley Software/Standard Distribution)

A UNIX operating system. It is also the basis of several other modern UNIX systems. Also see *SVR4*.

bss

The uninitialized data segment of an executable file produced by a UNIX linker. It contains data that has an address but contains no space. Therefore, no space is allocated until the program is loaded. In the executable file, a bss variable is assigned only a name, size, and location. Also see *text* and *data*.

built in function

Function bodies generated by the compiler are called *built in* functions. A built in function can be an optimized version of a standard library function, an added feature of the compiler, or a function used internally to implement such things as variable length argument lists.

bytecode

The portable form of object code produced from compiling Java programs. The *bytecode* is interpreted by the Java Virtual Machine to execute Java programs.

C89

The 1989 ANSI C standard.

C99

The 1999 ANSI C standard.

calling convention

See *calling sequence*.

calling sequence

The sequence of assembly language statements used to call a function. The sequence sets up the arguments to be passed, stores the return address so it can be found by the called function, makes the call, and then manages the return value (if any). This is also called the *calling convention*.

CCP (Conditional Code Propagation)

An optimization technique that discovers values that are constant for all possible paths of execution and uses this fact to detect and delete any code that cannot be executed.

cfront

The original version of C++ was implemented as an AT&T program named *cfront* that translated C++ source code into C source code.

class

1. In object-oriented programming, a class is an object type definition. Objects produced from it are said to be in the same class because they have the same interface and set of behaviors. 2. In Java, the file that contains a compiled class is called a *class file*, or simply a *class*.

clobber

If a storage location (usually a register) has been used as a temporary work area, causing it to no longer contain the expected value, the storage location is said to have been *clobbered*.

CNI (Cygnus Native Interface)

A facility for writing native Java methods in C++. Also see *JNI*.

code

A term used to refer to any form of a list of instructions to be executed on a computer. Code can be anything from human-readable programming source to machine-readable opcode bit patterns.

code propagation

See *CPP*.

coercion

The automatic conversion from one fundamental data type to another (without casting or making a function call).

COFF (Common Object File Format)

A standard format for object files that is portable across systems and known to different assemblers and linkers. Also see *ECOFF* and *XCOFF*.

COMDAT (Common Data)

A data or executable item (or set of items) that may be duplicated in more than one object file. The linker removes all but one of them when the object files are combined into a library or an executable. This is also referred to as *folding* or *comdat folding*.

common

The attribute of a global variable that is allocated to the *common block*.

common block

The GNU linker creates a common block as an area to allocate space for global variables. If identical global variables are declared in separate object files, they are resolved into a single variable in the common block. See *COMDAT*.

compilation unit

A single unit of source code that can be compiled into a single object file. It is often a single source file, but it also encompasses other source code that compiles with it (such as the `#include` files of a C program). This is also called a *translation unit*.

compiler

A set of software that reads the source (or text) of a computer program and translates the instructions into forms that then can be executed on a computer. A compiler is also called a *translator*.

copyleft

A general license that states that a program is free software and that all modified and extended versions of the software will also be free software. See *GPL*.

cross compile

Using a compiler to create executable files that can be executed on an entirely different platform.

CPP (C Preprocessor)

The preprocessor reads program source text and processes the directives to produce a modified version of the source.

cruft

As software ages and goes through cycles of bug fixes and upgrades, some of its code is no longer used but remains part of the source. Such code is know as *cruft*. The size of a piece of cruft can range from one or two useless lines to entire source modules. Removal of cruft can be difficult because it is often hard to identify.

CSE (Common Subexpression Elimination)

An optimization technique that recognizes duplicate expressions and reuses the value instead of performing the calculations again. Also called *GCSE*.

ctor

A common abbreviation of *constructor*. Also see *dtor*.

CVS (Concurrent Version System)

A version control system that maintains revision history information on text files. It is designed for access by many different people in widely separated locations.

data

The segment of an executable file produced by a UNIX linker that contains data with initial values. The segment contains items that have a name, a size, and is allocated space to contain a value. Also see *bss* and *text*.

DBX

An interactive debugger that can be used to track the execution of a program line by line. DBX is a command-line debugger, but in various incarnations it has an X GUI interface and an emacs interface.

DCE (Dead Code Elimination)

An optimization technique that removes any code that would never be executed.

dead code

During optimization, it is possible for some code to be left over that will never be executed. This is known as *dead code*. The optimizer should remove such code.

demangle

The process of extracting the descriptive information encoded in a mangled function name. See *mangle*.

deprecated

Any compiler option or feature that is no longer needed (or is considered inappropriate for some other reason) is declared as *deprecated*. It still exists but may be removed from a future version of the compiler.

dereference

Expressions may involve an address stored in a pointer. A pointer being used in this way is said to be *dereferenced*.

directive

1. A command in the source preceded by a hash (#) character that is to be acted upon by the preprocessor. 2. In assembly language, a directive is an instruction to

the assembler rather than an opcode that will produce code. An assembler directive is also called a *pseudo-op*.

distention
The name applied to certain Fortran language extensions that are now considered "ugly" and should not be used. Some of the distentions are supported in g77 via `-fugly-*` flags.

dtor
A common abbreviation for destructor. Also see *ctor*.

DWARF (Debugging With Attribute Format)
A format used for the insertion debugging information into object code.

DWARF2 (Debugging With Attribute Format 2)
A more recent version of DWARF, this format is used for the insertion of debugging information into object code.

dynamic library
See *library*.

ECOFF (Extended Common Object File Format)
A standard format for object files that is portable across systems and known to different assemblers and linkers. Also see *COFF* and *XCOFF*.

EH
Short for *exception handling*.

elaborate
In Ada, the final step prior to execution is to *elaborate* the code by inserting the necessary initial values and executable instructions, which often require the content of other compilation units in the same program. Also see *preelaborable*.

elaboration
In the Ada language, *elaboration* is name of the process requied to *elaborate* a package.

ELF (Executable and Linkable Format)
The Linux binary object file format that contains information for dynamically loading libraries as well as executable code. ELF is derived from, and very similar to, the COFF format.

elide

An *elided* function is one that produces its return value value by using the return location of the caller as its work space instead of creating its own internal work space and having the value copied into the return location later. Function calls may be elided by the optimizer.

entry point

The address inside an executable program where its execution is to begin is called the *entry point*.

fetch

When a computer reads an instruction from a program in memory and loads it into the CPU to execute it, this is known as an instruction *fetch*. Also see *prefetch*.

FPU (Floating Point Unit)

A hardware processor that works along with the CPU to perform floating-point operations. Computers without an FPU will require software to emulate floating-point operations.

folding

See *COMDAT*.

frame

See *stack frame*.

function

A function is a block of executable code that is assigned a name and can be called from another location. A function may also be defined with parameters to specify a list of argument values that can be passed to the function by the caller. Also see *member function* and *method*.

garbage collection

The process of a running program automatically recovering dynamically allocated memory that is no longer being used. There are many schemes for doing this, but all are considered garbage collection.

GCSE (Global Common Subexpression Elimination)

An optimization technique that recognizes duplicate expressions and reuses the value instead of performing the calculations again. Also called *CSE*.

GNAT (GNU Ada Translator)

The name of the original Ada front end that has now become a part of GCC.

GNATS (GNU Bug Tracking System)

An online system used to track bugs for GCC and other GNU software.

GOT (Global Offset Table)

A table inside an object file that contains a list of offsets that can be used to relocate the executable code. See *PIC*.

GPL (General Public License)

A license under which software is made into free software in the form of *copyleft*.

header

A header file is included in the source text file by the preprocessor executing an `include` directive. In C, C++, and Objective-C, it is traditional to name the files with a `.h` suffix.

Hollerith field

In Fortran, quoted strings are stored as a character count followed by the characters themselves. A string of characters can be created by using a Hollerith field, which is a length followed by the letter H and the string of characters (for example, `10HPhillips66`).

host

See *platform*.

i18n

A short form of the word *internationalization*, which begins with the letter *i*, followed by 18 letters, and ends with the letter *n*. Also see *l10n*.

if-conversion

An optimization procedure for modifying the generated code so that the path following the branch most likely to be taken is more efficient than the one taken less often.

immediate

An *immediate* value is a constant that is specified as an operand with an assembly language opcode.

include guard

It is customary to use the preprocessor conditional compilation commands to defined an environment variable that can be tested at the top of a header file to prevent it from being compiled more than once. If the variable is not yet defined, the header is compiled.

induction variable
A variable that is incremented during a loop. A loop counter.

inline
The entire body of a function (or other similar language element) is included at the point of the function call. That is, the function body is expanded *inline* in the code instead of existing only as a call to the function body existing elsewhere.

insn
A machine languages or RTL intermediate language instruction. There are special-purpose insns, but the most important ones form a sort of meta assembly language that can be translated into assembly language instuctions of the target machine.

instantiation
The creation of the instance of an object from a class definition.

intrinsic
In Fortran, an *intrinsic* function is a built-in function that appears to be part of the language because it can be used without being declared.

invariant expression
An expression inside a loop that evaluates to the same value every time is an *invariant* and, for optimization, can be moved outside the loop.

ISO (International Organization or Standardization)
An international standards organization founded in 1946, ISO's membership is composed of standards organizations, including ANSI, from 75 countries.

jar
An archive file that contains one or more Java class files. It also contains a manifest, which is a text file containing a list of the names of the classes in the *jar* file.

Java Virtual Machine
See *JVM*.

JNI (Java Native Interface)
A standard programming interface for writing Java native methods and embedding the JVM into native applications. Also see *CNI*.

JVM (Java Virtual Machine)

A program that is capable of reading a file in the standard Java bytecode format and executing the instructions found in the file. Porting the JVM and the standard set of classes to a platform effectively ports all Java programs to that platform.

l10n

A short form of the word *localization*, which begins with the letter *l* (ell), followed by 10 letters, and ends with the letter *n*. Also see *i18n*.

lexical analysis

Also called *lexical scan*, lexical analysis is the reading of the stream of input characters from a program source file and grouping them in such a way that they construct names, numbers, and punctuation. The unit made up of a collection of characters is called a *token*.

LGPL (Lesser General Public License)

A license used by some, but not all, GNU libraries. This license allows for the use of the library routines in proprietary programs, where the GPL does not.

library

A library is a single file that contains one or more object files that can be linked with other object files to create an executable program. A *static* library is one that contains modules that are attached permanently to an executable program by the linker. A static library is also called an *archive*. A *shared* library is one that contains modules that are attached temporarily to an executing program as it is loaded into memory to be run. A shared library is also called a *dynamic library*. An executable program that is dynamically linked is one that contains only references to the functions it will need to run, and when the program runs, it loads the functions from a shared library. Also see *static library* and *relative address*.

life analysis

The process of determining which values should remain in registers for later use, as well as determining which register can be used because the data it contains is no longer alive.

link editor

Same as *linker*.

linkage

When a call is made to a function, there must be a standard method for storing and retrieving the arguments passed to the function and the value received from its return. This kind of protocol is known as *linkage* and is the main problem to solve when mixing two languages.

linker

A platform-specific program that combines a set of object files (some of which must be extracted from libraries) to produce an executable program.

lvalue

An expression of any kind that resolves into the address of a location in memory. The term originates from *left value*, referring to the value on the left side of an assignment statement. Also see *rvalue*.

macro

In the preprocessor, a name and value declared by the `#define` directive is a *macro*, which can subsequently be used for text substitution in the source.

makefile

A file containing a set of rules used by the make utility to compile and link programs, as well as perform other tasks, based on the date- and timestamps of files. The makefile is usually named either `makefile` or `Makefile`.

mangle

The C++ (and Java) compilers modify the names of member functions (and methods) to produce a name that is unique according to the number and types of parameters it accepts. This process, known as *mangling*, allows for overloading of the simple member function (and method) names. Also see *demangle*.

manifest

See *jar*.

marshaling

The act of serializing (converting to a transmittable stream of bytes) the arguments to be passed to a remote function, and serializing the value to be returned from a remote function, is called *marshaling*. Converting a marshaled stream back into data is called *unmarshaling*. Also see *serialize*.

member function

In C++, a function that is defined inside a class is considered to be a member of the class and is called a *member function*. Unless the member function is declared as static, it is always called in the context of a specific object of the class and has a `this` pointer that can be used inside the function to refer to the object. A member function is to C++ what a method is to Java.

method

In Java, a *method* is a function defined inside a class and is a part of the class definition. Unless the method is declared as static, it is always called in the context of a specific object of the class and has a `this` pointer that can be used inside the method to refer to the object. A method is to Java what a member function is to C++.

MFC (Microsoft Foundation Class)

A class hierarchy that is a wrapper around the Win32 user interface API.

mirror

A site on the Internet that duplicates another to make files more available for download.

mnemonic

A name representing a value for the purpose of making it easier to remember. This term is often used to refer to the names assigned to CPU opcodes recognized by an assembler when translating assembly language into binary code. Also see *opcode*.

multilib

If a single target requires more than one version of a library, this is referred to as a *multilib*. For example, a particular platform may or may not have floating-point hardware installed, so the same library of math functions would need to compiled twice with different option settings, making it possible to link programs for either situation.

NaN (Not a Number)

The IEEE standard term for an invalid floating-point number. A number of this kind can be produced from underflow, overflow, or some other invalid floating-point operation.

NEXTSTEP

A computer operating environment that provides a GUI interface and can be used on HP, NeXT, Sun, and other computers. It was originally developed for the NeXT computer system.

NLM (Netware Loadable Module)

An executable program that has been formatted to be executed on the NetWare system.

NLS (Native Language Support)

The ability of the GCC compiler to output diagnostic messages in a language other than American English. NLS is the combination of i18n and l10n.

noop

An assembly language instruction that does nothing (no operation). It is often inserted as a filler byte in executable code or is used as the instruction at the target of a branch.

object

1. In object-oriented programming, an *object* is a collection of data items and the methods (or functions) used to operate on these data items. Also see *class*. 2. The output from the compilation process is the *object* file (or *object* code) because generating a file of that form is the objective of running the compiler or linker.

opcode

A single instruction to a computer's CPU. An opcode can be an instruction to add two numbers, load a number in a register, store a value in memory, or anything else that the hardware knows how to do. The opcode is the portion of the machine instruction that does not include the data. Also see *mnemonic*.

ordered comparison

An ordered comparison between two floating-point numbers is one in which an exception will be thrown if either value is NaN. Also see *unordered comparison*.

package

In Java, a package is a collection of classes. In Ada, a package is a collection of procedures.

pass

Each time the software reads through the input for parsing, optimization, code generation, preprocessing, or whatever, is known as a *pass*. A pass may modify the form of the input for the next pass, or it may only generate tables.

peephole optimization

An optimization technique that only looks at a few adjacent instructions to determine whether they can be replaced with a set of improved instructions.

PIC (Position Independent Code)
Code suitable for use in a shared library because it can be stored at any location in memory and executed from there. All its internal addresses are relative internal offsets or reference a global table. See *GOT*.

platform
A specific computer hardware and operating system combination. The compiler must be configured to run on a specific operating system, running on a specific hardware computer. A platform is also called a *host* or a *target*.

PMF (Pointer to Member Function)
A special data type in C++ that is capable of holding the address of a member function of a specific object.

POSIX
A UNIX standard specification that was formed by merging the IEEE standard with the Open Group's Single UNIX specification.

pragma
A command inserted in the source code that is a compiler-specific message that is ignored by all compilers that do not understand the message.

preelaborable
If an Ada compilation unit can be elaborated without requiring information from another unit, it can be elaborated in a standalone manner and is said to be *preelaborable*. Also see *elaborate*.

prefetch
When a computer reads an instruction from a program and loads it into the CPU in preparation to execute it, this is known as an instruction *fetch*. Many CPUs will simultaneously load several instructions, which is known as a *prefetch*.

preprocessor
A text processor that reads program source code and replaces names with numeric values (or other names), expands macros by textual substitution, and evaluates expressions to determine whether certain code is to be eliminated.

pseudo-op
See *directive*.

Ratfor (Rational Fortran)

A publicly available preprocessor of source code that allows Fortran written with C-like syntax to be converted into standard Fortran.

relative address

A *relative address* is an offset from a known location. This type of addressing is used in relocatable (shared library) modules because only the location of the top of the module itself is all that needs to be known for the executable code to work when it is loaded into memory. Also see *absolute address*.

relocatable

See *relative address*.

RM

For Ada, this is short for the *reference manual*, which is the document defining the Ada 95 standard.

RTL (Register Transfer Language)

The internal code generated from the source code of the language and from which the output assembly language is generated. While in RTL form, it is possible to perform optimization and other operations.

RTTI (Runtime Type Identification)

In object-oriented programming it is possible for an object of one type to masquerade as another. The RTTI facilities can be used to make a runtime determination of the true type of an object.

runtime

Also called the *runtime package*, the runtime is a collection of functions that are distributed with the compiler and linked to the compiled programs because they are called when the application is running.

rvalue

An expression of any kind that results in a single value. The term originates from *right value*, referring to the value calculated from the expression on the right side of an assignment statement. Also see *lvalue*.

scheduler

If a machine is capable of executing more than one instruction at a time, the instructions can be rearranged (scheduled) so that several fast instructions can be executed simultaneously with one slow one.

scope

The region in which a definition is known. In C, a variable defined inside a function has the entire function as its scope. A variable defined inside a block delimited by a pair of braces is known only inside that block, whereas a variable declared outside a function can be addressed by a number of functions.

semantics

The meaning of a programming language statement. The actual meaning of a statement can depend on its context. For example, the expression a+b could be the integer addition, floating-point addition, or even string concatenation. The process of determining the meaning is known as *semantic analysis*.

serialize

In Java, an object can be converted to a string of characters and transmitted (or stored for later retrieval) and converted back into an executing object. Also see *marshaling*.

sequence point

A point in the execution of a program when all evaluations have been completed and the variables all contain the correct results. At this point it is valid to begin evaluating any new expression. Some optimization techniques modify or reorder the sequence of operations between two sequence points.

shared library

See *library*.

sibling call

See *tail call*.

side effect

An operation of some sort (such as a function call or arithmetic expression) that makes some changes to data either in memory or in files. These changes are known as the *side effects operation*. Most side effects are intentional and are necessary to make a program work, but there are circumstances in which side effects can be detrimental.

slot scheduler
See *scheduler*.

Single UNIX Specification
See *POSIX*.

Smalltalk
An object-oriented language developed at Xerox PARC in the 1970s. Smalltalk was the programming language of the SIMULA interface system that introduced the mouse and windows.

spec file
A file that contains a set of rules controlling which arguments gcc is to pass to each subprocess as well as what form the arguments should take.

STABS (Symbol TABle directiveS)
Operators and data locations inserted into the source code of assembly language to provide debugging information. The assembler and linker then include these tables in the object code and executable programs for the purposes of debugging.

static library
See *library*.

SSA (Static Single Assignment)
A special form representing the logic flow through a block of code. SSA is used for certain types of optimization, such as the elimination of dead code. One of the advantages of SSA is the ability to track the values stored in registers.

stack frame
The area on the stack that holds local variables and the saved register values for the current function. The exact format depends on the processor and on the function-calling convention being used.

static link
An executable program that is *statically linked* is one that includes all the functions it needs. When the program is linked, the functions are extracted from the runtime library and copied into the linked program. Also see *shared library*.

static single assignment
See *SSA*.

stringize
The action by the preprocessor of converting a macro argument to a quoted string instead of simply inserting it into the source as it is.

strip
The `strip` command can be used on an executable file to remove all debugging information. Depending on the amount of debugging information compiled into the executable, the reduction in size can be dramatic.

stderr (Standard Error)
Every UNIX program begins with this output stream open, which by default is directed to the terminal. This stream is used mostly for error message output.

stdin (Standard Input)
Every UNIX program begins with this input stream open, which by default reads keystrokes from the keyboard.

stdout (Standard Output)
Every UNIX program begins with this output stream open, which by default is directed to the terminal. This stream is used mostly for the standard data ouptut from a program.

strength reduction
An optimization technique that replaces expensive operations with cheaper ones, such as replacing a multiplication operation with addition or a shift.

stub
A local function that, when called by a local program, packages the calling information and transmits the call to the actual function, which may be located on another computer.

subexpression
Part of an expression. For example, in the expression a * (b + c), the factor (b + c) is a subexpression. A subexpression can be very complicated or as simple as an address being loaded into a register.

APPENDIXES

SVR4 (System Five Release Four)

A version of UNIX produced by AT&T. SVR4 is the basis of many modern versions of UNIX. Also see *BSD*.

syntax

The physical structure of a programming language. The syntax determines the form of the language by enforcing rules that determine valid ordering and the structure of the text of the language itself.

tail call

If a function recursively calls itself as its very last statement, the logic can be changed to a loop instead of a call to save the amount of stack space required. This same optimization technique can be used when two or more functions recursively call one another—this kind of optimization is called *sibling call*.

target

See *platform*.

text

The segment of an executable file produced by a UNIX linker that contains the executable code. Also see *bss* and *data*.

thunk

A piece of code used to generate an address. Introduced in ALGOL 60 to pass arguments by name by generating code that would resolve addresses at runtime, today *thunk* is also used to refer to the act of overwriting a list of addresses with a new set of addresses.

time slice

The amount of time the operating system allows a process to run before it is halted and another process has its time slice.

token

See *lexical analysis*.

translation unit

Another name for *compilation unit*.

translator

Another name for a compiler, because the job of a compiler is to translate source code into executable code. See *compiler*.

trap
A hardware signal issued to a running program to indicate a program execution error has been detected by the hardware. This involves such things as floating-point division by zero and invalid memory addresses.

trigraph
A three-character sequence in standard C that translates into a single character. It was devised to enable programming in C for computers not supporting the full ASCII character set. There are nine trigraphs:

```
??=  #        ??(  [        ??<  {
??/  \        ??)  ]        ??>  }
??'  ^        ??!  |        ??-  ~
```

unalias
To remove all but one possible reference to a memory location is to *unalias* the location. See *aliasing*.

unordered comparison
An ordered comparison between two floating-point numbers is one in which an exception will not be thrown if either or both values are NaN. Also see *ordered comparison*.

unroll
To optimize code, a loop that is small enough and has a fixed number of iterations can be *unrolled* by having its code duplicated the number of times it would have iterated, and the iteration can be removed.

UTF-8 (Unicode Transformation Format)
This is also written as UTF8, Utf8, or just UTF. Unicode encoded in such a way that all ASCII characters are stored as only 8 bits, which means an ASCII text file can be treated as if it were UTF-8 encoded.

vague linkage
Information included in an object file that is needed for linking and running a program, but is something other than the data required to resolve address references. An example is the virtual function table in C++.

variadic macro

A *variadic* macro is one that has a variable number of arguments. The GCC preprocessor is capable of expanding macros with a variable number of arguments by storing the text of the argument list in a variable named __VA_ARGS__ .

vector

A contiguous collection of data items that are all the same type and size.

volatile

A location in memory that could be modified elsewhere (without the routine's knowledge) is considered *volatile*. This is important to a compiler because it is more efficient to hold things in registers than to load them from memory each time they are needed.

vtable (virtual function table)

Object-oriented language objects maintain internal tables, called *vtables*, containing the addresses of functions. By replacing these addresses, a subclass can override and replace selected functions (the virtual functions) of its parent class.

VXT

A dialect of Fortran that is very much like VAX Fortran and somewhat similar to Fortran 90.

weak alias

Same as *weak symbol*.

weak symbol

Having two or more global symbols of the same name will not cause a conflict as long as all but one of them are declared as being *weak symbols*. The linker ignores the definitions of the weak symbols and uses the normal global symbol definition to resolve all references, but the weak symbols will be used if the normal global symbol is not available. A weak symbol can be used to name functions and data that can be overridden by user code. A weak symbol is also referred to as a *weak alias*, or simply *weak*.

width

The term *width* is often used to refer to the relative size of a fundamental data type. For example, in C, a char may take up a single byte, whereas a short may require two bytes. In this case, the short is said to be wider than the char.

word

The size of the native integer on a machine. On a 16-bit machine, a word is 16 bits; on a 32-bit machine, a word is 32 bits.

whitespace

The whitespace characters are the ones that do not normally show up visibly and are ignored as input when compiling modern free-form languages. These are normally the space, tab, vertical tab, form feed, linefeed, and carriage return characters.

XCOFF (Extended Common Object File Format)

A standard format for object files that is portable across systems and known to different assemblers and linkers. Also see *COFF* and *ECOFF.*

Index

O

INTERNATIONAL CONTACT INFORMATION

AUSTRALIA
McGraw-Hill Book Company Australia Pty. Ltd.
TEL +61-2-9415-9899
FAX +61-2-9415-5687
http://www.mcgraw-hill.com.au
books-it_sydney@mcgraw-hill.com

CANADA
McGraw-Hill Ryerson Ltd.
TEL +905-430-5000
FAX +905-430-5020
http://www.mcgrawhill.ca

GREECE, MIDDLE EAST,
NORTHERN AFRICA
McGraw-Hill Hellas
TEL +30-1-656-0990-3-4
FAX +30-1-654-5525

MEXICO (Also serving Latin America)
McGraw-Hill Interamericana Editores S.A. de C.V.
TEL +525-117-1583
FAX +525-117-1589
http://www.mcgraw-hill.com.mx
fernando_castellanos@mcgraw-hill.com

SINGAPORE (Serving Asia)
McGraw-Hill Book Company
TEL +65-863-1580
FAX +65-862-3354
http://www.mcgraw-hill.com.sg
mghasia@mcgraw-hill.com

SOUTH AFRICA
McGraw-Hill South Africa
TEL +27-11-622-7512
FAX +27-11-622-9045
robyn_swanepoel@mcgraw-hill.com

UNITED KINGDOM & EUROPE
(Excluding Southern Europe)
McGraw-Hill Education Europe
TEL +44-1-628-502500
FAX +44-1-628-770224
http://www.mcgraw-hill.co.uk
computing_neurope@mcgraw-hill.com

ALL OTHER INQUIRIES Contact:
Osborne/McGraw-Hill
TEL +1-510-549-6600
FAX +1-510-883-7600
http://www.osborne.com
omg_international@mcgraw-hill.com

Printed in the United States
66640LVS00005B/2

9 780072 224054